# Quick Start

 ## Installing Quicken

Hard Disk Users

1. Start your computer as usual.
2. If you are using a 5.25-inch floppy drive, insert Install Disk 1.
   If you are using a 3.5-inch floppy drive, insert the Install Disk.
3. Change to the floppy drive with the Install Disk. (Type A: and press Enter. Or type B: and press Enter if you're using floppy drive B.)
4. Type install and press Enter.
5. Follow the instructions that appear on the screen. (Hint to current Quicken users: Install Quicken in the same directory as your previous version of Quicken.)

When installation is complete, put the Install Disk or Disks away in a safe place. To start Quicken, see the other side of this card.

Floppy Disk Users

If you don't have a hard disk, you must have two floppy drives, at least one of which is high-density. (High density means 1.44 megabytes for a 3.5-inch floppy drive, or 1.2 megabytes for a 5.25-inch floppy drive.)

1. Label a formatted, unused, high-density floppy disk "Quicken Program."
2. Start your computer as usual.
3. After the DOS prompt (A> or B>) appears, remove all disks from your drives.
4. Insert the "Quicken Program" disk in the high-density drive from which you plan to run Quicken after installation.
5. If your other drive is a 5.25-inch floppy drive, insert Install Disk 1 in it.
   If your other drive is a 3.5-inch floppy drive, insert the Install Disk in it.
6. Change to the floppy drive with the Install Disk. (Type A: and press Enter. Or type B: and press Enter if you're using floppy drive B.)
7. Type INSTALL and press Enter.
8. Follow the instructions that appear on the screen.

When installation is complete, put the Install Disk(s) away in a safe place. To start Quicken, see the other side of this card.

We welcome your comments on this card and the rest of the manual.

If you have comments or suggestions about our documentation, call our Reader Comment Line toll-free at 800-468-8487 (800-INTUIT-7) and leave a message.

$ Starting Quicken

New Quicken Users

Before you start Quicken, find the last bank statement for the bank account you want to set up in Quicken. You'll need to enter the ending date and closing balance from your last bank statement as a starting point for the bank account in Quicken.

If you have a hard disk:

Type Q and press Enter. The Q.BAT file created by the install program starts Quicken even when you're not in the drive or directory that contains Quicken.

After you start Quicken, use the First Time Setup Assistants to show you an overview of Quicken and set up your first account. (See "First Time Setup" on page 15 for more information.)

If you don't have a hard disk:

1. Insert the "Quicken Program" disk you created in your high-density drive. Insert a formatted, unused disk for data in your other drive.

2. Type Q and press Enter.

Why doesn't my mouse work?

Quicken 5 works with any Microsoft-compatible mouse. If you have problems when using your mouse with Quicken, make sure your mouse is installed correctly and the mouse driver software loaded. (See "Mouse problems" on page 529 for more information.)

Current Quicken Users

We recommend that you install Quicken 5 in the same directory as your previous version of Quicken. Just start Quicken as usual and start using Quicken 5 with your current data files. You will have a chance to back up each file before Quicken 5 opens it and you should let Quicken 5 make the backup before it updates your data. See page 477 for information about exactly what happens when you update.

What happened to the numbers on the Main Menu?

For people new to Quicken, we install a new menu style (SAA or Alt-key menus) based on pressing the key for a letter in contrasting type. For people upgrading from an earlier version of Quicken, we ordinarily install the familiar numbered menus (Function-key menus). If you don't see numbers on the Main Menu when you start Quicken, you can switch to the numbered menu style. Starting at the Main Menu:

1. Choose Set Preferences.
2. Choose Screen Settings.
3. Choose Menu Access, and then type 1 for Function-keys and press Enter.

You need to exit and restart Quicken to see the change in menu style.

More Questions?

If you are unsure what to do at any time using Quicken, press F1 to see a Help screen, or press Ctrl-F1 to choose a topic from the Help Index.

User Manual

Version 5 for IBM and PC Compatibles

Program created by

Craig Carlson

Eric C. W. Dunn

Susan Hinton

Daniel K. Wilks

Alex Young

Lun-Shin Yuen

Menlo Park, California

Manual and Help Writers   Dennise C. Brown
Andrea G. Julian
Denise Lau
Mervyn Lewis
Suzanne Schrader

Version 5 Development Team   Mari Latterell-Baker (Product Manager)
Greg Ceniceroz
Valesha Jones
Jim Joseph
Farah Risoen

User Manual Easy Overview

Introducing Quicken

Quicken saves you time and gives you control over your finances. Use it to track all your financial transactions, for home, business, or both.

Get started with Quicken by using it to track your checking account.

Fill out a check on a screen that looks just like a paper check.

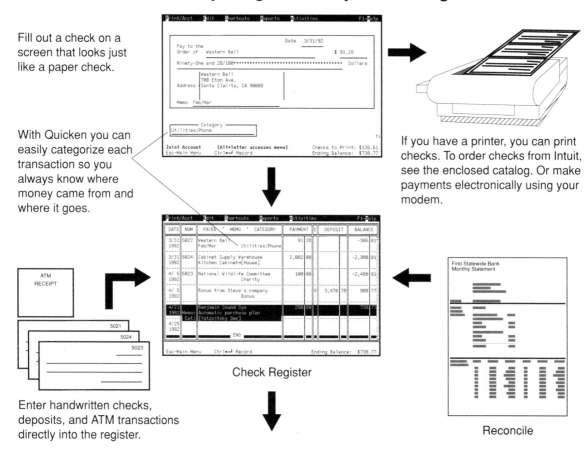

With Quicken you can easily categorize each transaction so you always know where money came from and where it goes.

If you have a printer, you can print checks. To order checks from Intuit, see the enclosed catalog. Or make payments electronically using your modem.

Check Register

Enter handwritten checks, deposits, and ATM transactions directly into the register.

Reconcile

Quicken automatically provides reports showing exactly how you spent your money by category, by month.

Later, use Quicken's six different account types to track all your finances.

Quicken has accounts designed specifically for each of the following:
- Checking, savings, and money market accounts
- Cash
- Credit Cards
- Investments
- Assets such as capital equipment or home basis
- Liabilities such as loans

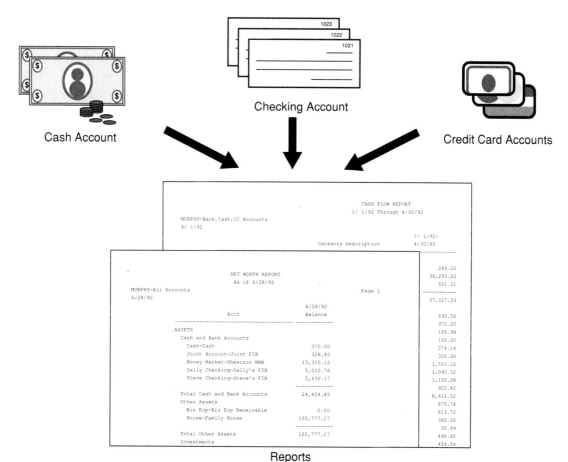

Cash Account

Checking Account

Credit Card Accounts

Reports

Capital Equipment
(Sample Asset Account)

Mortgage
(Sample Liability Account)

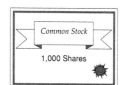

Investment Accounts

Contents

Section E. Applying Quicken to Your Needs

Section F. Managing Quicken

Section G. Appendices and Index

Chapter 1

Before You Begin

This short chapter tells you what you need to do before starting work with Quicken. Quicken leads you through the installation process, so it's easy even if you've never installed a program before. When you have finished with this chapter, you'll be ready to use Quicken.

You must install Quicken before you can run it.

You cannot simply use the DOS copy command to copy the files from the disks in the Quicken package. The Quicken program and help files are compressed to save space and must be expanded before you can use them. The install program expands the files automatically.

Quicken is not copy-protected, so you can make a copy by running the install program whenever you need it for your personal use. However, you may not make copies for other people.

If you want to know exactly what the install program puts on your hard disk, see "Installation on a Hard Disk" on page 491.

Attention Tandy DeskMate users: DeskMate users should follow the instructions in "Installing Quicken from the Tandy DeskMate Desktop" on page 7 *instead of* the instructions on pages 2 through 6 of this chapter.

What You Need

To use Quicken, you need the following equipment and supplies:

- IBM PC, XT, AT, PS/1, PS/2, or 100% compatible computer with a hard drive or two floppy drives, at least one of which is high-density (1.2- or 1.44-megabyte)
- 512K minimum memory
- DOS 2.0 or later
- Monochrome or color monitor
- Install Disks 1 and 2 (5.25-inch) or Install Disk (3.5-inch)
- One of the following on which to install Quicken and store data:
  - A hard disk
  - One unused, formatted high-density disk (either 1.2-megabyte 5.25-inch disk or 1.44-megabyte 3.5-inch disk) plus one unused disk formatted for your second drive

    See the recommendations on page 4 about whether you should format the disks as bootable (startup) disks.
- (Optional) Any printer

  (Note that "thermal" paper printers cannot print checks.)
- (Optional) Quicken checks (required only for printing checks)
- (Optional) A modem to send electronic payments through CheckFree

Installing Quicken on a Hard Disk

Follow these directions to install Quicken 5 on a hard disk. (If you do not have a hard disk, skip ahead to "Installing Quicken on a Floppy Disk" on page 4.)

If your installed copy is ever damaged, you can use the original Quicken install disks to reinstall it.

> **Installation does not affect existing Quicken data files.**
>
> Your existing Quicken data files are *not* affected in any way by this installation procedure. If you ever need to reinstall Quicken, just follow these same installation instructions again.

To install Quicken 5 on a hard disk:

1. Start your computer and stay in the root directory of your hard disk. The DOS prompt is probably C:\> or D:\>, depending on the letter of your hard disk drive.

2. Insert Install Disk 1 (or the 3.5-inch Install Disk) in your floppy disk drive.

3. Change to the floppy disk drive you put the disk in.
   - If it is Drive A, type A: and press the Enter (or Return) key.
   - If it is Drive B, type B: and press the Enter (or Return) key.

   The DOS prompt for the floppy disk drive (A:\> or B:\>) appears.

4. Type install and press the Enter key.

5. Follow the instructions that the install program displays on your screen.

   A message appears on the screen if you need to remove one disk and insert another. When installation is complete, you see a message telling you how to exit to DOS and start Quicken.

   During installation, the install program asks you to enter:
   - Whether you have a color screen
   - Your name (or the business name)
   - Type of drive (hard disk or floppy) to install on
   - Disk drive and directory to install in
   - Your printer brand and model
   - Whether you want to be reminded of upcoming bills

How to enter answers

- When Quicken displays the correct answer, indicate your approval by pressing the Enter key.

- When you have a list of choices, use the up and down arrow keys to select (point to) the correct answer, then press the Enter key.

  The printer list is too long to see all at once. Keep pressing PgDn to see the entire list.

  HINT: If the arrow keys and PgDn don't work, turn off the keyboard Number Lock.

- When you must type an answer, press the Enter key to record what you have typed.

  To change a typed answer, press Backspace or the left or right arrow keys and then retype.

Note: The install program checks to see whether you already have a copy of Quicken in a C:\QUICKEN4 (or C:\QUICKEN3) directory on your hard disk. If you don't, it prepares to install Quicken 5 in a new C:\QUICKEN5 directory. If you do, it prepares to install Quicken 5 in your old Quicken directory.

We recommend that you allow the program to install Quicken 5 in your old Quicken directory. Your Quicken 4 (or 3) program files will be replaced by the Quicken 5 program files. *Your data files are not affected in any way by installation.* If you want to keep your data in another directory or on a floppy disk, you can make the change later. (See "Changing Where Quicken Looks for Data" on page 457.)

6. Put all the original install disks away in a safe place.

    Do not try to use these disks to run the program. (If you type the command to start Quicken, you'll be required to install, instead.)

You are now ready to start Quicken. Skip to "What to Do Next" on page 6.

 # Installing Quicken on a Floppy Disk

To follow this installation procedure, you must have at least one high-density floppy drive (either 1.44-megabyte 3.5-inch or 1.2-megabyte 5.25-inch). Your second drive can be either high- or low-density.

You can install Quicken 5 on a high-density 3.5-inch or 5.25-inch floppy disk. *You cannot install it on regular (360-kilobyte) 5.25-inch floppy disks or regular (720-kilobyte) 3.5-inch floppy disks.*

Quicken 5 runs better on a hard disk.

Quicken 5 runs faster and more efficiently on a hard disk. If you have a hard disk, we recommend that you install Quicken on your hard disk rather than a floppy disk.

When you run Quicken on a two-floppy system, all your Quicken program files are on one high-density disk (the Quicken program disk). Your Quicken data files are on a separate disk (the data disk). You run Quicken from a high-density drive; you keep your data disk in your second drive.

Should you format the program and data disks as bootable (startup) disks? Here's what we recommend.

*   If you plan to run Quicken from a 3.5-inch high-density drive:
    -   Format a 3.5-inch high-density disk as a bootable disk. You will install Quicken on this disk. You'll be able to boot your computer with your Quicken program disk.
    -   Format a disk for your second drive as a nonbootable disk. You will store Quicken data on this disk.
*   If you plan to run Quicken from a 5.25-inch high-density drive:
    -   Format a 5.25-inch high-density disk as a nonbootable disk. You will install Quicken on this disk. There is not enough disk space for the additional files that make a disk bootable.
    -   Format a disk for your second drive as a nonbootable disk. You will store Quicken data on this disk.

If you aren't sure how to format a disk as bootable or nonbootable, see "To format a floppy disk:" on page 495.

To install Quicken 5 on a high-density floppy disk:

1. Label your formatted, unused, high-density disk "Quicken Program."

2. Start your computer as usual.

3. After the DOS prompt (A> or B>) appears, remove all disks from your drives.

4. Insert the unused "Quicken Program" disk in the high-density drive from which you plan to run Quicken.

5. Insert Install Disk 1 (or the 3.5-inch Install Disk) in the remaining drive.

6. Change to the floppy disk drive holding Install Disk 1 or Install Disk.
   - If it is Drive A, type A: and press the Enter (or Return) key.
   - If it is Drive B, type B: and press the Enter (or Return) key.

   The DOS prompt (A> or B>) for that drive appears.

7. Type install and press the Enter key.

8. Follow the instructions that the install program displays on your screen.

   The program displays a message if you need to remove one disk and insert another. When installation is complete, you see a message telling you how to exit to DOS and start Quicken.

   During installation, the install program asks you to enter:
   - Whether you have a color screen
   - Your name (or the business name)
   - Type of drive (hard disk or floppy) to install on
   - Floppy disk drive to install on
   - Your printer brand and model

How to enter answers

- When Quicken displays the correct answer, indicate your approval by pressing the Enter key.

- When you have a list of choices, use the up and down arrow keys to select (point to) the correct answer, then press the Enter key.

   The printer list is too long to see all at once. Keep pressing the PgDn key to see the entire list.

   HINT: If the arrow and PgDn keys don't work, turn off the keyboard Number Lock.

- When you must type an answer, press the Enter key to record what you have typed.

   To change a typed answer, press Backspace or the left or right arrow keys and then retype.

---

9. Put all the original install disks away in a safe place.

   Do not try to use these disks to run the program. (If you type the command to start Quicken, you'll be required to install, instead.)

You are now ready to start Quicken.

Cautions about running Quicken from a floppy disk

1. ***Do not remove the program disk from the drive while running Quicken.***
   Removing the Quicken program disk while Quicken is running could cause the program to stop and could lead to loss of data.

2. Eventually, your data disk will run out of disk space. For suggestions about what to do, read "If You Run Out of Disk Space" on page 496.

$ What to Do Next

New Quicken Users

1. Look over Chapter 2, *Getting Started with Quicken*, beginning on page 11. Be sure to read "Quicken Accounts and Files" on page 12.

2. Start Quicken (for instructions, see "Starting Quicken" on page 14).

   The Welcome to Quicken 5.0 window appears.

   Note: If the Main Menu appears instead of this window, choose Use Tutorials/Assistants and then choose First Time Setup.

3. Do all three activities described in the Welcome to Quicken 5.0 window in sequence. (For more information, see "First Time Setup" on page 15. Floppy-disk users cannot do the first two activities because the install program doesn't put sample data on the floppy disk.)

Then you'll be ready to enter data in the new bank account you've set up. If you'd like to read about entering data in a Quicken register, see Chapter 4, *Using the Register*, beginning on page 57.

Current Quicken Users

1. Look over Appendix B, *If You've Used an Earlier Version of Quicken*, beginning on page 477. It contains tables of the new features and changes in Quicken 5 with page references to sections in the manual where you can go to get complete information.

2. You may also want to lock at Appendix C, *Quicken Menus*, beginning on page 485. It contains maps of all the menus in Quicken 5.

3. **Important:** Follow the instructions in "Updating Data from Quicken 3 and 4" on page 477 to load your data into Quicken 5.

$ Installing Quicken from the Tandy DeskMate Desktop

Although Quicken is not a Tandy DeskMate-specific application, you can install and run it from the DeskMate Desktop by following the instructions given here.

Important: Follow these instructions instead of the preceding instructions.

DeskMate users should follow these instructions *instead of* the instructions given earlier in this chapter.

Before starting to install Quicken, remove any Quicken disks that might be in your floppy disk drives. Then restart your computer by turning power off and back on. (On some Tandy computers, restarting your computer also restarts DeskMate automatically.) You must install using Drive A.

Installing Quicken from DeskMate on a Hard Disk

1. Start DeskMate following the instructions in your Tandy DeskMate manual.

2. After the drive access light on Drive A goes out, insert the 5.25-inch Quicken Install Disk 1 (or the 3.5-inch Quicken Install Disk) in Drive A.

3. Select Install from the Desktop Menu.

   Now or later, if you see a DeskMate message, see "Messages from DeskMate During Installation" on page 9.

4. If the Display Menu dialog box appears, select a size and shape for the Quicken display menu and press Enter. Position the window where you want it on the Desktop using the arrow keys and press Enter. If you do not want to create a Quicken Menu, press the onscreen Cancel pushbutton.

5. Follow the instructions that the Install program displays on your screen.

   Quicken installs itself automatically. It displays messages when you need to remove one disk and insert another. You will see a screen that asks you to confirm the location for program files on your hard disk. By default, the Install program uses the subdirectory \QUICKEN5. We recommend that you install Quicken in this directory.

6. At the Desktop, select Redefine from the Desktop Menu.

   The Redefine Menu list box appears.

7. Select Quicken and press Enter.

   The Redefine Menu dialog box appears.

8. Be sure that Q.EXE (the name of the Quicken program file) is entered in the Program Name field.

9. In the Start-up Directory field, type the drive and directory in which you installed Quicken and press Enter.

   If you installed Quicken on Drive C in the QUICKEN5 directory, you would type c:\quicken5.

10. Store your original install disks in a safe place. You are ready to start Quicken.

Installing Quicken from DeskMate on a Floppy Disk

If you do not have a hard disk, you must have two floppy drives, at least one of which must be high density (1.44-megabyte 3.5-inch or 1.2-megabyte 5.25-inch).

Have ready one formatted, unused high-density disk for Drive B to hold the Quicken program. Label this disk "Quicken Program." You will keep your Quicken data on a separate formatted disk.

To install Quicken on a high-density floppy disk:

1. Start DeskMate following the instructions in your Tandy DeskMate manual.

2. Make sure the current directory (displayed at the top middle of the DeskMate screen) is A:\. If it is not, change the current directory to A:\ by choosing Change from the Directory Menu. Type A:\ in the Path field and press Enter (or Return).

   If you see the message "Critical Error," press Esc and try again. Be sure that after the letter A you type a colon (:) and then a backslash (\).

3. After the drive access light on Drive A goes out, insert Install Disk 1 (or the 3.5-inch Install Disk) in Drive A.

4. Press F7 and choose Install from the Desktop Menu.

   Now or later, if you see a DeskMate message, see "Messages from DeskMate During Installation" on page 9.

5. If the Display Menu dialog box appears, select a size and shape for the Quicken display menu and press Enter. Position the window where you want it on the Desktop using the arrow keys ($\rightarrow$, $\leftarrow$, $\uparrow$, or $\downarrow$) and press Enter. If you do not want to create a Quicken Menu, press the onscreen Cancel pushbutton.

6. Follow the instructions that the Install program displays on your screen.

   Quicken installs itself automatically. It displays messages when you need to remove one disk and insert another.

7. When the installation procedure is complete, store the original install disks in a safe place. Use only your Quicken Program disk to run the program.

Messages from DeskMate During Installation

As you install, you may see various DeskMate messages. The most likely reason for a message is that the system needs you to swap floppy disks in Drive A. You may need to insert the DeskMate disk or Install Disk 1. The message you see depends upon the version of DeskMate and your computer. Here are some messages, each one of which means that you need to swap disks:

- "Could not find new application on floppy disk."

  Insert Install Disk 1 in Drive A and press Enter. If this step does not resolve the problem, see below.

- "Please insert a disk containing the file DESKTOP.CFG into any drive."

  Insert the DeskMate disk in Drive A and press Enter.

- "Unable to locate file named INSTALL.PDM."

  Press Esc and insert Install Disk 1 in Drive A. Select F7 and choose Install again.

- "File Not Found. Unable to locate file DMCSR.XXX." where XXX can be various file extensions.

  You may see this message after Quicken is installed. Insert the DeskMate disk in Drive A and press Enter.

If you swap disks but still get the message "Could not find new application on floppy disk," DeskMate may think that Quicken has already been installed (even if you only started the procedure and are in the middle of it). Before you can continue installing Quicken, you must delete Quicken from DeskMate's list of installed programs.

To delete Quicken from DeskMate's list of installed programs:

1. Press the onscreen OK pushbutton at the message dialog box.

   DeskMate returns you to the DeskMate Desktop.

2. Exit DeskMate and then restart DeskMate. When you return to the DeskMate Desktop, press F7 and choose Delete from the Desktop Menu.

   The Delete Menu dialog box appears.

3. Click on the list box arrows with the mouse or use the up or down arrow keys to locate and select Quicken. Press Enter to delete Quicken from the list.

4. Start the installation procedure again.

How to Run Quicken from the DeskMate Desktop

After you install Quicken, see "What to Do Next" on page 6. When you're ready to start Quicken, use the following procedure, not the one in "Starting Quicken" on page 14.

- At the DeskMate Desktop, select the Quicken icon and press Enter.

  Or

- Choose Run from the File Menu, type Q in the Program Name field, and press Enter.

When you run Quicken from the Desktop, it works just the way this manual describes it.

Note: When you run Quicken from the Desktop, it reduces the memory available to Quicken by about 5% to 10%. If your data file becomes very large or if you request a long and complex report, Quicken may need more memory. Try running Quicken without DeskMate if possible. Exit from Quicken. Turn your machine off and on and start Quicken from the DOS prompt. (Go to the directory where you installed Quicken, type Q, and press ↵.) If you cannot run your computer without DeskMate or if you still need more memory, see "Not enough memory" on page 528.

Floppy disk users: Read "Cautions about running Quicken from a floppy disk" on page 6. It applies to Tandy DeskMate users.

Tandy 1000SL, 1000TL, and 1000RL Computers

Tandy 1000SL, 1000TL, and 1000RL computers come with DeskMate and the DeskMate Desktop built in. To install or run Quicken on these computers, you must start at the DeskMate Desktop.

To reach the DeskMate Desktop:

- Restart your computer (turn the power off and back on).

  Or

- At the DOS prompt, change to the directory that contains DeskMate (for example, type cd \desk and press Enter). Then type desk and press Enter.

Chapter 2

Getting Started with Quicken

This chapter helps you with first time setup and explains in general the way Quicken works. It's full of useful tips about procedures that you'll use throughout the program: choosing commands from menus, getting online help, using keyboard shortcuts, choosing items from lists, using a mouse, and using Quicken's built-in calculator.

If you haven't already installed Quicken, do so now following the steps in the preceding chapter. Then return to this chapter when you are ready to start Quicken for the first time.

Quicken Accounts and Files

In Quicken, the term "account" can refer to several different types of accounts: bank accounts (for checking, money market, or savings); credit card accounts; cash accounts; or special accounts for other types of assets, liabilities, and investments.

You create a Quicken account within a "data file," or simply "file." A file can contain as few as one account or as many as 255 accounts. This organization provides several important benefits as you enter transactions and request reports.

- You can assign transactions to categories (such as "rent," "utilities," "salary") and use those categories consistently for all accounts in the file.

- When you ask for a report, Quicken can consolidate data from any or all accounts in the file into a single report.

- A single transaction entry can show the transfer of money from one account to another account in the same file.

Most Quicken users need only one file. In fact, when you first use Quicken for personal finances, we recommend that you limit yourself to just one file. Later, you may want to have more than one file for these purposes:

- To separate personal finances from business finances (when these are entirely separate and have different checking accounts). Alternately, you can use Quicken classes, a feature that provides a second way to classify transactions, to separate your finances into personal and business even within one Quicken file.

- To separate personal or business accounts for each calendar year. (Not required; you must weigh the disadvantages of multiple files for this purpose.)

- To separate accounts for each business client (or you can use classes for this purpose within a single file).

Even these purposes do not necessarily mean that you need more than one file. So be sure to read "Do You Need More Than One File?" on page 453 for a more complete discussion before you decide to create additional files.

The figure on page 13 illustrates the structure of Quicken data in a file. You can see that keeping your data in a single file offers significant benefits.

Start with one or two bank accounts.

When you first use Quicken, limit yourself to one or two bank accounts for the first month or two. Many users find that a simple approach with fewer Quicken accounts serves their needs better than one with many Quicken accounts when they're getting started. Before you set up additional accounts, read the appropriate chapter (see the chapters in the section *Completing Your Financial Picture*, beginning on page 245).

Quicken File

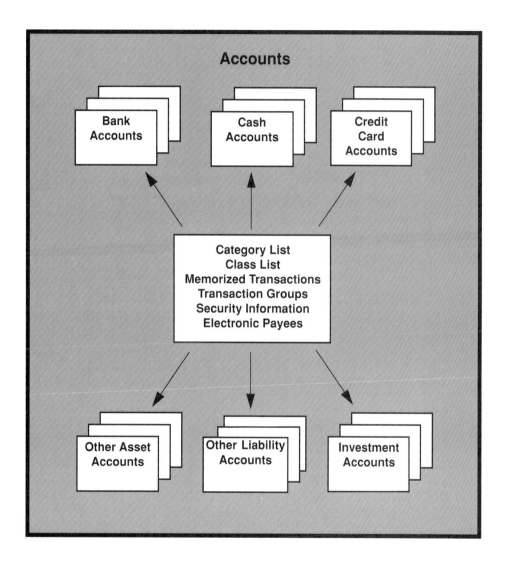

- A Quicken file contains many different accounts which all share the same lists of categories, classes, memorized transactions, transaction groups, security information, and electronic payees.

- Reports can consolidate the information from all accounts in one Quicken file into a single report.

- Bank accounts are the core of most finances; the rest of the accounts are optional.

$ Starting Quicken

Before you can start Quicken, it must already be installed on your hard disk or on floppy disks. (See Chapter 1, *Before You Begin*, beginning on page 1.)

This section tells how to start Quicken in the easiest and most usual way. For some special ways to start Quicken, see "Starting Quicken with Options" on page 496.

To start Quicken with a hard disk:

1. Turn on your computer if it is not already on.

2. When you see the C:\> prompt (assuming your hard disk is Drive C), type Q and press Enter.

To start Quicken without a hard disk:

1. Start your computer using a DOS startup ("bootable") disk.

   If your Quicken Program disk is bootable, use this.

2. Enter the date and time if your computer asks you for them. Quicken needs to know the correct date.

3. If you did not start your computer using your Quicken Program disk, insert this disk now in your high-density drive and display the DOS prompt (A> or B>) for that drive.

4. Type Q and press Enter to start Quicken.

5. When prompted for a data disk, insert a formatted disk in the *other* drive.

Remember:

Do not remove the Quicken Program disk until you have exited from Quicken.

If this copy of Quicken was installed in a new directory or on floppy disks, Quicken displays the First Time Setup window the first time someone starts Quicken. Otherwise, Quicken displays the Main Menu.

- If you are new to Quicken and have not yet set up any data file or account, continue with "First Time Setup" on page 15.

- If you are upgrading from an earlier version of Quicken and are ready to update your data files, see "Updating Data from Quicken 3 and 4" on page 477.

- For information about the Quicken Main Menu, read "Using Quicken's Menus" on page 16.

If you start Quicken and the screen is unreadable

If you should ever start Quicken and find that the screen is unreadable, it's probably because the Quicken program you are using is set for a color monitor, and you're using it on a monochrome monitor. To solve this problem, press Esc to make sure you are at the Main Menu and press P S C 1 to set the monitor type as monochrome. If this doesn't work, press 5 3 1 1 instead.

$ First Time Setup

The first time you start Quicken, you will see the Welcome to Quicken 5.0 window.

To go to the Quicken Main Menu, press Esc at this screen.

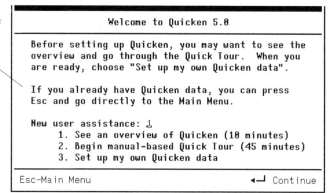

```
        Welcome to Quicken 5.0
_____
Before setting up Quicken, you may want to see the
overview and go through the Quick Tour.  When you
are ready, choose "Set up my own Quicken data".

If you already have Quicken data, you can press
Esc and go directly to the Main Menu.

New user assistance: 1
        1. See an overview of Quicken (10 minutes)
        2. Begin manual-based Quick Tour (45 minutes)
        3. Set up my own Quicken data
_____
Esc-Main Menu                          ◄┘ Continue
```

Note: If you have upgraded from an earlier version of Quicken, you see the Main Menu immediately instead of this window. If you want to use the aids available for new users, choose Use Tutorials/Assistants and then choose First Time Setup.

The Welcome window provides help to the first-time user of Quicken. If you have a hard disk, we recommend that you follow all three suggested steps in sequence. If you are running Quicken from floppy disks, you cannot do the first two, so start with choice 3 ("Set up my own Quicken data").

1. (Hard disk users only) See an overview of Quicken. The overview shows you several important screens and takes about ten minutes.

2. (Hard disk users only) Begin manual-based Quick Tour.

    When you choose this command, Quicken sets up sample data so you can follow the Quick Tour in the next chapter of this manual. Skip to "Choosing the Sample File" on page 33 of this manual to load the file and take the tour.

3. (Everyone) Set up my own Quicken data. Quicken helps you set up a data file and a bank account. For more information, see "Setting Up Your First File and Bank Account" on page 16.

Setting Up Your First File and Bank Account

Quicken guides you on screen when you're ready to set up your first data file and bank account.

At the Welcome window, choose 3 ("Set up my own Quicken data") and Quicken will help you do the following:

- Name and locate your first data file.
- Choose a standard list of categories for all accounts in this file. (To see the complete lists of Quicken's standard home and business categories, turn to "Standard Categories for Home and Business Use" on page 102.)
- Choose a type (bank, cash or credit card) for your first account and name your account.
- Record the balance and date as of your last statement.

You have a chance to review and change what you enter just before Quicken creates the file and account.

Tips for setting up your first file and account:

- Before you begin, have available your last bank statement (or the statement you will start with).

- If you're setting up the file for a business, you may want to use the business name as the file name (8 characters maximum).

- If you intend to keep both business and personal finances on Quicken, see the discussion in "Setting Up Additional Files" on page 453 before you set up your files. Depending upon your needs, it may be best for you to have one file or two. In any case, we suggest that you set up one file and work with it for a while before setting up a second file.

- Choosing one of the standard (home or business) lists of categories helps you get going with Quicken. You can always make changes to the list later.

Using Quicken's Menus

Using the Main Menu

Each time you start the program after first time setup, you start using Quicken by choosing the command you want from the Main Menu. You can return to the Main Menu by pressing Esc from any Quicken screen.

The Main Menu lists commands for Quicken's main activities.

Use the arrow keys to move the selection bar.

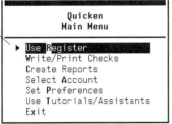

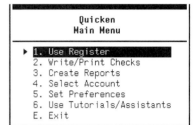

The Main Menu looks like this for new users of Quicken. One entire item (Use Register in this example) is "selected," or displayed in contrasting type. Other items have a single letter in contrasting type.

You can choose an item by pressing the key for the single letter in contrasting type. For example, press C to create reports.

The Main Menu looks like this if you installed over an earlier version, or if someone has chosen to display menus with function keys. (To change the way Quicken displays menus, see "Menu Access" on page 437.)

You can choose an item by pressing the key for the number (or letter) at its left. For example, press 3 to create reports.

Hint: If you can't see the highlighted letters in a command, adjust your monitor's brightness controls.

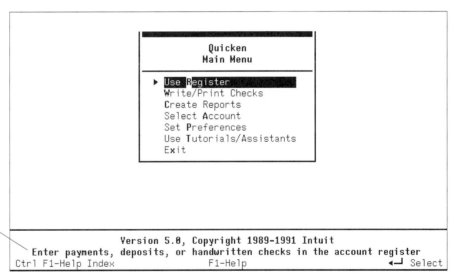

Each time you select a command on any menu, Quicken displays a description of the menu command at the bottom of the screen.

Choose a menu command in any one of these ways:

- Use the up arrow key (↑) or the down arrow key (↓) to select the command you want. (A command is selected when the selection bar is over it.) Then press Enter.

  OR

- Press the key for the highlighted letter or number of the command. (You don't have to press Enter.)

  OR

- With a mouse, move the pointer to the item and click (press the left button).

Main Menu Choices

Here's a brief summary of each command on the Main Menu. You'll find detailed information about these menu commands in the chapters and sections indicated.

Use Register

Takes you to the register for the account you are currently working with. (The Quicken register is much like your paper check register.) In a Quicken bank account, use the register to add checks you've written by hand, deposits, ATM withdrawals, bank fees, and other transactions. (See *Using the Register*, beginning on page 57.) In other types of accounts, the register is your primary work area, where you enter all types of transactions. (See the chapters in the section *Completing Your Financial Picture*, beginning on page 245.)

Write/Print Checks

Use to write checks that you want to print on your printer or to transmit electronically with your modem. (See *Writing Checks*, beginning on page 77; *Printing Checks*, beginning on page 85; or *Using CheckFree to Pay Bills Electronically*, beginning on page 219.) To enter checks you have written by hand, choose Use Register instead.

Create Reports

Displays the reports menu, where you can choose the type of financial report you want. You can produce financial summaries or detailed listings of your income and expenses, budgets, and more—all based on your Quicken records. (See *Personal, Business, and Investment Reports*, beginning on page 139.)

Select Account

Use to select the Quicken account you want to work with and to create new accounts. (See *Working with Multiple Accounts*, beginning on page 245.)

Set Preferences

Use to customize the program, set up your printer or printers, and set up electronic payment for CheckFree users. You may not have to change any settings since Quicken is set up to work with most PCs and printers. (See *Setting Preferences*, beginning on page 427.) Functions are also provided for setting up and maintaining additional Quicken files. (See *Managing Files*, beginning on page 449.)

Use Tutorials/Assistants

Choose Tutorials and Assistants to get help with first time setup, see an overview of the Quicken program, create a new file or account, or set up your file to do payroll. (See "Tutorials and Assistants" on page 23.)

Exit

Saves all your files and returns to DOS. (See "Leaving Quicken" on page 29 for important information about using the Exit command.)

If you have not set up your first file and account

Choose Tutorials/Assistants at the Main Menu and then choose First Time SetUp. Quicken can lead you through these steps.

Using the Pulldown Menus

In the Write Checks screen, the Register screen, and others, Quicken lists features on "pulldown menus."

If you are not in the register, press Esc as many times as needed to display the Main Menu. Then choose Use Register from the Main Menu.

Try out the pulldown menus now:

1. Once you're in the register, press Alt-A (that is, press and hold down the Alt key while you press the letter A) to display or "pull down" the Activities menu.

The menu bar at the top of the screen lists menu titles and the Help key. Each menu title has one highlighted letter.

The Activities menu is a pulldown menu.

Ctrl-W is a "Quick Key." You can choose the menu command by pressing the Quick Key without displaying the pulldown menu.

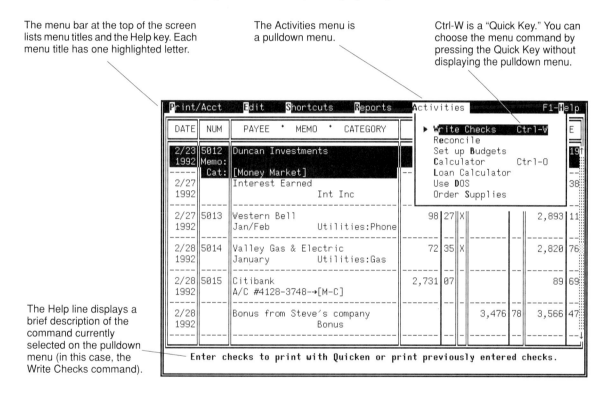

The Help line displays a brief description of the command currently selected on the pulldown menu (in this case, the Write Checks command).

When you press Alt and the highlighted letter in any pulldown menu title, Quicken displays the corresponding pulldown menu or pops up the Help window. If you have a mouse, click on a menu title to display the menu and then click on a command to choose it.

2. Press the left arrow key (←) to display the Reports menu.

Once you have a menu displayed, you can view the other menus on the menu bar by pressing the left (←) or right (→) arrow keys located to the right of your keyboard, as well as by pressing another Alt-key combination.

3. Now press the left arrow key to display each of the menus to the left of the Reports menu.

4. Press Alt-A to display the Activities menu again.

5. Now choose Write Checks from the Activities menu.

6. Press Esc to return to the Main Menu.

Try using Quick Keys as shortcuts for menu items.

Quicken displays "Quick Keys" to the right of many menu items. You can choose menu commands without first displaying a menu by simply pressing the appropriate Quick Key. A Quick Key is a Ctrl-key combination. Hold down the Ctrl key while you press the other key indicated. Once you become familiar with Quicken, you'll find that Quick Keys save you time. All of the Quick Keys are listed on a reference card in this manual. To practice using a Quick Key in a bank account register, press Ctrl-W to go to the Write Checks screen; then press Ctrl-R to return to the register.

$ Getting Help Information Fast

Computers can get you specific information faster than any paper manual. That's why Quicken has a comprehensive, fully indexed Help system. Once you are generally familiar with Quicken, you may decide to consult the Help routinely instead of this paper manual. Even if you rarely use the Help in other computer programs, give Quicken's Help a try.

Quicken Help speeds information to you in several ways:

Do this:	For this kind of information:
Press F1 anywhere.	When you press F1, Quicken shows you context-sensitive Help about the current screen, window, or menu. You can also press Alt-H for this kind of Help. You'll find the F1 key at the top or on the left of your keyboard.
Tab to a bold phrase and press Enter.	Most Help windows contain phrases in bold type or a different color (called "links") that you can use to move to Help on related topics. See "Moving to Help on Related Topics" on page 21 for more information about using links.
Press Ctrl-F1.	A detailed Help Index similar to the index at the back of this paper manual. You can use this Help Index to find information without picking up this manual.
Press F1 twice.	A Table of Contents that enables you to read Help topics in an order convenient for learning basic techniques, just like the contents of a book.
Press PgDn or the down arrow.	Some Help messages are too long to fit in the Help window. If this is the case, press PgDn or the down arrow as needed to see the entire message.

After you've received the help you need, press Esc to return to whatever you were doing before you asked for help.

Moving to Help on Related Topics

As you look at the Help window, you may notice one or more words in bold type or in a different color on your screen. This bold or colored text is a link to a related topic. Use Tab to select the link and then press Enter.

Here's a typical Help window and one of the related linked messages:

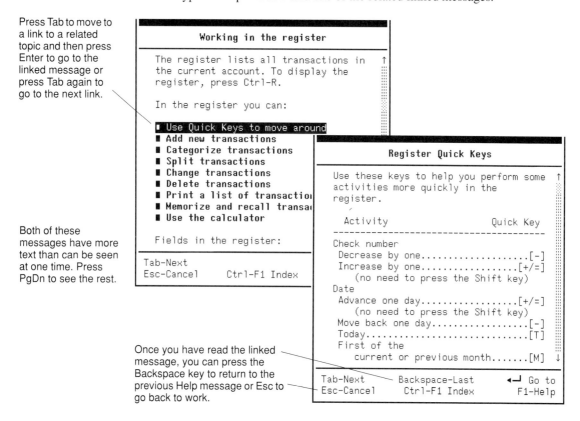

Press Tab to move to a link to a related topic and then press Enter to go to the linked message or press Tab again to go to the next link.

Both of these messages have more text than can be seen at one time. Press PgDn to see the rest.

Once you have read the linked message, you can press the Backspace key to return to the previous Help message or Esc to go back to work.

Using the Help Index

The Help system has its own index to use as you would use the index for this manual. You will find topics and subtopics to zero in on just the information you need. Press Ctrl-F1 anywhere in Quicken to go directly to the Help Index.

You can move around the Help Index in several fast ways:

Press Tab	To go to the next topic that is a link to a message. (Many topics have subtopics. When a topic has subtopics, it is the subtopics that are linked to messages.)
Press any alphabet key.	For example, press S to select the first topic that begins with that letter. If the first topic has subtopics, the first sub-topic is selected. This is similar to turning to the S tab in a paper dictionary.
Press PgDn or PgUp.	To see more topics in the index, page by page.
Press Ctrl-F to use Find.	To locate in the Help Index a word or phrase you have in mind.
Press Backspace.	To return to the Help message you just left.

This illustration may not show exactly the topics you will see. We add topics regularly in response to suggestions.

Give us your suggestions for Help! See "Your Suggestions for Help and the Manual" on page 30.

Press Esc to return to work.

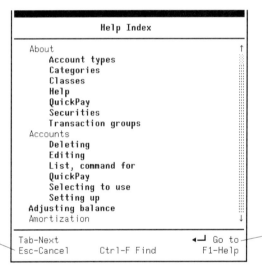

Press a letter to select the first topic that begins with the letter. If the first topic has subtopics, the first subtopic is selected. For example, type Y to select the first subtopic under "Year-end procedures."

Press - to see only first-level entries in the index (for example, About, Accounts, Adjusting balance. Press + to see first and second-level entries as shown here.

Use Tab or the arrow keys to select a topic, and press Enter to view the Help window for the selected topic.

Finding words or phrases in the Help Index

Another fast way to get to the information you need is Quicken's Find feature. Use Find at the Help Index to locate a topic that contains a word or phrase you have in mind.

To find a word in the Help Index:

1. Press Ctrl-F to display the Find window.

Type the word and press Enter.

```
Find: balance
    Ctrl-B Find back   Ctrl-N Find next
```

Repeat the search without redisplaying the Find window by pressing Ctrl-N (for the next occurrence) or Ctrl-B (for the previous occurrence).

2. Type a word or phrase and press Enter.

    Quicken finds the first topic in the index that includes the word.

3. You can repeat the search without redisplaying the Find window by pressing Ctrl-N to find the next occurrence. Go backwards in the Index by pressing Ctrl-B.

Type a partial phrase to save keystrokes or use combinations of these "wildcard characters" typed before, in the middle of, or after a phrase:

..   Two periods on one side, or both sides, or in the middle of the partial phrase to find the first topic that contains the partial phrase.

?   Question mark to substitute for any one character. (You can type more than one question mark.) Quicken finds the first topic that includes the partial phrase and any character in the position of the question mark.

Table of Contents Help for Basic Tasks

For information about one of the basic tasks in Quicken, press F1 twice to go to the Help Table of Contents.

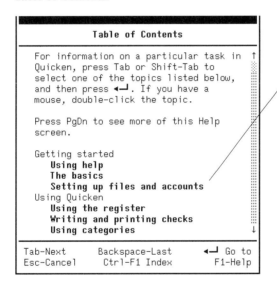

Use Tab or the up or down arrow key to select the task you need help with and press Enter.

Or double-click on a task with the mouse.

$ Tutorials and Assistants

Quicken provides teach-yourself demonstrations of its basic program features (called "tutorials" or "overviews"). You may already have used some of the tutorials and assistants during first time setup (see "First Time Setup" on page 15). If you haven't used them yet or want to try some again, you can do so at any time by choosing Tutorials/Assistants from the Main Menu.

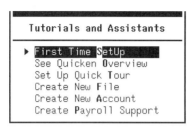

You can use as few or as many of the menu commands on the Tutorials and Assistants menu as you like. Then use this manual to find out more about Quicken's many useful features.

First Time Setup

Choose First Time Setup to return to the First Time Setup window. (See page 15.)

See Quicken Overview

When you choose this menu item, Quicken leads you through an overview of the program's features.

Set Up Quick Tour

Gets the sample data from your working copy of Quicken so that you can go through the Quick Tour in Chapter 3, beginning on page 31.

Create New File

This assistant shows you how to create a new file; that is, how to:

- Set up a new file.
- Choose a list of categories for the file.
- Set up a new account (bank, credit card, or cash) in the file.
- Enter a current balance for the account.

You have complete control over each stage of the setup process, so you can use this assistant to set up your actual data files. If you later decide you don't want to use the file you created, you can delete the file (see page 461).

You may decide to use this assistant just once to create your first Quicken file, or you may use it when you set up any new file. At some point, when you are more familiar with Quicken, you will probably prefer to create your files and accounts without using the assistant.

Create New Account

This assistant shows you how to create a new account; that is, how to:

- Set up a new account (bank, credit card, or cash) in the current file.
- Enter a current balance for the account.

Quicken asks you to enter the name of the new account, the type of account, and the balance. By watching the assistant set up the account, you can learn how to set up an account without the assistant.

If you later decide you don't want to use the account you created, you can delete the account (see page 250). You can also edit an account at any time to change its name or description.

Create Payroll Support
This assistant is for small businesses with employees to pay. See "Payroll Setup" on page 402 for more information.

Correcting Mistakes

It's easy to correct typing mistakes anywhere in Quicken, whether you are typing information in a window, entering new transactions, or reviewing transactions entered earlier.

Use the arrow keys (↑, ↓, ←, →) to position the cursor under the first character you want to change. Then make the correction by replacing, deleting, or inserting characters:

Replace Characters. Simply type new characters over the characters you want to replace.

Delete Characters. In overwrite mode, you can delete characters four ways:

• Press the spacebar to replace the character above the cursor with a space.

• Press Del (the Delete key) to delete the character at the cursor position. Any remaining characters on the line shift to the left.

• Press Backspace to delete the character to the left of the cursor. This leaves a blank in place of the character.

• Press Ctrl-Backspace to delete the entire contents of the current field.

Insert Characters. Move the cursor to the place where you want to begin inserting. Press Ins (the Insert key) to change from overwrite mode to insert mode. The cursor changes from a blinking line to a blinking rectangle. Type the characters you want to insert. The existing characters will move over to make room for the new characters. Press Ins again to stop inserting.

Shortcuts you can use inside a field

To move forward or backward one word at a time within a field, press Ctrl-→ or Ctrl-←. To move to the beginning or end of a field, press Home or End.

For information about changing or deleting whole transactions, see "Reviewing Checks You've Written" on page 81 and "Revising the Register" on page 65.

 # Keyboard Shortcuts for Quicken Lists

Quicken has several keyboard shortcuts that work in lists: for example, the Category and Transfer List window, the Class List window, the Select Account to Use window, the Select/Set Up File window:

Press the up or down arrow key	To move up or down in a list.
Press a letter key	If the list is long, press a letter to select the first name starting with that letter; for example, press A to choose Auto in the category list.
Ctrl-Ins at the Account, Category or Class lists	To add a new category or class. Pressing Ctrl-Ins is the same as choosing <New Category> or <New Class>.

 # Using a Mouse with Quicken

Quicken works with any Microsoft-compatible mouse. If your mouse doesn't work automatically with Quicken, see "Mouse problems" on page 529.

You can do the following things with a mouse in Quicken. See the figure on page 27 for examples of some of these techniques.

Right mouse button: Same as pressing Esc.

Left mouse button:

- Click a command on the Main Menu to choose it.

- Click a menu title on the pulldown menu bar to display the menu.

- Click a command on a pulldown menu to choose it.

- Click a key name at the bottom of a screen or window to carry out the function of that key. For example, you can click anywhere on the words "Ctrl ↵ Record" at the bottom of the register to record a transaction, or click "Esc-Main Menu" in the same screen to return to the Main Menu.

- Click a transaction in the register or an item in any list to select it. When you click a transaction in the register, Quicken selects it and also moves the cursor to the spot you clicked. ("Select" means mark it with the selection bar or highlight for further action.)

- Click the SPLIT label in the Num field of a selected transaction to display the Split Transaction window.

- Click the Cat: label in the Num field of a selected transaction to display the Category and Transfer List window.

- Double-click to choose any item from a list. For example, you can double-click a file name in the Select/Set Up File window to use that file.

- Hold down the mouse button on a transaction or list item and move the mouse vertically to scroll up or down in the register or in the list.

- Click the arrows on a vertical scroll bar to scroll to the next or previous transaction.

- Press the mouse button on a vertical scroll bar arrow and hold it down to scroll rapidly through the register or any list.

- Click above or below the ▓▓▓▓ to page up or page down (same as PgUp and PgDn). The po▓▓▓ represents your current position in the register or list.

- Drag the scr▓▓▓▓ ▓ical scroll bar to move to a different position in the list.

- Double-click ▓ ▓ ▓indow to move to related text.

- In a window th▓ ▓ n them to toggle. For example, you can click on an optic▓ ▓ gle from Yes to No.

Click a transaction or any item in a list to select it.

Click a menu title to ▓ mouse button when ▓ you can scroll up and ▓ the button when the c▓

▓lease the menu, ▓release ▓cted.

Click above or below the scroll box to page up or down.

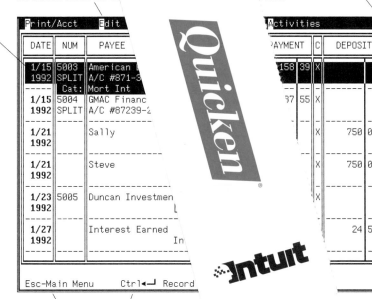

Click these words to return to the Main M▓ ▓ transaction. You can also click a key name ▓ ▓yed at the bottom of a screen instead of pressing the key itself.

Click a scroll bar arrow to scroll up or down one transaction.

$ Using the Calculator

Quicken includes its own calculator, which is accurate to eight decimal places. To display it, choose Calculator from the Activities menu, or press Ctrl-O. Quicken automatically turns on your keyboard's numeric lock so you can use the numeric keypad.

To operate:

- Using the numeric keypad or the numbers across the top of your keyboard, type numbers and operators (type + to add; − to subtract; * to multiply; / to divide). Use up to eight decimal digits. Your typing appears at the cursor.

  As soon as you type an operator, Quicken displays the value and the operator on the "paper" above the area that contains the cursor. The value remains in the cursor area, where you can type the next value over it. When you press Enter, the paper area displays the second value and the results of the calculation.

- To paste the result into the current field, press F9.

- Type C to clear the calculator.

- To perform a chain of calculations, do the first operation and press Enter. Then type an operator (+, −, *, or /) and press Enter. Quicken enters the calculated amount to start the new calculation.

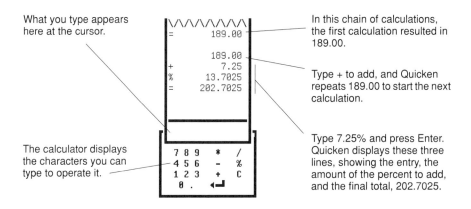

What you type appears here at the cursor.

The calculator displays the characters you can type to operate it.

In this chain of calculations, the first calculation resulted in 189.00.

Type + to add, and Quicken repeats 189.00 to start the next calculation.

Type 7.25% and press Enter. Quicken displays these three lines, showing the entry, the amount of the percent to add, and the final total, 202.7025.

- You can use the percent sign to add or subtract a percentage from an amount:

  - Type (or calculate) the amount; then press + or − (to add or subtract).

  - Type the percentage you want to add or subtract.

  - Type the percent (%) sign (for example, type 7.65%); press Enter to calculate.

  This example calculates and subtracts 7.65% from 3,500.00. The amount on the third line, 267.75, equals the amount to subtract.

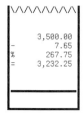

> **Use the special loan calculator to work out loan variables.**
>
> Quicken has a loan calculator that you can use to create payment schedules for your current loans or to set up "what if" scenarios to compare different loans based on a number of different loan variables. See "Using the Loan Calculator" on page 209.

Leaving Quicken

Quicken saves your data automatically when you exit. However, exiting does not back up your data.

If you leave Quicken without choosing Exit (for example, if you accidentally turn off the computer while running Quicken or if the electricity fails), the program has no opportunity to save all the files it needs. All but your most recent transactions will be safe, but the next time you start Quicken, the program will have to rebuild the incomplete files. The rebuild takes a few minutes. You may need to re-enter the last few transactions.

To make a backup (second) copy of your accounts as you leave Quicken, press Ctrl-E (that is, hold down the Control key and press the letter E). Quicken will guide you through the process to back up accounts in the current file and then exit to DOS. To make a quick backup without leaving the Quicken program, press Ctrl-B at the Main Menu. For more information on backing up your accounts, see "Backing Up a Quicken File" on page 458.

Important: Always choose Exit from the Main Menu before turning off your computer.

Quicken Terms vs. Traditional Accounting Terms

Quicken is a double-entry accrual accounting system. Quicken doesn't use traditional accounting terms like *chart of accounts* and *ledger* because many Quicken users don't understand these terms and they don't need to learn them to use Quicken.

> **Use Quicken income and expense categories to set up your chart of accounts.**
>
> The term *account* in Quicken means one of the asset or liability account types in a Quicken file. The traditional chart of accounts is equivalent to Quicken's list of income and expense categories. You can use Quicken's standard home or business categories or you can create categories that match your existing set of chart of accounts numbers. See "Setting Up a Chart of Accounts" on page 370 for more information.

Accounting term	Quicken term
chart of accounts	**Balance sheet accounts.** Balance sheet accounts (your assets, liabilities, and capital) are equivalent to Quicken accounts. *Working with Multiple Accounts*, beginning on page 245, explains how to set up your balance sheet accounts in Quicken. **Income statement (or profit and loss) accounts.** Income statement accounts (your revenue and expenses) are equivalent to Quicken *income and expense categories*. See "Setting Up a Chart of Accounts" on page 370.
close	If you wish to close and bar editing of historical transactions, simply use Quicken's transaction password to deny access to transactions prior to the close. (See "Setting a Transaction Password" on page 440.) However, Quicken does not require you to "close out your accounts" at the end of an accounting period.
general ledger	Posting to a ledger is equivalent to categorizing a transaction in a Quicken register or at the Write Checks screen. Quicken handles double-entry automatically when you use categories. *Using Categories*, beginning on page 101, explains how to set up and use Quicken income and expense categories. To see a ledger, print an itemized category report. (See "Itemized Categories" on page 143.) An itemized category report can list all the transactions in your file by category or you can limit the report to a single category.

Other Tips for Accounting Professionals

See the discussions in "Cash-Basis Bookkeeping" on page 370 and "Accrual Accounting: Timing of Income and Expenses" on page 383 to help you decide how to record your financial transactions: on a cash basis, modified cash basis, or accrual basis.

Browse through the sample applications in Section E, *Applying Quicken to Your Needs*, beginning on page 341, to see what Quicken can do; for example, accounts payable, accounts receivable, payroll preparation and tracking, balance sheets, job costing. Check the index at the back of this manual to look up any special applications you have in mind for Quicken.

Your Suggestions for Help and the Manual

Our goal is to make Quicken so easy to use and its manual and Help system so complete that no one will ever be delayed in getting work done. If you can't find the information necessary for your work, we need to improve our documentation. To leave us a message, call the toll-free Intuit Reader Comment line at 800-468-8487 (800-INTUIT-7). Thank you for your comments and suggestions.

Chapter 3

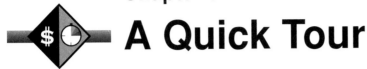

A Quick Tour

Getting a Hands-on Overview

This Quick Tour gives you hands-on experience using Quicken. You'll use a sample data file (which is installed on your hard disk when you install Quicken) to try out the various tasks you can perform using Quicken. Using sample data, you can explore the program freely with no worry about recording incorrect data in your own accounts. (Any changes or additions you make to the sample data will not be saved.) When you finish with this tour, you'll be ready to switch to your own file before entering your personal data.

How Long Does the Quick Tour Take?

Allow about an hour to complete the seven lessons of the Quick Tour. However, each lesson begins and ends at the Main Menu, so if you want to take a break, or even leave the Tour completely, you can do so easily at the end of any lesson.

What if you only have 10 minutes?

You can get started with Quicken even if you only have a few minutes to spend. If you have only 10 minutes, why not try the Quicken Overview? The Overview gives a brief demonstration of Quicken at work.

To see the Quicken Overview:

1. From the Main Menu, choose Use Tutorials/Assistants.

2. Choose See Quicken Overview.

Quicken's Main Menu

Quicken's Main Menu serves as a "home base" for the Quick Tour. Each lesson starts and ends at the Main Menu.

If your Main Menu looks different from this, showing numbers at the left of each menu item, you can change to this style of menu.

See "Using Quicken's Menus" on page 16.

```
┌─────────────────────────────┐
│ ███████████████████████████ │
│          Quicken            │
│         Main Menu           │
│─────────────────────────────│
│   Use Register              │
│   Write/Print Checks        │
│   Create Reports            │
│   Select Account            │
│ ▶ Set Preferences           │
│   Tutorials and Assistants  │
│   Exit                      │
└─────────────────────────────┘
```

You'll explore most of these menu items during this Quick Tour.

Tip for a Successful Tour

As part of the Quick Tour, you'll be moving your visual focus frequently:

- You'll read a step in the manual
- Then you'll look at the keyboard
- Then you'll look up at the screen
- Then you'll look back to the manual

It's easy to lose your place, so Quicken users who tried the Quick Tour suggest that a convenient technique is to check off each step as you complete it. That way, when you glance back at the manual, you can easily see which step is next, and you'll avoid the confusion of missing an essential step.

Starting your own Quicken file

Be sure to leave the sample file and create a separate file for your own data. Don't enter your personal data in the sample data file!

It may seem tempting to stop in the middle of the Quick Tour and start adding your own data to the sample file, rather than setting up a data file of your own. However, it is essential to leave the Quick Tour and set up your own file, because other Quicken assistants may write over the sample file.

So to avoid losing your data, set up your own Quicken file after you finish the Quick Tour. The Create New File assistant is there to help you with this task. For more information, see "Tutorials and Assistants" on page 23.

$ Lesson 1. Getting Started

In this lesson you'll learn:

- How to start Quicken from DOS
- How to set Quicken to look at the sample data file
- How to get around in Quicken
- How to use the Register screen

Starting Quicken

First, you'll start Quicken and open the sample data file that comes with Quicken. Follow these steps if taking the Quick Tour is the way you begin using Quicken. You can also reach the Quick Tour from the Main Menu at any time. (Choose Use Tutorials/Assistants, choose Set Up Quick Tour, then start at "To set Quicken to look at the sample data file:" on page 34.)

To start Quicken:

1. Enter Q to start Quicken at the DOS prompt for the drive where you installed Quicken (normally Drive C).

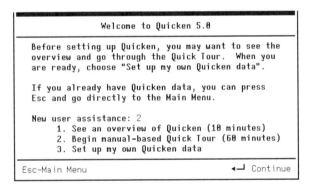

```
                  Welcome to Quicken 5.0

   Before setting up Quicken, you may want to see the
   overview and go through the Quick Tour.  When you
   are ready, choose "Set up my own Quicken data".

   If you already have Quicken data, you can press
   Esc and go directly to the Main Menu.

   New user assistance: 2
        1. See an overview of Quicken (10 minutes)
        2. Begin manual-based Quick Tour (60 minutes)
        3. Set up my own Quicken data

   Esc-Main Menu                          ◄┘ Continue
```

2. In the Welcome to Quicken window, type 2 and press Enter.

   Quicken returns to the Main Menu and flashes the message "Getting data." When the sample data file is ready, Quicken displays the "Ready To Begin Quick Tour" window.

3. Press Enter to begin the Quick Tour.

   Quicken takes you to the Select/Set Up File window.

Choosing the Sample File

For you to explore the sample data that was placed on your hard disk during installation, Quicken must be set to look at the sample file.

Note: Begin here if you start from Use Tutorials/Assistants on the Main Menu.

To set Quicken to look at the sample data file:

1. Select (highlight) the sample data file (~Sample) from the Select/Set Up File window and press Enter.

   (Usually, you'll see several files listed in the Select/Set Up File window. If you are taking the Quick Tour before you create any files, you may see only one file in the list, the sample data file (~Sample). In this case, the sample data file will already be selected, so you only need to press Enter.)

This is the Sample file for the Quick Tour. (You can recognize this file by the tilde symbol (~) in front of the name.)

This is the directory where the ~Sample file is stored.

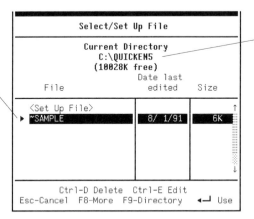

```
                 Select/Set Up File

               Current Directory
                  C:\QUICKEN5
                 (10028K free)
                            Date last
          File                edited    Size

        <Set Up File>
      ▶ ~SAMPLE              8/ 1/91     6K


          Ctrl-D Delete   Ctrl-E Edit
     Esc-Cancel  F8-More  F9-Directory   ◄┘ Use
```

Quicken displays the Select Account to Use screen. Notice that the sample data file contains six different accounts. (When you open your own data file, you'll also create one file containing several accounts.) Because these accounts are all part of one file, you treat them as a group:

- You can create reports that include information from all the accounts in a file.
- You can transfer funds from account to account within the file.
- You use one category list for all six accounts in the file.

2. Press Enter to choose Checking from the Select Account to Use screen.

   When Quicken displays this screen, Checking should be highlighted. If it isn't, use the arrow keys to select Checking, then press Enter (or double-click with the mouse)

The sample file contains six accounts. One file can hold all the accounts you'll need to get started in Quicken.

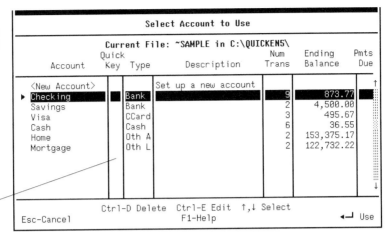

```
                        Select Account to Use

              Current File: ~SAMPLE in C:\QUICKEN5\
                     Quick                    Num    Ending    Pmts
          Account    Key   Type   Description Trans  Balance    Due

      <New Account>              Set up a new account              ↑
   ▶  Checking         Bank                        9     873.77  :::
      Savings          Bank                        2   4,500.00  :::
      Visa             CCard                        3     495.67  :::
      Cash             Cash                         6      36.55  :::
      Home             Oth A                        2 153,375.17  :::
      Mortgage         Oth L                        2 122,732.22  :::
                                                                  ↓

              Ctrl-D Delete   Ctrl-E Edit   ↑,↓ Select
      Esc-Cancel                  F1-Help                    ↵ Use
```

The Type column shows the type of account. For instance, Visa is a Credit Card account.

Starting your own data file

When you finish this tour, you're ready to set up your own data file, with your own accounts, to hold your own data. Starting your own file is an important step in using Quicken, so the Quicken program is set up to help you.

When you're ready to set up your own file, choose Use Tutorials/Assistants from the Main Menu, then choose Create New File. The Create New File assistant guides you through the process of creating your own data file. (See "Setting Up Your First File and Bank Account" on page 16.)

Getting Around in Quicken

You can use either the keyboard or a mouse to navigate in Quicken:

Check your NumLock?

The PgDn, PgUp, Home, and End keys won't work if you have the number lock (Num Lock) on. Num Lock is a toggle, so to turn off the number lock, press the Num Lock key.

- To use the keyboard, scroll up and down using the arrow keys; press PgUp and PgDn to move a screenful at a time.

- To use a mouse, scroll by clicking in the stippled scroll bar at the right side of the screen.

(To avoid confusion, this manual presents keystroke techniques in procedures. If you use a mouse, see "Using a Mouse with Quicken" on page 26.)

Quicken Screen Geography

When you choose Checking, Quicken opens the register for the sample data file's checking account. The Quicken register for a checking account resembles a paper check register. (If your screen does not look like this, press Esc to return to the Main Menu and choose Use Register.)

This is the menu bar. ——

Press Alt plus the highlighted letter to pull down the menus. For example, press Alt-S to display the Shortcuts menu.

Or, if you see function keys on the menu bar, press them instead: F4 for Shortcuts.

An empty transaction is selected (highlighted) at the end of the register.

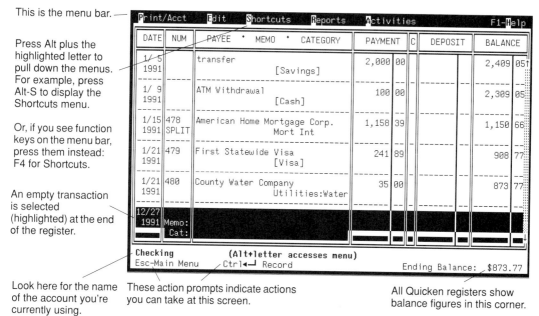

DATE	NUM	PAYEE * MEMO * CATEGORY	PAYMENT	C	DEPOSIT	BALANCE
1/ 5 1991		transfer [Savings]	2,000 00			2,409 05
1/ 9 1991		ATM Withdrawal [Cash]	100 00			2,309 05
1/15 1991	478 SPLIT	American Home Mortgage Corp. Mort Int	1,158 39			1,150 66
1/21 1991	479	First Statewide Visa [Visa]	241 89			908 77
1/21 1991	480	County Water Company Utilities:Water	35 00			873 77
12/27 1991		Memo: Cat:				

Checking   (Alt+letter accesses menu)
Esc-Main Menu   Ctrl◄┘ Record   Ending Balance: $873.77

Look here for the name of the account you're currently using.

These action prompts indicate actions you can take at this screen.

All Quicken registers show balance figures in this corner.

Once you know your way around the screen, press Esc to return to the Main Menu.

 # Lesson 2. Using the Check Register

In this lesson you'll learn:

- How to record a check in the register
- How to assign category information to a check
- How to use the Help system
- How to find a specific check in the register
- How to "split" a check used for purchases related to several categories

Entering a Check in the Check Register

The Register screen shows all the transactions for the Quicken bank account called "Checking," which is part of the Sample data file. The check register for a Quicken bank account looks just like a paper check register where you record financial transactions, such as payments, deposits, and ATM withdrawals.

To begin lesson 2, suppose that yesterday you went to Alameda Foods and wrote a $100 check for groceries (check number 3032). Now you want to record that transaction in the Quicken check register.

To add a transaction to the check register:

1. From the Main Menu, choose Use Register. When you enter the register, Quicken places the cursor in an empty transaction at the end of the register. The cursor should be in the Date field.

    (If the cursor is not at the end of the register, press Ctrl-End to reach that transaction. If the cursor is not in the Date field, use the arrow keys or Shift-Tab to move there.)

2. The highlighted text in the Date field of the empty entry is today's date. Press the minus key (−) to display yesterday's date.

    *   If nothing happens when you press the minus key, press the right arrow key to move the cursor under one of the date digits, then press the minus key.

    *   The minus key is the key to the right of the 0 (zero) key in the row of numbers across the top of your keyboard.

3. Press Tab to move to the Num field and enter the check number: 3032.

    If you press Tab twice by mistake and go past the Num field, press Shift-Tab to back up.

    Notice that this check number is in a different series from the other checks recorded in the register. The other checks were printed on Intuit checks, while this check was written by hand from your paper checkbook. There's no problem with using more than one series of check numbers at a time.

    (Because Quicken users can print out their check registers at any time, they often use their paper check registers only to record handwritten checks.)

4. Tab to the Payee field (the line above the Memo field) and enter Alameda Foods.

5. Tab to the Payment field and enter 100.

To display the pulldown menus, press Alt plus the highlighted letter.

This is the Payee field.

This line describes the selected command. For more information, press F1 for Help.

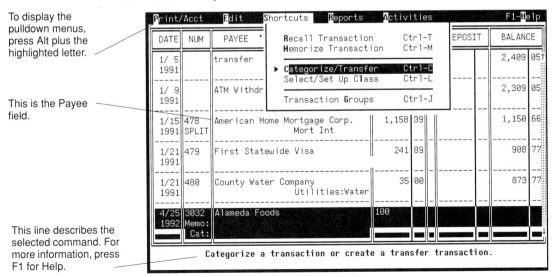

6. Tab repeatedly to move to the Category field.

(You skip the Balance field because Quicken computes the balance automatically when you record the transaction.)

Stay in the Category field and continue to the next section, where you'll enter a category for this check.

Categorizing the Check

If you wanted to track your expenses by hand, you might put all your grocery receipts in an envelope labeled "Groceries" and all your charge slips for gasoline in an envelope labeled "Gas." Then, at the end of the month, you'd tally up the contents of each envelope to find out how much you spent on each category.

You can do the same thing easily in Quicken by assigning a category name to each transaction ("categorizing" the transaction). For example, if you go grocery shopping once a week, and categorize each of those checks as "Groceries," at the end of the month you can create a report that shows how much you spent on groceries that month.

Categories are important because they let you label a group of related purchases, add together the total amounts spent on that group, and print those totals on reports.

Now you'll add information about what kind of expense the $100 check to Alameda Foods covered.

To categorize the check:

The $100 check you entered earlier should still be selected. (If not, move to it using the arrow keys.)

1. Press Ctrl-C to display the category list. (Hold down Ctrl, then press C.)

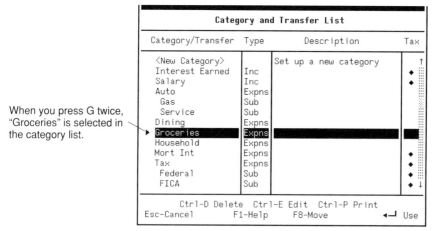

When you press G twice, "Groceries" is selected in the category list.

2. Press the letter G twice to select the category name Groceries, so this purchase will be grouped on your reports with other amounts you've spent this month on groceries.

   (If you are using a mouse, drag the mouse down the list of categories to select Groceries.)

3. Press Enter (or double-click) to categorize this transaction as Groceries.

Quicken inserts the category name "Groceries" in the Category field.

4. Press Ctrl-Enter (or click on Ctrl-Record at the bottom of the screen) to save this transaction.

   (The word RECORDING flashes in the lower-left corner of the screen, and you hear a beep.)

Saving in Quicken

In some programs, you have to "save" regularly or you may lose your work if you exit unexpectedly, such as when there's a power failure. Quicken automatically saves each transaction when you press Ctrl-Enter to record that transaction.

This automatic, transaction-by-transaction saving means that, in most cases, even if you leave Quicken unexpectedly, your data files will be up-to-date. (Of course, because your data files are a valuable resource that cannot be recovered unless you make backup copies, you will want to back up your data files regularly. See "Backing Up a Quicken File" on page 458.)

Using the Help System

Suppose you want to learn more about Quicken's categories. One convenient way to do so is to use the Help system. The following steps describe how to get Help for categories, but you can use the same techniques to learn about any aspect of Quicken.

To get Help about categories:

1. Press F1 (or Alt-H) to choose Help from the menu bar.

   Because you're in the register, you'll see "Working in the register" first.

2. Press Ctrl-F1 to see the Help Index.

   Notice that the index has two levels, like the index at the back of this manual. You can press − to see only first-level entries in the index and + to see second-level entries.

3. Press the down arrow key until "Categories" is highlighted; then press Enter.

If your screen doesn't look like this, you may still be at the screen-level help, instead of at the Help Index. Press Ctrl-F1 to reach the Help Index.

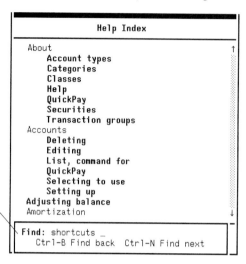

```
┌──────────────────────────────────────────────┐
│███████████████████████████████████████████████│
│                 Help Index                    ↑│
│  About                                          │
│       Account types                             │
│       Categories                                │
│       Classes                                   │
│       Help                                      │
│       QuickPay                                  │
│       Securities                                │
│       Transaction groups                        │
│  Accounts                                       │
│       Deleting                                  │
│       Editing                                   │
│       List, command for                         │
│       QuickPay                                  │
│       Selecting to use                          │
│       Setting up                               ↓│
│  Adjusting balance                              │
│  Amortization                                  │
├──────────────────────────────────────────────┤
│ Find: shortcuts _                               │
│    Ctrl-B Find back   Ctrl-N Find next          │
└──────────────────────────────────────────────┘
```

If an Index entry has subtopics, you can select only at the topic level. For example, you can select "Deleting" or "Editing" under "Accounts," but not "Accounts" itself.

Press Ctrl-F (Find) to search for any topic in the Help Index. If the first listing you find isn't the one you want, press Ctrl-F again to search for the next occurrence.

You can also reach a topic by pressing the first letter of the entry. For example, you can press the letter Y to reach "Year-end procedures."

4. Read the definition of categories in the "About categories" Help message.

5. Press PgDn to scroll, or click in the scroll bar (the stippled area at the right of the window), and read the rest of the information.

At the end of the Help message, you'll see a list of related topics. These are highlighted, or in a different color, to indicate that they are "links."

6. Choose any link to go to another Help topic. (Select by highlighting; then press Enter or double-click.)

7. Press Esc to return to the check register.

Exploring Help

Screen Help: Press F1 (or Alt-H) at any Quicken screen, window, or menu for context-sensitive Help about your current task. For example, if you are working on the Write Checks screen and need information about filling out a check, press F1 for specific help about writing checks.

Links: If you see a phrase in **bold** (or in a different color) while you are reading a Help message, you can tab to the phrase (called a "link") and press Enter to move to related text.

Help Index: You can also press Ctrl-F1 to browse through the Help Index for areas of Quicken you'd like to know more about.

Table of Contents Help: For a task-oriented list of Help topics, press F1 to reach context-sensitive help; then press F1 again. The Table of Contents Help is organized like an onscreen user manual, including topics such as "Setting up files and accounts."

Return: To return to the last topic, press Backspace.

To get Help about a field:

Let's practice getting information about the Payee field.

1. With your cursor in any transaction in the check register, press F1 for Help.

    First you'll see Help on the screen as a general topic: in this case, "Working in the register."

2. Press PgDn to display a list of fields in the register.

3. Type a p, use the arrow keys, or click in the scroll bar to move to the word Payee.

4. Press Enter (or double-click) to see Help for the Payee field.

5. Press Backspace (or click on the word Backspace) to return to the list of fields in the register.

6. For more practice using Help to get information about a field, try Memo or Category.

7. Press Esc to return to the check register.

Onscreen Help vs. This Manual

When should you use the Help system, and when should you use this manual?

You'll probably develop your own habits, but here are some guidelines:

Use the Help system when you want:	Use the manual when you want:
Information about a field you're filling in	Step-by-step instructions for a task
Guidance when you're asked to make a choice	An overview of how to use Quicken
A quick reminder on a topic you're familiar with	Ideas about new ways to use Quicken, with illustrated examples
To follow a chain of thought from topic to topic using links (words that are highlighted or show in a different color on your screen)	Systematic learning about Quicken

Searching for a Check

You can find a specific check in your check register in any of these ways:

*   Use the arrow keys to page through the register transaction by transaction.
*   Use the Find window to search for a check by any specific information, such as check number, payee, memo, category, or amount.
*   Use Go to Date to find a check by date.

Let's say you want to verify the amount of the check you wrote to the Central Market on 1/2/91, using Find.

To search for a check written to Central Market:

1. Press Alt-E to display the Edit menu.

2. Choose Find from the Edit menu.

3. In the Transaction to Find window, enter Central (in the Payee field, on the top line).

4. Press Enter repeatedly to move through the rest of the fields until Quicken displays the Search Direction window. (You can also use Tab to move through the fields, but only Enter will let you continue. Tab will cycle back through the fields again.)

5. Press Enter to choose option 1. Find Backwards. Quicken will go to the Central Market transaction for $185.98.

   Notice that you did not have to enter the entire payee. "Central" was enough to locate "Central Market."

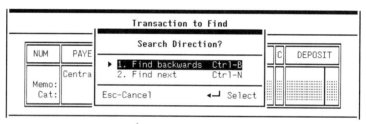

6. Leave this check selected and continue to the next section.

Finding a transaction by date

Another way to locate a specific check is to use Go to Date on the Edit menu:

1. Press Alt-E to display the Edit menu.

2. Choose Go to Date (or press Ctrl-G).

3. Fill in the date in the Go to Date window and press Enter.

Splitting a Check

Sometimes you use a single check to pay for purchases that include several categories. For instance, assume that your purchase at the Central Market actually included both groceries and power tools for use around the house. To separate these two amounts in your reports, you can split the transaction. Splitting a check lets you categorize part of the purchase as Groceries and part as Household.

To split the check:

1. The Central Market check is already selected, so press Alt-E to display the Edit menu and choose Split Transaction (or press Ctrl-S, the Quick Key to move directly from the register to the Split Transaction window).

   The Split Transaction window displays the category Groceries and the full amount of $185.98.

2. To split the transaction:

   a. Press Tab until you reach the Amount field. (If you're not moving, your finger may still be on the Ctrl key. Move up to the Tab key.)

   b. Enter 85.00. (It's OK to write in the same field as the current amount; you don't have to delete the 185.98 first.)

   c. Press Tab.

   The Amount field now shows the $85.00 spent on groceries.

   When you leave the first Amount field by pressing Tab, Quicken advances the cursor to the Category field on the second line of the split transaction and inserts the remainder of 100.98 in the Amount field. This is the amount spent on the power tools.

3. In the second Category field, type hou and press Tab.

   Quicken fills in the rest of the expense category because "Household" is on the category list. (This shortcut way of entering categories can be used in any Category field in Quicken.)

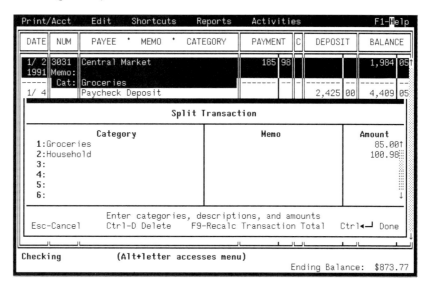

4. Press Ctrl-Enter twice:
   - Once to close the Split Transaction window
   - Once to save the changes you made to the transaction

Only the first category shows in the register when the Split Transaction window is closed.

| 1/ 2
1991 | 3031
SPLIT | Central Market
          Groceries | 185 | 98 | | | 1,984 | 05 |

5. Press Esc to return to the Main Menu.

Two favorite Quick Keys

Splitting a transaction and choosing a category are two tasks you perform repeatedly in Quicken. For these and other repetitious tasks, Quicken provides a shortcut, called a Quick Key. To use Quick Keys, hold down the Ctrl key and press the second key:

- Ctrl-S: Open the Split Transaction window (hold down the Ctrl key while pressing the S key)

- Ctrl-C: Display the Category list

Reminders: Can't quite recall the Quick Key you need? All the Quick Keys are listed on the Quick Key card included with this manual. For Help, press Ctrl-F1 for the Help Index and then Q for Quick Keys. Use the down arrow to choose the appropriate subtopic, such as "Register."

 # Lesson 3. Recalling a Memorized Check

Paying your bills each month requires writing many checks. Every check you write belongs to one of these three groups:

- Checks that are exactly the same each month (rent, a car payment)

- Checks that are the same except for the amount, which varies (telephone bill, department store charges)

- Checks that are unique for a given month (a gift to a niece, payment for a magazine subscription)

Because most of the checks you write belong to the first two groups, Quicken gives you a shortcut so you don't have to type the same information again and again.

Memorized Checks

Suppose you write a monthly check to pay the gas and electric bill. If you memorize the check the first time you write it, you can recall the same check every month from the memorized transactions list and just change the amount to pay the current bill.

You can recall a memorized check in the register or at the Write Checks screen. For this Quick Tour, you'll visit the Write Checks screen to practice recalling a memorized check.

To recall a memorized check:

1. Choose Write/Print Checks from the Main Menu.

The Write Checks screen is where you record checks that you want to print with Quicken. Notice that today's date is displayed in the Date field.

2. Press Alt-S to display the Shortcuts menu.

3. Choose Recall Transaction to see a list of previously memorized transactions.

This check was memorized without an amount because the monthly gas and electric bill varies.

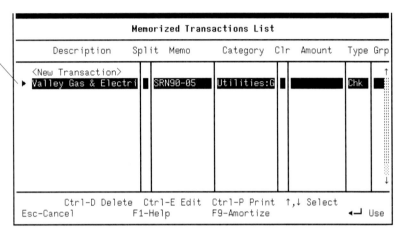

4. Press the down arrow key to select the Valley Gas & Electric check.

5. Press Enter to recall that check in the Write Checks screen.

6. In the $ (Amount) field, enter 34.17.

The address was memorized with this check, so when you recall the check, the address is included.

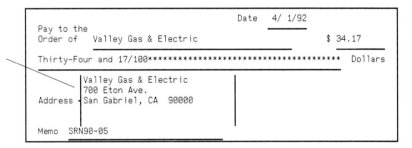

7. Press Tab. Quicken spells out the dollar amount on the next line.

If you knew that all future payments to Valley Gas & Electric would be $34.17, you could choose Memorize Transaction (from the Shortcuts menu) to rememorize the check with that amount. You can always memorize a transaction with a specific amount.

8. Press Ctrl-Enter to save the check.

(The word RECORDING flashes in the lower-left corner of the screen, and you hear a beep.)

Quicken displays a new blank check.

9. (Optional.) To print the check, use the sample checks from your Quicken package and follow the steps in *Printing Checks*, beginning on page 85.

10. Press Esc to return to the Main Menu.

Grouping memorized transactions

Later, when you've set up memorized transactions that you want to recall on the same date (for example, a group of bills that you pay at the same time each month), set up transaction groups and let Quicken keep track of when bills are due. (See *Entering Transaction Groups*, beginning on page 211.)

$ Lesson 4. Creating Reports

Let's use the sample data file to look at income and expenses for the month of January and to examine net worth as of the end of January. To get this information, create two reports:

- Cash flow, a summary of income and expenses
- Net worth, a summary of assets and liabilities

To create a cash flow report:

1. Start at the Main Menu:
   a. Choose Create Reports.
   b. Choose Personal Reports.
   c. Choose Cash Flow.

2. Fill in the fields in the Cash Flow Report window:
   a. Tab once to skip the optional report title.
   b. Change ***both*** dates to 1/91 so the cash flow report will include the correct transactions.

Tab past the Report Title field to accept the default title, "Cash Flow Report."

Change both dates to 1/91 so the report will include information from the first to the last of the month.

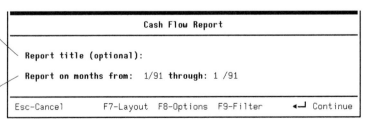

```
                          Cash Flow Report

    Report title (optional):

    Report on months from:  1/91 through: 1 /91

  Esc-Cancel        F7-Layout  F8-Options  F9-Filter     ◄┘ Continue
```

3. Press Enter to create the report.

4. Press PgDn to examine the report.

- Note categories showing large expenditures
- Note categories showing small expenditures
- Note the overall total at the end of the month

Note: If Quicken displays the No Items Found window, it searched for transactions in the date range you entered, but couldn't find any.

a. Press Esc to cancel the message.

b. Quicken displays the cash flow report with no transactions included.

c. Press Esc again and return to step 2. (Quicken's default dates show the current year, so to include only the sample transactions, be sure to enter 1/91 in both date fields.)

5. Press Esc repeatedly, until you return to the Main Menu.

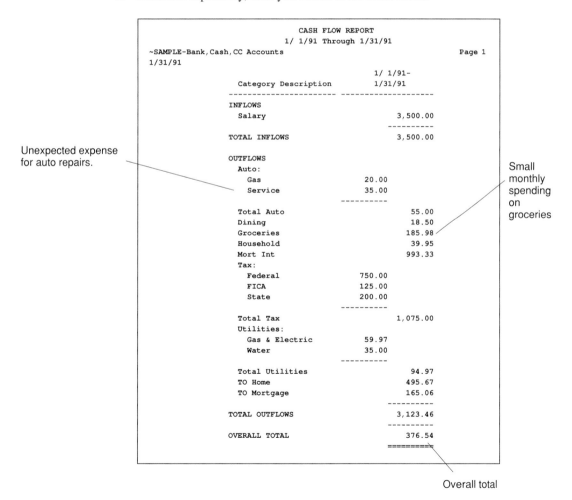

Unexpected expense for auto repairs.

Small monthly spending on groceries

Overall total

```
                          CASH FLOW REPORT
                     1/ 1/91 Through 1/31/91
   ~SAMPLE-Bank,Cash,CC Accounts                              Page 1
   1/31/91
                                             1/ 1/91-
                 Category Description          1/31/91
                 ----------------------    ------------------
                 INFLOWS
                    Salary                             3,500.00
                                                       ----------
                 TOTAL INFLOWS                         3,500.00

                 OUTFLOWS
                    Auto:
                       Gas                  20.00
                       Service              35.00
                                            ----------
                    Total Auto                            55.00
                    Dining                                18.50
                    Groceries                            185.98
                    Household                             39.95
                    Mort Int                             993.33
                    Tax:
                       Federal             750.00
                       FICA                125.00
                       State               200.00
                                            ----------
                    Total Tax                          1,075.00
                    Utilities:
                       Gas & Electric       59.97
                       Water                35.00
                                            ----------
                    Total Utilities                       94.97
                    TO Home                              495.67
                    TO Mortgage                          165.06
                                                       ----------
                 TOTAL OUTFLOWS                        3,123.46
                                                       ----------
                 OVERALL TOTAL                           376.54
                                                       ==========
```

To create a net worth report as of January 31:

1. Start at the Main Menu:

    a. Choose Create Reports.

    b. Choose Personal Reports.

    c. Choose Net Worth.

2. Fill in the fields in the Net Worth Report window.

If you tab past the report title field, Quicken will use the default title, "Net Worth Report."

Change the Report Balances date to 1/31/91.

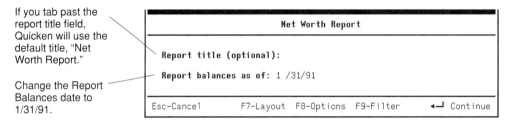

```
                        Net Worth Report


    Report title (optional):

    Report balances as of: 1 /31/91


  Esc-Cancel        F7-Layout  F8-Options  F9-Filter      ◄┘ Continue
```

3. Press Enter to create the report.

Quicken calculates the balance of all the accounts in the file as of the date you specify.

```
                              NET WORTH REPORT
                               As of 1/31/91
       ~SAMPLE-All Accounts                                        Page 1
       1/31/91
                                                      1/31/91
                                   Acct                Balance
       ----------------------------------- ------------
       ASSETS
         Cash and Bank Accounts
            Cash                                        36.55
            Checking                                   873.77
            Savings                                  4,500.00
                                                   ------------
            Total Cash and Bank Accounts             5,410.32

         Other Assets
            Home                                    153,375.17
                                                   ------------
            Total Other Assets                      153,375.17


       TOTAL ASSETS                                 158,785.49

       LIABILITIES
         Credit Cards
            Visa                                        495.67
                                                   ------------
            Total Credit Cards                          495.67

         Other Liabilities
            Mortgage                                122,732.22
                                                   ------------
            Total Other Liabilities                 122,732.22


       TOTAL LIABILITIES                            123,227.89


       TOTAL NET WORTH                               35,557.60
                                                   ============
```

4. Press PgDn to examine the report.

   This report shows multiple accounts. Setting up multiple accounts is an advanced use of Quicken; we recommend that you work with one checking account for a month or two before you set up additional accounts for items such as a savings account or a mortgage.

5. Press Esc repeatedly, until you reach the Main Menu.

 # Lesson 5. Adding a New Account

Suppose that you want to add a new account to the Sample data file. For example, you might want to add a new money market account.

What's the difference between a file and an account?

You might have a checking account, a savings account, a credit card account, and a money market account, all in one file called by your name, such as Alvarez. You combine a group of accounts into a single file, so you can create reports, such as a net worth report, that include balances from all your accounts.

For more information, press F1 twice to see Table of Contents help. Choose "Setting up files and accounts," then choose "About files" and "About accounts."

To add a new account to a Quicken file:

1. From the Main Menu, choose Select Account.

   Quicken displays the Select Account to Use screen.

2. Press the up arrow key to select <New Account>.

3. Press Enter.

Quicken has six account types.

Bank accounts include both checking and savings accounts.

Account names can be up to 15 characters long. Each account name must be unique.

4. Fill in the Set Up New Account window:

   a. At the Account Type field, press Tab to accept the default option: 1. Bank Account.

b. Enter **Money Market** as the name for this account.

c. Enter 20,000 for the opening balance as of today's date.

d. Press Tab to accept today's date, the default value. (If you want to change the date, enter a new date in this field.)

e. Enter an account number in the optional Description field.

5. Press Enter to set up the account.

6. Press the down arrow key to highlight the Money Market account you just added, and press Enter. (This will take you to the register for the Money Market account.)

7. Press Esc to return to the Main Menu.

Lesson 6. Transferring Money Between Accounts

When you have multiple accounts, you may want to transfer money from one account to another. Suppose you want to transfer money from your savings account to the new money market account. When you record the deposit as a transfer *to* the register of the money market account, Quicken automatically records a withdrawal *from* the savings account for the same amount.

Let's say you want to transfer $4,000 from your savings account to your money market fund. You start by recording the deposit in your money market account, then in the Category field, you create a transfer transaction by entering the name of the savings account. When you record a transfer in this way, Quicken automatically creates a parallel transaction in the savings account.

(Sometimes people wonder why they can't categorize transfers. Categories allow you to track income and expenses, however, and a transfer is only a way to record the movement of funds. No income or expense is created by a transfer. In this case, for example, you categorized the $4,000 as income when you deposited it in your savings account, and you'll categorize it as various expenses if you withdraw it from your money market fund.)

To create a transfer transaction:

1. From the Main Menu, choose Use Register.

Look in the lower-left corner of the screen to see the account name for this register. The account name should be Money Market. If it is *not* Money Market:

a. Esc to the Main Menu.

b. Choose Select Account.

c. Choose Money Market.

2. In the highlighted transaction, Tab to the Payee field (the first line, just above the Memo field) and enter **transfer from savings**.

(If you need to move backward, press Shift-Tab.)

Here's the name of the account that contains the other side of the transfer. Note the brackets around the transfer account name.

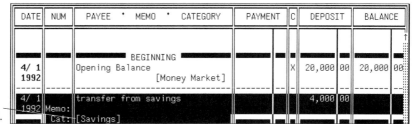

3. Press Tab until you reach the Deposit field, then type **4000**. Press Enter.

4. Tab to the Category field.

5. Press Ctrl-C to display the category and transfer list.

6. Select the account name [Savings] from close to the bottom of the list. One way to move quickly to [Savings] is to repeatedly press the first letter of the name (in this case, **S**).

Account names are enclosed in brackets to distinguish them from categories.

Press the letter S to move quickly to the Savings account. (If you press the left bracket ([ ) you will remain at the top of the list.)

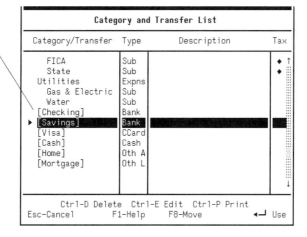

7. Press Enter.

Quicken inserts the account name [Savings] in the Category field of the selected transaction.

8. Press Ctrl-Enter to record, or save, the transaction.

9. Press the up arrow key to select the transaction again.

10. Press Alt-E to display the Edit menu and choose Go to Transfer. (Or press Ctrl-X.)

Look in the lower-left corner of the screen to see the account name: Savings. Quicken took you to the parallel entry in Savings, the withdrawal of the $4,000 that was deposited into the Money Market account.

When you entered the transfer in the Money Market account, Quicken automatically created this matching entry in Savings, with $4,000 in the Payment field.

DATE	NUM	PAYEE · MEMO · CATEGORY	PAYMENT	C	DEPOSIT	BALANCE
		▬▬▬ BEGINNING ▬▬▬				
1/ 1 1991		Opening Balance [Savings]		X	2,500 00	2,500 00
1/ 5 1991		transfer [Checking]			2,000 00	4,500 00
4/ 1 1992		transfer from savings [Money Market]	4,000 00			500 00

Here's the name of the account that contains the other side of the transfer.

Note how the running balance decreases by $4,000.00 after the transfer of money from Savings to the Money Market account.

11. You'll be working with the Checking account in the next part of the tour, so before you return to the Main Menu, set Quicken to look at the Checking account:

a. Press Alt-P to display the Print/Acct menu.

b. Choose Select/Set Up Account.

c. Select the Checking account and press Enter. (Quicken takes you to the register for the Checking account.)

d. Press Esc to return to the Main Menu.

Lesson 7. Balancing a Bank Statement

For the final lesson in this Quick Tour, you'll practice balancing, or reconciling, the January bank statement for the checking account. Here's the sample bank statement you'll use to check which items have cleared the bank.

Sample Bank Statement for Checking Account				
Last statement date:	12/27/90	Beginning balance:		2,230.00
This statement date:	1/27/91	Ending balance:		878.41
		Interest earned:		4.64
Payments:		5	Deposits:	1
477	1/1	59.97	1/4	2,245.00
478	1/15	1,158.39		
479	1/15	241.89	Withdrawals:	2
480	1/21	35.00	1/5	2,000.00
3031	1/2	185.98	1/9	100.00

To reconcile the account:

1. From the Main Menu, choose Use Register.

   Look in the lower-left corner of the screen to see the account name for this register. The account name should be Checking. If it is *not* Checking:

   a. Esc to the Main Menu.

   b. Choose Select Account.

   c. Choose Checking.

2. Press Alt-A to display the Activities menu.

3. Choose Reconcile.

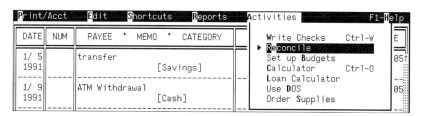

4. Enter the ending balance from the sample statement (on page 53) in the Bank Statement Ending Balance field.

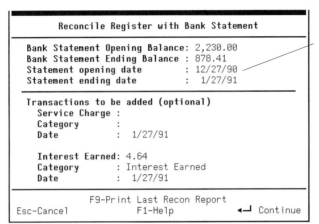

```
Reconcile Register with Bank Statement

Bank Statement Opening Balance: 2,230.00
Bank Statement Ending Balance : 878.41
Statement opening date        : 12/27/90
Statement ending date         :  1/27/91

Transactions to be added (optional)
  Service Charge :
  Category       :
  Date           : 1/27/91

  Interest Earned: 4.64
  Category       : Interest Earned
  Date           : 1/27/91

              F9-Print Last Recon Report
Esc-Cancel          F1-Help              ◄┘ Continue
```

If the dates on your screen are different, change them to the opening and ending dates from the sample bank statement.

5. Enter the interest amount and categorize it as Interest Earned. (Press Ctrl-C to display the category and transfer list.)

6. Press Enter repeatedly to move through the fields on this screen and continue to the next screen, the Reconciliation Summary screen.

To mark an item as cleared, highlight it and then press Enter. Quicken enters an asterisk (*) in the C (Cleared) field.

These two transactions have not cleared the bank, so don't mark them as cleared.

The Reconciliation Summary screen displays one line for each transaction.

```
Print/Acct    Edit    Shortcuts    Reports    Activities              F1-Help

 NUM   C    AMOUNT      DATE        PAYEE                  MEMO
            *      -100.00   1/ 9/91  ATM Withdrawal
 477    *       -59.97   1/ 1/91  Valley Gas & Electric  SRN90-05
 478    *    -1,158.39   1/15/91  American Home Mortgage
 479    *      -241.89   1/21/91  First Statewide Visa
 480    *       -35.00   1/21/91  County Water Company
 3031   *      -185.98   1/ 2/91  Central Market
 3032          -100.00   4/ 2/92  Alameda Foods
 *****          -34.17   4/ 2/92  Valley Gas & Electric  SRN90-05
►═════ ═ ════════════ ══════ ═════════════════════ ════════════════════
            *         4.64   1/27/91  Interest Earned

To Mark Cleared Items, press ◄┘   ▪      To Add or Change Items, press F9

                        RECONCILIATION SUMMARY
       Items You Have Marked Cleared (*)   Opening Bal Difference     0.00
       -------------------------------     Cleared (X,*) Balance    878.41
           7    Checks, Debits  -3,781.23  Bank Statement Balance   878.41
           2    Deposits, Credits 2,429.64 Difference                 0.00

 F1-Help      F8-Mark Range    F9-View Register    Ctrl-F Find  Ctrl F10-Done
```

Press F9 to see the register in full and make any necessary changes.

The amount in the Difference field changes with each item you mark as cleared.

7. In the list of transactions at the top of the Reconciliation Summary screen, mark as cleared each item that appears on the sample bank statement on page 53.

   - To mark an item as cleared, select the item and press Enter (or double-click).

   - When you press Enter, Quicken inserts an asterisk in the C (Cleared) field and moves the cursor to the next item.

   - Do not mark any item that isn't on the statement. For example, do not mark either the Valley Gas & Electric check for $34.17, or the check to Alameda Foods for $100, because they have not yet cleared the bank. (You know they haven't cleared the bank because they do not appear on the sample 1/27/91 statement on page 53.)

   - If you do mark an item by mistake, highlight it and press the spacebar to unmark it.

   As you mark items as cleared, watch how the amount in the Difference field changes. When you've finished marking all the cleared transactions, the value in the Difference field should be 0.00.

8. When the amount in the Difference field is zero, press Ctrl-F10.

   You have successfully balanced the account!

   Because this is sample data, if the account doesn't balance, it means you may have mismarked some transactions in step 7, or someone might have altered one or more of the transactions. In this case, Quicken will offer to make an adjusting entry. To accept the adjusting entry:

   a. Press Enter to accept the adjusting entry.

   b. Enter Y at the Adding Balance Adjustment Entry window.

   c. Press F10.

9. Press Enter to finish reconciliation and return to the register.

10. Press Esc to return to the Main Menu. (Enter X if you want to exit from Quicken.)

Where to Go Next

Now that you've seen the basics of Quicken, you're probably ready to start working in your own data file.

Starting your own file

Be sure to leave the sample file and create a separate file for your own data. Don't enter your personal data in the sample file because the sample file is not designed to hold real data. Your data is precious: it requires its own file and its own accounts.

To create your own Quicken file:

1. Choose Use Tutorials/Assistants from the Main Menu.

2. Choose Create New File. The Create New File assistant will walk you through the process of setting up your own file.

3. For more information about the Create New File assistant, see "Tutorials and Assistants" on page 23.

If you want to take the Quick Tour again...

You can take the Quick Tour again at any time, to refresh your knowledge of the program, to practice a particular task using Quicken, or to demonstrate Quicken to visiting friends and colleagues.

1. Choose Use Tutorials/Assistants from the Main Menu.

2. Choose Set Up Quick Tour.

3. Press Enter at the "Ready to Begin Quick Tour" message. Quicken creates new sample data, so you can start the Quick Tour again. Turn to "Choosing the Sample File" on page 33.

Note: How did the Quick Tour work for you? If something worked particularly well (or didn't work so well at all!), we want to know. Call Quicken's 24-hour Reader Comment Line at 800-468-8487 (800-INTUIT-7).

Chapter 4

Using the Register

You're familiar with using a paper check register to record transactions in your checking account. Use Quicken's register screen the same way, to keep a record of all activity that affects your checking account balance.

You add transactions to the register by entering the appropriate information and recording it. When you record a check at the Write Checks screen, Quicken automatically creates a register entry. You only need to add register entries for other activities that affect your account balance:

- Checks written by hand
- ATM (automatic teller machine) transactions
- Electronic transactions
- Deposits
- Checking account fees and interest

The Quicken register has several advantages over a paper check register:

- Quicken does all the math, so you will never make addition or subtraction errors.
- As you work, Quicken orders your transactions by date and check number.
- You can review or print the check register any time you want.

Note: Some people like to get started by entering transactions that occurred before they bought Quicken. If you want to start this way, see "Entering Year-to-Date Transactions" on page 75.

The Check Register

Choose Use Register from the Main Menu (or, if you are at the Write Checks screen, from the Activities menu). Quicken displays the check register, which looks like the register in your paper checkbook, with columns for payments and deposits.

Quicken puts your transactions in order by date.

Asterisks indicate checks you've written but not yet printed.

The C (Cleared) field shows transactions marked as cleared when you reconcile your account.

This double line appears when you have postdated transactions. All transactions dated after today are shown below it.

Number of printed check or handwritten check.

The payee or description appears on the top line of this field.

Any memo text appears here on the second line of the transaction.

You can enter a new transaction at the bottom of the register.

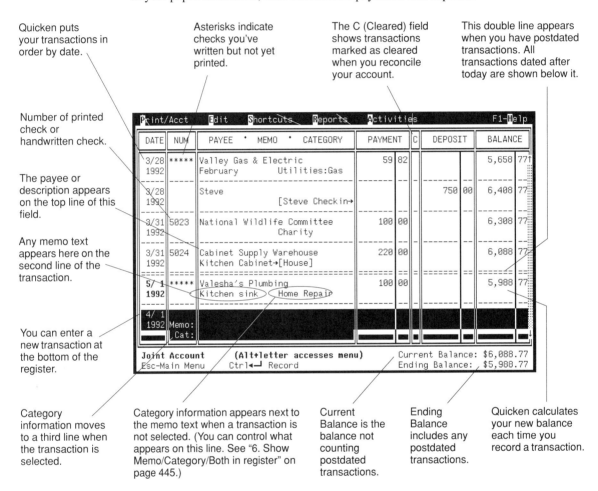

Category information moves to a third line when the transaction is selected.

Category information appears next to the memo text when a transaction is not selected. (You can control what appears on this line. See "6. Show Memo/Category/Both in register" on page 445.)

Current Balance is the balance not counting postdated transactions.

Ending Balance includes any postdated transactions.

Quicken calculates your new balance each time you record a transaction.

Note: Each Quicken account has a register associated with it. This chapter describes using the register for bank accounts. The basic steps for working in all Quicken registers are the same. Once you've learned to work with your check register, you'll know most of what you need to know about any Quicken register. You'll find illustrations of registers for other types of accounts, such as investment accounts, in the chapters about those accounts.

$ Adding Transactions to the Check Register

You enter transactions in the check register in much the same way you fill in a paper check register. You add new transactions in the blank entry at the very bottom of the register.

To add a transaction to the check register:

1. Display the register. (Choose Use Register from the Main Menu, or press Ctrl-R.)

2. If necessary, press Ctrl-End (hold down the Ctrl key and press the End key) to move to the blank entry at the end of the register.

3. Enter the information about the new transaction. (See "Fields in a Transaction" on page 60 for details about each field.)

    *   Press Enter or Tab to move the cursor from one field to the next.
    *   Use the left and right arrow keys to move the cursor one space at a time.
    *   If you make a mistake, see "Correcting Mistakes" on page 25.

4. When you have finished entering the transaction, press Ctrl-Enter or F10 to record it and make it a permanent part of your records.

    The word RECORDING flashes in the lower-left corner of the screen, and you hear a beep. You may also see the word MOVING flash on the screen, indicating Quicken is moving the entry to put it in order by date and check number. Some fast computers display these messages very briefly, so don't worry if you miss the messages.

Where did my transaction go?

Quicken sorted it by date. See "Quicken Sorts Transactions by Date and Check Number" on page 60.

Quicken Displays Memo and Category Fields on Separate Lines

Quicken places the cursor in the Date field of the next transaction. Only the current transaction shows Memo and Category fields on two separate lines. Once you record a transaction, Quicken shows both the Memo and Category fields on the second line, with Memo on the left and Category on the right.

Do I still need my paper register?

Once your transactions are recorded in your Quicken register, you no longer need to keep your paper register up-to-date. Use your paper register to record only those checks you write away from home, and then use the Cleared column in that register to check off when you add those transactions to your Quicken register.

Quicken Sorts Transactions by Date and Check Number

Each time you record a transaction, Quicken places it in the register in order first by date and then by check number within the date. After placing the transaction in the correct order, Quicken recalculates all subsequent balances.

This sorting keeps your records in order no matter when you enter transactions. Suppose the date at the end of the check register is 2/27/92 and you want to enter an ATM withdrawal made on 2/10/92. You can enter the transaction at the end of the register. When you press Ctrl-Enter to record, Quicken automatically moves the transaction to where it belongs. If you prefer to enter the new transaction in the correct sequence, press Ctrl-Ins to create a blank transaction above the current transaction.

Duplicate check numbers

Quicken can warn you if you enter a check number that duplicates a number already used in this account. See "5. Warn if a check number is re-used" on page 447.

Fields in a Transaction

Date   Enter the date of the transaction, either in full or by using one of the date shortcuts.

Date shortcuts

These special keys allow you to change the date quickly:

+ (plus key)	Move forward one day
− (minus key)	Move back one day
T	Today
M	First of Month
H	End of montH
Y	First of Year
R	End of yeaR

If you are in a Date field, press one of these keys once to fill in the associated date in the current month or year. Press the same key repeatedly to bring up the previous or next month or year (M and Y move backward; H and R move forward).

For example, if your cursor is in the register's Date field and the date shown is 3/15/92, press M to fill in the beginning of the month (3/1); press M again to fill in the beginning of the previous month (2/1). If you start at 3/1, however, M will fill in 2/1. (Don't worry about capitalizing these letters: m works just like M.)

The best way to become familiar with these keys is to experiment with them. If you find that you can't quickly get to the date you want using these keys, you can always enter the new date directly over the current date.

Use the slash (/) to move the cursor from one part of the date to the next (for example, to move from the day to the month or from the month to the year).

You can add postdated transactions to the register by entering a future date. These transactions appear in the register with the date selected and are separated from other transactions by a double line. (On a color monitor, postdated transactions appear in a different color.)

Num   If the transaction you're entering is a handwritten check, enter the check number. If the transaction is not numbered (for example, if it is a bank fee or ATM withdrawal), press Tab to skip this field.

When you record a check with a check number, Quicken moves to the next transaction and automatically fills in the same date and the next check number.

Number field shortcut

Use the + (plus key) to save time. Press + when the cursor is in the Num field to increase the number by one. The − (minus key) decreases the number.

Payee   Enter the payee's name (for a check), the word "Deposit" (for a deposit), or any phrase you want to identify the transaction (up to 31 characters).

Payment   If you're entering a payment, enter the amount in the Payment field. (A payment is any money subtracted from your account, including withdrawals, checks, or service charges.)

You can enter the amount without dollar signs or commas. If the amount has dollars and no cents, you don't have to enter the decimal point or zeros in the cents place (Quicken will add them for you). The maximum amount for any transaction is $9,999,999.99.

C (Cleared)   This field shows either X or * for transactions that have cleared the bank. Usually you'll use the Cleared field only when you reconcile your account. Skip this field when you're entering transactions. (See *Balancing Your Checkbook*, beginning on page 119, for more information on clearing transactions.)

Deposit   If you're entering a deposit, enter the amount in the Deposit field. (A deposit is any money added to your account, including deposits, interest, or transfers from another account.)

Memo
(Optional)   You can add a memo to the transaction to provide additional information for your own records. For example, you might enter an account number as a memo. Memos can also be used to determine which transactions are included in reports. For more information, see "Filtering Your Report Data" on page 180.

If you want to add a memo that is more than 31 characters long, press Ctrl-S to display the Split Transactions window, and enter your memo in the Memo field. When you reach the end of a line, Tab three times to move to the next line of the Description field. When you have finished, press Ctrl-Enter. If you use voucher checks, the contents of the first 15 lines of the Split Transaction window will print on the voucher.

Category Enter category (and class) information on the third line of the transaction. You
(Optional) can also "split" the transaction to assign parts of it to different categories. (Press Ctrl-S
to open the Split Transactions window.)

Using categories is optional, but recommended, because categories are the key to your
ability to control your finances. The categories you use influence the level of detail you
can see in reports and the ways you can sort your transactions. You can enter three types
of information in the Category field:

- *Category names.* Enter a category name to specify what the check is for. Using
  categories can help you track how you spend your money (for example, for rent,
  utilities, entertainment, groceries). Most Quicken users will want to use categories
  as much as possible to track their spending. If you selected Quicken's standard home
  or business categories at the First Time Setup window, you can press Ctrl-C to view
  these categories. Select the category you want, and press Enter. Setting up and using
  categories are described in "Setting Up Categories" on page 105 and "Categorizing
  Transactions" on page 107.

- *Class names.* Using classes is another way of classifying your expenses that is
  similar to, but distinct from, using categories. You typically enter a class name in
  addition to a category name. Enter a class name to specify who, where, or when
  (what time period) the check was for. Some Quicken users will benefit from using
  classes; others won't. If you manage properties, you could have a separate class
  name for each property. To determine whether you should use classes, see Chapter
  22, *Using Classes*, beginning on page 351.

- *Account names.* You can enter the name of another Quicken account to transfer
  money to that account. For example, you can write a check to your savings account
  and have Quicken automatically record the amount as a deposit in a Quicken account
  set up for your savings account. You can recognize transfers because the name of the
  account that money is transferred to or from appears in brackets: [Savings]. For more
  information, see *Transferring Money Between Accounts*, beginning on page 251.

Always enter a slash (/) in the Category field before entering the first class name. For
example, enter Utilities/Oak Street for a check to the utility company for a property on
Oak Street. "Utilities" is the category and "Oak Street" is the class. Quicken interprets
everything you enter before a slash as category or account information and everything
you enter after a slash as class information.

You can also assign the check to more than one category or class by splitting the
transaction. To try this, press Ctrl-S to open the Split Transaction window. For more
information, see "Splitting a Transaction" on page 67.

Reviewing the Register

You can review the check register at any time. You can move the selection bar through
the check register by transaction, by page, or by month, and go to the beginning or end
of the register by using the keys on the cursor keypad. To find specific transactions in the
register, you can use Quicken's Find and Go to Date features.

Scrolling Through the Register

Use the keys on the cursor keypad to move to other transactions in the check register.

To do this:	Press these keys:
Move up or down one transaction at a time	Up arrow; Down arrow
Move up or down one screenful at a time	PgUp; PgDn
Move to start of previous or next month	Ctrl-PgUp; Ctrl-PgDn
Move to start of register	Ctrl-Home
Move to end of register	Ctrl-End

Using Find

Find (Ctrl-F) helps you find specific transactions without scrolling through the entire register. You can find a transaction even if you don't know all the information contained in the transaction.

To find a specific transaction:

1. Choose Find from the Edit menu or press Ctrl-F to display this window.

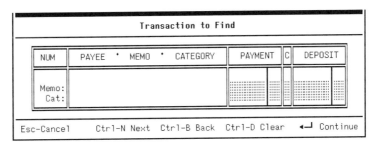

Note: If the Transaction to Find window already contains information, you can clear it by pressing Ctrl-D.

2. Enter a word, number, or phrase that matches part of the transaction you want to find, according to the rules described in "Fields in the Transaction to Find Window" on page 64.

    Note: To help locate the correct transaction, you can enter information in several of the fields. However, Quicken will find only transactions that meet *all* the criteria you specify in this window. Quicken searches all lines in a split transaction for matching information in the amount, memo, description, or category fields.

    In addition to entering information by hand, you can also select from the category (Ctrl-C), class (Ctrl-L), and memorized transaction (Ctrl-T) lists.

3. Quicken displays the Search Direction window:
    *   To have Quicken search backward (toward the beginning), press Ctrl-B.
    *   To search forward (toward the end) press Ctrl-N.

4. Several different transactions may all contain the information you requested. If the first transaction is not the one you want, continue to press Ctrl-B or Ctrl-N until you find the transaction you want. (Even though the Find window is closed, Ctrl-B and Ctrl-N remain active.)

   If Quicken reaches the end of the register without finding the transaction, it will start from the top and keep searching.

   Note: If Quicken doesn't seem to find the transaction you want, check to see if you're currently resting on that transaction.

Fields in the Transaction to Find Window

Num   Enter a check number to find a specific check.

Payee   Enter the exact or approximate payee name or description given to the transaction you want to find.

How Quicken matches text

If you don't know the full name, enter whatever part you know. For example, Smith will find Dr. Smith and William F. Smith, and phone will find Phoneland and Mountain Telephone Co.

If you need to find an exact match for the text you've entered, use Quicken's special match characters. You can also use these special characters to limit your search in other ways. For complete information, see "Using Match Characters to Limit Searches" on page 186.

You can use the match characters in the Payee, Memo, and Category fields.

Memo   Enter the memo text you want to find. Quicken first searches the transaction memos, then the split descriptions (if any) for matching text.

Category   Enter the category and class name you want to find. You can also search for account names in this field, if one was entered to transfer money to another account. You don't need to enter brackets ([ ]) around an account name to find a transfer.

Payment   To search for a transaction of a specific amount, enter the amount in the Payment field.

C (Cleared)   To search for uncleared transactions (transactions for which the cleared field is blank), enter a period (.). To search for reconciled transactions, enter an X. To search for transactions marked with an asterisk (cleared but not yet reconciled), enter an asterisk (*).

Deposit   To search for a deposit of a specific amount, enter the amount in the Deposit field.

Using Go to Date

The Go to Date feature lets you find transactions by date.

You can also use Go to Date to locate unprinted checks while you are at the Write Checks screen, and to locate transactions in any other type of Quicken account.

To go to a specific date in the register:

1. Select Go to Date from the Edit menu or press Ctrl-G.

   The Go to Date window appears.

2. Enter the date you want to find.

3. Press Enter.

   Quicken will go to the first transaction with the date you entered. If there is no transaction with the date you specify, Quicken will go to the one that is closest to that date.

Revising the Register

You can change any entry you made in the check register. You can change an existing transaction, insert a new transaction, void a transaction, or delete a transaction. When you finish making changes, press Ctrl-Enter to record the changes. Quicken recalculates all subsequent balances.

Caution: Exercise care when changing reconciled transactions (marked with an X in the C (Cleared) field). If you remove the X from the Cleared field or change the total amount of a reconciled transaction, you will alter Quicken's reconciled balance and create unexpected results when you reconcile.

To change a transaction:

1. Select the transaction you want to change in the register. (See "Reviewing the Register" on page 62.)

2. Press Tab or Enter to move the cursor to the field you want to change.

3. Use the arrow keys to position the cursor where you want to make the change.

4. Enter your changes right over the existing characters. (For more information, see "Correcting Mistakes" on page 25.)

5. Press Ctrl-Enter or F10 to record the change in the check register.

   Note: The only field in the register you cannot change by normal editing is the Balance field. Quicken calculates the account balance automatically, so if you need to change the balance, you must make an adjustment by adding or changing a payment or deposit in the register.

Changing dollar amounts

To change a dollar amount in the Payment or Deposit field, Tab to the field and enter the new amount. Quicken clears the previous amount from the field as soon as you enter the first digit of the new amount.

To insert a transaction:

1. Quicken inserts transactions above the cursor, so select the transaction below the place you want to insert a new transaction.

2. Choose Insert Transaction from the Edit menu (or press Ctrl-Ins).

   Quicken displays a blank transaction for you to complete. The date of the transaction is the same date as the following transaction. This date allows the inserted transaction to stay where you put it.

   If you change the date, Quicken's automatic sorting process may move this transaction. (Within a single date, Quicken sorts by check number.)

3. Press Ctrl-Enter or F10 to record the new transaction in the check register.

   The transaction is added to the register and Quicken recalculates all subsequent balances.

To void a transaction:

You may need to void a check for several reasons:
- If you need to stop payment on a check
- If you lose a check and write another to replace it
- If you have Intuit checks that didn't print correctly
- If you make an error on a paper check and discard it

By marking a check as void in the register instead of deleting it, you'll have accurate records for each numbered check.

Don't void an electronic payment.

If you void an electronic payment, Quicken cannot get the confirmation number it needs to stop the payment or transmit an inquiry about its status to CheckFree. Instead, choose Stop Payment Request from the Edit menu. For more information, see "Stopping Electronic Payments" on page 238.

---

1. Select the check you want to void.

   (If the check was one you wrote by hand and you haven't yet entered it in the register, select the blank entry at the end of the register and enter the date and check number.)

2. Choose Void Transaction from the Edit menu.

   Quicken inserts the word VOID before the payee name and puts an X in the C (Cleared) field, so the voided check won't interfere with reconciling.

> **Do you really want to delete this transaction?**
>
> Once a transaction is deleted or voided, you can't recover it. To give yourself an extra chance to be sure you are eliminating the right transaction (and not one you really want to keep), you can have Quicken request confirmation before deleting or voiding a transaction. See "3. Request confirmation when deleting or voiding a transaction" on page 445.

To delete a transaction:

1. Select the transaction you want to delete.

2. Choose Delete Transaction from the Edit menu (or press Ctrl-D).

3. If you have requested confirmation before deleting, Quicken displays the OK to Delete Transaction window.

- To delete the transaction, press Enter. Quicken removes the transaction from the register and recalculates all subsequent balances.

- If you don't want to delete the transaction, choose option 2, Do Not Delete (or press Esc). The transaction remains in the register.

> **Use a transaction password to protect against deletion.**
>
> To protect a specific transaction or group of transactions from being deleted accidentally or without authorization, you can create a transaction password. For instructions, see "Setting a Transaction Password" on page 440.

$ Splitting a Transaction

Sometimes you need to divide a transaction into more than one category. For example, a check to one department store might cover clothing, office supplies, and home furnishings. This section describes how to "split" a transaction by categorizing it with more than one category name (splitting a transaction with multiple classes works the same way).

When you split a transaction, you enter category names and amounts to identify each line of the split. You can enter this information when you first record a transaction, or you can add it later. With a split transaction, you have a record of each individual expense or income amount in addition to a record of the transaction total.

You can split transactions in any account register and at the Write Checks screen.

To display the Split Transaction window, press Ctrl-S. Quicken copies any category and class information already on the check or transaction to the first line of the Split Transaction window.

You can enter a description here or use the field to enter a long memo about the transaction.

Enter the amount of the transaction that is to be applied to each category in the Amount field. As you enter amounts, Quicken adds a balancing item if the total of the splits does not match the transaction amount.

Enter each category and class to which the transaction is to be applied in the Category field.

Press PgDn to bring more lines into view. You can enter up to 30 lines in this window.

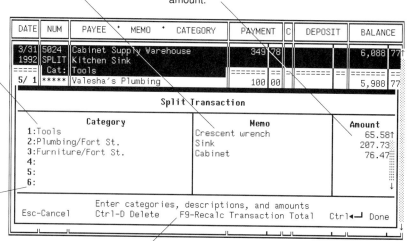

You can recalculate the transaction total. See "Recalculating the Transaction Total" on page 72.

Filling in a Split Transaction

You split transactions by entering items (using category and class names) and amounts in the Split Transaction window. You can enter this information when you first enter a transaction, or you can add it later.

To split a transaction:

1. Select the transaction you want to split.

2. Choose Split Transaction from the Edit menu (or press Ctrl-S) to display the Split Transaction window.

    Quicken copies any category and class names already entered in the Category field of the transaction to the first line of the Split Transaction window. The Amount field on the first line of the Split Transaction window shows the total amount of your check or other transaction.

3. *If no categories or classes show in the window,* enter the name of the first category or class for this transaction. Then press Enter twice to move to the Amount field.

   (You can enter the full name, enter part of the name and press Enter, or recall the name from the category or class list. If you're entering a class name, be sure to enter a forward slash (/) before the first class name.)

   If a category or class has been copied onto the first line, make any changes you want to the information and press Enter twice to move to the Amount field.

4. Enter the amount to apply to the first category.

   Don't worry about the total amount that is already in the field. Enter the amount for the first part of the split transaction right over it. If you're entering a small number over a large one, press the spacebar at the end of your number to erase the remaining numbers from the previous amount.

   Quicken subtracts the amount you entered from the total amount of the transaction and displays the remainder in the next Amount field.

5. Continue to add categories and amounts. When you finish, press Ctrl-Enter.

6. The Split Transaction window disappears and you can continue to fill in fields on your check or enter information in the register. When you have finished, press F10 or Ctrl-Enter to record the entire transaction.

   When a transaction has been split, the word SPLIT appears under the check number in the Num field of the register. On the Write Checks screen, the word SPLIT appears below the Category field. (The word SPLIT is simply a reminder: it doesn't appear on the printed check.)

To go to a new line in the Split Transaction window

Press Ctrl-End to go to the next blank line in the Split Transaction window.

Copying Information from One Line to Another

In some split transactions, you may want to repeat part of the information on one line in the Category field on the next line. You don't have to enter it again, just press the Quote key (' or "). You can use the Quote key to copy categories, subcategories, classes, subclasses, and memos.

For example, suppose you wrote one check to cover both personal and business supplies. If you enter one part of the purchase as supplies/business, you can assign the remainder to supplies/personal by entering "/personal. Press the Quote key for each category and class name that you want Quicken to copy from the previous line.

Quicken copies the
category name as
soon as you press
the Quote key (' or ").

```
                        Split Transaction
  ┌──────────────────────┬────────────────────┬─────────────┐
  │      Category        │       Memo         │   Amount    │
  │ 1:supplies/business  │ software           │    125.43↑  │
  │ 2:supplies/personal  │ desk accessories   │     85.10   │
  │ 3:                   │                    │             │
  │ 4:                   │                    │             │
  │ 5:                   │                    │             │
  │ 6:                   │                    │          ↓  │
  └──────────────────────┴────────────────────┴─────────────┘
           Enter categories, descriptions, and amounts
  Esc-Cancel    Ctrl-D Delete    F9-Recalc Transaction Total   Ctrl◄┘ Done
```

Including Transfer Information in a Split Transaction

You can include transfer information in a split transaction. This example shows a deposit to a checking account in which $53 is transferred from an investment account. When you enter the deposit here, a parallel transaction in the investment account automatically decreases that balance.

Note: You can enter either category or transfer information (but not both) in the Category field of the Split Transaction window. However, you can include transfer and class information on the same line. (For more information, see "How Transfers Work" on page 252.)

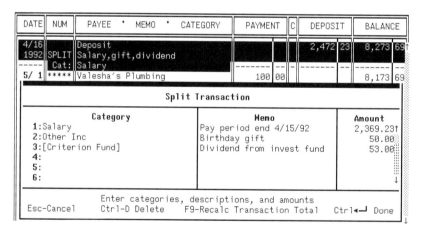

Entering Percentages in a Split Transaction

Usually, to split the amount of a single check between two or more categories, you enter dollar amounts in the Split Transaction window. However, sometimes you may want to allocate a split by percentage. In that case, you can split the transaction and have Quicken calculate the dollar amount to apply to each category.

To enter a percentage in a split transaction:

1. Select the transaction in the register.

2. Press Ctrl-S to open the Split Transaction window.

    When you open the Split Transaction window, you'll see the full amount of the check assigned to one category.

3. In the Amount field, enter the percentage you want assigned to that category (for example, 20%).

    When you press Enter, Quicken enters that percentage of the total amount in the Amount field on the first line and places the remainder on the next line.

    If you want to split the transaction further, repeat step 3.

Printing Information in Split Transactions

If you use voucher checks, Quicken prints the first 16 lines of information from the Split Transaction window on the voucher. (The split does not print on regular checks.)

Anything recorded on line 17 or below does not print on the voucher.

You can also print only the contents of the Description field on your vouchers. For more information, see "4. Print categories on voucher checks" on page 447.

Using the Split Transaction Window as a Calculator

You can use the Split Transaction window as a calculator to add up the total amount of the transaction.

If you press Ctrl-S before entering an amount for your check or other transaction, Quicken totals the amounts you enter in the Split Transaction window and displays the result in the Amount field on the check or in the Payment or Deposit field in the register.

If you've already entered an amount for your check or other transaction, you can tell when the amount you enter in the Split Transaction window doesn't equal the total amount of the transaction, because Quicken displays the difference in the Amount field on the next line. This is a useful way to double-check that you've entered the correct amounts in your split, and to see what amount hasn't been categorized.

Note: If the transaction is an income item (such as a paycheck) and you subtract expenses (such as various taxes), you must put a minus sign before each expense amount to create a total deposit.

To create a total deposit for an income item, place a minus sign before each expense amount (such as taxes).

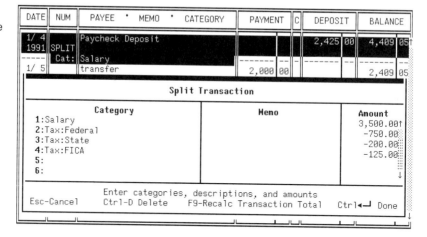

Recalculating the Transaction Total

Sometimes you may want the total amount of the transaction to change on the basis of the information you enter in the split. When you do, you can have Quicken recalculate the amount of the transaction on the basis of the contents in the Split Transaction window.

To recalculate the transaction total:

1.   In the Split Transaction window, enter amounts for the splits.

2.   Press F9 to recalculate the transaction total.

     Quicken recalculates the amounts entered in the Split Transaction window and inserts the total as the amount of the transaction.

3.   Press Ctrl-Enter to record the transaction as usual.

Deleting the balancing remainder

To recalculate without the balancing remainder item that Quicken adds, move the cursor to the remainder item and press Ctrl-D to delete it; then press F9.

Reviewing and Revising Split Transactions

To review or change a split transaction:

1. Select the transaction whose split you want to see and press Ctrl-S to open the Split Transaction window. (If you have a mouse, click once on the SPLIT label in the Num field.)

2. Make any changes you want in the Split Transactions window.

3. When you finish making changes, press Ctrl-Enter to save the split.

4. Press Ctrl-Enter again to record the entire transaction.

To delete the contents of the Split Transaction window:

1. Press Ctrl-S to open the Split Transaction window.

2. Press Ctrl-D to delete each individual line.

3. When you finish, press Ctrl-Enter. The word SPLIT will disappear from the unprinted check or the Num field in the register.

4. Press Ctrl-Enter to record the entire transaction.

$ Printing the Check Register

You can print transactions from all or part of your check register—a day, a week, a month, a year, or more. You will then have a printed record of the period of time covered.

To print transactions from the register:

1. Select Print Register from the Print/Acct menu (or press Ctrl-P).

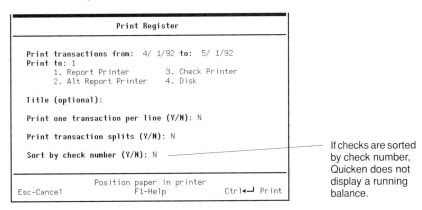

If checks are sorted by check number, Quicken does not display a running balance.

2. Fill in the fields in the Print Register window.

   For some of the items, Quicken's default values are displayed. To change these values, simply enter new information over them.

3. Press Ctrl-Enter to start printing the register.

Fields in the Print Register Window

Print Transactions From Enter the date range you want (inclusive). The default value is the first day of the current year and today's date. (See page 60 for date shortcuts.) The date fields are required, because they control which transactions will print.

Print To Enter the number of the printer you are using (1, 2, 3 or 4). Enter 4 if you want to print to disk.

Printing to disk creates an ASCII file that you can read into your word processor or other program. You can print the file using your word processor or you can use the DOS PRINT command.

At the DOS prompt, enter PRINT *filename*. If this is the first time you have used the PRINT command this session, DOS prompts for the name of the printer port. Enter the name of your printer port. If you don't know which port your printer is attached to, ask the person who set up your system or experiment with: PRN: LPT1: LPT2: COM1: COM2: LPT3:.

Alternately, you can use the DOS command TYPE. For example, if you named your register file CHECKREG, to print it out you would enter:

TYPE CHECKREG>LPT1

(If you can't find the file, look in QUICKEN5, or wherever you store your program files.)

Title (optional) Enter the title you want to have printed on the report. If you leave this blank, Quicken will title the report Check Register.

Print One Transaction per Line (Y/N) Quicken normally prints three lines for each transaction. If you want to print more transactions per page, enter Y. Quicken will abbreviate each transaction so that it fits on one line.

Print Transaction Splits (Y/N) Quicken normally does not print the contents of the split window for split transactions. If you have split transactions and want them printed, enter Y. For more information, see "Printing Information in Split Transactions" on page 71.

Sort by Check Number (Y/N) Quicken normally sorts first by date and then by check number. If you want the register to be sorted first by check number and then by date, enter Y.

Note: When checks are sorted by number, Quicken does not generate or display a running balance. (If there is a gap in the number sequence, Quicken displays an asterisk to the immediate left of the next number.)

Looking for missing checks?

Try the missing check report to find gaps in your check sequence:

- Press Alt-R.
- Choose Personal or Business.
- Choose Missing Check.

For more information, see "Missing Check" on page 145.

$ Entering Year-to-Date Transactions

You may want to start using Quicken by entering checks and other transactions you tracked manually before you bought Quicken. Entering such historical transactions is just like entering any other transaction in the register, but this section offers some tips to make the task go as quickly as possible.

Have you already reconciled?

If you've already used Quicken to record and reconcile transactions and now want to add year-to-date transactions to your Quicken bank account for reporting purposes, follow the steps in "Adding Year-to-Date Transactions" on page 136.

- Organize your manual records by month and enter one month at a time. Then reconcile each month after you enter the data for it. See *Balancing Your Checkbook*, beginning on page 119, for information about reconciling. If you have already entered more recent checks that have not cleared the bank, ignore them as you reconcile earlier months.

- To start, look at the first entry in the register: the Opening Balance transaction. Does the date and amount of the opening balance accurately reflect the amount of money in your account on the first date for which you are about to enter transactions? If not, change the date and amount of the opening balance.

  Suppose you want to enter transactions starting with January 1, 1992. Change the date of the opening balance to the date of your December 1991 bank statement and use the ending balance shown on your December 1991 statement as your opening balance amount. When you reconcile your January bank statement, you can add any missing transactions from the end of the previous year to the register.

- To start entering year-to-date transactions, go to the last entry in the register. Quicken automatically sorts your transactions by date, so you can enter them in any order.

> ### Remember to memorize!
>
> If you find yourself entering similar transactions, use the Memorize Transaction feature described in *Saving Time with Memorized Transactions*, beginning on page 195.

$ Advanced Techniques

Once you're familiar with the basics of using the check register, you may want to try using some of Quicken's advanced techniques:

- *Memorize and recall* reduces the effort involved in entering recurring transactions, such as paycheck deposits (see *Saving Time with Memorized Transactions*, beginning on page 195) and recurring reports (see "Memorizing a Custom Report Setup" on page 193).

- *Categories and classes* help you keep track of where your money is coming from and where it is going. (See *Using Categories*, beginning on page 101, and *Using Classes*, beginning on page 351.)

- *Confirming transaction changes* allows you to choose whether you want a confirmation before changing a transaction, deleting or voiding a transaction, or both. Note that changing the cleared status of a transaction may affect future reconciliations. (See "Transaction Settings" on page 444.)

- *Changing date styles* allows you to have dates displayed in the register with the day before the month (for example, 31/10/92). (See "Transaction Settings" on page 444.)

- *Showing memo only, category only, or both* allows you to choose which fields you want to see in the register. (See "Transaction Settings" on page 444.)

Chapter 5

Writing Checks

Having Quicken prepare your checks is a great convenience. Few banking tasks are more satisfying than receiving a stack of finished checks straight from your printer and ready for your signature.

Writing Checks with Quicken

Use the Write Checks screen to enter checks that you plan to print with Quicken. To enter other transactions, such as handwritten checks, deposits, or bank fees, use the register. When you record a check in Write Checks, Quicken automatically adds it to the check register. (Chapter 4, *Using the Register*, describes the check register in detail.)

You can write checks in any Quicken bank account: checking, money market, or savings. You can write checks on any schedule you prefer: throughout the month as bills arrive, or at regular intervals: weekly, biweekly, or monthly.

Intuit checks are accepted everywhere in the United States and Canada. See *Ordering Checks and Other Intuit Products*, beginning on page 471, for information about how to order different kinds of Intuit checks, or consult the catalog in your Quicken package.

$ The Write Checks Screen

The Quicken Write Checks screen looks like the paper checks you're used to filling out. When you choose Write/Print Checks from the Main Menu (or choose Write Checks from the Activities menu if you're at the register), you'll see a blank check.

Enter the payee as you want the name to appear on the check.

Today's date appears in month/day/year format.

Enter the amount. (Quicken spells it out for you on the next line.)

(Optional) Enter the payee's name and address if you want to mail the check in an Intuit window envelope.

(Optional) Enter a memo to send a message to the payee.

(Optional) Enter a category to which this check should be applied.

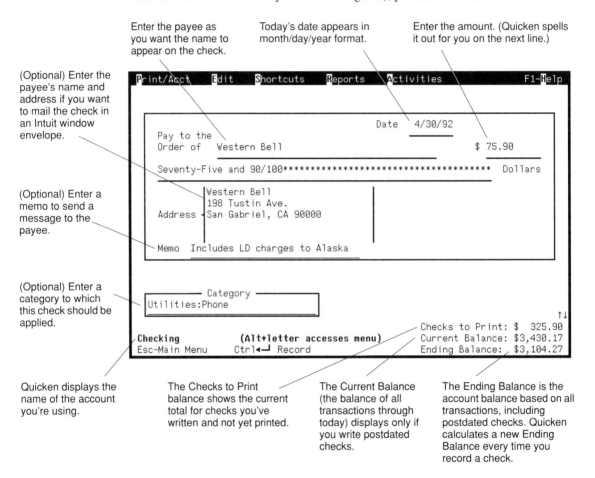

Quicken displays the name of the account you're using.

The Checks to Print balance shows the current total for checks you've written and not yet printed.

The Current Balance (the balance of all transactions through today) displays only if you write postdated checks.

The Ending Balance is the account balance based on all transactions, including postdated checks. Quicken calculates a new Ending Balance every time you record a check.

$ Filling Out a Check

Filling out a blank check on the screen is much like writing a check on paper. The Write Checks screen displays a check form, and you fill in the fields.

To write a check:

1. Display the Write Checks screen as described on the previous page.

2. Enter the information for this check in the appropriate fields.

Press Enter or Tab to move the cursor forward one field. Press Shift-Tab to move the cursor back one field.

- Make sure the date is correct (change it if you need to).
- Enter the payee's name and the amount of the check.
- The remaining fields are for optional information.

When you fill in the Amount field and press Enter, Quicken automatically spells out the amount on the next line.

When you've finished filling in the check, you're ready to record it.

3. To record the check, press Ctrl-Enter from any field. (Or just press Enter from the Category field, and Quicken asks if you want to record the check.)

Monthly checks

If you write the same checks regularly, Quicken can memorize the check information, eliminating tedious retyping. For example, you can have Quicken memorize checks that you write regularly for such things as rent, utilities, and credit card bills. For complete information, see *Saving Time with Memorized Transactions*, beginning on page 195.

Fields in a Check

Date The date in this field appears on the check when you print it, in the numeric format MM/DD/YY (for example: 7/12/92). To change the date, enter the new date over the date shown.

Spelling out the month on your check

If you prefer, you can have Quicken print the date in an alphabetic format on your checks, for example 7 Oct '92 or 25 Dec '91. See "3. Print months as Jan, Feb... on checks" on page 447.

To postdate a check, enter a future date. When you change the date, Quicken remembers the new date and enters it on your next check.

You can also have Quicken use this date to determine which checks to print. (For more information, see "Printing Your Checks" on page 91.)

Date shortcuts

These special keys allow you to change the date quickly:

+ (plus key)	Move forward one day
– (minus key)	Move back one day
T	Today
M	First of Month
H	End of montH
Y	First of Year
R	End of yeaR

If you are in a Date field, press one of these keys once to fill in the associated date in the current month or year. Press the same key repeatedly to bring up the previous or next month or year (M and Y move backward; H and R move forward).

For example, if your cursor is in the register's Date field and the date shown is 3/15/92, press M to fill in the beginning of the month (3/1); press M again to fill in the beginning of the previous month (2/1). If you start at 3/1, however, M will fill in 2/1. (Don't worry about capitalizing these letters: m works just like M.)

The best way to become familiar with these keys is to experiment with them. If you find that you can't quickly get to the date you want using these keys, you can always enter the new date directly over the current date.

Use the slash (/) to move the cursor from one part of the date to the next (for example, to move from the day to the month or from the month to the year).

Pay to the Order of Enter the name of the payee, or person to whom this check is being written, up to 40 characters. When you view this check later in the check register, the name appears in the Payee field.

Amount Enter the dollar amount of the check:

- Omit punctuation, such as dollar signs or commas.
- For a dollars-only amount, omit decimal point or zeros in the cents place. (If you enter 2000 and press Enter, Quicken displays 2,000.00.)

The maximum amount for any transaction is $9,999,999.99.

Address
(Optional) If you plan to mail the check in an Intuit window envelope, enter the payee's name and address. (If you don't want to enter an address, press Enter on the first address line to move the cursor to the Memo field.)

You can use up to five lines for the payee's name, address, city, state, and zip code.

> **Copy payee name in the Address field.**
>
> To copy the payee's name to the top line of the Address field, press the Quote key (' or ") in the first line. Then complete the rest of the address.

Memo
(Optional)

If you want to send a message to the payee or if you want to provide additional information on the check for your own records, you can enter it as a memo on the check. For example, you could enter the account number for a bill you are paying.

Memos can contain any letters, numerals, and punctuation marks.

If you plan to mail the check in an Intuit window envelope, be aware that the contents of this memo field will show through the window. If you want to include information on your check that should not show through the window, such as a charge card account number, you can set up an extra message field. The message field will appear to the right of the Address field. See "1. Extra message line on check (printed on check but not recorded)" on page 446.

Category
(Optional)

You can enter three types of information in the Category field: category and subcategory names, class and subclass names, and the names of transfer accounts.

You can have Quicken create an automatic entry in another account by entering the name of the account here.

You can also split the transaction to assign parts of it to different categories. (Press Ctrl-S to open the Split Transaction window.)

For more information about entering category, class, and transfer accounts, see page 62.

Check Number

Note that there is no place for the check number on the Write Checks screen. Quicken checks are prenumbered, because most banks require this in order to be able to stop payment. Quicken adds the correct check number to the register when the check is printed. Until checks are printed, they are shown with five asterisks (*****) in the Num field of the register.

Reviewing Checks You've Written

Once you've written and recorded your checks, you can review checks in two ways:

- Scrolling through the checks at the Write Checks screen
- Reviewing them in the register (see "Reviewing the Register" on page 62)

Note: Once you've printed a check, you cannot review it at the Write Checks screen. Use the register to review printed checks.

To review checks at the Write Checks screen:

1. Display the Write Checks screen.

   To picture how Quicken organizes your unprinted checks, think of them as a continuous scroll of checks like the ones you insert in a tractor-feed printer. Checks are always in chronological order, and there is always a blank check at the bottom of the stack.

2. Use the PgUp and PgDn keys to bring the checks you want to review into view, one at a time.

To see:	Press these keys:
The preceding check	PgUp
The next check	PgDn
The first check	Ctrl-Home
The last check (a blank check)	Ctrl-End

   You can also use Find and Go to Date to locate the exact check you want. See "Using Find" on page 63 and "Using Go to Date" on page 65.

   PgDn doesn't work?

   If the PgDn, PgUp, Home, and End keys don't work, you probably have the number lock (Num Lock) on. To turn off the number lock, press the Num Lock key.

Revising Checks You've Written

If you want to revise entries in your check register, you can:

- Change a check
- Delete a check

Try void instead of delete.

To keep your records complete, you may want to void a check instead of deleting it. When you delete a check, you have no record of that check or its number. (You void a check at the register, not at the Write Checks screen.) For more information, see "To insert a transaction:" on page 66.

To change a check:

1. Select the check you want to change.

2. Press Tab or Enter to move the cursor to the field you want to change.

3. Use the arrow keys to position the cursor where you want to make the change.

4. Enter your changes right over the existing characters. Use the techniques described in "Correcting Mistakes" on page 25.

5. When you've finished making changes to a check, press Ctrl-Enter to record the check.

   Quicken scrolls the next check into view.

   If you want to cancel your changes without recording them, press Esc. When Quicken asks if you want to record the changes, choose option 2, Cancel Changes and Leave.

To delete a check:

1. Select the check you want to change.

2. Choose Delete Transaction (Ctrl-D) from the Edit menu.

   Quicken displays the OK to Delete Transaction window so that you can confirm that the check should be deleted.

3. Choose Delete Transaction (or press Enter).

Use a transaction password to protect against deletion.

If you want to protect a specific transaction or group of transactions from being accidentally deleted or deleted by an unauthorized person, you can create a transaction password. For instructions, see "Setting a Transaction Password" on page 440.

$ Writing Postdated Checks

To write a postdated check, follow the same process as for writing a regular check, except for changing the date. By postdating, you can schedule checks for future payment. You can also forecast how much money you need in the coming weeks. Later, when you print checks, you can have Quicken print checks dated through a specific date.

To write a postdated check:

1. At the Write Checks screen, change the current date to the future date when you want to print the check.

2. Fill in the check as described earlier in this chapter. When it is complete, press Ctrl-Enter to record the check.

Postdated checks appear in the register with the date selected and are separated from other transactions by a double line.

When you have postdated checks in your account, Quicken calculates a Current Balance as well as an Ending Balance and displays it at the bottom of the screen. The Current Balance shows the balance in your account before any postdated transactions. The Ending Balance shows the balance after all postdated transactions.

Using Postdating for Accounts Payable

You can use postdating to produce up-to-date accounts payable reports. To do this, write postdated checks for all bills as you receive them. Postdate each check for a few days before you want to mail the check and pay the bill.

Your register will show how much money you need to cover your known bills. "Checks to Print," at the bottom of the Write Checks screen, shows the total of your unprinted checks. To see the total accounts payable amount, produce an account balances report, which shows the unprinted checks.

For a detailed description of managing accounts payable with Quicken, see "Accounts Payable" on page 384.

$ Related Features

You now know the basics of writing, recording, and reviewing checks with Quicken. In later chapters you'll learn about additional check-writing features you can use, including how to:

Print checks. (See *Printing Checks*, beginning on page 85.)

Memorize and recall transactions, which makes it easy to write checks for recurring bills. (See *Saving Time with Memorized Transactions*, beginning on page 195.)

Assign checks to categories and classes, which helps you keep track of where your money is going. (See *Using Categories*, beginning on page 101, and *Using Classes*, beginning on page 351.)

Make electronic payments. (See *Using CheckFree to Pay Bills Electronically*, beginning on page 219.)

Chapter 6

Printing Checks

When you use Quicken to write checks, you print them on special personalized checks designed to work with Quicken. (You can order these checks from Intuit.)

If you have a continuous-feed printer, use the sample checks enclosed in the Quicken package for practice. If you remove the tractor strips from the sides of the sample checks and tear them into groups of three, you can use them for practice with a page-oriented (laser) printer.

If you have entered checks and haven't printed them yet, Quicken reminds you by displaying a message at the bottom of the Main Menu when you start Quicken. If you're using Billminder, you'll also see a reminder at the DOS prompt when you start your computer. (For more information, see "Automatic Reminders" on page 441.)

$ Ordering Checks

To order your personalized Intuit checks, use the order form attached inside the catalog that came with this package or print an order form on your printer. (To print an order form, choose Order Supplies from the Activities menu.)

Intuit checks offer you several advantages:

*   The checks come with your name, address, account number, bank name, check numbers, and all the information required by financial institutions. Intuit guarantees they will be accepted everywhere your checks are accepted now.

- They are economical, fit all printers, and come in a variety of sizes. If you have a laser printer, you can order special laser checks.

- Some continuous-feed printers waste the first check because of the way the forms tractor operates. If yours does, order the continuous Forms Leaders, which allow your printer to print on the very first check.

- You can use your company logo on your checks. See "Logo Service" on page 473 to order Intuit checks preprinted with your logo.

- All Intuit checks fit one of the two sizes of Intuit double-window envelopes. Both your address and the payee's address appear in the windows, eliminating the need to address envelopes.

$ Looking at an Intuit Check

See the catalog in your Quicken package for pictures of the kinds of checks you can order from Intuit. (Laser checks do not have the tractor strips you see in this example.)

Intuit checks are personalized with your name and address. You can even use your company logo.

Intuit checks contain all information needed by financial institutions.

Check numbers are preprinted on the checks. After you print a check, this number replaces the asterisks in the Num field of the check register.

On continuous checks, position numbers on the tractor strips help you align the checks correctly in your printer using Intuit's patented, automatic alignment feature.

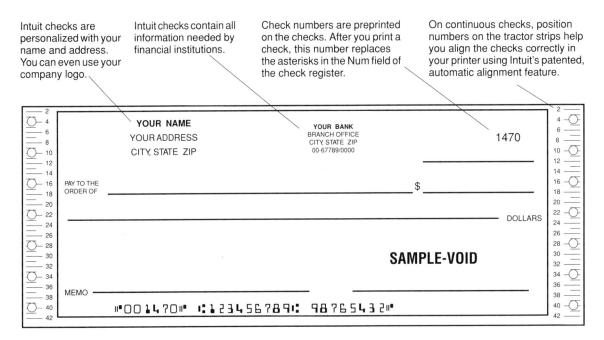

Note: This example and the example on page 89 are approximations of real Intuit checks. An Intuit check is larger and has a colored background pattern like most bank checks.

Printer Setup

Quicken is ready to work with the printer you chose during installation. It assumes the printer is connected to parallel printer port 1 (LPT1).

Using Standard Printer Settings

Unless you know your printer is connected to a serial port, or you did not tell Quicken the name of your printer for checks when you installed, it's a good idea to try printing with Quicken before making any setup changes. Since Quicken comes ready to work with most printers, you'll probably find that you won't have to change anything.

Changing Printer Settings

If your printer is connected to a serial port or if you did not tell Quicken the name of your printer for checks when you installed, turn to "Printer Settings" on page 428 for instructions on how to change the printer settings.

Choosing the correct printer

To check on your printer settings, choose Change Printer Styles from the Print/Acct menu, then choose Settings for Printing Checks. Your current check printer is selected in the Select Check Printer window (for example, HP Deskjet), and your current style, pitch, and orientation are selected in the window for your printer (for example, 10 cpi, Portrait). For more information, see "Printer Settings" on page 428.

You can use Quicken with up to three different printers or with one printer set up to work in three different ways. You can set different printer options for checks and for printing reports. If you want to use different settings for printing checks and printing reports, see "Printer Settings" on page 428 for instructions.

$ Positioning Checks in Your Printer

If you have a traditional printer that uses continuous form paper, follow the steps under "Printing a Sample Check" to test that the checks are aligned correctly.

Using the first check

Some continuous-feed printers waste the first check. If yours does, you may want to order the continuous Forms Leader, which allows your printer to print on the very first check. For more information, see "More Time-Saving Products" on page 473.

Note: If you have a laser printer, skip this test because Quicken aligns laser checks automatically. Turn to "Printing Checks Using a Laser Printer" on page 90.

Printing a Sample Check

Quicken lets you print a sample check to make sure the checks are properly aligned in your printer. Using Intuit's patented automatic alignment feature, you don't have to align checks by trial and error.

To print a sample check:

1. Insert the checks into your printer just as you would any continuous computer paper.

2. Turn on the printer and make sure that the printer is on line.

3. Choose Write/Print Checks from the Main Menu.

   If you do not currently have any checks to print, press Ctrl-Enter to record a blank check before proceeding to the next step.

4. Press Alt-P to display the Print/Acct menu and choose Print Checks (or press Ctrl-P).

   Quicken displays the Print Checks window.

5. At the Print To field, press Enter to accept option 3, Check Printer, unless you want to use a different printer this time.

   To use a different printer, enter the number for the printer you want to use and press Enter.

6. At the Print All/Selected Checks field, press Enter to accept the default A (All).

7. At the Type of Checks field, enter the number that indicates the type of check you are testing. (For more about types of checks, see "Fields in the Print Checks Window" on page 94.)

8. Press F9 to print a sample check, read the message, and then press Enter.

   Quicken prints the sample check and then displays the Type Position Number window.

   Note: *Do not* move the checks up or down in the printer to correct the alignment. Quicken will do this for you.

9. Without moving the checks in the printer, look at the printed sample check.

You will see XXXX's entered in the Date and Amount fields, "PAYEE" entered in the Pay To The Order Of field, and "This is a void check" entered in the Memo field. If the check is aligned correctly, the type should rest just above the lines on the check.

10. If the sample check printed correctly, press Enter. Go on to step 4 under "Telling Quicken to Print Checks" on page 92.

If the sample check did ***not*** print correctly, go on to step 11 below.

11. Look at the line labeled POINTER LINE that has just printed on the check.

The arrows at each end of the line point to numbers printed along the edges of the check. Note the number that the arrows point to—this is the position number.

Note: If the pointer line wraps from one line to another on your check, either the pitch or the indent setting of the check printer needs to be adjusted. See step 12 and "Common Printing Problems and Solutions" on page 97.

12. Enter the position number in the Type Position Number window and press Enter.

Quicken advances the checks in the printer and prints another sample check.

The vertical positioning of the second check should be almost perfect. If a half-line adjustment is needed (for example, if the printing is slightly above the line), use the knob on the side of your printer to move the check up a half line.

13. Make any side-to-side positioning adjustments by hand, moving the paper clamps as necessary.

If the printing is too far to the right or left, move the checks to the right or left.

14. **Important:** Note the correct position of the check for future positioning.

> ### Using a visual alignment cue
>
> Look for a way to align a visible part of your printer, such as the sprocket cover or type head, with one of the position numbers at the edge of the check. Make a note of this visual alignment cue. (Or put a small piece of tape at this spot on your printer.) You can use this visual cue to align your checks each time you insert them in your printer and you won't have to go through the process of printing a sample check again.

15. When your checks are aligned correctly, press Enter at the Type Position Number window.

    Quicken displays the Print Checks window.

16. To print your first batch of checks, go on to step 4 under "Telling Quicken to Print Checks" on page 92.

> ### Do I need to align each time I print?
>
> After you've completed the alignment process once, your printer will stay aligned. You don't need to go through the alignment process again each time you want to print checks.
>
> You only need to use the pointer line method the first time. After that, verify your printer alignment by looking at the information on the check. If the date and payee are aligned, you're ready to print.

Printing Checks Using a Laser Printer

Intuit's laser checks come ready to be inserted in your laser printer paper tray. Laser standard and laser wallet checks are grouped three per sheet; laser voucher checks come one per sheet.

Note: Sample continuous checks are included in your Quicken package. If you want to test them in your laser printer, separate the checks into groups of three and completely remove the tractor strips.

To insert checks in your laser printer:

1. Insert a stack of check pages in the paper tray in the same way you would insert printed letterhead stationery. (Refer to your printer manual for information on how to load letterhead in your paper tray.)

2. Press Alt-P to display the Print/Acct menu.

   a. Choose Change Printer Styles.

   b. Choose Settings for Printing Checks.

   Quicken displays three windows: the Check Printer Settings window, the Select Check Printer window, and a window listing styles available for your printer.

3. Choose the style and check printer you want to use:

   • If the correct printer is selected, choose the style you want and press Enter to display the Check Printer Settings window.

   • If you want to change the printer, press Esc to leave the style list, then choose the printer you want and press Enter. Then select the style you want and press Enter to display the Check Printer Settings window.

4. The settings in the Check Printer Settings window should be correct for the printer you selected. Press Ctrl-Enter (or F10) to accept these settings.

   If you need to change the settings, see "Printer Settings" on page 428.

   You are now ready to print checks.

To print checks with your laser printer:

1. Choose Print Checks from the Print/Acct menu. (Or press Ctrl-P.)

2. Fill in the Print Checks window.

   (See "Fields in the Print Checks Window" on page 94.)

3. Press F9 if you want to print a sample check.

   If the sample doesn't print correctly, you may need to change printer settings. See "Printer Settings" on page 428.

Printing partial pages of checks?

If you have a laser printer with a manual feed tray, you can print on partial pages (sheets that have only one or two checks on them). Follow the onscreen instructions to insert the page normally or sideways in the manual feed tray. Then press F9 at the Enter Check Number window, and enter 1 or 2 to indicate how many checks are in the manual feed tray.

(You may want to order InkJet Forms Leaders to help with printing partial pages of checks on inkjet printers. See page 473.)

💲 Printing Your Checks

You can print a batch of checks as soon as you've written them, or you can wait and print them at another time. For example, you can write checks at the Write Checks screen at various times throughout the month, but wait and print them only once or twice each month. Or you can write all the checks you will need for the coming month, and print them only when they are due. You can also print postdated checks before they are due.

All checks are printed in the order of their due date; that is, the date you entered on them at the Write Checks screen.

The Print Checks Window

At the Write Checks screen, choose Print Checks from the Print/Acct menu.

Specifies the printer you want to use (default is 3).

Set the type of checks you want to print on in this field. For more information, see "Fields in the Print Checks Window" on page 94.

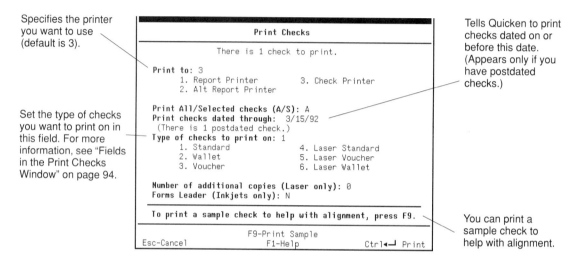

```
                              Print Checks

                      There is 1 check to print.

        Print to: 3
               1. Report Printer        3. Check Printer
               2. Alt Report Printer

        Print All/Selected checks (A/S): A
        Print checks dated through:  3/15/92
          (There is 1 postdated check.)
        Type of checks to print on: 1
               1. Standard              4. Laser Standard
               2. Wallet                5. Laser Voucher
               3. Voucher               6. Laser Wallet

        Number of additional copies (Laser only): 0
        Forms Leader (Inkjets only): N

        To print a sample check to help with alignment, press F9.

                         F9-Print Sample
        Esc-Cancel             F1-Help             Ctrl◄┘ Print
```

Tells Quicken to print checks dated on or before this date. (Appears only if you have postdated checks.)

You can print a sample check to help with alignment.

Telling Quicken to Print Checks

You tell Quicken what checks to print in the Print Checks window. If any checks print incorrectly, you can have Quicken reprint them during the printing procedure described here, or later as needed. (See "Reprinting Printed Checks" on page 96.)

Changing the date on your check

Quicken automatically prints the same date on the check that you recorded when you wrote the check. You can change this default so that Quicken supplies the date when you print the check. See "2. Change date of checks to date when printed" on page 447.

To print checks:

1. Make sure your printer is turned on and is on line. Also make sure the checks are inserted in it and are aligned correctly.

   See "Positioning Checks in Your Printer" on page 87.

2. At the Write Checks screen, choose Print Checks from the Print/Acct menu.

3. Fill in the fields in the Print Checks window. (See "Fields in the Print Checks Window" on page 94.)

4. When you've finished filling in the window, press Ctrl-Enter (or F10).

5. If you left the setting at **A** to print all checks, Quicken displays the Enter Check Number window.

   If you entered **S** to select specific checks, Quicken displays the Select Checks to Print window. Enter the numbers of the checks you want to print and press Enter.

   (See "Fields in the Print Checks Window" on page 94.) Quicken displays the Enter Check Number window.

Press F9 to print only the first check.

If you have set up for a laser printer, you may see a different F9 option to print on a partial page.

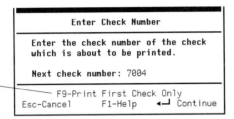

```
        ┌────────────────────────────────────────────┐
        │▀▀▀▀▀▀▀▀▀▀▀▀▀▀▀▀▀▀▀▀▀▀▀▀▀▀▀▀▀▀▀▀▀▀▀▀▀▀▀▀▀▀▀▀│
        │           Enter Check Number                │
        │                                            │
        │  Enter the check number of the check        │
        │  which is about to be printed.              │
        │                                            │
        │  Next check number: 7004                    │
        │                                            │
        │      ── F9-Print First Check Only           │
        │  Esc-Cancel     F1-Help    ◄┘ Continue      │
        └────────────────────────────────────────────┘
```

6. Look at the number on the check that is about to be printed. (You may have to lift the printer cover to see the check number.)

   If the number is not right, correct the check number in the Next Check Number field.

7. When the number is correct, press Enter.

   Quicken starts printing your checks.

How to stop your printer

If you notice a problem while your checks are being printed, stop the printing process by pressing the Esc key. To discontinue printing altogether, press the Esc key again and answer any questions Quicken asks.

If your printer continues to print after you press Esc, it probably has a "buffer." A buffer enables a printer to keep printing even after the computer tells it to stop. To stop this kind of printer quickly, turn its power switch off.

Examining Printed Checks

After the checks have finished printing, Quicken asks if the checks printed correctly. Examine the checks to see if any were not aligned correctly.

If the checks printed correctly:

1. If the checks printed correctly, press Enter.

   Quicken returns to the Write Checks screen, where you can continue writing checks.

If the checks didn't print correctly:

1. Examine your printer to see if the checks jammed or the printer ran out of checks.

   Some of the checks may not have printed or may have printed incorrectly. Fix any printer feed problems or check the alignment of the checks in your printer.

   (If one of the checks contains a misspelling or an incorrect amount, go to the Write Checks screen to edit the transaction, then reprint the check.)

2. Type the number of the first check that printed incorrectly (or did not print) and press Enter.

   Quicken marks the remaining checks as unprinted and returns to the Print Checks window.

3. Press Enter to display the Enter Check Number window again.

4. Make sure the check number now shown in the window is the next check in your printer and press Enter.

5. When all checks have printed correctly, press Enter.

Fields in the Print Checks Window

Print To Type the number of the printer to which you are printing. Usually the number is 3 for the Check Printer. However, if you have more than one printer, or if you have set your printer to print in more than one way, you may need to change this setting. (For more information, see "Printer Settings" on page 428.)

Print All/ Selected Checks You can print all checks (A) in the unprinted check list (through the indicated date, if you have postdated checks), or you can select the checks you want to print (S). Quicken normally prints all the checks in the list. If you want to print all the unprinted checks, you don't need to change this setting.

To select individual checks to print, enter **S** (for Selected). If you also want to set a date to define which checks are printed, enter it in the next field. (See the discussion of "Print Checks Dated Through" below.) Quicken displays a window listing all the checks you've written and not yet printed, in chronological order. If you don't see the check you want to select, use the PgUp and PgDn keys to bring more checks into view. Use the arrow keys to select the check, and then press the spacebar.

Quicken preselects checks dated on or before the indicated date.

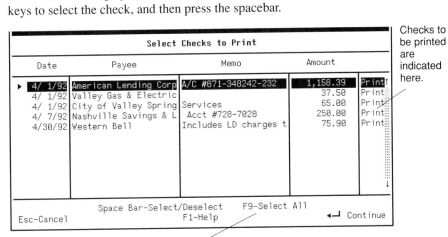

Checks to be printed are indicated here.

Press F9 to select all checks. Press F9 again to select no checks. Then you can use the spacebar to exclude or to print individual checks.

Print Checks Dated Through   This item does not appear in the window unless you have written postdated checks. Quicken inserts today's date here. If you want to print some or all of the postdated checks, you can enter the new date over the date shown. Any checks dated after this date will not be printed.

Note: You can set the date and then select specific checks to print. Quicken will use the date to preselect checks to print, but you can override the selection in the Select Checks to Print window.

Type of Check   Enter the type of check you are using and (if you have a laser printer) the number of copies to be printed. Once you've set the check type, Quicken remembers it so you won't have to reset it each time you print checks.

Enter the number of the type of check you are using:

1. Standard   These are standard 3 1/2-inch-high checks.

2. Wallet   These 2 5/6-inch-high checks have a removable stub on the left.

3. Voucher   Voucher checks have a 3 1/2-inch voucher between checks.

4. Laser Standard   These are 3 1/2-inch checks designed to fit the paper tray of your laser printer (three checks to a page).

5. Laser Wallet   These checks are the same size as the checks in your checkbook and fit the paper tray of a laser printer.

6. Laser Voucher   These voucher checks fit the paper tray of a laser printer.

Additional Copies   If you have a laser printer, you can tell Quicken to print multiple copies of each check. The setting in this window specifies the number of additional copies: 0, 1, 2, or 3. Select additional copies only if you have purchased multi-part laser voucher checks (multi-part checks are not available in the three-per-page laser format).

InkJet Forms Leader If you are using an inkjet printer to print partial pages, you can use an InkJet Forms Leader to enable you to print a partial page of checks. Enter a Y if you are using an InkJet Forms Leader. (If you have a continuous-feed printer and are using a Forms Leader, you don't need to enter anything in this field. Quicken doesn't need to know about a continuous Forms Leader.)

F9 Print Sample Check Press F9 to print a sample check and check the alignment in your printer. For more information, see "Printing a Sample Check" on page 88.

Reprinting Printed Checks

With Quicken, you can easily reprint any check at any time, for any reason.

Note: You can set the date and then select specific checks to print. Quicken will use the date to preselect checks to print, but you can override the selection in the Select Checks to Print window.

To reprint a check:

1. Start at the check register and find the check you want to reprint.

2. Type an asterisk (*) in the Num field.

   Quicken replaces the check number with a row of asterisks and considers the check unprinted.

3. Go to the Write Checks screen and print the check as usual.

Note: To prevent Quicken from printing a check you've written but not yet printed, delete the asterisks from the Num field in the register.

Missing an address?

When you change a check number to asterisks to reprint a check, remember that any address the original check had was deleted after the check was first printed. To replace an address on the check, go to Write Checks and press PgUp as needed to display the check. Then enter the address and press Ctrl-Enter to record the check.

Common Printing Problems and Solutions

This section describes some of the most common printing problems and their solutions.

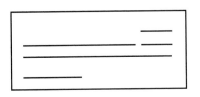

Problem: Printer doesn't print.

Solution: Check your equipment.

- Connect the cable securely to the printer and the computer.
- Make sure Quicken is set to print to the correct printer port. (See "Print to" on page 430.)
- Make sure your printer is turned on and is on line.

If the printer still doesn't print, try changing the print setting from LPT1: to PRN:

Problem: Check prints too high or too low (on any type of printer).

Solution: If the first *continuous* check prints too high or too low, Quicken needs to realign your checks.

- See "Positioning Checks in Your Printer" on page 87.

If the first three *continuous* checks print correctly, but subsequent checks print too low, the printer may be set to skip down past the perforation on standard paper.

- Turn this feature off. See your printer manual for how to set dip switches or use control codes to turn off "Skip perforation."

On a *laser* printer, if the first check prints too high or too low, adjust the printer settings in Quicken.

- Select the correct printer on the printer list. See "Printer Settings" on page 428.

On a *laser* printer, if checks print correctly on the first sheet but print several lines off on subsequent sheets, the printer is not using its default settings *or* a reverse line feed control code must be added.

- Set the printer itself to its default form length or lines per page setting (usually 60). See your printer manual.
- Add the Reverse Line Feed control code from your printer manual to the "start of page" control characters. See "Entering Printer Control Codes" on page 433.

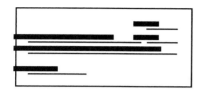

Problem: All text is too far left on check.

Solution: Move continuous-feed checks to the left by hand, moving the paper clamps as necessary.

For a *laser* printer, add an indent to move text to the right. See "Indent" on page 432.

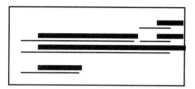

Problem: All text is too far right on continuous-feed check.

Solution: Move checks to the right by hand, moving the paper clamps as necessary.

• If the problem persists when the checks are all the way to the right, change the indent setting to 0. See "Indent" on page 432.

Problem: All text is too far right on laser check.

Solution: A nonzero indent is set in the Check Printer Settings window.

• Change the indent setting to 0. See "Indent" on page 432.

Problem: Text is OK on the left side, but doesn't reach the right side.

Solution: The pitch setting in the Check Printer Settings window is wrong. Change Print pitch to 12.

• See "Print pitch" on page 432.

Or

Use the printer's standard, nonproportional font.

• Remove the font cartridge, if there is one. Or, change font settings on the front of the printer to the default font.

• Turn the printer off for 30 seconds and then back on. (Try this even if there's no cartridge or font settings.)

Problem: Text is too long on left and right sides, or wraps from one line to the next (for example, if the date prints on the left) on continuous checks, or runs off the page on laser checks.

Solution: The pitch setting in the Check Printer Settings window is wrong. Change Print pitch to 10.

- See "Print pitch" on page 432.

Or

A nonzero indent is set in the Check Printer Settings window, but your printer can print only 80 characters (96 at 12 pitch) before it automatically advances a line.

- Change the indent setting to 0. See "Indent" on page 432.

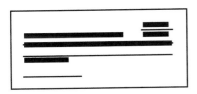

Problem: Lines of text print too close together.

Solution: Your printer is set to print 8 lines per inch, instead of 6.

- Change the lines per inch setting on your printer itself to 6 lines per inch. See your printer manual to determine how to change this setting.

Problem: Too much space between lines of text.

Solution: Printer generates an extra line feed at the end of each line or at every carriage return.

- Turn off automatic line feed in your printer settings (not in the Quicken printer settings). See your printer manual for details on its printer settings.

- Note to Tandy printer owners: Use the MODE LFOFF command at the DOS prompt and change Quicken's printer settings from LPT1: to PRN:

Problem: Printer control codes print on the check instead of controlling the printer.

Solution: Always use the backslash (for example \27) when entering printer control codes, and be sure all control code characters are entered correctly.

- See "Entering Printer Control Codes" on page 433.

Problem: Text is squeezed together on check; letters are narrow.

Solution: Compressed type is turned on. The printer may be using settings from a previous software program or from control codes set in Quicken for compressed type.

- Turn printer off and on to clear its memory of settings.
- If the problem persists, look up the compressed type control codes in your printer manual. Remove those codes from the Printer Control Codes window. See "Entering Printer Control Codes" on page 433.

If you continue to have problems, see your printer manual or call Intuit's technical support group. (See *Contacting Intuit*, beginning on page 525.)

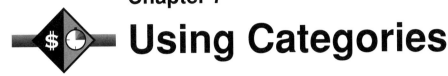

Using Categories

This chapter tells you how to set up and use categories to specify exactly what types of income and expenses your transactions cover. A home user might have expense categories for items such as food, mortgage interest paid, and utilities. Income categories might include items such as salary, bonuses, interest income, and dividends. A business can use categories to assign transactions to its chart of accounts.

When you categorize transactions, you can take full advantage of Quicken reports. For example, you can produce a report that totals all tax-related income and expenses by category for each month in a year. Some Quicken reports are specially designed to sort and total transactions by categories.

About Categories

Quicken categories are highly flexible and much easier to use than the rigid category structures found in most traditional finance and accounting software. You can name your categories using words, numbers, or characters in any combination. After you create an account, you can set up categories before you categorize transactions, or set them up "on the fly" as you enter transactions. You can enter categories in some or all of your transactions.

If you work with an accounting professional

Accountants consider your list of income and expense items part of a "chart of accounts."

Standard Categories for Home and Business Use

When you create a new Quicken file, you can select standard categories for home or for business use. If you choose to use these categories, you can delete any you don't want, change names or descriptions, or add categories to meet your needs. Page 103 lists Quicken standard categories for home and business use. The standard category list also has tax schedule names and line numbers assigned to tax-related categories. See page 417 for a list of the tax schedule information for standard home, business, and investment categories.

If you set up a file without choosing standard categories, see "Adding Standard Categories to a File" on page 117.

The category and transfer list sorts categories by type (income or expense) and then by category name.

Standard Categories for Investment Use

The investment categories, which all begin with an underline (for example, _DivInc), appear on your category list automatically (whether or not you selected standard categories) as soon as you add an investment account. You cannot delete these categories nor edit their names. You *can* change their descriptions, which are what ordinarily appear on Quicken reports.

Name	Type	Description
_DivInc	Inc	Dividend
_IntInc	Inc	Investment Interest Inc
_LT CapGnDst	Inc	Long Term Cap Gain Dist
_Other Inc	Inc	Other Income
_RlzdGain	Inc	Realized Gain/Loss
_ST CapGnDst	Inc	Short Term Cap Gain Dist
_UnrlzdGain	Inc	Unrealized Gain/Loss
_Accrued Int	Exp	Accrued Interest
_IntExp	Exp	Investment Interest Exp

Standard Home Categories

Income Categories

Name	Description
Bonus	Bonus Income
Canada Pen	Canadian Pension
Div Income	Dividend Income
Gift Received	Gift Received
Int Inc	Interest Income
Invest Inc	Investment Income
Old Age Pension	Old Age Pension
Other Inc	Other Income
Salary	Salary Income

Expense Categories

Name	Description
Auto	Automobile Expenses
Fuel	Automobile Fuel
Loan	Auto Loan Payment
Serv	Automobile Service
Bank Chrg	Bank Charge
Charity	Charitable Donations
Childcare	Childcare Expense
Christmas	Christmas Expenses
Clothing	Clothing
Dining	Dining Out
Dues	Dues
Education	Education
Entertain	Entertainment
Gifts	Gift Expenses
Groceries	Groceries
Home Rpair	Home Repair & Maint.
Household	Household Misc. Exp
Housing	Housing
Insurance	Insurance
Int Exp	Interest Expense
Invest Exp	Investment Expense
Medical	Medical & Dental
Misc	Miscellaneous
Mort Int	Mortgage Interest Exp
Other Exp	Other Expenses
Recreation	Recreation Expense
RRSP	Reg Retirement Sav Plan
Subscriptions	Subscriptions
Supplies	Supplies
Tax	Taxes
Fed	Federal Tax
FICA	Social Security Tax
Other	Misc. Taxes
Prop	Property Tax
State	State Tax
Telephone	Telephone Expense
UIC	Unemploy. Ins. Commission
Utilities	Utilities
Gas & Electric	Electric
Water	Water

Standard Business Categories

Income Categories

Name	Description
Gr Sales	Gross Sales
Other Inc	Other Income
Rent Income	Rent Income

Expense Categories

Name	Description
Ads	Advertising
Car	Car & Truck
Commission	Commissions
Freight	Freight
Int Paid	Interest Paid
L&P Fees	Legal & Prof. Fees
Late Fees	Late Payment Fees
Office	Office Expenses
Rent Paid	Rent Paid
Repairs	Repairs
Returns	Returns & Allowances
Taxes	Taxes
Travel	Travel Expenses
Wages	Wages & Job Credits

Notes:

- The standard list that comes with Quicken includes a few common subcategories for Auto, Taxes, and Utilities. Quicken indents a subcategory in the list under the name of the category it belongs to. You can use subcategories to add detail to reports (see "Entering Subcategory Information in a Transaction" on page 111).

- One way to group categories on the category list and in reports is to use subcategories. Here's a second approach to get categories to appear on adjacent lines in the reports: give them category names that are alphabetically next to each other. For example, to get home repairs, utilities, and mortgage to appear next to each other, give them names such as H_repairs, H_utilities, and H_mortgage. Similarly, you can force a category to show up last in reports by beginning the name with an underline: for example, _Appliances.

What Kind of Categories Do You Need?

Whether you want to modify the standard Quicken list of home or business categories or start from scratch, here's a tip to help you get started. When you start thinking about what categories you want to use, make a list of questions you would like Quicken reports to answer.

If you are tracking your home finances, you might want Quicken reports to tell you:

- How much do I spend each month on food, mortgage interest, tuition, or charity? These items are your expense categories.

- How much do I receive each month in salary and bonuses, dividends, interest income, or rent from investment properties? These items are your income categories.

If you own a small business, you might want Quicken reports to answer these kinds of questions:

- What are my top three sources of income?

- What is my current tax status?

- What is the cost to me of the goods I sell?

- How much do I spend to make a sale?

(You'll find some suggested lists of category names for specific purposes in the chapters in the section *Applying Quicken to Your Needs*, beginning on page 341.)

You categorize transactions by entering the category names in a Category field. When you categorize transactions, you can:

- Prepare for your tax returns by creating a report that sorts all tax-related income and expenses by form name and line number. (See "Tax Summary" on page 144 and Chapter 26, *Preparing Your Income Taxes*, beginning on page 415.) You can export this report to tax preparation software. (See Chapter 26, *Preparing Your Income Taxes*, beginning on page 415.)

- Set up budget amounts for each category and quickly compare your actual expenses with your budget amounts by creating a budget report. (See Chapter 21, *Budgeting Your Income and Expenses*, beginning on page 341.)

- Maintain a chart of accounts. A chart of accounts is a list of categories for income and expenses. (If you are familiar with accounting terms, note that categories are income and expense accounts, as in a chart of accounts. Quicken uses the term categories to avoid confusion with the use of the word accounts to describe how your transactions are organized in bank, cash, credit card, asset, or liability accounts.)

In addition, you can categorize different parts of the same transaction with multiple category names. Categorizing one transaction with multiple categories or classes is called "splitting" a transaction. To find complete information about split transactions, see "Splitting a Transaction" on page 67.

Setting Up Categories

When you set up a category, you tell Quicken the category name you want to use and provide an optional description for it. (If you haven't already done so, first set up your Quicken file and first account. See *Getting Started with Quicken*, beginning on page 11.)

Quicken maintains a category and transfer list that includes the names of all the categories and accounts in the current Quicken file. Whenever you set up a new category or account, Quicken adds it to the list. To see the list, press Ctrl-C at the register or the Write Checks screen.

You can set up your category names before you enter transactions, or you can set them up as you enter transactions. When you type a new category name in a transaction, Quicken lets you set up the category on the fly.

Note: Quicken includes account names at the end of the category and transfer list because you can choose an account name to create an automatic transfer between accounts. ***Quicken cannot categorize a transfer transaction.*** A transfer transaction has the name of the source or destination account in the Category field. If you really need all transactions to have categories, do not use the automatic transfer feature. Instead enter a transaction in each account. See Chapter 15, *Transferring Money Between Accounts*, beginning on page 251, for complete information about transfers between accounts.

To set up a new category:

1. At the register or Write Checks screen, choose Categorize/Transfer from the Shortcuts menu (or press Ctrl-C) to display the Category and Transfer List window.

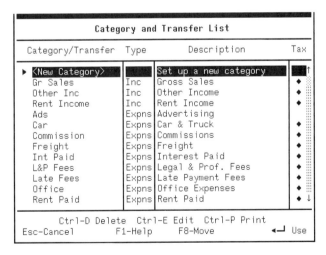

2. Select <New Category> at the top of the category list and press Enter (or press Ctrl-Ins).

3. In the Name field of the Set Up Category window, enter a category name.

   You can use up to 15 characters. See "Fields in the Set Up Category Window" next for complete information about each of the fields in the Set Up Category window.

4. Select a category type: Income (I), Expense (E), or Subcategory (S).

   For information about subcategories, see "Adding Subcategories" on page 109.

5. (Optional) Enter a description of the category (up to 25 characters) in the Description field.

6. (Optional) If the category contains tax information, enter Y (Yes) in the Tax-related field.

7. (Optional) Press F9 to choose a tax schedule and line description from lists.

   Note: The two tax fields affect two different reports. You can flag a category as tax-related for the tax summary report, and/or you can assign it a tax line for the tax schedule report.

8. Press Ctrl-Enter to add the category name to the list.

Fields in the Set Up Category Window

Category   Category names can be very specific or very general. You could have a general category called Utilities for keeping track of the gas, electric, and water bills you pay, or you could have specific categories called Gas, Electric, and Water.

You can enter numbers and uppercase and lowercase characters in any combination, but Quicken doesn't allow you to create two category names differentiated only by case. For example, you can create a category named "Utilities" or "utilities," but not both. If you want to use numbers for category names, see "Setting Up a Chart of Accounts" on page 370.

Quicken reports sort categories in alphabetical order by description or category name. To change the way Quicken displays category information in reports, see "6. In reports, print category Description/Name/Both" on page 447.

Income, Expense,   Income categories are for items that increase your account balance (for example, salary,
or Subcategory   interest, dividends, or a bonus). Expense categories are for items that decrease your account balance (for example, travel, food, utilities, and gasoline).

Using an expense category for an increase

Sometimes you should use an expense category for a transaction that increases your account balance. For example, if you categorize a clothing purchase with the expense category Clothing, you would categorize a credit for the return of a clothing purchase with the same expense category Clothing. The net result of a credit for returned merchandise is a decrease in your clothing expenses on a summary report.

Subcategories add more detail to a category. (See "Adding Subcategories" on page 109.)

Quicken uses the category type when you create reports. In many reports, Quicken organizes income and expense categories separately and provides totals for each. For more information, see Chapter 9, *Personal, Business, and Investment Reports*, beginning on page 139.

Description
(Optional)

Quicken reports normally list the category description, if there is one, rather than the category name. If there is no description, it prints the name. See "6. In reports, print category Description/Name/Both" on page 447 to change the way categories show up in reports.

For most categories, you don't need a description. For example, Groceries is already descriptive enough. But for other categories, you might need more information than can fit in the 15-character limit for a category name. If you are using Quicken in your business, you may want to use numbers or abbreviations for category names (such as 431-A) and then use the description to tell what the category includes. If you are using numbers for category names, see "Setting Up a Chart of Accounts" on page 370.

Tax-related
(Optional)

Enter Y (Yes) for Tax-related if the category is used when you do your taxes. (When you use Quicken for business, all categories are used for taxes.) Salary and Bonus are typical tax-related income categories. Taxes paid, charitable donations, and medical expenses are typical tax-related expense categories. For a discussion of using Quicken in preparing your tax returns, see "Assigning Categories to Tax Forms" on page 416. When you flag a category as tax-related, Quicken includes it in the tax summary report.

Tax Schedule
(Optional)

Press F9 to choose a tax schedule name and line description from lists. Quicken uses the tax schedule names to create a useful tax schedule report that shows line by line information for your tax schedules. You can export this report to tax preparation software. For more information, see "Assigning Categories to Tax Forms" on page 416.

$ Categorizing Transactions

You can categorize any transaction, but Quicken does not require you to use categories. You can categorize a transaction at the time you enter the transaction in the Write Checks or Register screen, or later as you review transactions. If you don't categorize a transaction, it appears as "Other" under INCOME, EXPENSES, INFLOWS, or OUTFLOWS in reports. (See "Searching for Uncategorized Transactions" on page 188.)

Each transaction has a Category field where you can enter category information. If you want to categorize part of a transaction with one category and part with another, you do so by "splitting" the transaction. To split a transaction and enter multiple categories and amounts, choose Split Transaction from the Edit menu. For example, a check written to a drugstore for $35 might actually cover a $20 expense for a prescription and $15 for office supplies. (See "Splitting a Transaction" on page 67 for more information.)

You enter a category in either of these two ways:

• Choose the category name from the category and transfer list (see the next section).

OR

- In the Category field of a transaction, type the category name or the first few letters of the name (enough to distinguish it from other categories) and press Tab. (See "Typing a Category Name" on this page.)

Choosing a Category from the Category and Transfer List

When you're not sure of the exact category name you want to use in a transaction, you can choose one from the category and transfer list (Ctrl-C).

The cursor doesn't have to be in the Category field when you choose a category from the list. Quicken automatically inserts the category you choose in the Category field of the current check or selected transaction no matter where the cursor is in the transaction. In a split transaction, Quicken inserts the category name on the line that contains the cursor.

To choose a category from the category list:

1. Choose Categorize/ Transfer from the Shortcuts menu, or press Ctrl-C, or click the "Cat:" label in the Num field of a selected transaction.

Choosing a subcategory name from the list inserts the category and subcategory names together in the Category field of a transaction, like this:

Auto:Fuel

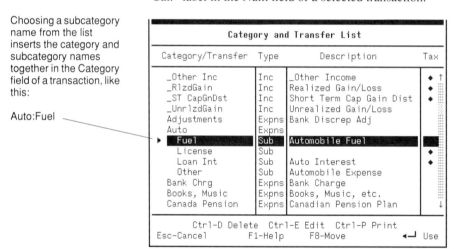

2. To insert a category name from the list into the first empty category field of the current transaction, select the category you want and press Enter. (If you have a mouse, you can double-click on the category name.)

   See "Keyboard Shortcuts for Quicken Lists" on page 26 for shortcuts to select an item in any Quicken list.

Typing a Category Name

If you already know the category name you want to use, you can insert it quickly in the Category field of the transaction by typing the first few letters (enough to distinguish it from other categories) and then pressing Tab. Quicken checks the letters you type against the category list and inserts the name in the Category field. If the name is not in the list or is not unique, Quicken lets you select from the list or add the new name you typed to the list. If you type a new category name and a new subcategory name, Quicken lets you set up both names, one after the other. For example, suppose your category list contains these names:

- Automobile
- Food
- Foreign Travel

If you enter:	Quicken inserts:
au in the Category field	Automobile
foo in the Category field	Food
fo in the Category field	The abbreviation is ambiguous, so Quicken asks if you want to add it or select it from the list. If you choose to select the category from the list, Quicken selects "Food" because it's the first category that starts with the letters fo.

$ Requiring Categories for All Transactions

You can set Quicken to require that all new transactions be categorized. This setting is helpful later when you create reports because it helps ensure that all spending is attributed to a category. Otherwise, summary reports group all uncategorized transactions together as "Other." (See "Searching for Uncategorized Transactions" on page 188.)

To require that all new transactions be categorized:

1. Choose Set Preferences from the Main Menu.

2. Choose Transaction Settings from the Set Preferences menu.

3. In the Require Category on Transactions field, enter Y (Yes).

4. Press Ctrl-Enter to save the changed setting.

$ Adding Subcategories

Subcategories provide more detail about a category; they are useful if you want your reports to group and subtotal similar categories. For example, you could add the subcategories Gas & Electric and Water to provide detail about a category called Utilities.

Think about reports before you set up subcategories.

Take some time to experiment with the kinds of reports you want to create before setting up many subcategories. In this way, you'll learn how to get the results you want without wasting time. In general, a simple approach is best.

To set up a subcategory:

1. Choose Categorize/Transfer from the Shortcuts menu (or press Ctrl-C).

2. In the Category and Transfer List window, select the name of the category or subcategory to which you want to add a subcategory.

3. Press Ctrl-Ins.

   Quicken displays the Set Up Category window with the category type preset to Subcategory (S).

4. Enter a subcategory name in the Name field. You can use up to 15 characters.

5. (Optional) Enter a description of the subcategory in the Description field. You can use up to 25 characters.

6. (Optional) If the subcategory contains tax information, enter Y (Yes) in the Tax-related field.

7. (Optional) In the Tax Schedule field, press F9 to choose a schedule name from a popup menu.

8. Press Ctrl-Enter to add the subcategory to the category you selected in step 2.

You can add a subcategory while you are entering a transaction.

You can also add a subcategory to an existing category in a transaction. In the Category field of the transaction, type the existing category name, a colon (:), and the new subcategory name. Press Tab to enter the information and choose option 1 (Add to Category List) when Quicken displays the Category Not Found window. You can then enter the information for the new subcategory in the Set Up Category window and press Ctrl-Enter to return to the transaction.

You probably will not run into Quicken's limit on the number of subcategory levels that you can create for a category. Remember that too many levels may make your reports unnecessarily complex. It's hard to think of examples where even two subcategory levels are helpful. Nevertheless, there is a limit and it depends on the total number of characters when all the levels are used in a transaction. The Category field of a transaction can hold only 31 characters, so the total number of characters for combined subcategory levels cannot exceed 31 (including the colon separator that Quicken inserts between subcategory levels).

For example, the total number of characters for all levels in the following sequence of category and subcategories is 22 (including two colon separators). Note that the Category field of the transaction could hold nine additional characters (up to the limit of 31).

Notice how Quicken separates the category and subcategory names in the Category field with a colon.

```
--------- ------||---------------------------------- ------- -- --|------- -- -------- ---:
  8/10 ||       ||Crystal Springs Utilities               487 66||       ||        ||     :
  1991 ||Memo:  ||                                               ||       ||        ||     :
  ---- ||Cat:   ||Utilities:Water:Summer                         ||       ||        ||     :
```

You can add up to 15 subcategory levels under a category. (You would have to limit the category name and the 15 subcategory names to one character each.) In the preceding example, the two subcategory levels (Utilities:Water:Summer) do not exceed the 31-character limit. Here's how the category and two subcategory levels appear in the category list.

A family living in a drought area might want to track summer and winter water expenses.

Category and Transfer List			
Category/Transfer	Type	Description	Tax
Utilities	Expns	Utilities	↑
Electricity	Sub	Electricity	
Water	Sub	Water	
Summer	Sub	Includes garden usage	
Winter	Sub	Minimal garden usage	

Entering Subcategory Information in a Transaction

You enter a subcategory in either of these ways:

- Choose the subcategory name from the category list (Ctrl-C), as described in "Choosing a Category from the Category and Transfer List" on page 108.

  OR

- In the Category field of a transaction, type the main category name, a colon (:), and the subcategory name (or the first few characters of the name). If you type only the first few characters of a name, press Tab to complete it.

When you choose a subcategory from the list, Quicken separates the category and subcategory names in the Category field with a colon (:). (See above.)

To save time:

- Enter just the subcategory in the Category field. If the subcategory name is unique in the list, Quicken fills in the main category and the subcategory.

- If the subcategory name is unique, you can type just enough letters to distinguish it and press Tab. Quicken fills in the entire sequence of category and subcategory names that precede the subcategory in the list.

Changing and Deleting Categories

You change category information or delete a category from the category list:

- When you change a category name, Quicken automatically changes it in all transactions categorized with the old name.

- When you delete a category, Quicken deletes it from the category list and erases the name from the Category field of any transactions currently assigned to it. For this reason, don't delete a category name as a step in changing it. Instead, change it as described below.

- When you delete a subcategory, Quicken changes any existing transactions so that they are categorized with the next higher-level category. For example, if your category list includes Utilities:Water:Winter, and you delete the subcategory Winter, existing transactions will be categorized simply Utilities:Water.

To change a category name, type, or description:

1. Choose Categorize/Transfer from the Shortcuts menu (or press Ctrl-C).

2. Select the category you want to change.

3. Press Ctrl-E to edit the information for that category.

Note that you can't enter a category name that is already in use at the same level. Use the technique described in "Merging Two Categories" on page 115.

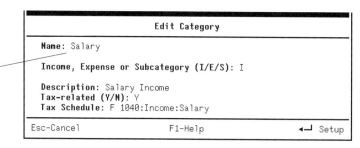

```
                         Edit Category

     Name: Salary

     Income, Expense or Subcategory (I/E/S): I

     Description: Salary Income
     Tax-related (Y/N): Y
     Tax Schedule: F 1040:Income:Salary

  Esc-Cancel                 F1-Help              ◄┘ Setup
```

4. In the Edit Category window, make your changes to the category information. "Fields in the Set Up Category Window" on page 106 describes each of the fields, which are identical to the fields in the Set Up Category window.

5. Press Ctrl-Enter to record the changed category information.

To delete a category:

1. Choose Categorize/Transfer from the Shortcuts menu (or press Ctrl-C).

2. Select the category you want to delete.

3. Press Ctrl-D.

   A message asks you to confirm that you really want to delete the category.

4. Press Enter.

   Quicken deletes the category from the list and erases it from the Category field of any transactions assigned to it.

Note: You cannot delete a category that has subcategories. Delete the subcategories first and then the main category.

Moving Categories in the List

After working with Quicken a while, you may find that you want to move the names in the category list. You can change a category into a subcategory, change a subcategory into a category, or move a subcategory from one category to another. See "Example: Moving a Category So It Becomes a Subcategory" on page 114.

Note: When you change the name or level of a category, Quicken automatically changes the name in each of the transactions that you've categorized with the old name.

To move a category or subcategory:

1. Choose Categorize/Transfer from the Shortcuts menu (or press Ctrl-C).

2. Select the category or subcategory in the list and press F8.

   When you press F8, Quicken moves a selected subcategory up one level and inserts a colon in front of it (for example, Utilities : Water). Quicken moves a selected category to the top of the list because a main category is already at the highest level (for example, : Utilities). If the category or subcategory has subcategories, you will see a plus symbol at the end of the category name (for example, : Utilities+) at this stage of the move (any subcategories will move with the selected category or subcategory).

3. Use PgUp, PgDn, or the arrow keys to move the selected category or subcategory to a new place in the list (to a target category or subcategory).

   When you reach the target category or subcategory, Quicken displays the category or subcategory you want to move next to the target name like this:

   Entertain : Dining

   To change a subcategory to a main category, move it all the way to the top of the list.

4. Press Enter.

   Quicken moves the category or subcategory and updates the alphabetic order of the list. Any subcategories that belonged to the category or subcategory you moved stay with it. The category or subcategory you moved remains selected in the list.

   If a subcategory belongs to an income category before you promote it to a category, it becomes an income category. If it belongs to an expense category, it becomes an expense category.

Note: When you move a subcategory from an expense parent to an income parent, you change its type. If you then promote it to the main category level, check that it has the type you want. See "To change a category name, type, or description:" on page 112.

Example: Moving a Category So It Becomes a Subcategory

In this example, we move the expense category Telephone so it becomes a subcategory of another expense category, Utilities.

We've selected the category and pressed F8. Quicken has moved the category to the top of the list.

The category name has a colon in front of it to indicate that you can move it now. If a plus symbol appears at the end of the name, the category you selected has subcategories that belong to it and will move with the category.

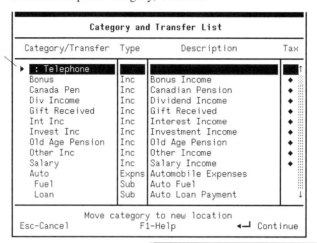

Now we've moved down to the Utilities category.

When you reach the target category, the category you want to change into a subcategory appears next to the target category.

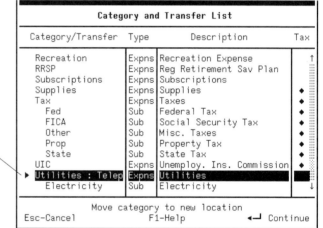

When you press Enter with the target category selected, Quicken updates the list and selects the new subcategory.

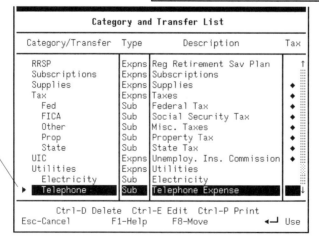

Merging Two Categories

After you use categories for a while, you might find you have two very similar categories that you want to merge into one. Before you begin the merge procedure, decide which category name you want to discard and which category name you want to keep. Don't worry about losing the category information in any transactions currently categorized with the category name you will discard. At the end of the merge procedure, Quicken updates the transactions with the category you want to keep.

Note: Quicken cannot merge two categories if one of them has subcategories.

To merge two categories:

1. Choose Categorize/Transfer from the Shortcuts menu (or press Ctrl-C).

2. Select the category or subcategory that you don't want to use anymore and follow the steps in "To move a category or subcategory:" on page 113 to make it a subcategory of the category or subcategory name you want to keep.

   For example, suppose you want to discard the category name Antiques and keep the category name Collectibles. Move the Antiques category so it is a subcategory of Collectibles.

3. Delete the category or subcategory that you want to discard. (Select it and press Ctrl-D).

   In the example, you would delete Antiques.

   Quicken automatically assigns the category name you are keeping to each of the transactions that you had previously categorized with the discarded name. Now all those transactions will have the name you've decided to keep. In the example, all transactions that were assigned to Antiques will now be assigned to Collectibles.

Printing the Category List

You can print the category list, including descriptions, income or expense type, tax-related status, and tax schedule information.

To print the category list:

1. Choose Categorize/Transfer from the Shortcuts menu (or press Ctrl-C).

2. Press Ctrl-P to print the category list.

3. (Optional) Change the setting in the Print Category and Transfer List window to print to an alternate printer or to disk.

4. Press Ctrl-Enter.

$ Copying the Category List from One File to Another

All the accounts in one Quicken file share the same category list. You can copy the category list from one Quicken file to another by exporting the categories to a separate file, and then importing the separate file with the categories into the second Quicken file. Quicken adds the imported categories to the category list in the second Quicken file.

To export categories from a Quicken file to a new export file:

1. Select the Quicken file that contains the category list you want to copy.

2. Choose Export from the Print/Acct menu.

3. In the DOS File field of the Export Transactions to QIF File window, enter a name for the export file.

4. Ignore the Export Transactions dates. They only matter when you're exporting transactions.

5. Make sure the setting is N (No) for Export Transactions, Export Accounts, and Export Memorized Transactions.

6. Make sure the setting Y (Yes) for Export Categories and Classes.

7. Press Ctrl-Enter.

    Quicken exports the categories and classes from the current file to a QIF file.

To import the exported categories into the second Quicken file:

1. Select the Quicken file to which you want to copy the category list.

2. Choose Import from the Print/Acct menu.

3. In the DOS File field, specify the name of the export file that you just created.

4. Make sure the setting is N (No) for Import Transactions, Import Accounts, and Import Memorized Transactions.

5. Ignore the option for Special Handling for Transfers.

6. Make sure the setting is Y (Yes) for Import Categories and Classes.

7. Press Ctrl-Enter.

    Quicken imports the QIF file. It adds new categories and classes (if any) to the existing category and class lists in the current file.

For details about the QIF file format, see "Exporting and Importing Data" on page 500.

For information about exporting transactions from one account to another with the Export and Import commands, see"Copying Data from One File to Another" on page 464.

For information about exporting budget amounts from one account to another with the Export Budget and Import Budget commands, see "Copying Budget Amounts from One File to Another" on page 347.

Adding Standard Categories to a File

If you set up a Quicken file without standard home or business categories and you want to add them later, you can do so at any time.

To add the standard home or business categories to a file:

1. Make sure the file to which you want to add standard categories is the current file. If it is not, use Select/Set Up File to change the current file.

2. In the Write Checks or Register screen, choose Import from the Print/Acct menu.

3. Enter HOME.QIF or BUSINESS.QIF as the file name.

   HOME.QIF and BUSINESS.QIF are files included with your Quicken program that contain Quicken's standard home and business categories.

4. Press Enter to begin importing.

   Quicken adds the standard home or business categories to the category list already in the file.

Chapter 8

Balancing Your Checkbook

When your bank statement arrives, use Quicken to balance your checkbook, or "reconcile."

The goal of reconciling is to make sure that you and the bank agree about the state of your account on a certain date. As of the statement date, your records and the bank's records should agree, showing the same:

- Transactions (both number and amount of deposits and withdrawals)
- Total dollar amount (your account balance)

Can't find those last few pennies?

Quicken allows you to reconcile to the degree of accuracy that works for you. You can track down every cent if you prefer, but Quicken does not require you to balance to the penny. See "Having Quicken Adjust for Differences" on page 128.

$ When the Bank Statement Arrives

When your bank statement arrives, follow the basic stages listed here to reconcile your account. You'll find detailed steps for these stages in this chapter. First we'll walk through the basic reconciliation for an account that balances immediately. Most of the time, that's the only part of this chapter you'll need. After that, you'll find specific help for some common situations that require special attention.

The overall goal of reconciliation is to bring your Quicken records into balance with your bank records:

- Stage 1: You enter balances and dates from your bank statement to Quicken.
- Stage 2: You mark individual transactions as cleared.
- Stage 3: Quicken reconciles all the transactions you marked and notifies you whether the account balances or requires adjustment.

Basic stages to reconcile your bank account

1. Start reconciling at the Reconcile Register window. (See page 121.)

2. Mark the transactions that have cleared your bank account in the reconcile list at the top of the Reconciliation Summary window. (See page 122.)

3. Complete reconciliation at the bottom of the Reconciliation Summary window:
   - Compare the total of cleared items in the list with those on your bank statement and check the Difference amount. (See page 125.)
   - When the totals match and the Difference amount is zero, your account balances and reconciliation is complete.
   - (Optional.) Create and print a reconciliation report.

Reconciling for the first time?

Plan to spend a little extra time on your first reconciliation, because you're bringing your Quicken records and your bank records into balance for the first time. Experienced Quicken users say that once you resolve any discrepancies found in the first reconciliation, succeeding months proceed quickly and smoothly. (See "Reconciling for the First Time" on page 133.)

Perhaps you'd like to practice before you start reconciling your own account. If so, the Quick Tour lets you walk through the steps using sample data. At the Main Menu, choose Use Tutorials/Assistants, then Set Up Quick Tour. In this manual, turn to "Lesson 7. Balancing a Bank Statement" on page 53.

If you prefer online help, press F1 twice for Table of Contents help, then choose "Balancing your checkbook."

Stage 1. Starting Reconciliation

The first step in reconciling your account is to enter general information about balances and dates from your bank statement to your Quicken records.

Is this the account you want to reconcile?

Look in the lower-left corner of your screen for the current account name. If this account is not the one you want to reconcile, press Ctrl-A and select the correct account from the list.

To begin reconciling your account:

1. Starting at the register, choose Reconcile from the Activities menu.

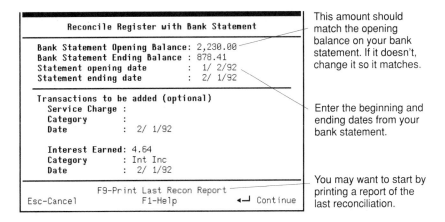

This amount should match the opening balance on your bank statement. If it doesn't, change it so it matches.

Enter the beginning and ending dates from your bank statement.

You may want to start by printing a report of the last reconciliation.

2. Compare the Bank Statement Opening Balance shown in the window with the opening balance shown on your bank statement. (Your bank statement might call this amount the "previous" or "beginning" balance.)

- The amount in the Bank Statement Opening Balance field should be the same as the opening balance on your statement. (This amount is the total of all previously reconciled items in this register, those items marked with an X).

- If the amounts differ, enter the opening balance shown on your statement over the one shown in the window. (This will create an Opening Balance Difference which you can resolve later. See "#3: An Opening Balance Difference Amount Exists" on page 132.)

3. Find the ending balance on your bank statement and enter it in the Bank Statement Ending Balance field. (Your bank statement might call this amount the "new" or "current" balance.)

4. The Statement Opening and Statement Ending dates in the Reconcile Register window should match the dates on your statement. If they don't match, change the dates in the window to match your statement.

5. If your bank statement lists a service charge or interest earned, fill in the Service Charge or Interest Earned fields:

   a. Enter the amount in the Service Charge or Interest Earned field. (If your statement lists more than one service charge, enter the total of all service charges here.)

   b. (Optional.) Categorize the Service Charge or Interest Earned amount.

   c. The Date field for these charges defaults to one month after last month's date. You can alter this date by typing over it.

6. When you've finished filling in the window, press Ctrl-Enter.

   Quicken displays the Reconciliation Summary window. The top half of the window shows the reconcile list, a list of uncleared transactions in your account.

Finding missing checks

Use the Missing Check Report to help locate checks that are missing or out of sequence. From the register, press Alt-R to display the Reports pulldown menu, choose Personal Reports, then Missing Check.

 # Stage 2. Marking Cleared Transactions

In stage 2, you record specific information about individual transactions. The purpose of stage 2 is to go through the transactions your bank has cleared and mark them in the reconcile list at the top of the Reconciliation Summary window.

An asterisk (*) appears in the C (Cleared) column for each marked transaction.

To unmark a transaction, select it and then press the spacebar. Quicken removes the *.

Quicken notes Service Charges and Interest Earned in the reconcile list, but these transactions will not appear in your register until you complete reconciliation.

As you check off cleared transactions, Quicken tallies them in this field, totaling the quantity and dollar amount of each type of transaction.

```
 Print/Acct    Edit     Shortcuts    Reports    Activities              F1-Help
┌────────┬─┬────────────┬───────┬─────────────────────┬──────────────────────┐
│  NUM   │C│  AMOUNT    │ DATE  │       PAYEE         │        MEMO          │
├────────┼─┼────────────┼───────┼─────────────────────┼──────────────────────┤
│        │*│   2,425.00 │ 1/ 4/92│Paycheck Deposit    │                     ↑│
│        │*│  -2,000.00 │ 1/ 5/92│transfer            │                      │
│        │*│    -100.00 │ 1/ 9/92│ATM Withdrawal      │                      │
│   477  │*│     -59.97 │ 1/ 1/92│Valley Gas & Electric│SRN90-05             │
│   478  │*│  -1,158.39 │ 1/15/92│American Home Mortgage│                     │
│   479  │*│    -241.89 │ 1/21/92│First Statewide Visa │                     │
│   480  │*│     -35.00 │ 1/21/92│County Water Company │                     │
│   3031 │*│    -185.98 │ 1/ 2/92│Central Market       │                     │
│▶══════ │═│════════════│═══════│═════════════════════│══════════════════════│
│        │*│       4.64 │ 2/ 1/92│Interest Earned      │                     ↓│
└────────┴─┴────────────┴───────┴─────────────────────┴──────────────────────┘
 To Mark Cleared Items, press ↵       ▪        To Add or Change Items, press F9

                          RECONCILIATION SUMMARY
      Items You Have Marked Cleared (*)
      ----------------------------------------  Cleared (X,*) Balance    878.41
         7    Checks, Debits     -3,781.23      Bank Statement Balance   878.41
         2    Deposits, Credits   2,429.64      Difference                 0.00

 F1-Help       F8-Mark Range      F9-View Register    Ctrl-F Find  Ctrl F10-Done
```

If you need to change a transaction during reconciliation, press F9 to toggle to the register.

Quicken keeps a running comparison of the $ total of items marked cleared and the Bank Statement Balance.

To mark cleared transactions:

1. Select (highlight) a transaction in the reconcile list that is listed on your current bank statement.

2. Mark the transaction as cleared:

   a. Verify that the transaction amount matches the amount listed on the bank statement.

   b. Press Enter to mark the item as cleared.

   Quicken enters an asterisk in the C (Cleared) field. (If you mark an item as cleared by mistake, you can remove the asterisk by highlighting the item and pressing the spacebar.)

3. Place a checkmark on the bank statement beside each item as you mark it in the reconcile list. This written checkmark helps you locate items that appear on the statement but may be missing from your Quicken register.

4. Repeat steps 1 through 3 until you have marked all the transactions that appear on your current bank statement.

   If you need to find a transaction in the reconcile list, press Ctrl-F (Find). For more information, see "To find transactions in the reconcile list:" on page 124.

   If you find transactions that contain incorrect amounts or other errors, change them now in the check register, using the steps in "To change transactions in the reconcile list:" on page 124.

   If you find a transaction listed on your bank statement that is not shown in the reconcile list, enter it now in the check register, using the steps in "To enter transactions missing from the reconcile list:" on page 124.

5. When you have finished marking cleared transactions, the amount in the Difference field should be zero. Continue with "Stage 3. Completing Reconciliation" on page 125.

Marking a range of items

If your statement shows an uninterrupted sequence of check numbers, you can quickly mark them as cleared:

1. Press F8.

2. In the Mark Range of Check Numbers as Cleared window, enter the beginning and ending check numbers of the range.

3. Press Enter.

Quicken marks each check in the range with an asterisk.

To find transactions in the reconcile list:

When you look at the reconcile list, you only see some of your transactions at a time. Use the Find Item window to locate any transactions that aren't currently displayed.

1. Press Ctrl-F (Find) to display the Find Item window.

2. Fill in the Find Item window with one of the following types of information:

    • Date (including slashes, such as 3/12/92)
    • Dollar amount (including dollar sign or decimal point, such as $312 or 45.72)
    • Check number (such as 3024)

3. Press Enter to begin the search.

To change transactions in the reconcile list:

1. Select the transaction you want to change.

2. Press F9 to view that transaction in the register.

3. Enter any changes directly in the fields of the transaction. (Use Tab to move forward through the fields; Shift-Tab to move backward.)

4. Press F9 to return to the reconcile list.

To enter transactions missing from the reconcile list:

1. Press F9 to view the register.

2. Press Ctrl-Ins to insert an empty transaction above the current transaction.

3. Enter the missing transaction.

4. Enter an asterisk (*) in the C (Cleared) field to mark the transaction as cleared.

5. Press Ctrl-Enter to record the transaction. (Quicken will move the transaction to its correct place in the register sequence when it sorts the transactions by date.)

6. Repeat steps 2 through 5 to insert any other missing transactions.

7. Press F9 to return to the reconcile list.

    The transactions you just entered now appear in the list. Because you entered the transactions as cleared, they already have an asterisk beside them in the reconcile list.

What does Quicken do when I mark transactions as cleared?

As you mark off cleared transactions, Quicken tallies them, entering the number of each type of transaction and the total amounts for each in the Reconciliation Summary at the bottom of the window. Quicken also keeps a running comparison of the dollar total of cleared transactions with the bank balance on your statement.

Stage 3. Completing Reconciliation

When you've finished checking off cleared transactions, look at the Difference amount in the Reconciliation Summary. Compare the amount or amounts in your Reconciliation Summary with the three following situations:

* #1: The Difference amount is zero
* #2: The Difference amount is not zero
* #3: An Opening Balance Difference amount exists

#1: The Difference Amount Is Zero

If the Difference amount is zero, you've reconciled the current bank statement successfully. Congratulations, your account balances!

How does your bank list interest earned and service charges?

Quicken includes interest earned in the number of credit items and the total credit amount, and service charges in the number of debit items and the total debit amount.

If your bank lists interest earned and service charges separately from the totals of your deposits and withdrawals, Quicken's totals will not match your statement. In this case, ignore the total counts and dollar amounts: if your Difference amount is zero, your account balances.

The final step is to complete reconciling your account.

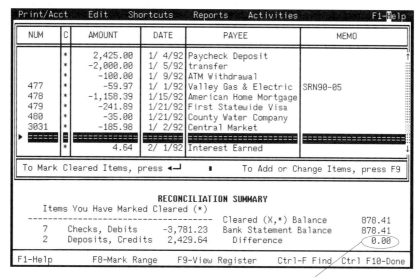

When the Difference amount is zero, you've balanced your account.

To complete reconciliation when your account balances:

1. If the Opening Balance Difference is zero, press Ctrl-F10 to complete reconciliation. Now you know that the balance in your Quicken check register is accurate as of the latest bank statement.

Quicken congratulates you.

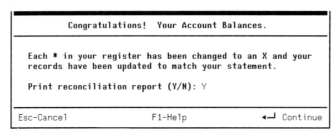

2. If you want to print a reconciliation report, enter Y.

3. (Optional.) Fill in the fields in the Print Reconciliation Report window:

This report is only stored until the next time you reconcile.

If you want to save this report in an ASCII file, choose 4 to print it to disk.

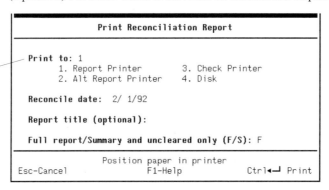

a. Enter your choice of printer.

b. Quicken inserts today's date as the Reconcile date. You can change this date if you want the report to show a different date, such as the last day of the month.

c. To use the default title, "Reconciliation Report," skip the Report Title field.

d. In the Full Report field, enter F for a full report; S for a summary report.

e. Press Ctrl-Enter to print.

Note: If you examine the check register now, you'll find that an X appears next to each reconciled transaction in the C (Cleared) column.

What's on the reconciliation report?

The reconciliation report summarizes both your cleared transactions from the current reconciliation and the uncleared transactions in your register.

A full report lists totals and all transactions; a summary report lists totals and uncleared transactions only. You can print this report now, or right before you reconcile the next time. Once you begin to reconcile again, Quicken writes over the contents of this report, so if you think you might want to refer to it, print it now.

#2: The Difference Amount Is Not Zero

If the Difference amount is not zero, your account doesn't balance for the current bank statement period.

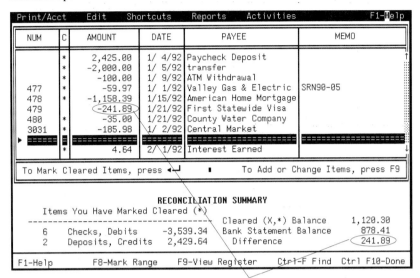

This Difference amount is a running comparison of the total items marked cleared and the total items shown on the bank statement. Here, the Difference amount happens to match the amount of a transaction that is not marked as cleared in the list.

What went wrong?

If your account doesn't balance, check for these common errors:

- Incorrect number of payments marked as cleared
- Incorrect number of deposits marked as cleared
- Incorrect dollar amounts on some items

You have two options when your account doesn't balance:

- Have Quicken fix it. Modify your Quicken balance to agree with the bank's by recording an adjustment transaction. (Skip to "Having Quicken Adjust for Differences" on page 128.)

- Fix it yourself. Research the difference between your check register and the bank statement and correct it. (Skip to "Finding and Correcting a Current Statement Difference" on page 129.)

Is the difference a multiple of 9?

If the difference is a multiple of 9, check to see if you've transposed two digits.

For example, suppose you entered $6.72 instead of $6.27. (The difference is $.45, a multiple of 9.) In this case, correct the transaction amount.

Having Quicken Adjust for Differences

You might decide to ignore the difference between your check register and the bank statement. This will save you time when the amount is small and you feel it is not worth your time to track it down.

Even though you decide to ignore the difference, you'll want to have Quicken enter an adjustment for the amount of the difference. That way you'll start with accurate totals the next time you reconcile your account.

Caution: Be careful about having Quicken make an adjustment to bring your register into balance with the bank's ending balance. Making an adjustment could introduce an error into your Quicken register equal to the size of the difference. In some circumstances, this difference could cause you to overdraw your account. Unless the difference is very small, it's usually safer to go through your transactions, locate the problem, and correct the difference. (See "Finding and Correcting a Current Statement Difference" on page 129.)

To have Quicken adjust for the difference:

1. Press Ctrl-F10 (Done) at the Reconciliation Summary window.

    If there is a Difference amount to resolve, Quicken displays a window summarizing the current problem and giving the amount of the difference.

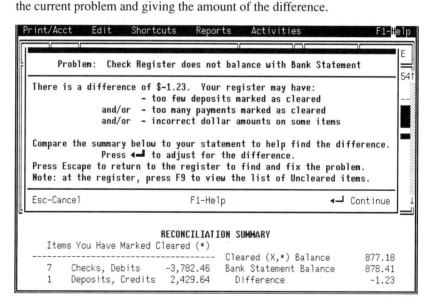

2. Press Enter to continue if you want Quicken to adjust for the difference. (You can delete the adjustment transaction later if you find the error.)

    Press Esc if you want to return to the Reconciliation Summary window to track down the difference on your own. (See "Finding and Correcting a Current Statement Difference" on page 129.)

3. At the Adding Balance Adjustment Entry window:

- Enter Y (Yes) if you want Quicken to enter an adjustment transaction. (You can categorize this transaction if you want.)
- Enter N (No) if you want to complete reconciliation without adjusting for the Difference amount, resolving the discrepancy yourself.

Quicken tells you the amount of the adjustment it will create.

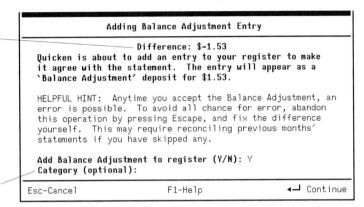

```
         Adding Balance Adjustment Entry

                    Difference: $-1.53
Quicken is about to add an entry to your register to make
it agree with the statement. The entry will appear as a
'Balance Adjustment' deposit for $1.53.

HELPFUL HINT:  Anytime you accept the Balance Adjustment, an
error is possible.  To avoid all chance for error, abandon
this operation by pressing Escape, and fix the difference
yourself.  This may require reconciling previous months'
statements if you have skipped any.

Add Balance Adjustment to register (Y/N): Y
Category (optional):

Esc-Cancel                F1-Help              ← Continue
```

You can enter a category name to assign this transaction to a category.

Quicken creates a cleared transaction, using the difference between your cleared items and the bank statement as the amount, and reconciles your account. Quicken adds this balance adjustment transaction to the register.

Be aware of outstanding uncleared transactions.

If the balance shown on your bank statement is greater than the one shown in your paper checkbook and you don't see earlier cleared transactions on your statement, be cautious about assuming that the bank balance is correct. You could have additional outstanding checks that have not yet cleared the bank from earlier months. Be sure to enter these in the check register.

 # Finding and Correcting a Current Statement Difference

To check your reconciliation against the bank statement in a systematic way, follow these steps:

1. Count the number of debit items listed on your bank statement and compare that number with the total number of "Checks, Debits" items checked off in the reconcile list.

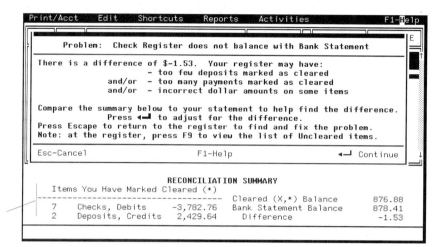

Check this chart for the total number and dollar amount of items that you have checked off.

Debits include checks, transfers out of the account, ATM withdrawals, service charges and fees, and automatic payments. Some statements count the total number of debits for you; some list service charges and ATM withdrawals separately.

If the count does not agree, you have a problem with the number of debits marked as cleared. Skip to "To Find a Problem with the Number of Items" on page 131.

2. Count the number of credit items listed on your bank statement and compare that number with the total number of "Deposits, Credits" items checked off in the reconcile list.

   Credits include direct deposits, transfers into the account, ATM deposits, and interest earned. Some statements count the total number of credits for you; some list interest earned and ATM deposits separately.

   If the count does not agree, you have a problem with the number of credits marked as cleared. Skip to "To Find a Problem with the Number of Items" on page 131.

3. If there's no problem with the number of items marked as cleared, compare the dollar amount of the "Checks, Debits" total with the total debits shown on your bank statement.

   If the totals do not agree, you have a problem with the dollar amount of debits. Skip to "To Find a Problem with the Dollar Amount of Items" on page 131.

4. Compare the dollar amount of the "Deposits, Credits" total with the total credits shown on your bank statement.

   If the totals do not agree, you have a problem with the dollar amount of credits. Skip to "To Find a Problem with the Dollar Amount of Items" on page 131.

Looking for a specific transaction?

When you're in the reconcile list at the top of the Reconciliation Summary screen, press Ctrl-F to display the Find Item window. You can search for a check by its date, dollar amount, or check number.

To Find a Problem with the Number of Items

To find a problem with the number of items:

- If you know the problem is the number of debits, look only at payments.
- If you know the problem is the number of credits, look only at deposits.

Check one or more of the following possibilities:

- **You missed recording an item in the check register.**
  Press F9 to display the register and enter any transactions that appear on the bank statement but not in the list of uncleared items. Enter an asterisk (*) in the C (Cleared) column to mark the item as cleared.

- **You missed marking an item as cleared.**
  Find any items listed on the bank statement that you neglected to clear and mark them in the list to clear them.

- **You mistakenly marked an item as cleared.**
  Examine the reconcile list to see if you accidentally marked an item not included on the statement. If you did, press the spacebar to remove the asterisk and "unclear" it.

To Find a Problem with the Dollar Amount of Items

To find a problem with the dollar amount of items:

- If you know the problem is the dollar amount of debits, look only at payments.
- If you know the problem is the dollar amount of credits, look only at deposits.

Check one or more of the following possibilities:

- **You probably recorded all items, but typed an amount incorrectly.**
  Compare all amounts shown in the reconcile list with the amounts shown on your statement. If you find an incorrect amount, press F9 to display the register, find that transaction, and correct the amount.

- **The bank made a mistake by processing a transaction for a different amount than you wrote it for.**
  Adjust the balance by entering a transaction (or let Quicken make the adjustment for you as described in "Having Quicken Adjust for Differences" on page 128.) Then contact your bank. The bank will make an adjustment that will appear on your next statement. Because this adjustment will appear as an already cleared item in the check register, your account will be off by the same amount at the end of the next reconciliation. Have Quicken make another adjustment when you finish reconciling the next statement.

Reconciling the Account After Correcting Errors

As you change cleared items or make corrections to the amounts of items, Quicken updates the Difference amount and the totals for the items you have marked as cleared. When the Difference amount is zero, your account balances. See "Stage 3. Completing Reconciliation" on page 125.

If the account still doesn't balance, you might want to double-check your work. In particular, make sure that all items on the bank statement are correctly recorded in the check register and are marked as cleared. If you still can't locate the problem, there may be an error on your bank statement and you should contact your bank.

#3: An Opening Balance Difference Amount Exists

Even if you have reconciled the current bank statement successfully, you may still need to resolve an Opening Balance Difference. If the opening balance from your bank statement differed from the amount Quicken expected as your previously reconciled balance (or your starting balance, if this is your first reconciliation), you need to account for the difference so Quicken can reconcile your account accurately.

Does the Difference amount equal the Opening Balance Difference?

If you have an Opening Balance Difference, check to see if that amount is the same as the amount in the Difference field.

If so, your account is basically balanced. Check to see if the Opening Balance difference was caused by a missing check. If so, press F9, add that check to your register, mark it as reconciled (X), and continue with reconciliation.

What is an Opening Balance Difference?

An Opening Balance Difference is the difference between the total of the previously reconciled items in the register and the previous balance shown in the current bank statement.

```
 Print/Acct    Edit    Shortcuts    Reports    Activities           F1-Help
 ┌──────┬─┬─────────┬───────┬────────────────────┬──────────────────┐
 │ NUM  │C│ AMOUNT  │ DATE  │      PAYEE         │      MEMO        │
 ├──────┼─┼─────────┼───────┼────────────────────┼──────────────────┤
 │►     │*│ 2,425.00│1/ 4/92│Paycheck Deposit    │                  │
 │      │*│-2,000.00│1/ 5/92│transfer            │                  │
 │      │*│  -100.00│1/ 9/92│ATM Withdrawal      │                  │
 │ 477  │*│   -59.97│1/ 1/92│Valley Gas & Electric│SRN90-05         │
 │ 478  │*│-1,158.39│1/15/92│American Home Mortgage│                 │
 │ 479  │*│  -241.89│1/21/92│First Statewide Visa │                 │
 │ 480  │*│   -35.00│1/21/92│County Water Company │                 │
 │ 3031 │*│  -185.98│1/ 2/92│Central Market      │                  │
 └──────┴─┴─────────┴───────┴────────────────────┴──────────────────┘
 ┌──────────────────────────────────┬──────────────────────────────┐
 │ To Mark Cleared Items, press ⏎  ▐ │  To Add or Change Items, press F9│
 └──────────────────────────────────┴──────────────────────────────┘
                      RECONCILIATION SUMMARY
   Items You Have Marked Cleared (*)   Opening Bal Difference   -200.00
   ----------------------------------  Cleared (X,*) Balance     873.77
      7    Checks, Debits   -3,781.23  Bank Statement Balance    873.77
      1    Deposits, Credits 2,425.00  Difference                  0.00
 F1-Help     F8-Mark Range   F9-View Register   Ctrl-F Find  Ctrl F10-Done
```

This Opening Balance Difference indicates a problem with previously reconciled items.

For example, if you took the opening balance for this account from your paper checkbook instead of your last bank statement, the amount you entered might have included an uncleared transaction.

Quicken counts each item with an X in the C (Cleared) field of the check register as a previously reconciled item. The reconciled balance in Quicken is the total of all previously reconciled items.

Resolving an Opening Balance Difference

The correct way to resolve an Opening Balance Difference depends on the cause of the discrepancy. The reconciled balance might differ from the previous balance shown on the bank statement for several reasons:

- This is the first time you've reconciled your Quicken bank account. In this case, Quicken uses the new account balance you entered for the account as the opening balance for this month's reconciliation. You may have entered a new account balance that differed from the actual amount in your account. (See "Reconciling for the First Time" below.)

- You've been using Quicken and reconciling your accounts, and you decided to add year-to-date information so your reports can include a full year's data. After you enter these items, you change your balance forward so your register's ending balance is correct. (See "Adding Year-to-Date Transactions" on page 136.)

- You started reconciling with a current bank statement, but you haven't reconciled each of the previous month's statements. (See "Catching Up If You Skipped Reconciling" on page 134.)

Once you've resolved the Opening Balance Difference, your reconciliation is complete.

$ Reconciling for the First Time

The first time you reconcile, you may encounter a few predictable problems. If you take the time to fix them, succeeding reconciliations should proceed smoothly. To reconcile your account accurately, check two things:

- Have I entered all uncleared transactions in my account?
- Was my opening balance correct?

When you set up your bank account in Quicken, you entered a new account balance in the Set Up New Account window. If you took this balance from your paper check register instead of from a bank statement, it may not have reflected the actual amount of money in your account.

When you get your next bank statement, if you find that the opening balance on your statement does not match the Bank Statement Opening Balance in the Reconcile Register window, you can update your starting balance to reflect the amount that was actually in your account.

For example, suppose the balance in your paper checkbook was $200 on January 1, 1992, when you started using Quicken. You used that $200 as your starting balance in Quicken, and then entered the transactions shown in your paper register for 1992. But three checks (totaling $80) that you wrote in December 1991 had not yet cleared the bank. (You didn't enter them in Quicken because they were December transactions, and you started with January entries.) However, the opening balance on your January 15 bank statement is $280, because it includes the $80 of earlier transactions.

To reconcile the first time:

1. Enter all uncleared transactions in your account. (See "To enter transactions missing from the reconcile list:" on page 124.)

2. Update your opening balance to reflect the amount that was actually in your account:

    a. In the check register, press Ctrl-PgUp to move to the opening balance transaction at the top of the register.

    b. Tab to the Deposit field and enter the opening balance from your bank statement.

    c. Press Ctrl-Enter to record the transaction. (Quicken will display a caution message because you are modifying a cleared transaction.)

    d. Press Enter to acknowledge the message.

Catching Up If You Skipped Reconciling

If you have used Quicken for a number of months and have just decided that you want to reconcile, you might ***not*** want to go back and reconcile your Quicken account against the bank statements for each of the previous months. You can skip reconciling for some months. However, your records might not be as accurate as they would be if you reconciled monthly.

For example, suppose that you have decided to start reconciling with your June bank statement. You have been entering transactions in Quicken since January of the same year. You can approach reconciliation in two ways: month by month or all at once.

Catching Up Month by Month

The most accurate way to catch up is to reconcile each month separately. Start with January, then continue month by month from February through June. See "When the Bank Statement Arrives" on page 120.

Note: Because this method is the most accurate, it is the recommended method for reconciliation.

Catching Up All at Once

The other way to catch up is to reconcile the bank statements for January to June in one step, treating the entire time period as one large month. You might also need to enter previously cleared transactions that were never entered in your Quicken account. This method updates the reconciled balance through the period covered by the current statement (June, in this example).

Note: This method is not recommended because, with many more transactions being cleared at once, any error will be harder to locate.

To reconcile previous statements all at once:

1. Choose Reconcile from the Activities pulldown menu.

   When you set up your bank account in Quicken, you entered an opening balance in the Set Up New Account window. The opening balance amount should have been the ending balance from your latest bank statement at the time you started using Quicken (your December statement, if you started using Quicken in January). You'll see that opening balance amount now in the Bank Statement Opening Balance field of the Reconcile Register window.

   (Of course, that Bank Statement Opening Balance will not match the opening balance on your current (June) statement. In this case, leave the Bank Statement Opening Balance field set to the December amount.)

2. In the Bank Statement Ending Balance field of the Reconcile Register window, enter the ending balance from the current bank statement (June, in this example).

3. In the reconcile list, mark the transactions shown on the bank statements for the period covered by your Quicken check register (January to June, in this example). See "Stage 2. Marking Cleared Transactions" on page 122.

4. If any transactions shown on the bank statements are missing, enter them now in the check register as described on page 123. In addition, correct any mistakes that you discover now.

5. When you have finished marking the earlier transactions as cleared, the Difference amount in the Reconciliation Summary window should be zero.

6. Press Ctrl-F10 at the Reconciliation Summary window to reconcile the transactions that appeared on bank statements from January to June.

   If you examine the check register now, you'll find that an X appears next to each reconciled transaction in the C (Cleared) field.

   Your account balances and you're ready for next month's bank statement (July, in this example).

If you've entered all the missing transactions and there is still a Difference amount, you or your bank may have made an error at an earlier date. If the difference is fairly small, you can have Quicken enter an adjustment transaction when it completes the reconciliation. Then your records will match the next time you reconcile your account. If the difference is large and you cannot account for it, you may want to ask your bank to determine which balance is accurate.

Adding Year-to-Date Transactions

Perhaps you've used Quicken to record and reconcile transactions and print reports, and now you decide those reports would be more useful to you if they included data from the whole year. You decide to add earlier transactions to your Quicken records.

Intermittent reconciliation

If you think you may want to reconcile past months, either of the two methods outlined in "Catching Up If You Skipped Reconciling" on page 134 will work if you enter past transactions *before* you reconcile.

However, if you have already reconciled the current month, and then decide to go back and reconcile earlier months, you will encounter some difficulties. (For example, if you reconciled June and then decided to reconcile January through May.)

In this situation, we recommend that you reconcile *forward* only: use the previous months' data for reporting only and continue reconciling with July's statement.

If you've used Quicken to record and reconcile transactions and now want to add earlier transactions to your Quicken bank account, you can do so.

To add earlier transactions to Quicken:

1. Make note of the ending balance in your account before you begin to enter earlier transactions.

2. Change the date and amount of the opening balance in the account to reflect the opening balance on the first date for which you are about to enter transactions.

    For example, say your opening balance is now dated June 1 and is in the amount of $450. You will be adding transactions starting January 1. Your records show that on January 1 you had $210 in your account. So you change the date of the opening balance to January 1, and the amount to $210.

3. Enter all the earlier transactions in your register, just as you would enter any current transactions.

4. When you have finished entering transactions, the ending balance should be the same as it was when you started. (That is, it should equal the amount you noted in step 1). If it is not, you have made an error. The error could be in your opening balance as of January, you could have omitted one or more transactions, or you could have made an error when recording the amount of a transaction. You can find and locate the error, or adjust the opening balance. For example, if your ending balance at step 1 was $1,500 and is $1,475 at step 4, you should increase the opening balance by $25 to make your account balance.

5. The next time you reconcile, the opening balance on your bank statement will be different from the one shown in the Reconcile Register window. Enter the bank opening balance over the one shown in the window.

6. Before reconciling your current month, press Enter to display the register. Mark all of the earlier transactions you entered in step 3 as already cleared: enter an X in the C (Cleared) column for each transaction.

When you finish marking the earlier transactions as cleared, the Opening Balance Difference shown at the bottom of the window should be zero. Now you can go ahead and reconcile for the current month.

If you accidentally change or delete a cleared transaction:

If you accidentally change or delete a cleared transaction, you can correct your mistake the next time you get your bank statement and reconcile.

1. From the register, choose Reconcile from the Activities menu.

2. Change the amount in the Bank Statement Opening Balance field to the correct opening balance shown on your statement.

3. Fill in the other fields as you normally would, and press Ctrl-Enter to continue.

Quicken displays a message warning that the total of the previously cleared items in the register does not match the bank statement opening balance.

4. Press Enter to continue.

5. Note the amount for Opening Balance Difference shown at the bottom of the window. This should equal the net total of the previously cleared transactions you changed or deleted.

6. Edit or reenter each changed or deleted transaction in the register as necessary.

- If the C (Cleared) field for the transaction is blank, type an X in it and press Ctrl-Enter.
- If the C (Cleared) field already has an X in it but the amount is incorrect, type the correct amount and press Ctrl-Enter.

The amount in the Opening Balance Difference field should change to zero.

7. Press F9 to view the reconcile list and continue with normal reconciliation.

Chapter 9

Personal, Business, and Investment Reports

Quicken reports give you useful information about your transactions. Many reports are based on your assignments of transactions to categories (see Chapter 7, *Using Categories*, beginning on page 101). This chapter explains how to create and print reports.

If you find that the preset personal, business, and investment reports don't meet your needs exactly, you can customize them. Once you've customized a report format, you can memorize it for repeated use. For complete information about customizing and memorizing reports, see Chapter 10, *Customizing Reports*, beginning on page 167.

$ Personal Reports

Quicken has seven personal reports:

- Cash flow report (page 140)
- Monthly budget report (page 142)
- Itemized categories report (page 143)
- Tax summary report (page 144)
- Net worth report (page 144
- Missing check report (page 145)
- Tax schedule report (page 146)

This section briefly describes each personal report and shows an example of all but the monthly budget report (shown elsewhere on page 349) and the tax summary report (which resembles the itemized category report).

To create a personal report, follow the steps in "Basic Steps to Create a Report" on page 162.

Cash Flow

A cash flow report summarizes the money you have received for each income category, the money you have spent for each expense category, and transfers to and from each asset, liability, and investment account. This report covers only transactions in your bank, cash, and credit card accounts. It is based on the summary report (page 171).

A typical cash flow report groups these items under INFLOWS:

- Income categories
- Transfers *from* asset, liability, and investment accounts.

It groups these items under OUTFLOWS:

- Expense categories
- Transfers *to* asset, liability, and investment accounts.

A cash flow report normally excludes transfers between your bank, cash, and credit card accounts. Quicken excludes these transfers because they cancel each other out. For example, suppose you use a credit card account to track your credit card charges and payments. A check that you use to pay your credit card bill would appear in a cash flow report under outflows as a transfer from your checking account to your credit card account, and under inflows as a transfer to your credit card account from your checking account. Quicken excludes both transfers from the report because they cancel each other out, and because the report includes the categorized expenses from credit card charges you entered in the credit card account. (See Chapter 19, *Tracking Credit Cards*, beginning on page 323, for details about using credit card accounts.)

You can change the accounts included in a report. See "Filtering the Transactions in a Report by Account" on page 180.

These are transfers to bank, cash, or credit card accounts *from* accounts named "Biz Exp" and "Marmona Fund."

"Other" appears on the report when at least one transaction is not assigned to a category. To learn how to track down uncategorized transactions, see "Investigating Items in Reports" on page 189.

These are transfers from bank, cash, or credit card accounts *to* accounts named "Auto Loans," "House," "Marmona Fund," and "Mortgage."

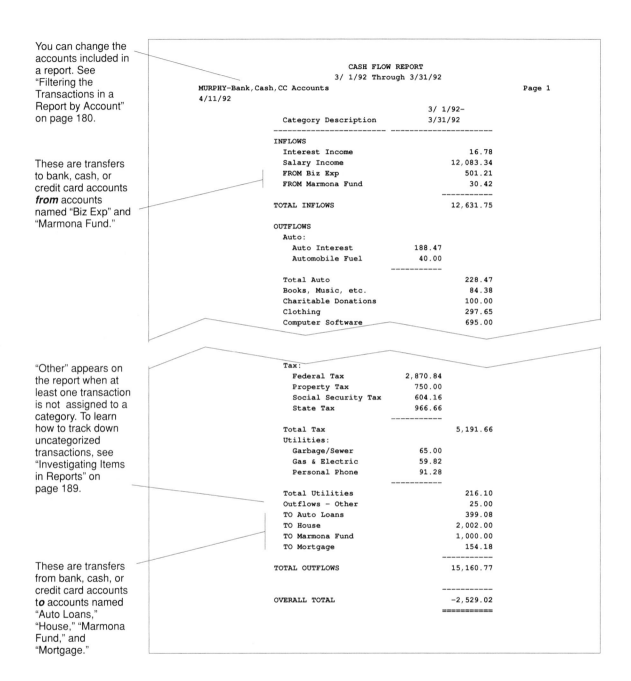

```
                              CASH FLOW REPORT
                          3/ 1/92 Through 3/31/92
     MURPHY-Bank,Cash,CC Accounts                                Page 1
     4/11/92
                                                3/ 1/92-
                    Category Description         3/31/92
     -------------------------     ------------------------

     INFLOWS
        Interest Income                            16.78
        Salary Income                          12,083.34
        FROM Biz Exp                              501.21
        FROM Marmona Fund                          30.42
                                              -----------
     TOTAL INFLOWS                             12,631.75

     OUTFLOWS
        Auto:
           Auto Interest           188.47
           Automobile Fuel          40.00
                                 -----------
           Total Auto                            228.47
        Books, Music, etc.                        84.38
        Charitable Donations                     100.00
        Clothing                                 297.65
        Computer Software                        695.00

        Tax:
           Federal Tax           2,870.84
           Property Tax            750.00
           Social Security Tax     604.16
           State Tax               966.66
                                 -----------
        Total Tax                              5,191.66
        Utilities:
           Garbage/Sewer           65.00
           Gas & Electric          59.82
           Personal Phone          91.28
                                 -----------
        Total Utilities                          216.10
        Outflows - Other                          25.00
        TO Auto Loans                            399.08
        TO House                               2,002.00
        TO Marmona Fund                        1,000.00
        TO Mortgage                              154.18
                                              -----------
     TOTAL OUTFLOWS                            15,160.77

                                              -----------
     OVERALL TOTAL                             -2,529.02
                                              ===========
```

Monthly Budget

A monthly budget report compares the money you spend and receive each month with your monthly budgeted amount for each category. Like a cash flow report, it covers only transactions in your bank, cash, and credit card accounts. It is based on the budget report (page 173).

Before you can create a monthly budget report, you must set up budget amounts for your income and expense categories.

For instructions on how to set up budget amounts and for a sample monthly budget report, see Chapter 21, *Budgeting Your Income and Expenses*, beginning on page 341.

Itemized Categories

An itemized category report lists transactions from all your accounts, grouped and subtotaled by category. This report is based on the transaction report (page 169).

This report can be very lengthy if you have many transactions. It's usually more useful if you filter it for a small number of categories or even a single category. (See "Filtering the Transactions in a Report by Category" on page 181 and "The Filter Transactions Window" on page 183.)

If you want an itemized category report filtered for tax-related categories, create a tax summary report instead (page 144).

The itemized category report, unlike the cash flow and budget reports, includes transactions from all accounts in your file.

The report normally lists income transactions first. This example was filtered to show only two selected expense categories.

```
                              ITEMIZED CATEGORY REPORT
                                1/ 1/92 Through 3/31/92
          MURPHY-All Accounts                                              Page 1
          4/ 9/92

           Date    Acct    Num     Description    Memo     Category    Clr  Amount
           -----  -------  ------  -------------- --------- -----------  -  --------

                   INCOME/EXPENSE
                     EXPENSES
                       Charitable Donations
                       --------------------
           1/ 7  Joint Ac 5002    American Heart F          Charity     X   -100.00
           2/ 8  Joint Ac 5009    American Cancer           Charity         -100.00
           3/31  Joint Ac 5023    National Wildlif          Charity         -100.00
                                                                           ---------
                       Total Charitable Donations                           -300.00

                       Dining Out
                       ----------
           1/16  Sally Ch 371    California Cafe  Lunch w/Kat Dining    X    -42.87
           1/21  AMX             Sam's Restaurant Steve Lunch Dining    X    -34.67
           1/23  AMX             Park Restaurant            Dining      X    -85.00
           1/30  AMX             Hacienda                   Dining      X    -53.00
           2/ 1  AMX             Spring Garden    Sally Lunch Dining    X    -24.00
           2/12  AMX             Valley Springs B           Dining      X    -43.00
           2/13  AMX             Pat's                      Dining      X    -31.00
           3/ 2  AMX             Acapulco                   Dining           -85.96
           2/ 5  M-C             Harvey's                   Dining      X    -23.00
           2/21  M-C             Duke of Edinburg           Dining          -125.00
           3/12  M-C             Duke of Edinburg           Dining           -62.58
           3/20  M-C             Chart House                Dining           -75.00
           1/25  Cash                                       Dining           -60.00
           1/31  Cash                                       Dining          -100.00
           2/ 1  Cash            S Valley Springs H         Dining          -120.00
           2/ 5  Cash            Joe's Burgers              Dining           -10.00
           3/ 4  Cash            Misc. Lunches              Dining           -60.00
           3/11  Cash            Stuart's Steak H           Dining          -120.00
                                                                           ---------
                       Total Dining Out                                   -1,155.08
                                                                           ---------
                     TOTAL EXPENSES                                       -1,455.08

                                                                           ---------
                   TOTAL INCOME/EXPENSE                                   -1,455.08
                                                                           =========
```

This example does not show transfers and balances forward; normally, they follow Total Income/Expense.

Tax Summary

A tax summary report lists transactions assigned to tax-related categories, grouped and subtotaled by category. This report uses transactions from all your accounts. It is the same as an itemized category report (page 143) filtered for tax-related categories only.

Net Worth

A net worth report shows your total assets minus your total liabilities as of today, using the balances from all your accounts. For an accurate report, create accounts for all your assets and liabilities. The report is based on the account balances report (page 173).

To see your net worth as of a different date, enter that date in the Net Worth Report window before you create the report. Or, after you create the report, use Set Title & Date Range (see page 175).

If you have set up investment accounts, the net worth report shows the market value of your investments based on the most recent prices you entered prior to the report date.

```
                              NET WORTH REPORT
                               As of 3/31/92
     MURPHY-All Accounts                                    Page 1
     4/ 9/92
                                                   3/31/92
                                    Acct            Balance
     --------------------------------------- ------------
     ASSETS
       Cash and Bank Accounts
         Cash                                        370.00
         Joint Account                             1,034.06
         Money Market                             13,315.12
         Sally Checking                            4,910.76
         Steve Checking                            3,430.17
                                                ------------
       Total Cash and Bank Accounts              23,060.11

       Other Assets
         Biz Exp                                       0.00
         House                                    155,777.17
         Sally's 401(k)                            4,731.11
                                                ------------
       Total Other Assets                        160,508.28

       Investments
         Marmona Fund                              7,575.20
         Sally's IRA                              13,958.62
         Steve's IRA                              13,639.67
         Yotzvitsky Sec                           14,403.57
                                                ------------
       Total Investments                          49,577.06
                                                ------------
     TOTAL ASSETS                                233,145.45

     LIABILITIES
       Credit Cards
         AMX                                          65.47
         M-C                                       2,018.21
                                                ------------
       Total Credit Cards                         2,083.68

       Other Liabilities
         Auto Loans                               17,396.23
         Mortgage                                132,612.44
                                                ------------
       Total Other Liabilities                   150,008.67
                                                ------------
     TOTAL LIABILITIES                           152,092.35
                                                ------------
     TOTAL NET WORTH                              81,053.10
                                                ============
```

Missing Check

The missing check report lists payments in the current account by check number, so you can easily spot a break in a sequence of check numbers. It lists missing check numbers as well as duplicate check numbers. This report is based on the transaction report (page 169).

```
                            MISSING CHECK REPORT
                           3/ 1/92 Through 3/31/92
        MURPHY-Joint Account                                    Page 1
        4/ 9/92

          Date    Num      Description        Memo          Category       Clr Amount
          -----  ------  ----------------  ---------------  ------------------- - ---------

                  Joint Account
                  -------------
          3/ 3  5018    Marmona Fund       Buy additional  [Marmona Fund]      -1,000.00
          3/ 2  5019    County of Santa Cor 909 Exmoor Way Tax:Prop             -750.00

                  *** Missing Check 5020   ***

          3/ 8  5021    City of Valley Spri Services        Utilities:Garbage     -65.00
          3/14  5022    San Francisco Opera Fall Season     Entertain            -250.00
          3/15  5023 S  American Lending Co A/C #871-34824 --SPLIT--           -1,158.39
          3/15  5024 S  GMAC Financing      A/C #87239-278 --SPLIT--             -587.55
          3/28  5025    Valley Gas & Electr February        Utilities:Gas         -59.82

                  *** Duplicate Check 5025   ***

          3/31  5025    Cabinet Supply Ware Kitchen Cabine [House]             -2,002.00
          3/31  5026    National Wildlife C                 Charity              -100.00
          3/31  5027    Western Bell        Feb/Mar         Utilities:Phone       -91.28
                                                                               ---------
                  Total Joint Account                                          -6,064.04
                                                                               =========
```

If a check number is missing in the sequence, Quicken lists it as a "Missing Check" item.

If a check number is duplicated in the sequence, Quicken lists it as a "Duplicate Check" item.

Tax Schedule

The tax schedule report lists transactions assigned to categories (and transfers to accounts) that have tax schedule information (see Chapter 26, *Preparing Your Income Taxes*, beginning on page 415). The transactions are grouped by tax schedule or form and then by line. This report is based on the transaction report (page 169).

You can print this report to disk as a file that can be read by tax software. At the Print Report window, enter 6 in the Print To field (see "Printing Reports" on page 164).

If you have Quicken investment accounts, the capital gains report (page 157) and investment income report (page 158) provide additional tax information.

This report groups taxable income and expenses by tax schedule or form and then by line description.

Use this report to prepare tax returns by hand or with tax preparation software.

```
                                 TAX SCHEDULE REPORT FOR 1992
                                    1/ 1/92 Through 3/31/92
        MURPHY-All Accounts                                              Page 1
        4/11/92

          Date   Acct     Num     Description     Memo      Category   Clr  Amount
         -----  --------  ------  --------------  ---------  ---------  -  ---------
                Form 1040
                ---------
                  IRA contribs-deductible
                  -----------------------
          2/17 Steve Ch 586    Rawson Total Ret 1992 IRA co [Steve's IRA]  X  -2,000.00
                                                                            ----------
                     Total IRA contribs-deductible                          -2,000.00

                Schedule A
                ----------
                  Real estate tax
                  ---------------
          3/ 2 Joint Ac 5019   County of Santa  909 Exmoor  Tax:Prop          -750.00
                                                                            ----------
                     Total Real estate tax                                    -750.00

                  Cash charity contributions
                  --------------------------
          1/ 7 Joint Ac 5002   American Heart F            Charity     X      -100.00
          2/ 8 Joint Ac 5009   American Cancer             Charity            -100.00
          3/31 Joint Ac 5026   National Wildlif            Charity            -100.00
                                                                            ----------
                     Total Cash charity contributions                        -300.00

                Schedule B
                ----------
                  Interest income
                  ---------------
          1/27 Joint Ac INT    Interest Earned             Int Inc     X       24.56
          2/27 Joint Ac INT    Interest Earned             Int Inc     X       21.19
          1/12 Money Ma        Shearson/Lehman/            Int Inc     X       81.15
          2/12 Money Ma        Shearson/Lehman/            Int Inc     X       83.97
          2/ 7 Sally Ch        Interest Earned             Int Inc     X       52.01
          1/15 Steve Ch        Interest Earned             Int Inc     X       12.78
          2/15 Steve Ch        Interest Earned             Int Inc     X       20.00
          3/16 Steve Ch        Interest Earned             Int Inc     X       16.78
          1/10 Sally's  IntInc Guren Cor        Semiannual  _IntInc            75.00
                                                                            ----------
```

$ Business Reports

Quicken has eight business reports:

- P & L statement (page 148)
- Cash flow report (page 149)
- A/P by vendor report (page 149)
- A/R by customer report (page 150)
- Job/project report (page 151)
- Payroll report (page 152)
- Balance sheet (page 153)
- Missing check report (page 153)

This section briefly describes and shows an example of each business report but the cash flow and missing check reports (which are identical to the personal versions).

To create one of the business reports, follow the steps in "Basic Steps to Create a Report" on page 162.

You can customize any of the business reports. See *Customizing Reports*, beginning on page 167, for information about customizing and memorizing reports.

P & L Statement

A P & L (profit and loss) statement summarizes your income and expenses by category, using all your accounts. This type of report is sometimes called an income statement. It groups and totals income categories at the top, followed by expense categories. This report is based on the summary report (see page 171).

```
                        PROFIT & LOSS STATEMENT
                        1/ 1/92 Through 1/31/92
     DESIGN-All Accounts                                        Page 1
     2/10/92
                                              1/ 1/92-
                   Category Description       1/31/92
                   ------------------------   ------------------------
                   INCOME/EXPENSE
                     INCOME
                       Design                          7,813.50
                       Interest Inc                      144.45
                       Production                       2,429.51
                                                      -----------
                     TOTAL INCOME                       10,387.46

                     EXPENSES
                       Advertising                        248.00
                       Auto:
                         Gas                125.34
                         Leasing            208.56
                         Tickets             23.00
                                           -----------
                       Total Auto                         356.90
                       Computer                           444.40
                       Contractor                         120.00
                       Federal Express                     91.24
                       Insurance                          186.35
                       Meals & Enter                      157.24
                       Mechanical Prep                    166.00
                       Paper                              708.76
                       Payroll:
                         FICA               319.36
                         FUTA                80.00
                         Gross            5,150.74
                         Medicare           74.70
                         SUI                40.00
                                           -----------
                       Total Payroll                    5,664.80
                       Photocopying                        67.95
                       Photostats.                         72.70
                       Postage                            246.00
                       Printing                         1,079.44
                       Reference Materials                 45.50
                       Rent Paid                          400.00
                       Telephone                          131.90
                                                      -----------
                     TOTAL EXPENSES                     10,187.18

                                                      -----------
                   TOTAL INCOME/EXPENSE                    200.28
                                                      ===========
```

The net amount here is your net profit or loss for the period.

Cash Flow

The business cash flow report is identical to the personal cash flow report (see page 140).

Note: Cash flow reports are not related to cash-basis accounting. For information on reports to use with cash-basis accounting, see "Cash-Basis Bookkeeping" on page 370.

A/P by Vendor

An A/P (or "accounts payable") by vendor report summarizes the dollar amount of unprinted checks for all your bank accounts by payee. Quicken generates a column for each month of the period for which you have unprinted checks. For a detailed discussion of using Quicken to do accounts payable, see "Accounts Payable" on page 384.

Note: The A/P by vendor report contains information from unprinted checks only. If you are not using Quicken to write checks, you can still use the A/P by vendor report by entering your accounts payable at the Write Checks screen. Just be sure to type the check number in the NUM column of the register when you eventually write the check by hand. However, if you are tracking accounts payable on an accrual basis by using a liability account, create the summary report described in "Accrual-Basis Accounts Payable Reports" on page 389.

The A/P by vendor report includes unprinted checks only.

Do not use this report if you are tracking accounts payable on an accrual basis by using a liability account.

```
                          A/P (UNPRINTED CHECKS) BY VENDOR
                               4/ 1/92 Through 5/31/92
         DESIGN-Bank Accounts                                    Page 1
         3/31/92

                                                          OVERALL
                    Payee             4/92      5/92        TOTAL
         ------------------------  ----------  --------  ----------
         Chris Jacobson              -961.15      0.00    -961.15
         First Statewide Bank      -2,641.60      0.00  -2,641.60
         Insurance Shield              0.00    -585.00    -585.00
         Richard Long              -1,058.20      0.00  -1,058.20
         Valley Real Estate          -400.00      0.00    -400.00
                                   ----------  --------  ----------
         OVERALL TOTAL             -5,060.95   -585.00  -5,645.95
                                   ==========  ========  ==========
```

A/R by Customer

An A/R (or "accounts receivable") by customer report summarizes outstanding balances for each customer by month. This report is designed for users who keep track of individual invoices in a Quicken asset account for A/R. It is restricted to transactions with a "blank" cleared status, so you should clear all paid invoices and payment transactions in the accounts receivable register by typing an asterisk (*) in the C (for Cleared) column. If you use the balance forward method, you'll want to produce a custom report. You'll find more information about using Quicken for accounts receivable in "Accounts Receivable" on page 393.

When you have completed the information in the A/R by Customer window, Quicken displays a window in which you can select the accounts to be included in this report.

If you want to exclude an account from this report, select it and press the spacebar. You can also press the spacebar to include more accounts.

Quicken preselects all the asset accounts. You probably need to include only your A/R account.

```
┌─────────────────────────────────────────────────────────────────┐
│                  Select Accounts to Include                       │
│                                                                   │
│                                              Include              │
│     Account      Type     Description       in Report            │
│  ───────────────────────────────────────────────────────         │
│ ▶ First Statewide│Bank │Business Checking │                       │
│   AR             │Oth A│Accounts Receivable│ Include │            │
│   Cap Equip      │Oth A│                  │ Include │             │
│   American Exp   │CCard│                  │                       │
│   AP             │Oth L│Accounts Payable  │                       │
│   Payroll-FICA   │Oth L│FICA Withholding  │                       │
│   Payroll-FWH    │Oth L│Federal Withholding│                      │
│   Payroll-SWH    │Oth L│State Withholding │                       │
│   Sales Tax      │Oth L│Sales Tax Payable │                       │
│                                                                   │
│                  Space Bar-Include/Exclude                        │
│ Esc-Cancel     F1-Help     F9-Select All    ◄─┘ Continue          │
└─────────────────────────────────────────────────────────────────┘
```

When you have finished, press Enter to start the report.

The following shows a sample A/R by customer report.

Tip: Memorize the A/R report after creating it. By recalling the memorized report, you'll avoid having to reselect the A/R account or accounts.

```
                              A/R by Customer
                          3/ 1/92 Through 4/30/92
       DESIGN-AR                                            Page 1
       4/30/92

                                                    OVERALL
                    Payee          3/92      4/92    TOTAL
       ───────────────────────  ─────────  ─────────  ─────────
       Ace Computer Sales         404.99    376.97    781.96
       Balloon Adventures           0.00    705.66    705.66
       Blaine Associates          589.03    571.95  1,160.98
       Computer Waves             679.45    595.41  1,274.86
       Engineering Control          0.00    446.19    446.19
       Osborne Studios            682.12  2,059.75  2,741.87
       Reynolds Markets           818.55      0.00    818.55
       Robinson Shoes             463.84    350.00    813.84
                                ─────────  ─────────  ─────────
       OVERALL TOTAL            3,637.98  5,105.93  8,743.91
                                =========  =========  =========
```

Job/Project

A job/project report summarizes your income and expenses by category with a column for each class, using all your accounts. This report can be used to show total income and expenses by job, project, property, department—whatever you have set up classes for. (You'll find specific information about using Quicken for bookkeeping by job and project in "Reporting by Job, Property, Client, Project, or Department" on page 372. If you manage properties, you can use this report to report on income and expenses by property. See "Rental Properties" on page 359.)

Here's a sample job/project report that shows total income and expenses for three projects. Class names were set up for each project and were assigned to all income and expense transactions related to that project. Transfers were filtered out.

```
                            Job/Project Report
                         2/ 1/92 Through 4/30/92
  DESIGN-All Accounts                                                  Page 1
  4/30/92

                                                                      OVERALL
        Category Description   Job 4-Computer Job 5-Engineer Job 6-Osborne   TOTAL
  ----------------------------- --------------- --------------- --------------- ---------------

  INCOME/EXPENSE
    INCOME
      Design                      3,007.69        2,110.00        3,263.50        8,381.19
      Mailing Lists                 725.00            0.00            0.00          725.00
      Mechanical Preparation        257.25          195.75          271.50          724.50
      Photography                     0.00            0.00          300.00          300.00
      Photostats                      0.00            0.00          200.00          200.00
      Printing                    1,412.72          546.00          540.00        2,498.72
      Production                    144.00          986.67          200.00        1,330.67
      Shipping/Postage              107.75          183.25          158.39          449.39
                                --------------- --------------- --------------- ---------------
    TOTAL INCOME                  5,654.41        4,021.67        4,933.39       14,609.47
    EXPENSES
      Advertising Space            667.90            0.00            0.00          667.90
      Art Supplies                   9.36            0.00            0.00            9.36
      Contract Labor                 0.00            0.00          585.00          585.00
      Federal Express Services      90.50          146.25           70.40          307.15
      Mailing Lists                658.00            0.00            0.00          658.00
      Mechanical Preparation       179.25          129.25           80.00          388.50
      Paper Supplies                 0.00          700.00           95.12          795.12
      Photocopying                  84.00            0.00            0.00           84.00
      Photostat Services             0.00            0.00          166.00          166.00
      Printing Services            483.72          265.50          161.50          910.72
                                --------------- --------------- --------------- ---------------
    TOTAL EXPENSES               2,172.73        1,241.00        1,158.02        4,571.75
                                --------------- --------------- --------------- ---------------
  TOTAL INCOME/EXPENSE           3,481.68        2,780.67        3,775.37       10,037.72
                                =============== =============== =============== ===============
```

Payroll

A payroll report summarizes your income and expenses by category with a column for each payee (employees and payroll tax payees). This report is designed specifically to work with both Intuit's payroll program QuickPay and the method of using Quicken for payroll described in "Payroll" on page 401. It assumes that you have assigned all payroll transactions to categories or accounts beginning with the word "Payroll."

This column shows your payments of payroll taxes.

This row shows gross wages for each payee (one payee per column).

This row shows your total payroll expenses for this time period.

```
                                    PAYROLL REPORT
                               1/ 1/92 Through 4/30/92
   DESIGN-All Accounts                                                 Page 1
   5/12/92
                                        First Statewide          OVERALL
      Category Description  Chris Jacobson  Bank        Richard Long    TOTAL
   -----------------------  --------------  --------------  -------------  --------------
   INCOME/EXPENSE
     EXPENSES
       Payroll:
         FICA                    610.48        0.00        666.96       1,277.44
         FUTA                    160.00        0.00        160.00         320.00
         Gross                 9,846.16        0.00     10,756.80      20,602.96
         Medicare               142.80        0.00        156.00         298.80
         SUI                     80.00        0.00         80.00         160.00
                             ------------  ------------  ------------  ------------
       Total Payroll         10,839.44        0.00     11,819.76      22,659.20
                             ------------  ------------  ------------  ------------
     TOTAL EXPENSES          10,839.44        0.00     11,819.76      22,659.20

                             ------------  ------------  ------------  ------------
   TOTAL INCOME/EXPENSE     -10,839.44        0.00    -11,819.76     -22,659.20

   TRANSFERS
     TO Payroll-FICA              0.00    -1,812.11        0.00      -1,812.11
     TO Payroll-FWH               0.00    -2,349.35        0.00      -2,349.35
     TO Payroll-MEDI              0.00      -465.14        0.00        -465.14
     FROM Payroll-FICA       1,220.96        0.00      1,333.92       2,554.88
     FROM Payroll-FUTA         160.00        0.00        160.00         320.00
     FROM Payroll-FWH        1,304.32        0.00      1,337.28       2,641.60
     FROM Payroll-MEDI         285.60        0.00        312.00         597.60
     FROM Payroll-SUI           80.00        0.00         80.00         160.00
     FROM Payroll-SWH           99.36        0.00        130.96         230.32
                             ------------  ------------  ------------  ------------
     TOTAL TRANSFERS         3,150.24    -4,626.60      3,354.16       1,877.80

                             ------------  ------------  ------------  ------------
   OVERALL TOTAL            -7,689.20    -4,626.60     -8,465.60     -20,781.40
                             ============  ============  ============  ============
```

The final amount in this row shows the net increase in your accrued payroll liabilities.

The TRANSFERS TO items show decreases in your accrued payroll liabilities. For example, each time you record a FICA payment in your checking account, Quicken automatically transfers the amount to the Payroll-FICA account, where it decreases the balance you owe.

The TRANSFERS FROM items show increases in your accrued payroll liabilities. For example, each time you record a paycheck, Quicken automatically transfers the FICA contribution amounts to your checking account from the Payroll-FICA account, where it increases the balance you owe for FICA.

Balance Sheet

A balance sheet shows your assets and liabilities as of today. This report combines the balances from all your Quicken accounts in the current file. It groups and totals the balances in your asset accounts (bank, cash, investment, and other asset accounts) and in your liability accounts (credit card and other liability accounts).

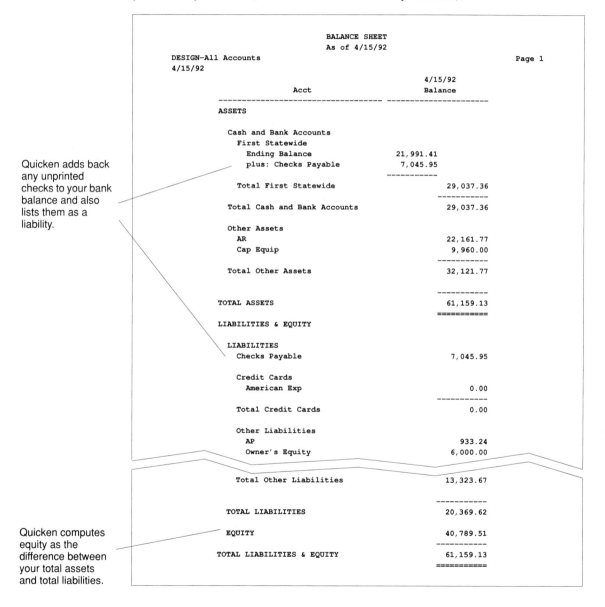

Quicken adds back any unprinted checks to your bank balance and also lists them as a liability.

Quicken computes equity as the difference between your total assets and total liabilities.

```
                              BALANCE SHEET
                               As of 4/15/92
         DESIGN-All Accounts                                    Page 1
         4/15/92
                                                 4/15/92
                               Acct              Balance
         ------------------------------------    ----------------------
         ASSETS

            Cash and Bank Accounts
               First Statewide
                  Ending Balance        21,991.41
                  plus: Checks Payable   7,045.95
                                        -----------
               Total First Statewide                    29,037.36
                                                        -----------
            Total Cash and Bank Accounts                29,037.36

            Other Assets
               AR                                       22,161.77
               Cap Equip                                 9,960.00
                                                        -----------
            Total Other Assets                          32,121.77

                                                        -----------
         TOTAL ASSETS                                   61,159.13
                                                        ===========
         LIABILITIES & EQUITY

            LIABILITIES
               Checks Payable                            7,045.95

            Credit Cards
               American Exp                                  0.00
                                                        -----------
            Total Credit Cards                              0.00

            Other Liabilities
               AP                                         933.24
               Owner's Equity                           6,000.00

            Total Other Liabilities                     13,323.67

                                                        -----------
         TOTAL LIABILITIES                              20,369.62

            EQUITY                                      40,789.51
                                                        -----------
         TOTAL LIABILITIES & EQUITY                     61,159.13
                                                        ===========
```

Missing Check

This report is identical to the personal missing check report (page 145).

$ Investment Reports

The investment reports are based on transactions entered in Quicken investment accounts (see Chapter 17, *Getting Started with Investment Accounts*, beginning on page 265). Quicken has five investment reports:

- Portfolio value report (page 154)
- Investment performance report (page 155)
- Capital gains report (page 157)
- Investment income report (page 158)
- Investment transactions report (page 160)

This section briefly describes and shows an example of each investment report. To create an investment report, follow the steps in "Basic Steps to Create a Report" on page 162.

You can customize any of the investment reports. See *Customizing Reports*, beginning on page 167, for information about customizing and memorizing reports.

Portfolio Value

The portfolio value report shows the value of each security on a specified date. This report shows the following information:

- Number of shares (to the nearest 0.01).

- Most recent price per share recorded in Quicken as of that date. Quicken marks estimated prices with an asterisk (*).

- Your cost basis for the security. (Quicken displays 0.00 if you did not enter the cost basis of your first transaction for the security.)

- Unrealized (paper) gain or loss in dollars.

- Market value on the date of the report.

When you choose Portfolio Value at the Investment Reports menu, Quicken displays the Portfolio Value Report window.

Enter a number here to tell Quicken how to subtotal this report.

To include all investment accounts in this report, enter A here (in place of C).

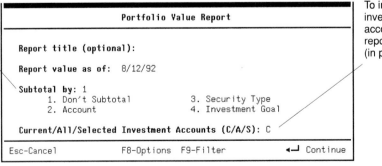

```
                         Portfolio Value Report

  Report title (optional):

  Report value as of:  8/12/92

  Subtotal by: 1
          1. Don't Subtotal           3. Security Type
          2. Account                  4. Investment Goal

  Current/All/Selected Investment Accounts (C/A/S): C

  Esc-Cancel          F8-Options  F9-Filter          ◄┘ Continue
```

The report is similar to the Update Prices and Market Value screen (page 296) but shows the unrealized gain in dollars (instead of as a percentage), and has options for subtotaling by account, security type, or investment goal.

This example includes all investment accounts and is subtotaled by account.

```
                         PORTFOLIO VALUE REPORT BY ACCOUNT
                                 As of 1/31/92
    MURPHY-All Investment Accts                                    Page 1
    1/31/92

          Security        Shares  Curr Price  Cost Basis  Gain/Loss   Balance
    -------------------  --------  ----------  ----------  ---------  ----------

    Marmona Fund
      Marmona Fund        265.37     22.680      5,920.54      98.19    6,018.73
                                                ----------  ---------  ----------
    Total Marmona Fund                            5,920.54      98.19    6,018.73

    Sally's IRA
      First Statewide C 10,224.65    1.000 *   10,224.65       0.00   10,224.65
      Guren Corp Bond      20.00    105.    *    2,075.00      25.00    2,100.00
      McKendry MMF      1,624.51      1.000      1,624.51       0.00    1,624.51
                                                ----------  ---------  ----------
    Total Sally's IRA                            13,924.16      25.00   13,949.16

    Steve's IRA
      Marmona Fund        206.54     22.680      4,608.04      76.42    4,684.46
      Rawson Totl Retur   252.32     23.950      5,992.79      50.47    6,043.26
                                                ----------  ---------  ----------
    Total Steve's IRA                            10,600.83     126.89   10,727.72

    Yotzvitsky Sec
      Benjamin Sound Sy   100.00    48 1/4 *     5,090.00    -265.00    4,825.00
      McKendry MMF      2,386.72      1.000      2,386.73       0.00    2,386.73
      Zarya Software      100.00    46 7/8 *     3,760.00     927.50    4,687.50
                                                ----------  ---------  ----------
    Total Yotzvitsky Sec                         11,236.73     662.50   11,899.23
                                                ----------  ---------  ----------
    Total Investments                            41,682.26     912.58   42,594.84
                                                ==========  =========  ==========
```

Prices followed by asterisks (*) are estimated prices for the report date.

Investment Performance

The investment performance report shows the average annual total return of your securities during a specified time period. This return takes into account dividends, interest, and other payments you receive as well as increases and decreases in the market value of your securities. Loosely speaking, if the average annual total return is, say, 10%, you're doing as well with the investment as with a bank account that pays 10% interest.

When you choose Investment Performance at the Investment Reports menu, the Investment Performance Report window appears.

For an accurate report, be sure Quicken has prices for (1) the day **before** the start date and (2) the end date.

Enter a number here to tell Quicken how to subtotal this report.

Enter Y here to see beginning and ending market values and a list of all transactions (such as purchases) that represent cash flowing in or out of your investments.

To include all investment accounts in this report, enter A here.

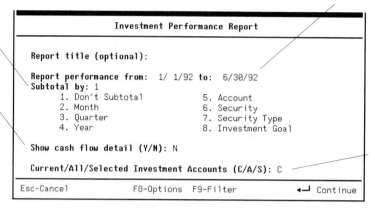

```
┌──────────────────────────────────────────────────────────────────┐
│ ████████████████████████████████████████████████████████████████ │
│                  Investment Performance Report                     │
│ ─────────────────────────────────────────────────────────────────│
│                                                                    │
│ Report title (optional):                                           │
│                                                                    │
│ Report performance from:  1/ 1/92 to:  6/30/92                     │
│ Subtotal by: 1                                                     │
│         1. Don't Subtotal         5. Account                       │
│         2. Month                  6. Security                      │
│         3. Quarter                7. Security Type                 │
│         4. Year                   8. Investment Goal               │
│                                                                    │
│ Show cash flow detail (Y/N): N                                     │
│                                                                    │
│ Current/All/Selected Investment Accounts (C/A/S): C                │
│ ───────────────────────────────────────────────────────────────── │
│ Esc-Cancel            F8-Options  F9-Filter          ◄┘ Continue   │
└──────────────────────────────────────────────────────────────────┘
```

When the average annual total return is greater than 10,000% or less than -99.9%, or when the timing of cash flows prevents Quicken from calculating a figure, Quicken displays a message that one or more calculations appear as N/A (not available).

Technical note: The average annual total return is the internal rate of return (IRR) for your investment. It equals the discount rate at which all the cash flows associated with the investment have a net present value of zero.

This example includes all investment accounts and is subtotaled by security.

```
                    PERFORMANCE REPORT BY SECURITY
                      1/ 1/92 Through 6/30/92
    MURPHY-All Investment Accts                          Page 1
    8/12/92
                                                   Avg. Annual
                    Description                    Tot. Return
    ---------------------------------------------  ------------

    Total Benjamin Sound 2                               4.8%

    Total Benjamin Sound Sys                            28.6%

    Total First Statewide CD                             0.0%

    Total Guren Corp Bond                                7.8%

    Total Marmona Fund                                  35.9%

    Total McKendry MMF                                   5.0%

    Total Rawson Totl Return                            17.9%

    Total SIRA Technology                              186.8%

    Total Zarya Software                                21.2%
```

Capital Gains

The capital gains report lists realized gains on securities you've sold. It shows long-term and short-term capital gains for securities sold during a specified time period. (For capital gains distributions from mutual funds, use the investment income report. For capital gains from covering short sales, use the investment income report (summaries) and the investment transaction report (detail).)

To get an accurate capital gains report, you must tell Quicken the date or dates you bought the shares you sold, and the actual cost basis of those shares. If you haven't already done so, you can enter this information in the investment register after you make the sale. See "Entering Prior History for Investments" on page 319.

If you sold only part of your shares of a security in one account, Quicken assumes that the shares you sold are the ones you've held the longest (FIFO—first in, first out). If you have designated other shares as the ones you sold, use separate lot numbers to identify the shares. See "Different Lots for a Security in One Account" on page 314.

Quicken does not distinguish "wash sales" from other sales. (A "wash sale" is a sale at a loss within 30 days of your acquiring the same security. Special tax rules apply.)

When you choose Capital Gains at the Investment Reports menu, the Capital Gains Report window appears.

Enter a number here to tell Quicken how to subtotal this report.

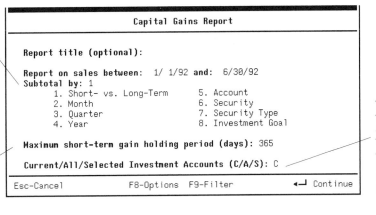

To select only those investment accounts with taxable capital gains, enter S here. (For example, do not include IRAs.)

Quicken's preset holding period for short-term capital gain is 365 days or less. You can change this period.

To use this report for Schedule D (after you've entered all prior history for any security you've sold), subtotal by short-term vs. long-term gain. Select only those accounts that have taxable capital gains (for example, exclude IRAs). You can memorize the report with these settings so you won't have to reselect the accounts each time (see "Memorizing a Custom Report Setup" on page 193).

This example is for one account and is subtotaled by short-term vs. long-term gain.

```
                              CAPITAL GAINS REPORT
                             1/ 1/92 Through 6/30/92

        MURPHY-Yotzvitsky Sec                                           Page 1
        8/12/92

             Security      Shares  Bought    Sold   Sales Price  Cost Basis  Gain/Loss
             ----------   --------  --------  -------  -----------  ----------  ----------
                          SHORT TERM
             SIRA Technolo    200  2/12/92  5/14/92    2,315.00    1,775.00     540.00
             McKendry MMF   64.39 12/31/91  6/ 1/92       64.39       64.39       0.00
                                                      -----------  ----------  ----------
                          TOTAL SHORT TERM            2,379.39    1,839.39     540.00

                          LONG TERM
             Zarya Softwar     50 10/29/85  6/24/92    2,525.00    1,880.00     645.00
                                                      -----------  ----------  ----------
                          TOTAL LONG TERM             2,525.00    1,880.00     645.00
                                                      -----------  ----------  ----------
                          OVERALL TOTAL               4,904.39    3,719.39   1,185.00
                                                      ===========  ==========  ==========
```

If you sell shares of a money market fund, the sale appears on the report, but there is no gain or loss because the price is always 1.

Investment Income

The investment income report summarizes your income and expenses by category, using transactions in your investment accounts. It shows dividend income (taxable and nontaxable); interest income (taxable and nontaxable); short-term and long-term capital gains distributions; realized gain or loss for both normal sales and short sales; unrealized gain or loss (as an option); and margin interest, accrued interest, and other investment expense during a specified time period.

When you choose Investment Income at the Investment Reports menu, the Investment Income Report window appears.

Enter a number here to tell Quicken how to subtotal this report.

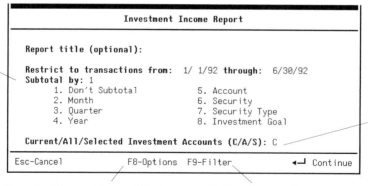

```
                    Investment Income Report
        ─────────────────────────────────────────────────────

        Report title (optional):

        Restrict to transactions from:  1/ 1/92 through:  6/30/92
        Subtotal by: 1
              1. Don't Subtotal          5. Account
              2. Month                   6. Security
              3. Quarter                 7. Security Type
              4. Year                    8. Investment Goal

        Current/All/Selected Investment Accounts (C/A/S): C
        ─────────────────────────────────────────────────────
        Esc-Cancel          F8-Options  F9-Filter          ◄┘ Continue
```

To select only those investment accounts with reportable income, enter S here. (For example, do not include IRAs.)

Normally, this report does not display unrealized capital gains. Press F8 if you want this option.

To filter the report for securities you know have special tax treatment, press F9.

If you want to use this report to gather information for Schedule B, be sure you've entered all investment transactions for the year. Select only those accounts for which you must report income (for example, exclude IRAs). Subtotal by security. Do not select the option to include unrealized gains. Create one report for all your reportable income, both taxable and tax-exempt. Then create a second report, using filters to include only securities that generate reportable but tax-exempt income. Again, subtotal by security.

This example is for all investment accounts and is not subtotaled.

Capital gains distributions appear on this report, **not** on the capital gains report.

Realized gains from both short sales and normal sales appear on this report.

Unrealized gains appear on this report only if you have chosen this option.

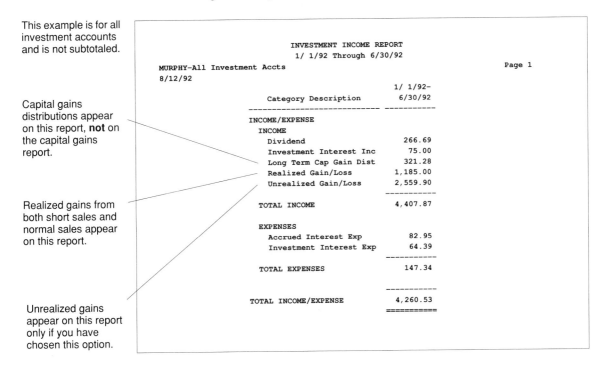

```
                            INVESTMENT INCOME REPORT
                             1/ 1/92 Through 6/30/92
        MURPHY-All Investment Accts                                    Page 1
        8/12/92
                                                      1/ 1/92-
                            Category Description       6/30/92
        ------------------------------------------   -----------
        INCOME/EXPENSE
          INCOME
            Dividend                                    266.69
            Investment Interest Inc                      75.00
            Long Term Cap Gain Dist                     321.28
            Realized Gain/Loss                        1,185.00
            Unrealized Gain/Loss                      2,559.90
                                                     -----------
          TOTAL INCOME                                4,407.87

          EXPENSES
            Accrued Interest Exp                         82.95
            Investment Interest Exp                      64.39
                                                     -----------
          TOTAL EXPENSES                                147.34

                                                     -----------
        TOTAL INCOME/EXPENSE                          4,260.53
                                                     ===========
```

Investment Transactions

The investment transactions report lists transactions from your investment accounts. It shows how transactions during a specified time period have affected either the market value or the cost basis of your investments and the cash balance in your investment accounts.

When you choose Investment Transactions at the Investment Reports menu, the Investment Transactions Report window appears.

Enter a number here to tell Quicken how to subtotal this report.

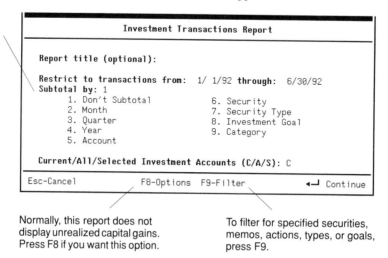

```
              Investment Transactions Report


    Report title (optional):

    Restrict to transactions from:  1/ 1/92 through:  6/30/92
    Subtotal by: 1
            1. Don't Subtotal           6. Security
            2. Month                    7. Security Type
            3. Quarter                  8. Investment Goal
            4. Year                     9. Category
            5. Account


    Current/All/Selected Investment Accounts (C/A/S): C

  Esc-Cancel              F8-Options  F9-Filter            ↵ Continue
```

Normally, this report does not display unrealized capital gains. Press F8 if you want this option.

To filter for specified securities, memos, actions, types, or goals, press F9.

If you do not include unrealized (paper) gains, the report shows the change in cost basis of your investments between the beginning and end of the period. On the other hand, if you select the option of including unrealized gains, the report shows the change in the market value of your investments between the beginning and end of the period.

Here is a sample investment transactions report for one account, which does not include unrealized gains.

```
                            INVESTMENT TRANSACTIONS REPORT
                               5/ 1/92 Through 6/30/92
MURPHY-Yotzvitsky Sec                                                           Page 1
8/13/91
                                                                    Invest.      Cash +
                                                                    Value        Invest.
  Date  Action   Secur     Categ    Price    Shares   Commssn    Cash
  ----- -------  -------   -------  -------- -------- --------  --------- --------- ---------
        BALANCE  4/30/92                                            0.00  13,051.18  13,051.18

  5/12 Div       Zarya Soft Dividend                               10.00             10.00

  5/14 Sell      SIRA Techn           12       200     85.00   1,775.00  -1,775.00
                          Realized Gain/Loss                      540.00             540.00

  5/15 Buy       Benjamin S        53 3/8      300    165.00 -16,177.50  16,177.50
  5/15 XIn           -Cash- [Margin L                          13,852.50          13,852.50

  5/31 ReinvDi McKendry M          1.000    10.763                -10.76      10.76
                          Dividend                                 10.76             10.76

  6/ 1 MargInt      -Cash- Investment Interest Exp               -64.39            -64.39
  6/ 1 Sell      McKendry M         1.000    64.39                64.39     -64.39
  6/ 6 Div       Benjamin S Dividend                             45.00              45.00
  6/11 Buy       McKendry M         1.000       45               -45.00      45.00
  6/15 StkSpli Benjamin S                        2:1
  6/15 StkSpli Benjamin S                        2:1

  6/24 Sell      Zarya Soft          52          50     75.00  1,880.00  -1,880.00
                          Realized Gain/Loss                     645.00            645.00

  6/28 Buy       McKendry M         1.000     2,525            -2,525.00   2,525.00

  6/30 ReinvDi McKendry M          1.000    10.992               -10.99      10.99
                          Dividend                                10.99             10.99
                                                              --------- --------- ---------
        TOTAL   5/ 1/92 -  6/30/92                                 0.00  15,049.86  15,049.86

        BALANCE  6/30/92                                           0.00  28,101.04  28,101.04
```

A reinvested dividend shows up as a buy transaction on one line, followed by an income transaction on the next line.

In general, complex transactions appear on several lines, with one line for each component of the transaction.

The Cash column shows the change in the cash balance of your account or accounts as a result of each transaction.

For each transaction, the Invest. Value column shows the change in cost basis of the security if unrealized gains are not included, or the change in market value if unrealized gains are included.

The balance is the current cost basis or market value of all the securities.

For each transaction, the Cash + Invest. column shows the sum of the amounts in the Cash and Invest. Value columns.

Basic Steps to Create a Report

When you create a report in Quicken, Quicken uses the most common settings, so most of the time you won't have to change anything.

To create a report:

1. Choose Create Reports from the Main Menu or choose Reports (Alt-R) from any register, the Write Checks screen, or the Report screen.

   Quicken displays the Reports menu.

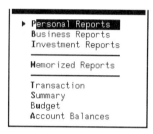

2. Choose a report type: Personal Reports, Business Reports, Investment Reports, Memorized Reports, Transaction, Summary, Budget, or Account Balances.

   ### Notes

   - The preset personal, business, and investment reports are designed to show the information most users want. All personal and business reports are just special variations of the basic transaction, summary, budget, or account balances report.

   - You need to memorize a report before you can recall it with the Memorized Reports command. See "Memorizing a Custom Report Setup" on page 193.

3. If you chose Personal Reports, Business Reports, Investment Reports, or Memorized Reports, Quicken displays a submenu of report names. Choose the name of the report you want.

   Quicken displays a setup window for the report you chose. (The windows for some reports have more fields than the one below).

The report will use transactions from the first day of this month . . .

. . . to the last day of this month.

For some reports you see a single date.

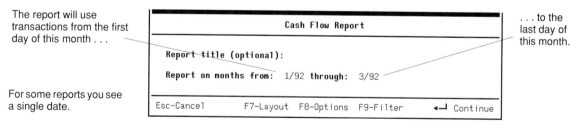

You can use the F7, F8, and F9 keys to customize a report before Quicken displays it on the screen. Chapter 10 describes the report options (see page 167).

4. (Optional) Enter a title for the report.

If you don't specify a title, Quicken uses the report name (for example, cash flow).

5. (Optional) Change the beginning and ending dates. You can type over the current date, or use the + and − keys to increase or decrease the day or month shown.

6. (Optional) Change any other fields that may be in the window.

7. Press Ctrl-Enter or F10 to create the report.

If you're creating an A/R by customer report, Quicken asks you to specify which accounts to include in the report. (For more information, see "A/R by Customer" on page 150.)

Quicken starts searching the account registers to find transactions that meet the criteria you've set, then displays the report onscreen. This process may take some time, depending on the size of your registers and the complexity of your criteria. See "Not enough memory" on page 528 if Quicken reports a memory problem.

Use the pulldown menus to customize the report. See "Basic Steps to Customize Reports" on page 168.

In some reports you can select any amount to find more information about it. See "Investigating Items in Reports" on page 189.

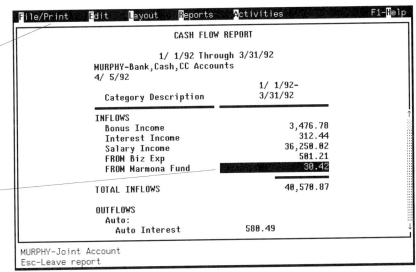

Note: If you have an EGA/VGA monitor and you select 43-line register/reports in Screen Settings, Quicken displays reports in 43-line mode.

8. To view more of the report on the screen, see "Working with Wide Reports" on page 164.

9. (Optional) To change the report in any way or carry out a number of other actions, use the pulldown menus at the top of the screen. The options available at the Report screen are described in Chapter 10, *Customizing Reports*, beginning on page 167.

10. (Optional) Print the report you see on the screen or save it as a file on disk. See "Printing Reports" on page 164.

11. When you want to leave the report, press Ctrl-R to go to the register or Ctrl-W to go to the Write Checks screen. Or press Esc to return to the report setup window.

Working with Wide Reports

There is virtually no limit to the width and length of Quicken's reports. Although some reports may fit entirely on your screen or on one printed page, others may be much wider or much longer.

Bringing More of a Report onto the Screen

To move:	Press:
Right one column	Tab or right arrow
Left one column	Shift-Tab or left arrow
Up one row	Up arrow
Down one row	Down arrow
Right one screen	Ctrl-right arrow
Left one screen	Ctrl-left arrow
Up one screen	PgUp
Down one screen	PgDn

If you have a mouse, use the scroll bars to display the parts of a report that don't fit on your screen.

If you're creating a report that lists specific transactions, some of the columns are set to half width so that you can see all the columns on the screen at once. However, the contents of some columns may be cut short. If you want to see the full contents of each column, choose Full Column Width from the Layout menu. This command changes the view of the report to full column width, and increases the total width of the report from 80 to 132 characters. To print the report, you'll need to use compressed type or a wide carriage. For more information, see "Printing Wide Reports" on page 165.

Printing Reports

You can print any Quicken report on paper or as a disk file.

To print a report:

1. (If you're printing on paper) Make sure your printer is turned on, is online, and contains paper.

2. Create the report as described in "Basic Steps to Create a Report" on page 162.

3. When Quicken displays the report onscreen, choose Print Report from the File/Print menu.

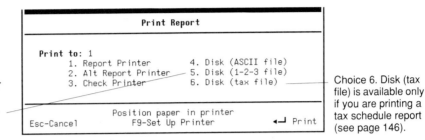

To create a file to transfer data to a spreadsheet, select 5. Disk (1-2-3 file). See "Printing to Disk" below.

Choice 6. Disk (tax file) is available only if you are printing a tax schedule report (see page 146).

4. Make sure the Print To field shows the printer or disk format you want to use. (If you need to change the printer settings, press F9; see "Printer Settings" on page 428.)

   For more information about saving the report as an ASCII, Lotus 1-2-3, or tax file, see "Printing to Disk" below.

5. Press Enter to print the report.

Printing Wide Reports

If a report is too wide to fit within the 80 characters of your computer screen, it's too wide to fit across an 8.5-inch-wide sheet of paper printed at the normal 10 characters per inch (80 characters per line). However, if the report is not more than 132 characters wide, it will fit on the paper in compressed type (usually 17 characters per inch). Alternatively, if you have a wide carriage, it will fit on wide paper at 10 characters per inch.

To use compressed type when printing Quicken reports, you must first choose this style as one of your printer styles. For more information, see "Printer Settings" on page 428.

If you have a laser printer that prints landscape style (horizontally), you can print even wider reports (up to 176 characters per line in compressed type). To use the landscape compressed style, you must first choose it as one of your printer styles.

If you print a report that is too wide to fit across a sheet of paper, Quicken prints the report in vertical strips, each sized for your paper. When the report is finished, you can tape the sheets of paper together to produce a wide, printed-out report. Quicken prints reports like this automatically. You don't have to do anything except tape the report together when it is finished.

Printing to Disk

You can print any report to a disk file if you want to use it with another program. At the Print Reports window, choose the format you want. After you choose a format, Quicken asks you to specify a path (optional) and a DOS filename.

- If you don't specify a path, Quicken creates the file in the current directory (for most people, the current directory is C:\QUICKEN5 or wherever Quicken is located).

- If you do specify a path, it must be for an existing directory.

ASCII Text File

Choose ASCII file format when you want an ordinary ASCII text file to use with a word-processing program.

- You may specify an extension as part of the DOS filename (for example, BALSHEET.REP). Quicken does not add an extension.

- If you specify a number of lines per page other than 0, Quicken inserts a header with a page number after that many lines.

- If the report is too wide to fit within the width you specify, Quicken treats the extra text just as though it were printing to paper that is not wide enough: it places the text after the portion that fits.

1-2-3 File

Choose 1-2-3 file format when you want a report in Lotus 1-2-3 import format.

Quicken creates a file with the extension .PRN. Lotus 1-2-3 format can be read directly into Lotus 1-2-3 or a compatible spreadsheet program. (Use the File Import Numbers command in Lotus 1-2-3.) Once you have the data in Lotus, type /WCS (for Worksheet Column Setwidth) to adjust the column width so you can see more of your data.

To use the .PRN file in Excel, first rename it using the DOS RENAME command so its extension is .CVS. For example, to rename BALSHEET.PRN, at the DOS prompt type

rename balsheet.prn balsheet.cvs

Use a blank Excel spreadsheet and open the CVS file. Then save the spreadsheet as an Excel file.

If you plan to use your Quicken data regularly with Lotus 1-2-3 or a compatible spreadsheet, you will find additional capabilities available with the Quicken Transfer Utility. For more information, see "Quicken Transfer Utility" on page 475.

Tax File

Choose tax file format to export a tax schedule report (page 146) to tax preparation software such as TurboTax and TaxCut.

- In the Print To Disk window, you may specify an extension as part of the DOS filename.

- Leave the lines per page as 0 and the width as 80.

See the instructions that accompany your tax preparation software for how to use the data file.

Chapter 10

Customizing Reports

This chapter tells how to create custom reports with Quicken. Custom reports let you determine exactly what information is included, and how that information is organized.

Each personal and business report is based on one of the four basic reports:

- Transaction report
- Summary report
- Budget report
- Account balances report

When you customize a personal or business report, you can choose from among all the possibilities available in the basic report on which it is based. (The missing check and tax schedule reports are exceptions; you can customize them within narrow limits.) If you prefer, you can start with a basic report and create the report you want.

All reports, including investment reports, allow you to choose display options (such as not showing cents) and to filter (limit) transactions to those meeting your criteria.

This chapter also explains how to memorize a customized report setup for repeated use, how to investigate the transactions that make up the report, and how to hide temporarily some line items in reports.

Note: Budget reports are special because they require that you first set up budget amounts. We describe setting up a budget and creating budget reports in Chapter 21, *Budgeting Your Income and Expenses*, beginning on page 341.

Basic Steps to Customize Reports

You follow the same basic steps to customize most types of Quicken reports. (Budget reports are different. See Chapter 21, *Budgeting Your Income and Expenses*, beginning on page 341. For investment and basic reports, the report setup window allows you to make choices before you create the report, but you can also customize the report as described below.)

To customize a report:

1. Create a report as described in "Basic Steps to Create a Report" on page 162.

2. After Quicken displays the report, use the pulldown menus at the top of the screen to make any of the following types of changes to your report. Each time you make a change, Quicken redisplays the report.

   • Change the title and date range for the current report. Choose Set Title & Date Range from the Edit menu.

   • Filter (that is, limit) the transactions in the current report by account, payee name, category, class, memo, dollar amount, transaction type, cleared status, or tax-related status. See "Filtering Your Report Data" on page 180.

   • Change the layout of items in the current report. Layout options include row and column headings, column width, the ability to summarize or redisplay items in the report, and much more. See "Changing the Layout and Display of a Report (Layout Menu)" on page 175.

3. When you want to leave the report, press Ctrl-R to go to the register or Ctrl-W to go to the Write Checks screen. You can also choose Register or Write Checks from the Activities menu.

In addition, you can use the pulldown menus at the top of the report screen to do any of the following things:

• Choose Print Report from the File/Print menu to print the current report or save it as a file on disk. (See "Printing Reports" on page 164.)

• Choose Memorize Report from the File/Print menu to save the current report setup for repeated use. (See "Memorizing a Custom Report Setup" on page 193.)

• Choose QuickZoom from the File/Print menu to examine the transactions that make up the amounts in a transaction, summary, or budget report, or any report based on those reports. (This feature is not available for investment or account balances reports. See "Investigating Items in Reports" on page 189.)

• Choose Calculator from the Activities menu to use the Calculator. (See "Using the Calculator" on page 28.)

• Choose a different report type from the Reports menu (Alt-R).

$ Four Basic Reports

Quicken has four basic reports:

- Transaction report (page 169)
- Summary report (page 171)
- Budget report (page 173)
- Account balances report (page 173)

Transaction

A transaction report lists transactions from one or more registers. Unlike a summary report, it shows individual transactions. This report can be sorted and subtotaled in a number of different ways, such as by time period, category, class, payee, or account.

The itemized category report and the tax summary report are based directly on the basic transaction report. The missing check report, tax schedule report, and investment transactions report are modified versions of the basic transaction report.

To create a transaction report, follow the steps in "Basic Steps to Create a Report" on page 162.

When you choose Transaction at the Reports menu, Quicken displays the Create Transaction Report window.

Enter a number here to tell Quicken how to subtotal this report. For descriptions of each time period choice, see "Column Headings" on page 178.

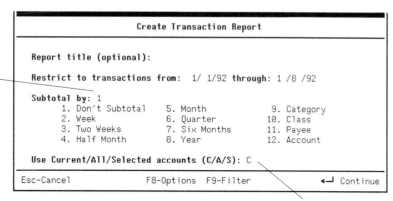

```
                       Create Transaction Report

  Report title (optional):

  Restrict to transactions from:  1/ 1/92 through: 1 /8 /92

  Subtotal by: 1
          1. Don't Subtotal    5. Month          9. Category
          2. Week              6. Quarter        10. Class
          3. Two Weeks         7. Six Months     11. Payee
          4. Half Month        8. Year           12. Account

  Use Current/All/Selected accounts (C/A/S): C

  Esc-Cancel            F8-Options  F9-Filter           ↵ Continue
```

For information about options and filters, see "Changing the Layout Before You Display a Report" on page 179 and "Filtering Your Report Data" on page 180.

To include all (A) or selected (S) accounts in this report, enter the appropriate letter here.

This example is not subtotaled. It lists transactions in four selected accounts.

Quicken normally sorts transactions by account and then by date. Accounts are in the same order that they appear on the account list.

```
                              TRANSACTION REPORT
                           1/ 1/92 Through 1/ 8/92
     DESIGN-Selected Accounts                                     Page 1
     1/ 8/92
     Date   Acct    Num     Description     Memo       Category   Clr  Amount
     -----  ------- ------  --------------- ---------- ---------- - ----------
            BALANCE 12/31/91                                          50,480.03
     1/ 1 First St 3025    MacWorld        1-year subs Reference    X    -20.00
     1/ 1 First St 3026    Western Office E Fax machine [Cap Equip] X   -950.00
     1/ 1 First St 3027    Valley Real Esta            Rent Paid    X   -400.00
     1/ 5 First St 3028 S  Richard Long                --SPLIT--       -1,058.11
     1/ 5 First St 3029 S  Chris Jacobson              --SPLIT--         -961.16
     1/ 6 First St 3030    Standard Busines 2021       [AP]         X   -200.00
     1/ 6 First St 3031    Chevron USA     A/C#12345   [AP]         X    -76.17
     1/ 8 First St 3032    Valley Toyota   Honda Accor [AP]         X   -104.28
     1/ 1 AR       1028 S  Robinson Shoes              --SPLIT--          684.81
     1/ 1 AR       1029 S  Reynolds Markets            --SPLIT--        1,539.19
     1/ 1 AR       1030 S  Ace Computer Sal            --SPLIT--          618.46
     1/ 1 AR       1031 S  Osborne Studios             --SPLIT--        1,051.22
     1/ 1 AR       1032 S  Tower Concerts              --SPLIT--          441.91
     1/ 1 AR       1033 S  Blaine Associate            --SPLIT--          856.00
     1/ 1 Cap Equi         Western Office E Fax machine [First Statewi   950.00
     1/ 1 AP               Western Bell    A/C#318-258 Telephone        -131.90
     1/ 1 AP            S  Stats 801       1209        --SPLIT--         -37.70
     1/ 1 AP            S  Amory Paper & Su 159014     --SPLIT--         -61.11
     1/ 1 AP               Graphic Details             Contractor/Job  -120.00
     1/ 1 AP               Small Business B            Ins Exp          -36.20
     1/ 2 AP            S  Federal Express A/C#1111-22 --SPLIT--         -91.24
     1/ 3 AP               LaserExpress    2438        Printing/Job 4   -74.00
     1/ 4 AP               Labels Unlimited            Paper/Job 7      -73.55
     1/ 4 AP               Sinclair Printin            Mechanical Pre   -15.50
     1/ 5 AP               Insurance Shield A/C#2822304 Ins Exp        -150.15
     1/ 6 AP               Standard Busines 2021       [First Statewi   200.00
     1/ 6 AP               Chevron USA                 [First Statewi    76.17
     1/ 6 AP               Sinclair Printin            Mechanical Pre   -15.00
     1/ 7 AP               LaserExpress    2899        Photocopying/J   -19.00
     1/ 8 AP               Valley Toyota   Honda Accor [First Statewi   104.28
                                                                      ----------
           TOTAL   1/ 1/92 -  1/ 8/92                                  1,926.97

           BALANCE  1/ 8/92                                           52,407.00

           TOTAL INFLOWS                                               6,522.04
           TOTAL OUTFLOWS                                             -4,595.07
                                                                      ----------
           NET TOTAL                                                   1,926.97
                                                                      ==========
```

Summary

A summary report summarizes transactions from your accounts by category or whatever else you choose for the row headings. Unlike a transaction report, it does not show individual transactions.

The cash flow report, P & L statement, A/P by vendor report, A/R by customer report, job/project report, and payroll report are based directly on the basic summary report. The investment income report is a modified version of the basic summary report.

To create a summary report, follow the steps in "Basic Steps to Create a Report" on page 162.

When you choose Summary at the Reports menu, Quicken displays the Create Summary Report window.

Enter a number here to tell Quicken what row headings to subtotal by. See "Row Headings" on page 178.

Enter a number here to tell Quicken what column headings to subtotal by. See "Column Headings" on page 178.

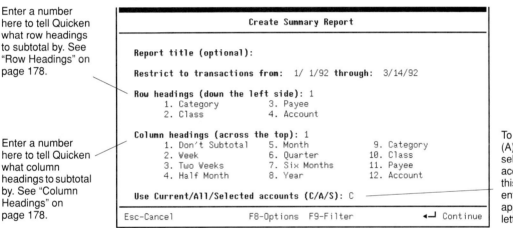

```
                    Create Summary Report

  Report title (optional):

  Restrict to transactions from:   1/ 1/92 through:  3/14/92

  Row headings (down the left side): 1
          1. Category          3. Payee
          2. Class             4. Account

  Column headings (across the top): 1
          1. Don't Subtotal   5. Month           9. Category
          2. Week             6. Quarter        10. Class
          3. Two Weeks        7. Six Months     11. Payee
          4. Half Month       8. Year           12. Account

  Use Current/All/Selected accounts (C/A/S): C

  Esc-Cancel              F8-Options  F9-Filter          ◄┘ Continue
```

To include all (A) or selected (S) accounts in this report, enter the appropriate letter here.

For information about options and filters, see "Changing the Layout Before You Display a Report" on page 179 and "Filtering Your Report Data" on page 180.

A summary report can have a separate column for each time period, category, class, payee, or account. This example shows one column for each month in the date range.

This example is for selected accounts. You can change the accounts included.

This example uses categories for row headings. You can change row headings to classes, payees, or accounts instead of categories.

Quicken indents subcategories by level under the main category. If you use classes for row headings, Quicken handles subclasses the same way.

Quicken groups uncategorized income or expenses under "Other."

Quicken groups all transfers to and from other accounts.

If an included account has an Opening Balance during the period, Quicken calls it a "balance forward" because you brought an existing balance forward into Quicken.

```
                         SUMMARY REPORT BY MONTH
                         1/ 1/92 Through 2/28/92
      MURPHY-Selected Accounts                               Page 1
      3/14/92
                                                           OVERALL
       Category Description        1/92         2/92        TOTAL
      --------------------------  ------------  ------------  ------------
       INCOME/EXPENSE
         INCOME
           Interest Income             93.93       103.97       197.90
           Salary Income            7,083.34     7,083.34    14,166.68
                                   -----------  -----------  -----------
         TOTAL INCOME              7,177.27     7,187.31    14,364.58

         EXPENSES
           Clothing                 1,023.38         0.00     1,023.38
           Computer Software          397.52         0.00       397.52
           Entertainment               0.00       300.00       300.00
           Gift Expenses               0.00       592.34       592.34
           Insurance                  65.74        65.74       131.48
           Recreation Expense        319.51         0.00       319.51
           Steve's Hobbies           397.58       431.39       828.97
           Tax:
             Federal Tax           1,770.84     1,770.84     3,541.68
             Social Security Tax     354.16       354.16       708.32
             State Tax               566.66       566.66     1,133.32
                                   -----------  -----------  -----------
             Total Tax             2,691.66     2,691.66     5,383.32
           Expenses - Other           25.00         0.00        25.00
                                   -----------  -----------  -----------
         TOTAL EXPENSES            4,920.39     4,081.13     9,001.52
                                   -----------  -----------  -----------
       TOTAL INCOME/EXPENSE        2,256.88     3,106.18     5,363.06

       TRANSFERS
         TO Cash                    -300.00      -300.00      -600.00
         TO Joint Account         -1,500.00    -1,500.00    -3,000.00
         TO Steve's IRA                0.00    -2,000.00    -2,000.00
         FROM Joint Account          400.00       400.00       800.00
                                   -----------  -----------  -----------
       TOTAL TRANSFERS            -1,400.00    -3,400.00    -4,800.00

       BALANCE FORWARD
         Money Market             12,350.00         0.00    12,350.00
                                   -----------  -----------  -----------
       TOTAL BALANCE FORWARD      12,350.00         0.00    12,350.00
                                   -----------  -----------  -----------
       OVERALL TOTAL              13,206.88      -293.82    12,913.06
                                   ===========  ===========  ===========
```

There are several things to notice about summary reports. Look at the sample summary report above as you read the following:

• A summary report normally displays category or class descriptions rather than names. (You can change this if you want through Other Settings. See "6. In reports, print category Description/Name/Both" on page 447.) If a category or class has no description, Quicken displays the category or class name.

- Quicken totals any uncategorized deposits covered by the date range as "Income– Other." It groups uncategorized payments as "Expenses–Other."

- Similarly, if you have used subcategories for some transactions within a category, but not for others, the report will have an "Other" line. For example, the report would have an "Other" line if some transactions were categorized as Dues:Personal and other transactions were categorized as Dues without a subcategory.

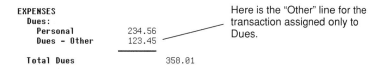

- A summary report groups income and expense items in separate INCOME and EXPENSES sections, followed by TRANSFERS and BALANCES FORWARD, unless you select the cash flow option (see "Other Options" on page 176). A summary report lists Opening Balance transactions and other "self-transfer" transactions in the BALANCES FORWARD section.

Budget

After you set up budget amounts, a budget report compares your actual expenses against your budgeted expenses for each category. You have a choice of different time periods as column headings. See Chapter 21, *Budgeting Your Income and Expenses*, beginning on page 341, for complete information about setting up budget amounts and creating budget reports.

Account Balances

An account balances report lists and totals the balances for all accounts in the current file. If you have investment accounts, the balances for those accounts include unrealized gains. The result shows the net worth of your Quicken accounts.

The personal net worth report (page 144) and business balance sheet (page 153) are based directly on the account balances report. The portfolio value report (page 154) is a modified version of the account balances report.

To create an account balances report, follow the steps in "Basic Steps to Create a Report" on page 162.

When you choose Account Balances at the Reports menu, Quicken displays the Create Account Balances Report window.

Enter a number here to tell Quicken what intervals to use as column headings. For descriptions of each choice, see "Column Headings" on page 178.

Tip: To see only beginning and ending balances for any period of up to one year, choose 8. Year.

If you choose intervals of None, the balances are as of the ending date.

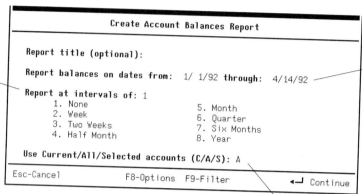

```
┌─────────────────────────────────────────────────────────────┐
│ ▄▄▄▄▄▄▄▄▄▄▄▄▄▄▄▄▄▄▄▄▄▄▄▄▄▄▄▄▄▄▄▄▄▄▄▄▄▄▄▄▄▄▄▄▄▄▄▄▄▄▄▄▄▄▄▄▄▄ │
│                                                             │
│              Create Account Balances Report                 │
│                                                             │
│  Report title (optional):                                   │
│                                                             │
│  Report balances on dates from:  1/ 1/92 through:  4/14/92  │
│                                                             │
│  Report at intervals of: 1                                  │
│        1. None              5. Month                        │
│        2. Week              6. Quarter                      │
│        3. Two Weeks         7. Six Months                   │
│        4. Half Month        8. Year                         │
│                                                             │
│  Use Current/All/Selected accounts (C/A/S): A               │
│                                                             │
│  Esc-Cancel        F8-Options  F9-Filter        ◄┘ Continue │
└─────────────────────────────────────────────────────────────┘
```

To include only the current (C) or selected (S) accounts in this report, enter the appropriate letter here.

Tip: Choose selected accounts to see account balances subtotaled by class or by security. See "Filtering the Transactions in a Report by Account" on page 180.

If you want Quicken to include "Checks Payable" (unprinted checks) under "ASSETS" and "LIABILITIES" in an account balances report, be sure to enter an ending date for the report that is later than any of your postdated checks in the register.

This example is for selected investment accounts.

To show balances for each security, as in this example, ask for detail for each account (page 181).

```
                        ACCOUNT BALANCES REPORT BY YEAR
                              As of 3/31/92
        MURPHY-Selected Accounts
        4/14/92                                               Page 1

                                      1/ 1/92          3/31/92
                          Acct        Balance          Balance
        --------------------------  --------------   ---------------
        ASSETS
          Investments
            Sally's IRA
              First Statewide CD     10,224.65        10,224.65
              Guren Corp Bond         2,100.00         2,097.50
              McKendry MMF            1,543.26         1,636.47
              -Cash-                      0.00             0.00
                                     -----------      -----------
            Total Sally's IRA        13,867.91        13,958.62

            Steve's IRA
              Marmona Fund            4,608.04         5,157.39
              Rawson Totl Return      5,992.79         8,482.28
                                     -----------      -----------
            Total Steve's IRA        10,600.83        13,639.67
```

The Report Screen Menus

The Report screen has special menus to help you work with reports:

File/Print	For Print Report, see Chapter 9 (page 164). For Memorize Report, see page 193. For QuickZoom, see page 189.
Edit and Layout	Commands on these menus are described in this section.
Reports	Commands on this menu are covered in Chapter 9 (page 139).
Activities	Commands on this menu are already familiar to you.

Changing the Data in a Report (Edit Menu)

Choose Edit (Alt-E) at the Report screen to change the data in a report.

Set Title & Date Range

Use this command to change the report title and to set the date range of the transactions included in the report.

The title can include numbers, letters, and other characters. You can use the + and – keys to increase or decrease the beginning and ending dates for the report.

Filter Transactions

Use the Filter Transactions command to limit the transactions in the report according to the criteria you specify. See "Filtering Your Report Data" on page 180 for details.

Accounts; Categories; Classes

Use the Accounts, Categories, and Classes commands on the Edit menu to select the account, category, and class names to include in the report. See "Filtering Your Report Data" on page 180 for information.

Changing the Layout and Display of a Report (Layout Menu)

Choose Layout (Alt-L) at the Report screen to hide or display certain information in the report or change the report format. Not all commands on the Layout menu work for all report types.

In addition to the budget reports, investment performance report, and capital gains report, Quicken has three basic report types:

Summary	**Transaction**	**Account Balances**
Cash flow	Investment transactions	Net worth
Payroll	Itemized categories	Balance sheet
A/P by vendor	Tax summary	Portfolio value
A/R by customer	Missing check	
P & L statement	Tax schedule	
Investment income		
Job/Project		

Hide Cents/Show Cents

Use this toggle to omit or display cent amounts in a report.

Hide Split/Show Split

For noninvestment transaction reports only (see list on page 175). Use this toggle to omit or display split transaction detail.

Hide Transactions/Show Transactions

For noninvestment transaction reports only (see list on page 175). Use this toggle to omit or display transaction detail. The Hide Transactions setting shows only the total dollar amount of transactions that meet the other criteria you've specified. The Show Transactions setting lists all the transactions that meet the criteria you've specified.

Other Options

Choose this command to display the Report Options window.

Note: Quicken displays only the report options that make sense for the report that you are creating, so the window you see may look different from this one.

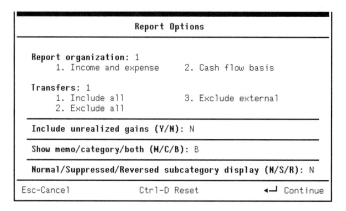

Report organization. For summary and budget reports, and for transaction reports subtotaled by category, you have two options:

Income and Expense Totals income, expense, and transfer transactions in separate sections of your report.

Cash Flow Basis Groups and totals Inflows (including income and transfers into the account) and Outflows (including expenses and transfers out of the account). For example, suppose you have a property asset account called "House," and you treat home improvement transactions as transfers to that account. To treat those transfers as spending and get a more accurate picture of your total expenditures, select Cash Flow Basis.

For noninvestment account balances reports, you have two different options:

Net Worth Prints your net worth as the last item.

Balance Sheet Adds an equity line item in the LIABILITIES section, so that Total Liabilities and Equity exactly balances ASSETS. Equity is the difference between assets and liabilities and is the value of the owner's or owners' stake in the business.

Transfers. For summary and transaction reports, you have three transfer options:

Include All	Includes all transfers from and to the accounts included in the report. For an example of a report that includes all transfers, see "Summary" on page 171.
Exclude All	Omits transfers from the report. For an example of a report without transfers, see "P & L Statement" on page 148.
External Transfers Only	Omits transfer transactions that essentially cancel each other out in the report. For an example of a report that excludes transfer transactions between accounts in the report, see "Cash Flow" on page 140.

Include unrealized gains. These options appear only if you have set up investment accounts.

Yes (Y)	On transaction reports, Quicken generates additional transactions to represent the impact of price changes for securities. On summary reports, Quicken adds an income or inflows line for Unrealized Gain/Loss.
No (N)	Quicken includes unrealized gains only for account balances reports.

Show Memo/Category/Both. These options appear only for transaction reports (see list on page 175):

Memo (M)	Creates a column for the Memo field only.
Category (C)	Creates a column for the Category field only.
Both (B)	Creates columns for both the Memo and the Category fields.

Normal/Suppressed/Reversed subcategory display. You can change the way Quicken shows subcategories and subclasses in a noninvestment summary report (see list on page 175):

Normal (N)	Subcategories appear indented under their main category.
Suppressed (S)	Quicken does not show subcategories and subclasses in a report. The amounts are combined into a total for the category or class.
Reversed (R)	Quicken groups the items in the report first by subcategories, with the main categories grouped under them. For example, if you have transactions categorized as Medical:Insurance and House:Insurance, you can use this option to generate a report totaling expenses for Insurance.

Sort Transactions

For noninvestment transaction reports only (see list on page 175). Use this command to change the order of transactions in the report. You can sort the transactions in the report by Account, Date (descending), Check Number (descending), or Amount (ascending). If the report is subtotaled (see "Row Headings" below), Quicken sorts the transactions within each subtotaled group by the Sort Transactions setting.

Row Headings

For noninvestment summary reports, all transaction reports except tax schedule, and all investment reports except investment income.

Quicken can base a summary report on categories, classes, payees, or accounts. Choose the item you want Quicken to base the report on from the Row Headings menu. For example, a summary report based on payees lists payees as row headings in the left column and displays totals for each payee. For an example of a summary report based on payees, see "A/P by Vendor" on page 149.

If you want your summary report to include categories or classes but not subcategories or subclasses, see "Other Options" on page 176.

On a transaction or investment report, choose how you want Quicken to group transactions or investment data from the Row Headings menu. You can group and subtotal transactions by week, two weeks, half month, month, quarter, six months, year, category, class, payee, or account. If you don't subtotal, Quicken simply lists transactions by account, date, check number, or amount, without groups or subtotals, according to the setting of the Sort Transactions command (see "Sort Transactions" on page 177).

Note: If you subtotal by category and your transactions have subcategories, Quicken sorts, groups, and subtotals by each subcategory within each category. Similarly, if you subtotal by class and your transactions have subclasses, Quicken sorts, groups, and subtotals by each subclass within each class. See "Other Options" on page 176 for information about suppressing subcategories and subclasses.

Column Headings

For summary, budget, and noninvestment account balances reports only. Choose the item that you want Quicken to use as column headings from the Column Headings menu. When Quicken creates the report, it includes a separate column for each Column Heading item. If you choose One Column, Quicken creates a report with a single column.

You can format a summary report with a separate column for each time period, category, class, payee, or account. (The investment income report has different options.) For an example of a summary report with months for column headings, see "Summary" on page 171.

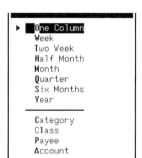

This is the Column Headings menu for summary reports. The Row Headings menu for transaction reports is almost identical to this menu.

Other reports have Column Headings or Row Headings menus with fewer or different options.

You can format a budget report with a separate column for each time period for which you want to compare actual income and spending with budgeted income and spending. For an example of a budget report with months for column headings, see "A Sample Monthly Budget Report" on page 349.

You can format an account balances report with a separate column for each interval at which you want Quicken to calculate your net worth. Quicken can format an account balances report so that it has a separate column for each week, two weeks, half month, month, quarter, six months, or year.

How Quicken defines report time periods	
Week	Runs Sunday through Saturday
Half month	Runs from the 1st to the 15th and from the 16th to the last day of the month
Month	Starts on the first of the month
Quarter	Includes three consecutive calendar months, starting with January 1, April 1, July 1, and October 1
Six months	Starts on the first of the month you specify and ends on the last day of the month six months later

Full Column Width/Half Column Width

For noninvestment transaction reports only (see list on page 175). Choose this command to shrink or expand report columns to half or full width.

Expand

For noninvestment summary, budget, and account balances reports only. Use Expand to display an item that you have summarized using the Collapse command. See "Collapsing Items in Reports" on page 190 for more information.

Collapse

For noninvestment summary, budget, and account balances reports only. Use Collapse to summarize a report item. See "Collapsing Items in Reports" on page 190 for more information.

Changing the Layout Before You Display a Report

You can define your report layout before you display a report.

For personal and business reports, press F7 at the report setup window to display the Create Report window for the appropriate basic report. For investment and basic reports, the window offers you layout options.

Depending on the report, you can choose options for row headings, column headings, subtotaling, or reporting at intervals.

For additional options, press F8. The options available vary by report.

See "Hide Transactions/Show Transactions" on page 176.

See "Hide Split/Show Split" on page 176.

See "Hide Cents/Show Cents" on page 176.

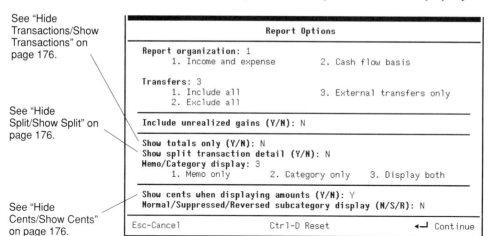

```
                          Report Options

 Report organization: 1
          1. Income and expense        2. Cash flow basis

 Transfers: 3
          1. Include all              3. External transfers only
          2. Exclude all
 ─────────────────────────────────────────────────────────────
 Include unrealized gains (Y/N): N
 ─────────────────────────────────────────────────────────────
 Show totals only (Y/N): N
 Show split transaction detail (Y/N): N
 Memo/Category display: 3
          1. Memo only     2. Category only    3. Display both
 ─────────────────────────────────────────────────────────────
 Show cents when displaying amounts (Y/N): Y
 Normal/Suppressed/Reversed subcategory display (N/S/R): N
 ─────────────────────────────────────────────────────────────
 Esc-Cancel              Ctrl-D Reset              ◄┘ Continue
```

See "Other Options" on page 176 for explanations of all other options shown here.

Filtering Your Report Data

You can limit the transactions to be included in your reports by telling Quicken to "filter" the report transactions. You can tell Quicken what must be true about a transaction in order for it to be included in a report. For example, you can tell Quicken to include only transactions with a specific payee, or only transactions with a specific payee that have been reconciled and cleared in your accounts. You can have Quicken report only on payments from your accounts, or only on deposits.

Filtering the Transactions in a Report by Account

You can see what accounts are selected for the report in the third line of the report. To change the accounts selected for the report, choose Edit (Alt-E) at the Report screen, and then choose Accounts from the Edit menu. The option marked with a check on the Accounts menu is the currently selected option.

Current

Quicken uses only transactions in the current account when compiling the report. The current account is the one named at the lower-left corner of the register, Write Checks screen, or Report screen.

All

Quicken uses all the accounts in the current Quicken file when compiling the report.

Selected

Choose Selected if you want to select specific accounts for the report from a list of accounts in the current file.

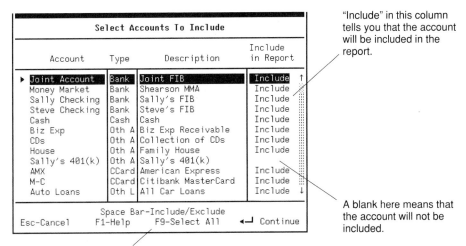

"Include" in this column tells you that the account will be included in the report.

Press the spacebar to change whether the selected account is included or excluded.

Press F9 to include or exclude all accounts at once.

A blank here means that the account will not be included.

To include or exclude an account, select the account name in the list and press the spacebar. When you've finished marking the accounts to be included or excluded from the report, press Enter to display the report.

Note: For account balances reports, you have three choices when selecting accounts to include. You can include the account, include the account and show class or security detail, or exclude the account. When you include detail for an account, the report shows subtotals by class for a noninvestment account or by security for an investment account. Pressing the spacebar cycles through the three choices: Include, Detail, and a blank.

Filtering the Transactions in a Report by Category

To change the categories and transfer accounts selected for the report, choose Edit (Alt-E) at the Report screen, and then choose Categories from the Edit menu. The option marked with a check on the Categories menu is the currently selected option.

Selected

Choose Selected if you want to select specific categories and transfer accounts to include in this report.

Press the spacebar to change whether the selected category is included or excluded.

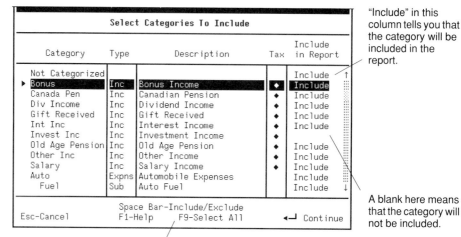

"Include" in this column tells you that the category will be included in the report.

A blank here means that the category will not be included.

Press F9 to include or exclude all categories at once.

To exclude a category, subcategory, or transfer account name from the report, select it in the list and press the spacebar.

Once you've selected categories to be included and excluded from your reports, Quicken remembers the settings. Any time you choose Selected from the Categories menu, Quicken uses the same settings unless you change them or recall a memorized report with selected categories.

All

Quicken includes all categories in the report (except in the tax schedule and tax summary reports).

Filtering the Transactions in a Report by Class

Selected

Choose Selected if you want to select specific classes to include in this report.

You include and exclude classes just as you do categories. For more information, see the preceding discussion about selecting categories.

All

Quicken includes all classes in the report.

The Filter Transactions Window

Choose Edit (Alt-E) at the Report screen, and then choose Filter Transactions from the Edit menu to display the Filter Transactions window.

Note: Quicken displays only the filter options that make sense for the report you are creating, so the window you see may look different from this one.

See page 185 for descriptions of special filters for investment reports.

```
┌──────────────────────────────────────────────────────┐
│■■■■■■■■■■■■■■■■■■■■■■■■■■■■■■■■■■■■■■■■■■■■■■■■■■■■■■■■■■│
│                   Filter Transactions                │
│                                                      │
│ Restrict report to transactions matching these criteria │
│      Payee contains   :                              │
│      Memo contains    :                              │
│      Category contains:                              │
│      Class contains   :                              │
│ ──────────────────────────────────────────────────── │
│ Tax-related categories only    (Y/N): N              │
│ Below/Equal/Above (B/E/A):    the amount:            │
│ Payments/Deposits/Unprinted checks/All (P/D/U/A) : A │
│ ──────────────────────────────────────────────────── │
│ Cleared status is                                    │
│ Blank ' ': Y  Newly cleared '*': Y   Cleared 'X': Y  │
│ ──────────────────────────────────────────────────── │
│ Esc-Cancel          Ctrl-D Reset         ◄┘ Continue │
└──────────────────────────────────────────────────────┘
```

Press Ctrl-D to reset all entries in this window to their default settings.

The report will include only the transactions that meet all the criteria specified in this window.

Payee contains

Enter a full or partial payee name to include transactions with Payee fields that contain what you type. For information about different kinds of filters, see "Using Match Characters to Limit Searches" on page 186.

Quicken searches are not case-sensitive.

When Quicken looks for a match, it does not differentiate between upper- and lower-case letters. It also ignores any spaces before or after the phrase you type.

Memo contains

Enter full or partial memo text to include transactions with Memo fields that contain what you type. Quicken searches all Memo fields in registers, including those in Split Transaction windows. For information about different kinds of filters, see "Using Match Characters to Limit Searches" on page 186.

Category contains

Enter a full or partial category or transfer account name to include transactions with Category fields that contain what you type. (You don't have to type brackets around the transfer account name.) You can also press Ctrl-C to choose the category or transfer account name from the category and transfer list. For information about different kinds of filters, see "Using Match Characters to Limit Searches" on page 186.

Class contains

Enter a full or partial class name to include transactions with Class fields that contain what you type. You can also press Ctrl-L to choose the name from the class list. For information about different kinds of filters, see "Using Match Characters to Limit Searches" on page 186.

Tax-related categories only

Enter Y (for yes) if you want the report to include only transactions that have been applied to tax-related categories.

If you don't specify tax-related only, the report includes transactions that are applied to both tax-related and non-tax-related categories, and transactions that have not been applied to any categories.

Note: If you filter on categories or classes, select categories or classes to include, or request tax-related categories for a transaction report, Quicken shows split detail whether you request it or not.

Below/Equal/Above: the amount

Select Below (B), Equal (E), or Above (A) to indicate whether you want to restrict transactions in a report for amounts below, equal to, or above a certain amount. Then enter the amount. Quicken treats all amounts as positive amounts for the purpose of restricting by amount.

Payments/Deposits/Unprinted checks/All

Select All (A) if you want the report to include all transactions. Select Payments (P) if you want the report to include payments only (including checks). Select Deposits (D) if you want the report to include deposits only. Select Unprinted Checks (U) if you want the report to include unprinted checks only. For this report, a payment is any transaction that decreases the balance of a cash or asset account, or that increases the balance of a credit card or liability account.

Cleared status is Blank, Newly cleared (*), or Reconciled (X)

Quicken initially enters a "Y" next to each of the cleared status settings. Leave these settings unchanged unless you are creating a report specifically to show which of your transactions are cleared or uncleared.

Transactions in the register can have one of three different cleared statuses. An "X" in the C (for Cleared) column indicates that the transaction has been cleared and reconciled with your account. An asterisk (*) indicates that the transaction has been marked cleared in the register, but has not yet been reconciled. No character in the C (for Cleared) column indicates that the transaction has not been marked cleared.

You can have Quicken report on transactions with a specific cleared status by entering Y (for Yes) next to each cleared status that you want Quicken to include in the report. For example, if you want a report using only transactions that have been reconciled, enter Y next to the Reconciled (X) setting and enter N (for No) next to the Newly Cleared (*) and Blank settings.

The Filter Investment Transactions window

Quicken has a special Filter Investment Transactions window for an investment report that allows you to include or exclude actions, securities, security types, or goals.

Note: Quicken displays only the filter options that make sense for the investment report you are creating, so the window you see may look different from this one.

```
┌─────────────────────────────────────────────────────────────┐
│■■■■■■■■■■■■■■■■■■■■■■■■■■■■■■■■■■■■■■■■■■■■■■■■■■■■■■■■■■■■■■■■■│
│                 Filter Investment Transactions               │
│                                                              │
│  Restrict report to transactions matching these criteria     │
│      Security contains:                                      │
│      Memo contains    :                                      │
│  ──────────────────────────────────────────────────────────  │
│      Select actions to include...       (Y/N): N             │
│      Select securities to include...    (Y/N): N             │
│      Select security types to include... (Y/N): N            │
│      Select investment goals to include... (Y/N): N          │
│                                                              │
│   Esc-Cancel          Ctrl-D Reset           ◄┘ Continue     │
└─────────────────────────────────────────────────────────────┘
```

Any time you enter Y to select items to include, Quicken remembers the settings and uses them unless you change them or recall a memorized investment report with selected items. If you enter N, Quicken again includes all the items when producing your investment reports.

Security contains

Enter the full or partial name of a security if you want to report only on that security. You can enter the exact name or press Ctrl-Y and choose from the security list. For information about different kinds of filters, see "Using Match Characters to Limit Searches" on page 186.

How to exclude cash from investment reports

You can easily filter any investment report to include only transactions associated with a security. In the Security Contains field of the Filter Investment Transactions window, enter two periods (..). The two periods tell Quicken to include a transaction only if the SECURITY column is filled in. Quicken then excludes all cash transactions and totals that are not associated with a security.

Select actions to include

Enter Y in this field if you want to select specific actions to include in this report.

When you leave the Filter Investment Transactions window, Quicken displays a window in which you can select the actions to be included in the report. Initially, all actions are included. To exclude an action from the report, select it and press the spacebar.

Select securities to include

Enter Y in this field if you want to select specific securities to include in this report.

When you leave the Filter Transactions window, Quicken displays a window in which you can select the securities to be included in the report. Initially, all securities are included. To exclude a security from the report, select it and press the spacebar.

Select security types to include

Enter Y in this field if you want to select specific security types to include in this report.

When you leave the Filter Investment Transactions window, Quicken displays a window in which you can select the security types to be included in the report. Initially, all security types are included. To exclude a security type from the report, select it and press the spacebar.

Select investment goals to include

Enter Y in this field if you want to select specific investment goals to include in this report.

When you leave the Filter Investment Transactions window, Quicken displays a window in which you can select the investment goals to be included in the report. Initially, all investment goals are included. To exclude an investment goal from the report, select it and press the spacebar.

Choosing a Report Filter Before You Display the Report

You can choose your report filter before you display a report.

For personal and business reports, first press F7 at the report setup window to display the Create Report window for the appropriate basic report. Then press F9 to filter.

For basic and investment reports, press F9 at the report setup window to filter.

Quicken displays Filter Transactions windows similar to the ones described earlier in this section (page 183 and page 185).

Using Match Characters to Limit Searches

As described in "The Filter Transactions Window" on page 183, you can use payee, memo, category, class, security, action, security type, or investment goal information to limit the transactions in reports. When you enter this information in the Filter Transactions window, Quicken normally reports on any transactions that contain the word or phrase you type.

In addition, you can use special characters in the Filter Transactions window to do the following:

- Include only transactions that match the word or phrase you type exactly.
- Exclude certain transactions from a report.
- Limit the search in other ways.

Match character	Description
=	Exact match
..	Match that contains unspecified characters at the beginning, middle, or end of the text you type. Examples: ..nn, nn.., n..n
?	Match with one unspecified character
~	Exclude all matches for the text that follows

For example, if you enter utilities in the Memo Contains field in the Filter Transaction window, the report includes transactions with memos such as "March utilities" or "Utilities for cabin." If you enter utilities in the Category Contains field, the report includes transactions with "utilities" in the category (or subcategory) name, including all transactions for subcategories of those categories.

If you enter =utilities in the Category Contains field in the Filter Transaction window, the report includes only transactions with the exact text "Utilities" in the Category field. It excludes transactions for subcategories of the category "Utilities."

If you enter utilities.. in the Memo Contains field, the report includes only those transactions in which "Utilities" is the first text in the Memo field. If you enter ..utilities, the report includes only those transactions in which "Utilities" is the last text in the Memo field. Similarly, if you want to report on all transactions categorized as either "Mortgage Int" (for mortgage interest) or "Mortgage Prin" (for mortgage principle), enter mort.. in the Category Contains field. Quicken includes all transactions for any category starting with "Mort."

You can also use a question mark to substitute for any one character. For example, if you have two cars and you designate expenses for them in the Class field as "Auto1" and "Auto2," you could enter auto? in the Class Contains field to have Quicken find all transactions that have "Auto" followed by any single character in the Class field. You can use more than one question mark if you want to substitute for more than one character.

Excluding Specific Transactions

When using a match, you can tell Quicken to exclude particular transactions by typing a tilde (~). For example, if you want all transactions except those having the phrase "utilities" anywhere in the Memo field, enter ~utilities in the Memo Contains field.

Searching for Uncategorized Transactions

If you enter ~.. Quicken excludes all transactions except those that are empty in the specified field. For example, if you enter ~.. in the Category Contains field, Quicken includes only those transactions that are uncategorized. Uncategorized transactions show up as "Other" in the INFLOWS, OUTFLOWS, INCOME, or EXPENSES section of a summary or budget report.

On the other hand, if you enter .. (two periods) without the tilde, Quicken includes transactions only if the specified field is filled in. For example, if you enter .. (two periods) in the Category Contains field, Quicken excludes uncategorized transactions.

Examples of Matches with Special Characters

The following chart shows some examples of what your report can include with and without using special match characters.

If you enter:	The report includes:	The report does not include:
tax	tax, Tax, TAX, taxable, tax deduction, Tax:State, surtax, new tax loss	rent, utilities
~tax	rent, utilities	tax, Tax, TAX, taxable, tax deduction, Tax:State, surtax, new tax loss
=tax	tax, Tax, TAX	taxable, tax deduction, Tax:State, surtax, new tax loss, rent, utilities
~=tax	taxable, tax deduction, Tax:State, surtax, new tax loss, rent, utilities	tax, Tax, TAX
tax..	tax, Tax, TAX, taxable, tax deduction, Tax:State	surtax, new tax loss, rent, utilities
..tax	tax, Tax, TAX, surtax, property tax	taxable, tax deduction, Tax:State, new tax loss, rent, utilities
t..x	trix, tx, tkx, t——x, tax, Tax, TAX	taxable, tax deduction, Tax:State, surtax, new tax loss, rent, utilities
t?x	tkx, tax, Tax, TAX	trix, tx, t——x, taxable, tax deduction, Tax:State, surtax, new tax loss, rent, utilities
..	tax, rent, utilities, and so on	transactions with nothing in this field
~..	transactions with nothing in this field	tax, rent, utilities, and so on

Note: If your matches do not behave as described above, check your Transaction Settings (see "Transaction Settings" on page 444). Enter N (No) in the field for "7. Exact matches on finds and filters."

> ### Use match characters when searching with Quicken's Find feature.
>
> You can use Quicken's ability to match with special characters when you tell
> Quicken to "Find" a specific transaction at the Write Checks screen or in a Register.
> For more information, see "Using Find" on page 63.

$ Investigating Items in Reports

You can use the QuickZoom command to examine the transaction detail In
noninvestment summary, transaction, and budget reports.

Use the arrow keys to select an amount in the report for investigation. For example, if
you are curious about what individual transactions are represented by an "Actual"
amount in a budget report, select the amount in the "Actual" column and choose
QuickZoom from the File/Print menu. (You can also press Ctrl-Z, press the Enter key, or
double-click on the amount).

When you use QuickZoom to examine an amount in a summary or budget report,
Quicken displays a Transaction List window with one line of information for all the
transactions that make up that amount. When you use QuickZoom to examine an item on
a transaction report, Quicken takes you to the account register with that transaction
selected. (Press Ctrl-M to memorize a custom report setup before you use QuickZoom if
you want to recreate the report after viewing or editing transactions in the register.)

To investigate the amount for Interest Income in a cash flow report:

1. Select the amount for Interest Income in the report.

Select the amount
you want to
investigate and
choose QuickZoom
at the File/Print
menu (or press
Ctrl-Z) to display a
Transaction List
window.

If you have a
mouse, double-click
the amount.

If you use
QuickZoom on a
transaction report,
Quicken displays
the register.

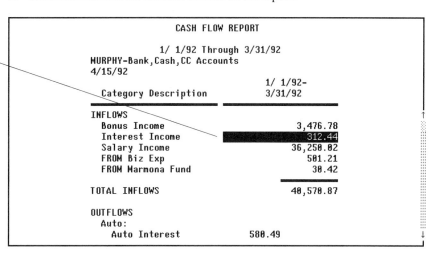

```
                      CASH FLOW REPORT

                 1/ 1/92 Through 3/31/92
           MURPHY-Bank,Cash,CC Accounts
           4/15/92
                                          1/ 1/92-
               Category Description        3/31/92

           INFLOWS
              Bonus Income                 3,476.78
              Interest Income                312.44
              Salary Income               36,250.82
              FROM Biz Exp                   501.21
              FROM Marmona Fund              38.42

           TOTAL INFLOWS                  48,570.87

           OUTFLOWS
              Auto:
                 Auto Interest      580.49
```

2. Press Ctrl-Z to explore the item.

Quicken displays a list of the transactions that make up that amount with columns for date, check number, description, category, cleared status, amount information.

If you need to see more of a transaction in the list, select it and press Enter to go to that transaction in the account register.

```
┌─────────────────────────────────────────────────────────────────┐
│                       Transaction List                           │
│                                                                   │
│    Date     Num      Desc           Cat       ·Clr    Amount      │
│                                                                   │
│ ▶ 1/27/92  INT   Interest Earned Int Inc       X         24.56 ↑  │
│   2/27/92  INT   Interest Earned Int Inc       X         21.19    │
│   1/12/92        Shearson/Lehman Int Inc       X         81.15    │
│   2/12/92        Shearson/Lehman Int Inc       X         83.97    │
│   2/ 7/92        Interest Earned Int Inc       X         52.01    │
│   1/15/92        Interest Earned Int Inc       X         12.78    │
│   2/15/92        Interest Earned Int Inc       X         20.00    │
│   3/16/92        Interest Earned Int Inc       X         16.78    │
│                                                                ↓  │
│                         ↑,↓ Select                                │
│   Esc-Cancel                                 F9-Go to register    │
└─────────────────────────────────────────────────────────────────┘
```

Use QuickZoom to find out which transactions are uncategorized.

If you see an item labeled "Other" (for example, Income - Other) on a summary report, select the item and choose QuickZoom. The Transactions List window displays all transaction that are uncategorized and therefore grouped under "Other."

Note: Quicken cannot explore an item that has detail hidden with Collapse as described in the following section. You need to Expand the collapsed item and try again.

$ Collapsing Items in Reports

You can use the Collapse command to summarize all detail for a row heading in a noninvestment summary, budget, or account balances report without changing the totals for the report. You can collapse any category, class, or payee row heading, including the totals for the major report sections (for example, TOTAL INFLOWS, TOTAL OUTFLOWS, TOTAL ASSETS, and TOTAL LIABILITIES). Use the arrow keys to select the row heading that you want to collapse. To restore collapsed report detail, select the collapsed item and choose Expand from the Layout menu.

To collapse the subcategory names in a cash flow report:

1. Select the name of a category with subcategories in the report (for example, Tax).

If you have a mouse, you can double-click an item to collapse it and again to expand it.

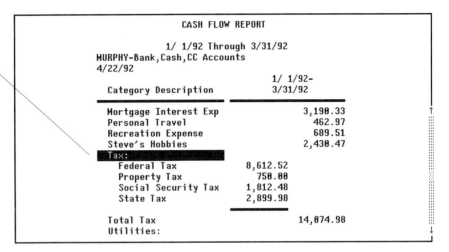

```
                        CASH FLOW REPORT

                     1/ 1/92 Through 3/31/92
             MURPHY-Bank,Cash,CC Accounts
             4/22/92
                                             1/ 1/92-
                 Category Description         3/31/92

                 Mortgage Interest Exp          3,190.33
                 Personal Travel                  462.97
                 Recreation Expense               689.51
                 Steve's Hobbies                2,430.47
                 Tax:
                   Federal Tax        8,612.52
                   Property Tax         750.00
                   Social Security Tax 1,812.48
                   State Tax           2,899.98

                 Total Tax                      14,074.98
                 Utilities:
```

2. Choose Collapse from the Layout menu.

   Quicken summarizes the subcategory amounts in one row item (for example, Total Tax).

Quicken summarizes all the subcategories that were listed in the report under Tax and lists them as a single item, Total Tax.

```
                        CASH FLOW REPORT

                     1/ 1/92 Through 3/31/92
             MURPHY-Bank,Cash,CC Accounts
             4/22/92
                                             1/ 1/92-
                 Category Description         3/31/92

                 Mortgage Interest Exp          3,190.33
                 Personal Travel                  462.97
                 Recreation Expense               689.51
                 Steve's Hobbies                2,430.47
                 Total Tax                     14,074.98
                 Utilities:
                   Garbage/Sewer        130.00
                   Gas & Electric       197.14
                   Personal Phone       277.07

                 Total Utilities                  604.21
                 Outflows - Other                  25.00
```

If you memorize a report after choosing Collapse, the report you recall is collapsed the same way.

3. Now let's say that you want to hide the Total Tax row heading. Select Total Tax and choose Collapse from the Layout menu.

Quicken summarizes your tax expenses in a row called "Outflows - Collapsed."

If you had collapsed an income category, Quicken would have created an item called Inflows - Collapsed.

If the report had been organized by income and expense, the items would be called Expenses - Collapsed and Income - Collapsed.

```
                  CASH FLOW REPORT

                1/ 1/92 Through 3/31/92
        MURPHY-Bank,Cash,CC Accounts
        4/22/92
                                   1/ 1/92-
           Category Description     3/31/92

           TO House                     2,897.67
           TO Marmona Fund              1,000.00
           TO Mortgage                    284.84
           TO Steve's IRA               2,000.00
           TO Yotzvitsky Sec            1,775.00
           Outflows - Collapsed        14,074.98

           TOTAL OUTFLOWS              40,511.21


           OVERALL TOTAL                   59.66
```

4. To take the collapse one level further, you can select the heading or "total" line for an entire report section and choose Collapse from the Layout menu.

Quicken hides all the detail in the section without changing the report totals. The detail is summarized in the TOTAL row heading. For example, you could select the OUTFLOWS or TOTAL OUTFLOWS row item in a cash flow report and hide all expense category names, select the INCOME or TOTAL INCOME row item in a summary report and hide all income category names, or select the ASSETS or TOTAL ASSETS row item in an account balances report and hide all asset account names.

If you have a mouse, you can double-click a report section title to collapse it and again to expand it.

```
                  CASH FLOW REPORT

                1/ 1/92 Through 3/31/92
        MURPHY-Bank,Cash,CC Accounts
        4/22/92
                                   1/ 1/92-
           Category Description     3/31/92

           INFLOWS
             Bonus Income               3,476.78
             Interest Income              312.44
             Salary Income            36,250.02
             FROM Biz Exp                 501.21
             FROM Marmona Fund             30.42

           TOTAL INFLOWS              40,570.87

           TOTAL OUTFLOWS             40,511.21

           OVERALL TOTAL                  59.66
```

Memorizing a Custom Report Setup

After you customize a report, you can memorize it so you can get a report using the same report instructions time after time. This feature is most useful for customized reports, especially reports that use filters. You can also change a memorized report and then rememorize it with the changes.

Note: Quicken does not memorize a date range, budget amounts, or the printer.

To memorize a report, just create a report as you normally would and press Ctrl-M to memorize it at any report window that has Ctrl M-Memorize at the bottom.

For example, suppose you want to create a summary report showing only discretionary expenses. You choose Summary at the Reports menu and press F10 to create the report. To change the categories selected for the report, you choose Edit (Alt-E) at the Report screen, and then choose Categories at the Edit menu. Use the Selected option on the Categories menu to select the categories you want to include in the report. Then press Ctrl-M to memorize the custom report setup for repeated use.

Note: When you memorize a report, you must enter a report title. If you use the same title again, Quicken warns that you are about to overwrite an existing memorized report.

Recalling a Memorized Report

After you have memorized a report, you can recall it. When you recall a report, it's really the report definition you are recalling (including any formatting, options, and filters you've specified). Quicken displays windows similar to the usual report windows so you can change the recalled instructions if you want. When you are satisfied with the instructions, Quicken searches for transactions and prepares the report as usual.

If you change the instructions for a memorized report, you can rememorize it with the same title or you can give the altered report a new title and memorize it again. (Change a memorized report the same way you would any other report.) If you don't rememorize a report whose definition you have changed, it retains the original definition the next time you recall the report.

To recall a memorized report:

1. At the Main Menu, choose Create Reports and then Memorized Reports.

You can also start at the Write Checks screen or the register, and then choose Memorized Reports at the Reports menu.

Quicken displays a list of the reports you have memorized.

You can delete the memorized report. Press Ctrl-D to delete.

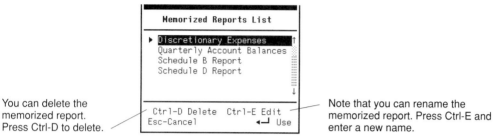

Note that you can rename the memorized report. Press Ctrl-E and enter a new name.

2. Select the report you want to use.

You can change the layout (F7), options (F8) or filter(F9) and then rememorize (Ctrl-M) the report with the new setup.

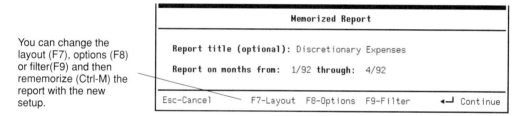

3. Press Ctrl-Enter or F10.

Quicken searches for transactions and displays the report.

Chapter 11

Saving Time with Memorized Transactions

Every month you handle many predictable transactions, such as:

* Mortgage payments
* Utility bills
* Paycheck deposits

Quicken helps you handle these repeated transactions quickly and accurately. You only need to enter the transaction once. Then have Quicken memorize it. The next time you want to enter that transaction, specify which transaction you want, and Quicken enters it for you automatically.

You can memorize any transaction you have entered at the Write Checks screen or in a register. You can memorize a whole check or create a template, memorizing only certain parts of the transaction (for example, the payee and category). A template allows you to memorize information that is predictable and later add information that changes. (For example, everything about a check to pay a utility bill is predictable except the amount.) If you split a transaction, Quicken memorizes the contents of the split along with the rest of the transaction.

If you're considering a loan, the loan calculator will let you compare the result of varying the interest rate or number of payments. And once you decide on a loan, use amortization to automatically track both principal and interest.

$ Memorizing a Transaction

When you have Quicken memorize a transaction, a copy of the transaction is saved in a separate list. You start by filling out the fields on a check at the Write Checks screen or in a transaction in a register. (You can also enter information in the Split Transaction window.) Then you tell Quicken to memorize what you've entered.

Note: You can memorize transactions in any Quicken account register. Quicken stores all memorized transactions for a given file in the one list, so you can use the same memorized transactions with any of your Quicken accounts (except investment accounts).

To memorize a transaction:

1. Enter the information you want memorized at the Write Checks screen or in the register.

2. Choose Memorize Transaction from the Shortcuts menu (or press Ctrl-M).

   Quicken highlights the information you entered and asks you to confirm that you want the information memorized.

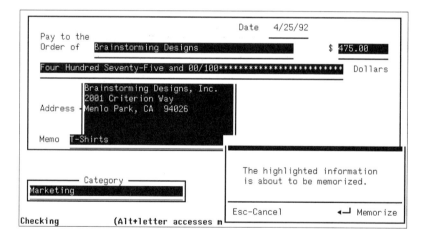

3. Press Enter to confirm that you want Quicken to memorize the highlighted information.

   Quicken memorizes the transaction and adds it to the memorized transactions list. (To see this list, choose Recall Transaction from the Shortcuts menu, or press Ctrl-T.)

4. To complete the transaction and add it to the register, simply continue entering information. When you have finished, press Ctrl-Enter to record the transaction, as usual.

Note: You can memorize transactions at any time:

*   Before you enter them in the register or Write Checks screen
*   While you are entering them in the register or Write Checks screen
*   After you've entered them in the register or Write Checks screen

To memorize a transaction before entering it in the register, choose <New Transaction> from the memorized transactions list. Fill in the information about the transaction in the Edit/Setup Memorized Transaction window.

To memorize a check or other transaction that has already been recorded, select the transaction you want to memorize, then choose Memorize Transaction from the Shortcuts menu. Quicken memorizes all the information entered in the transaction except the date (and the check number, if you're recording the transaction in the register).

 # Examples of Memorized Transactions

This section offers examples of some typical transactions you may want Quicken to memorize. Note that Quicken does not memorize the date. When you use a memorized transaction, the current date appears on the check and in the register.

These are all examples of transactions in a checking account. However, you can memorize transactions in all types of Quicken accounts. You can also memorize the contents of split transactions.

Whole Check Method

Here's a check where all the information stays the same from month to month. Quicken memorizes the highlighted information. If you split the transaction, Quicken memorizes the contents of the split as well.

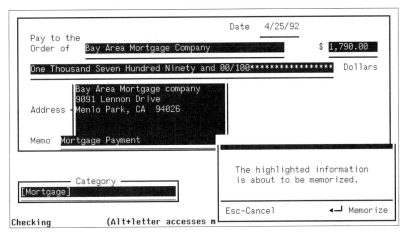

Template Method

When you have a check that has some information that stays the same from month to month, and some information that changes, use the template method.

Some repeated transactions, such as telephone and utility bills, have the same payee, memo, and category, but the dollar amount varies. In this case, you can either memorize the check with the current amount, and change that amount when you recall the check, or memorize the check without an amount, and then fill in the amount when you recall the check. (If you memorize a transaction from the register without an amount, Quicken will ask you to specify whether it is a payment or a deposit.)

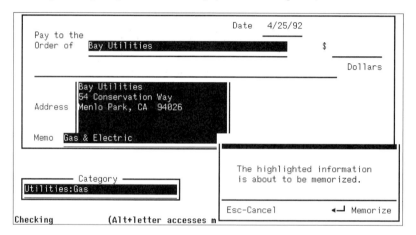

Memorizing Deposits and Payments

You can also use this method to enter recurring deposits and payments in the register. (Quicken memorizes the transaction's cleared status, which is useful for service charges.)

$ **Recalling a Memorized Transaction**

You can recall a memorized transaction at the Write Checks screen or in any Quicken account register. When the transaction you recall is a check that you want Quicken to print, you can recall it at the Write Checks screen or in the register (enter ***** in the Num field). If an address was memorized with the check, it is recalled as part of the information. However, you'll see the address only if you review the check at the Write Checks screen.

You can recall groups of memorized transactions all at once by setting up a transaction group. For more information, see *Entering Transaction Groups*, beginning on page 211.

To recall a memorized transaction:

1. Choose Recall Transaction from the Shortcuts menu (or press Ctrl-T).

The memorized transactions list shows transactions in alphabetical order by payee.

The Split column lists an S for a split transaction; A for an amortized transaction.

```
                          Memorized Transactions List

         Description      Split  Memo      Category  Clr  Amount   Type Grp

    ▶ <New Transaction>    ▇ ▇                        ▇              ▇    ↑
      Bay Utilities        S Gas & Elect Utilities:G            Epm
      Brainstorming Design S T-Shirts    Marketing      475.00  Chk
      Citibank               A/C #4128-3 [Joint Acco            Pmt
      City of Valley Sprin   Services    Utilities:G     65.00  Chk
      Duncan Investments                 [Savings]      400.00  Chk
      GMAC Financing       A A/C #87239- [Auto Loans    325.00  Epm
      Paycheck             S Sally's     Salary       1,582.11  Dep
      Shearson/Lehman/Hutt               Int Inc               Pmt
      Steve                              [Checking]     750.00  Dep
      Western Bell                       Utilities:P           Chk   ↓

           Ctrl-D Delete  Ctrl-E Edit  Ctrl-P Print  ↑,↓ Select
      Esc-Cancel          F1-Help       F9-Amortize           ◄┘ Use
```

The Type column tells you whether a transaction is a check you can print, a handwritten check, a deposit or an electronic payment.

2. Select the transaction you want, and if you do not need to make any changes to it, press Enter to recall it to the Write Checks screen or the current register, depending on which you are using.

Entering memorized transactions quickly

Save time by typing the first few letters of the payee name (enough to make the payee unique) in the Payee field and pressing Ctrl-E. Quicken fills in the rest of the memorized transaction. If your entry matches more than one memorized transaction, Quicken displays the memorized transactions list.

Or you can type a letter or two and press Ctrl-T. When the memorized transactions list appears, Quicken highlights the first transaction beginning with the letter or letters you typed. If this is the transaction you want, press Enter to accept it. If not, use the arrow keys to move up and down the list until the transaction you want is selected; then press Enter. (You can also type the first letter to move around in the list.)

Changing a Memorized Transaction

To change a memorized transaction:

1. Select Recall Transaction from the Shortcuts menu (or press Ctrl-T).

Select
<New Transaction> to
create a new memorized
transaction.

Electronic
payment

Check that
you can
print using
Quicken

Handwritten
check

Deposit

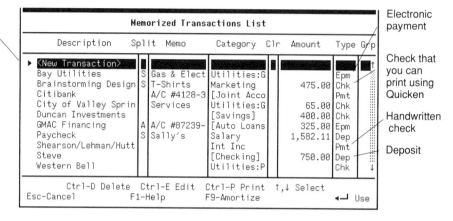

2. Select the memorized transaction you want to change and press Ctrl-E to edit.

3. Make changes while the transaction is displayed in the Edit/Set Up Memorized Transaction window.

You can change the Payee name, amount of Payment or Deposit, cleared status (C), Memo, or Category in this window.

Asterisks here mean
that this item is a check
you can print using
Quicken.
(>>>>> mean this is an
electronic payment.)

Press Ctrl-C to display
the category list from
this window.

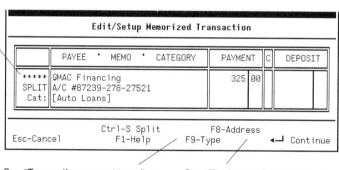

See "To specify payment type:" on
page 201.

See "To change the address of a
memorized transaction:" on page
201.

Note: You can use the Edit/Set Up Memorized Transaction window to edit any type of transaction *except* an investment transaction.

To split a memorized transaction:

1. From the Edit/Set Up Memorized Transaction window, press Ctrl-S to display the Split Transaction window. (See "Splitting a Transaction" on page 67.)

2. Change or enter information about the split transaction as you normally would.

3. Press Ctrl-Enter to memorize the split transaction.

To change the address of a memorized transaction:

1. From the Edit/Set Up Memorized Transaction window, press F8 to display the Memorized Transaction Address window.

(Optional.)
Enter an account number or other information that will identify this payment to the merchant. See "Checks and Reports Settings" on page 446 for more information.

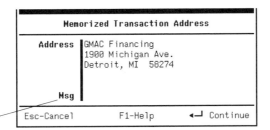

2. Change or enter the address, up to five lines.

3. Press Enter to memorize the address (and optional message).

To specify payment type:

Payment type affects how you can recall and use a memorized transaction. For instance, if you decide you want to create a check from a transaction you initially entered in the register, you must change payment type from 1. Payment to 2. Check.

1. From the Edit/Set Up Memorized Transaction window, press F9 to view the Select Memorized Payment Type window.

(You can edit payment type for any memorized transaction except a deposit transaction memorized with an amount.)

Option 4 (Deposit) appears on this list only if the transaction was memorized without a specific amount.

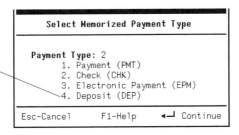

2. Enter the number that corresponds to the payment type you want:

   - Enter 1 for Payment if this is a manual check, one you are not going to print.
   - Enter 2 for Check if this a check you plan to print later. (Quicken places ***** in the Num field.)
   - Enter 3 for Electronic Payment if you plan to use CheckFree to pay this bill. (Quicken places >>>>> in the Num field.)
   - Enter 4 for Deposit if this transaction is a deposit. (When Quicken recalls a deposit transaction into the register, the cursor is automatically placed in the Deposit field.)

3. Press Enter to return to the Edit/Set Up Memorized Transaction window, and then press Ctrl-Enter to record the new payment type.

   Note: You can also change payment type in the register, by changing the contents of the Num field.

Using Percentages in a Memorized Split Transaction

Usually, to split the amount of a single check between two or more categories, you enter dollar amounts in the Split Transaction window. However, sometimes you may want to allocate a split by percentage, instead. In that case, you can create a template transaction, split the transaction, and assign percentages to each category. Then, each time you recall the template transaction and fill in a real amount, Quicken calculates the dollar amount to apply to each category.

For instance, if two people living at your house want to split the phone bill 60%/40%, Quicken can calculate the amount each person should pay. Because you won't know the exact amount until you get the phone bill, you would memorize a template transaction with a split showing the 60%/40% division. Then, when the phone bill comes, recall the check and fill in the actual amount, and Quicken calculates how much each person owes.

Basic steps for using percentages in a memorized split transaction

1. Set up a template transaction.
2. Recall the memorized transaction to pay the bill.

To set up a template transaction:

1. Choose Recall Transaction from the Shortcuts menu (or press Ctrl-T).
2. Select <New Transaction> at the top of the list and press Ctrl-E to open the Edit/Set Up Memorized Transaction window.
3. Fill in the fields for a template transaction.
   a. Enter the company name in the Payee field.
   b. Enter 100 in the Payment field. (This 100 represents 100 percent of the payment, not $100.)
   c. Press F9 to choose the type of transaction. Enter 2 to create a check to be printed.

4. Press Ctrl-S to open the Split Transaction window.

Enter the percentages for each part of the split.

Once you memorize this transaction as a percentage, the Amount field becomes the Percent field.

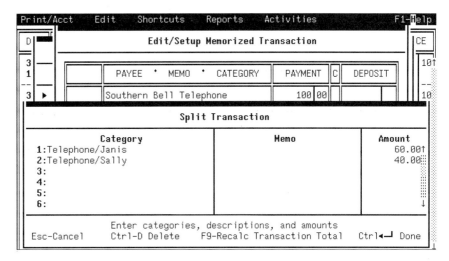

Press Ctrl-Enter twice (first to leave the Split Transaction window and then to leave the Edit window).

Quicken asks if you want to memorize the transaction as an amount or a percentage.

5. Enter P to choose percentage.

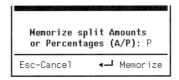

Quicken memorizes this transaction with percentages.

6. Look at this transaction in the memorized transactions list. Quicken shows 100% in the Amount field for this transaction, rather than a dollar amount.

Notice the S in the Split column and % in the Amount column: this transaction was memorized with percentages rather than amounts.

```
┌──────────────────────────────────────────────────────────────────┐
│                    Memorized Transactions List                     │
├──────────────────────────────────────────────────────────────────┤
│    Description    Split  Memo      Category   Clr  Amount  Type Grp│
│                                                                    │
│  Brainstorming Design S T-Shirts   Marketing     475.00  Chk   ↑   │
│  Citibank             A/C #4128-3 [Joint Acco            Pmt   2   │
│  City of Valley Sprin  Services   Utilities:G     65.00  Chk   2   │
│  Duncan Investments              [Savings]       400.00  Chk   1   │
│  GMAC Financing       A A/C #87239- [Auto Loans  325.00  Chk   2   │
│  Paycheck             S Sally's   Salary       1,582.11  Dep       │
│  Shearson/Lehman/Hutt             Int Inc               Pmt       │
│▶ Southern Bell        S           Telephone/J    100.%   Chk       │
│  Steve                            [Checking]     750.00  Dep   1   │
│  Western Bell                     Utilities:P            Chk   2   │
│                                                                 ↓  │
├──────────────────────────────────────────────────────────────────┤
│       Ctrl-D Delete  Ctrl-E Edit  Ctrl-P Print  ↑,↓ Select         │
│  Esc-Cancel          F1-Help      F9-Amortize          ←┘ Use      │
└──────────────────────────────────────────────────────────────────┘
```

To recall the memorized transaction to pay the bill:

1. Start at the empty transaction at the bottom of the register.

2. Choose Recall Transaction from the Shortcuts menu (or press Ctrl-T).

3. Choose the memorized transaction from the list.

4. Enter the dollar amount you want Quicken to divide into the percentages stored in the split transaction.

Payee name.

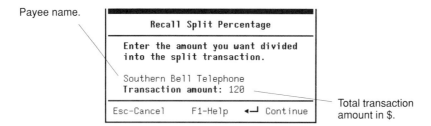

Total transaction amount in $.

Quicken enters a transaction for the dollar amount you specify, with the dollar amount split according to the percentages stored in the memorized transaction.

Press Ctrl-S to see the amounts assigned to each part of the split transaction.

In this Split Transaction window, Quicken calculates the dollar amount corresponding to the percentages you stored in the memorized transaction.

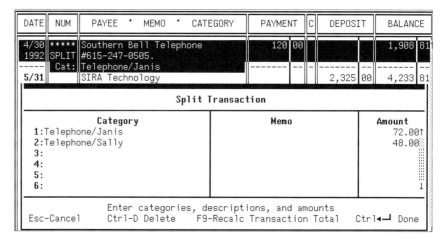

Using percentages in splits as a calculator

You can also start with a transaction for a specific dollar amount and use the percentage feature to calculate percentages to split between categories.

For example, you might create a transaction to divide the electricity bill:

1. Recall the memorized transaction for the electricity bill.

2. Press Ctrl-S to open the Split Transaction window.

3. Enter the first category in the split: Electricity/Janis.

4. Tab over to the Amount column and enter the percentage for the first person: 60%.

5. Press Enter.

6. Quicken calculates that percentage of the total and enters the dollar amount in the Amount column, then enters the remainder on the second line.

7. Enter the category for the second person: Electricity/Sally.

Deleting a Memorized Transaction

To delete a transaction from the memorized transactions list:

1. Choose Recall Transaction from the Shortcuts menu (or press Ctrl-T).

2. Select the transaction you want to delete.

3. Press Ctrl-D.

   Quicken warns that you are about to delete a memorized item.

4. If you are sure this is what you want to do, press Enter to delete the transaction.

Printing the Memorized Transactions List

To print the memorized transactions list:

1. Choose Recall Transaction from the Shortcuts menu (or press Ctrl-T).

   Quicken displays the memorized transactions list.

2. Press Ctrl-P while the memorized transactions list is open.

   Enter the number that corresponds to the printer you are using and press Ctrl-Enter to begin printing the memorized transactions list.

$ Amortization

Memorized transactions save you time in making predictable transactions, including mortgage payments. Once you memorize your mortgage payment transaction, you can use amortization to track loan balances and payments for fixed-rate mortgages. Each time you record a payment made on the loan, Quicken updates the dollar amount of payments made, and calculates the amount credited to principal and interest.

Note: Quicken's amortization is based on scheduled payments. Do not set up a loan for amortization if you plan to make early payment of principal.

Basic steps for using amortization

1. Set up a loan for amortization:

   a. Define a loan transaction as a memorized transaction.

   b. Fill in the amortization information.

   c. Display the payment schedule to see the breakdown of principal and interest amounts.

2. Record a payment:

   a. When it's time to make a payment, select the transaction in the memorized transaction list.

   b. Display the Split Transactions window in the register to see how much of the payment was applied to principal and how much to interest.

To set up a loan for amortization:

1. Memorize a transaction for the loan payment. (See "Memorizing a Transaction" on page 196.)

2. Select that transaction in the memorized transactions list.

3. Press F9 to amortize.

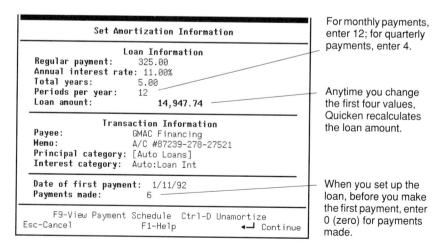

For monthly payments, enter 12; for quarterly payments, enter 4.

Anytime you change the first four values, Quicken recalculates the loan amount.

When you set up the loan, before you make the first payment, enter 0 (zero) for payments made.

4. Fill in the first four Loan Information fields.

   Based on the information you enter, Quicken calculates the loan amount.

5. Quicken fills in the Transaction Information fields from your memorized transaction, but you can change them here.

6. Fill in the Date of First Payment field.

7. Fill in the Payments Made field.

   When you first set up the loan, before you make the first payment, enter 0. Quicken will update the Payments Made number as you record payments on this loan.

   If this is an existing loan (you've already made payments), enter the number of payments made so far.

8. Press Enter to record this amortization information.

   Quicken displays the memorized transaction list.

```
                    Memorized Transactions List

         Description      Split  Memo      Category   Clr  Amount   Type Grp

     <New Transaction>                                                       ↑
     Bay Utilities         S Gas & Elect Utilities:G            Epm
     Brainstorming Design  S T-Shirts     Marketing      475.00 Chk
     Citibank                A/C #4128-3 [Joint Acco            Pmt
     City of Valley Sprin    Services    Utilities:G     65.00 Chk
     Duncan Investments                  [Savings]      400.00 Chk
   ▶ GMAC Financing        A A/C #87239- [Auto Loans    325.00 Chk
     Paycheck              S Sally's     Salary       1,582.11 Dep
     Shearson/Lehman/Hutt              Int Inc                 Pmt
     Steve                             [Checking]      750.00 Dep
     Western Bell                      Utilities:P            Chk    ↓

          Ctrl-D Delete  Ctrl-E Edit  Ctrl-P Print  ↑,↓ Select
     Esc-Cancel          F1-Help      F9-Amortize            ◂┘ Use
```

An A (Amortized) appears in the Split column of the transaction.

9. Press F9 twice to see the loan payment schedule.

```
                 Approximate Payment Schedule

         Date     Pmt   Principal    Interest     Balance

   ▶                                             14,947.74 ↑
      1/11/92   1      187.98      137.02     14,759.76
      2/11/92   2      189.71      135.29     14,570.05
      3/11/92   3      191.45      133.55     14,378.60
      4/11/92   4      193.20      131.80     14,185.40
      5/11/92   5      194.97      130.03     13,990.43
      6/11/92   6      196.76      128.24     13,793.67
      7/11/92   7      198.56      126.44     13,595.11 ↓

              Ctrl-P Print  ↑,↓ Select
      Esc-Cancel            F1-Help          ◂┘ Continue
```

Based on the information you provide, Quicken calculates the breakdown of each payment into principal and interest amounts.

To record a payment:

1. When it is time to record a payment on the loan, choose Recall Transaction from the Shortcuts menu (or press Ctrl-T).

2. Choose the loan transaction from the memorized transactions list.

   Every month, when you record the loan payment transaction, Quicken updates the amounts applied to both principal and interest, calculated according to the amount and term of the loan.

3. Choose Split Transaction from the Edit menu (or press Ctrl-S) to view the amounts applied to principal and interest for this payment.

   (When you reach the total number of payments scheduled for this loan, Quicken will remind you that this is the last payment. After the last payment is made, you will not be able to recall this transaction again.)

Quicken automatically fills in the categories from the loan transaction you memorized.

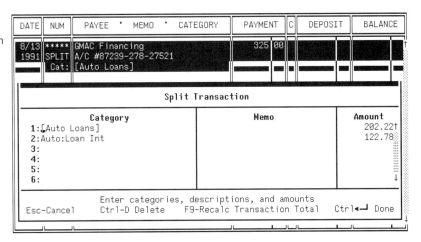

To undo a mistaken loan payment

Each time you recall the loan payment transaction into the register, Quicken increases the number in the Payments Made field by one. (See the Set Amortization Information window on page 195.)

If you accidentally record an extra loan payment, take these steps to reverse it:

1. Return to the Set Amortization Information window.

2. Reset the number in the Payments Made field and press Enter to record the change.

3. Delete the recalled transaction from the register.

The next time you record a payment, Quicken will calculate the principal and interest amounts for the corrected number of payments.

Using the Loan Calculator

Use the Loan Calculator to do "what if" calculations, to see the effect of changing the amount of the loan, the interest rate, or the number of payments.

1. Choose Loan Calculator from the Activities menu.

2. Fill in the fields in the Loan Calculator window.

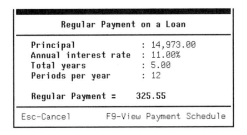

```
          Regular Payment on a Loan

  Principal             : 14,973.00
  Annual interest rate  : 11.00%
  Total years           : 5.00
  Periods per year      : 12

  Regular Payment =      325.55

 Esc-Cancel        F9-View Payment Schedule
```

When you press Tab after entering Periods per Year, Quicken calculates the Regular Payment amount.

3. Press F9 to view the Payment Schedule.

How many more loan payments?

If you prepay the principal on a loan, you may wonder how long it will take to pay off the loan. Use these steps to find out how many years are left:

1. On the Approximate Payment Schedule, scan down the Interest column until you find the interest amount that most closely matches the interest due on your next payment.

2. Notice the payment number of that payment.

3. Subtract that payment number from the number of the last payment to get the number of payments left.

4. Divide by twelve to get the number of years remaining.

Chapter 12

Entering Transaction Groups

Once you have memorized some transactions, you can use transaction groups to have Quicken handle those transactions you routinely enter at the same time.

What Is a Transaction Group?

Transaction groups are batches of recurring transactions that you pay or add to your account at the same time. For example, you may have a mortgage payment, phone bill, electric bill, and car payment all due around the beginning of each month. Quicken lets you group these transactions and reminds you when their scheduled date arrives. When you tell Quicken to pay them, Quicken enters the entire group for you automatically. This automatic entry saves you time and keystrokes, yet you retain complete control. Once Quicken has entered the transactions, you can edit them, changing information such as amounts, or deleting any that you don't want to pay.

A group can consist of a single transaction, such as a mortgage payment, or many, such as that group of predictable bills you pay at the end of the month. You can change the groups, adding or deleting transactions whenever you want.

Basic Steps to Use Transaction Groups

1. Set up one or more transaction groups.

   First, memorize any transactions you want to include in a group.

   When you set up a transaction group, you use three windows:
   • The Select Transaction Group to Execute window
   • The Describe Group window
   • The Assign Transactions to Group window

2. Recall the transaction group when you're ready to use it (for instance, to enter a group of checks to pay monthly bills).

3. Maintain your transaction groups:
   • Add more transactions to a group
   • Change transaction group information
   • Delete transaction groups

Automatic reminders about bill-paying

In addition to saving you time, transaction groups can serve a scheduling function. This is optional, but useful for recurring expenses for which you may not receive bills. For example, you may owe a monthly mortgage payment, a quarterly tax payment, or a semi-annual insurance premium. You could set up a transaction group (with one entry) for each of these transactions (a total of three groups). Quicken can then remind you when they must be paid.

This reminder appears at the bottom of the screen when the Main Menu is displayed. The reminder begins to appear in advance of the scheduled date for the group. You can adjust how far in advance the reminder appears. (For more information, see "How many days in advance" on page 443.)

In addition, if you have a hard disk and you have installed Billminder, you will also see a reminder when you first turn on your computer. Billminder appears above the DOS prompt. In this way, Quicken reminds you of scheduled groups, even without running Quicken. If you don't use your computer often, you can increase the time in advance Billminder will remind you.

For more information, see *Setting Preferences*, beginning on page 427.

Setting Up a Transaction Group

You set up a new transaction group by describing the group and then assigning memorized transactions to it.

To include a transaction in a group for automatic entry, you must first memorize that transaction. (See *Saving Time with Memorized Transactions*, beginning on page 195.) Once Quicken has memorized the transactions you want to include, you can set up the transaction group.

You can set up as many as twelve different groups.

Using a transaction group to print checks

If you want to create a transaction group to print checks, the transactions assigned to the group must be memorized as checks. (You can recognize checks in the memorized transactions list by the word "Chk" in the Type column.)

You can create printable checks in two ways:

- Memorize the transaction at the Write Checks˙screen.

- Press Ctrl-E to edit the transaction from the memorized transactions list, then press F9 and choose option 2, Check.

To set up a transaction group:

1. Choose Transaction Groups from the Shortcuts menu (or press Ctrl-J).

   The Select Transaction Group to Execute window lists all your current transaction groups and allows you to define new transaction groups.

Source of the transaction group number.

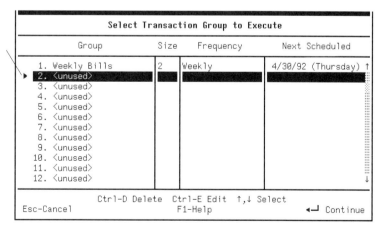

2. Select the first <unused> group and press Enter.

The Describe Group window allows you to set characteristics for each transaction group.

Group number.

Enter a name for this transaction group.

Enter a number to indicate how often you want the group to be scheduled.

Enter the date when you want to be reminded that the group is due.

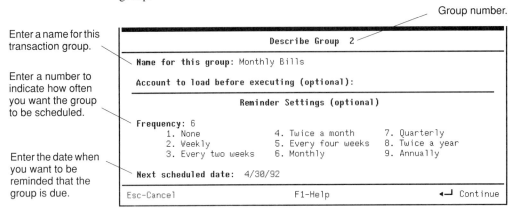

```
                        Describe Group  2

 Name for this group: Monthly Bills

 Account to load before executing (optional):

                      Reminder Settings (optional)

 Frequency: 6
       1. None              4. Twice a month     7. Quarterly
       2. Weekly            5. Every four weeks  8. Twice a year
       3. Every two weeks   6. Monthly           9. Annually

 Next scheduled date:  4/30/92

 Esc-Cancel                      F1-Help               ←┘ Continue
```

3. Enter information about the new transaction group in the Describe Group window. See "Fields in the Describe Group Window" on page 215 for information about each field.

4. When you finish defining the group, press Ctrl-Enter.

Quicken displays the Assign Transactions to Group window, listing all the transactions you memorized previously.

Quicken displays all the available memorized transactions.

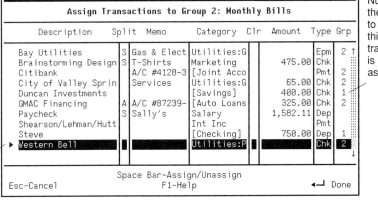

```
        Assign Transactions to Group 2: Monthly Bills

    Description     Split  Memo      Category  Clr  Amount  Type Grp

 Bay Utilities      S Gas & Elect Utilities:G            Epm  2 ↑
 Brainstorming Design S T-Shirts   Marketing     475.00  Chk  2
 Citibank             A/C #4128-3 [Joint Acco           Pmt  2
 City of Valley Sprin  Services    Utilities:G    65.00  Chk  2
 Duncan Investments               [Savings]     400.00  Chk  1
 GMAC Financing     A A/C #87239- [Auto Loans    325.00  Chk  2
 Paycheck           S Sally's     Salary       1,582.11  Dep
 Shearson/Lehman/Hutt              Int Inc               Pmt
 Steve                            [Checking]     750.00  Dep  1
▶Western Bell                    Utilities:P            Chk  2
                                                            ↓

                       Space Bar-Assign/Unassign
 Esc-Cancel                      F1-Help               ←┘ Done
```

Number of the group to which this transaction is assigned.

Select a transaction and press the spacebar to assign it to the new transaction group.

5. Select the first transaction you want to include in the group.

6. Press the spacebar to assign the selected transaction to the group.

The group number appears in the Group (Grp) column. (To unassign the transaction, press the spacebar again.)

Repeat steps 5 and 6 until all transactions you want to include have been assigned to this group.

7. When you finish assigning transactions to the group, press Enter.

You have finished setting up your transaction group, and you can now recall it at any time.

Assigning the same transaction to several groups

You can assign a memorized transaction to more than one group. For example, you might want to have an employees' transaction group and a transaction group for salespeople on commission. You can include checks to the same employees in both groups by memorizing the check transaction twice so that it will appear on the memorized transactions list twice. Then assign one of the memorized transactions to one group, and the remaining one to another.

Fields in the Describe Group Window

Name   Enter a description of the group, such as "Monthly Bills." This name will help you select the group from the list of account groups.

Account to Load   Specify the account that you want Quicken to use when you recall this transaction group. Quicken will automatically load the account when you recall the transaction group. If you leave this field blank, Quicken recalls the transactions into the account you are using when you recall the group. Leave the field blank if you expect to use the transaction group with more than one account.

Frequency   Enter the number that indicates how often you want the group to be scheduled. Leave this field set to 1 (None) if the group doesn't have a regular frequency.

Next Scheduled Date   Enter the date you first want to be reminded that the group is due. You will see a reminder when you start Quicken, based on the frequency you choose.

Even if you entered 1 (None) in the Frequency field, you can still specify a date when you want Quicken to post a reminder for you.

This is also the default date that will be entered on each transaction in this group, unless you change it in the Transaction Group Date window after you recall the transaction group.

Note: When the scheduled date arrives, Quicken will remind you that the group is due. Quicken does not recall the group until you tell it to. You control when the transactions are entered.

Recalling a Transaction Group

Recalling a transaction group tells Quicken to automatically enter the entire group in the current account register (or the register of the account you specified in the Account to Load field). You can then make any changes you want, such as adding dollar amounts. If the transactions are checks, you can print them in the same way you would print any Quicken check.

To recall a transaction group:

1. Choose Transaction Groups from the Shortcuts menu (or press Ctrl-J).

Quicken displays a list of the transaction groups you set up.

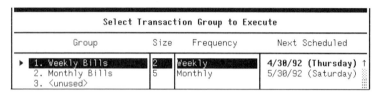

2. Select the transaction group you want to recall and press Enter.

(If you specified an account when you set up the transaction group, Quicken loads that account now.)

The date in the Transaction Group Date window is the date that Quicken gives the transactions when it enters them in the register.

If you want a
different date,
type over the date
displayed.

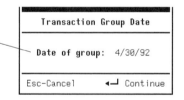

3. To enter these transactions in the register, press Enter.

Quicken displays a Recording message as it records each check. When all transactions in the group have been entered in the account register, you see the Transaction Group Entered confirmation message.

4. Press Enter to continue. If you want to make changes to the transactions, do so just as you would to any transactions in the register. (For instance, add amounts to any transactions saved without dollar amounts.) Remember to press Ctrl-Enter when you have completed changes to a transaction to record the changes in the register.

5. If the transactions include checks to be printed and you want to print them now, press Ctrl-W to display the Write Checks screen.

The total dollar amount of the checks in this group appears in the Checks to Print field.

When you're ready to print these checks, press Ctrl-P. (For more information, see *Printing Checks*, beginning on page 85.)

Adding to a Transaction Group

Once you set up a transaction group, you can add transactions to it whenever you want. First, memorize the transactions you want to add. (See *Saving Time with Memorized Transactions*, beginning on page 195.)

To add memorized transactions to a group:

1. Choose Transaction Groups from the Shortcuts menu (or press Ctrl-J).

   Quicken displays the Select Transaction Group to Execute window.

2. Select the transaction group you want to edit and press Ctrl-E.

   Quicken displays the Describe Group window, showing information about the group.

3. Press Ctrl-Enter to confirm the Describe Group window and display the list of memorized transactions you can assign to the group.

4. Assign transactions by selecting the ones you want and then pressing the spacebar, just as you would if you were setting up a new group.

5. When you finish adding transactions to the group, press Enter.

   The memorized transactions you assigned are added to the group. (Notice the increase in the number of transactions listed in the Size column of the Select Transaction Group to Execute window.)

 # Changing a Transaction Group

You can change a transaction group at any time. For example, you might want to change the group description or select a different scheduling frequency.

To change a transaction group:

1. From the Shortcuts menu, choose Transaction Groups.
   Quicken displays the Select Transaction Group to Execute window.

2. Select the group you want to change and press Ctrl-E to edit.

3. Make whatever changes you want in the Describe Group window.
   When the changes are complete, press Ctrl-Enter.

4. In the Assign Transactions to Group window, use the spacebar to assign transactions to the group or to remove transactions from the group.

5. Press Enter when you finish.

Deleting a Transaction Group

You can also delete a transaction group. When you delete a transaction group, you remove it permanently from your records. The memorized transactions included in the group remain in the memorized transactions list. (However, if you delete a memorized transaction from the memorized transactions list, Quicken automatically removes it from the transaction group.)

To delete a transaction group:

1. Choose Transaction Groups from the Shortcuts menu (or press Ctrl-J).

    Quicken displays the Select Transaction Group to Execute window.

2. Select the group you want to delete.

3. Press Ctrl-D to delete.

    Quicken warns you that you are about to permanently delete the group.

    •   Press Enter to confirm that you want to delete the group

    OR

    •   Press Esc to cancel the deletion.

Chapter 13

Using CheckFree to Pay Bills Electronically

CheckFree lets you pay any bill electronically, using your personal computer and a modem. This technology for paying bills was developed by the CheckFree Corporation of Columbus, Ohio. Paying bills electronically works like this:

- You send payment instructions to CheckFree via modem.
- CheckFree sends the payment to any individual, organization, or corporation in the United States (except some government organizations).

You can use CheckFree regardless of where you bank, and you don't have to make any special arrangements with your bank to use CheckFree.

The CheckFree Corporation is the nation's leading provider of electronic payment services. Intuit and CheckFree are pleased to offer their mutual users the opportunity to use Quicken to connect directly with the CheckFree payment service. Note that CheckFree is an independently owned company and is not affiliated with Intuit. To use CheckFree, you must sign up with the CheckFree Corporation. For details, see "Before You Start" on page 223.

$ How CheckFree Works

When you use Quicken to pay bills through CheckFree, you start a series of events:

1. You enter an "electronic payment" transaction in Quicken, much as you enter a paper check at the Write Checks screen or register. Your transaction includes a date (called the "scheduled date") on which you want payment to be made.

2. Using your modem and the communications options in Quicken, you transmit your payment instructions to CheckFree well before the scheduled date.

3. Quicken dials the CheckFree Processing Center and transmits your instructions. Your Quicken check register is updated as soon as the electronic transmissions are completed.

4. The CheckFree Processing Center returns a confirmation number, which Quicken stores in the check register with each transaction.

5. The way the CheckFree Processing Center makes the payment depends on the merchant you're paying:

   a. CheckFree prints and mails a paper check on your behalf to the merchant or individual and then receives funds electronically from your bank on the payment date you specified. Your bank statement will list the merchant name, payment amount, and date for this type of transaction, instead of attaching a canceled check as a receipt.

   b. CheckFree mails a laser-printed check drawn on your bank account to the merchant or individual. The check contains information such as your account number and address. If your checks are returned with your bank statement, this laser-printed check from CheckFree will be returned like any other paper check.

   c. If the merchant is set up to receive electronic payments via one of CheckFree's payment networks, CheckFree initiates an electronic payment directly from your bank account to the merchant. Your bank statement will list the merchant name, payment amount, and date for this type of transaction, instead of attaching a canceled check as a receipt.

   Typically, CheckFree mails checks to merchants three or four days before the scheduled date, although your account will never be debited prior to the scheduled payment date. CheckFree makes an electronic payment on the date you schedule.

6. You receive confirmation of the payment both in your bank statement and in the statement you receive from the merchant (if the merchant ordinarily sends statements).

$ About CheckFree

The CheckFree payment service provides convenience and security. It's convenient because you don't need stamps or envelopes and you don't have to print and sign checks. The CheckFree service is secure because each user has a personal account number (also called a "Personal Security Code") and has complete control over access to this number. You enter all data offline and your financial records reside only in your computer. You send only payment instructions to CheckFree.

Many small businesses use CheckFree; however, it is not specifically designed for business use. (For example, it cannot pass invoice numbers through to merchants.) If you are undecided about the relative benefits of paying bills through CheckFree, give it a try. The first month is free.

Allow Extra Time for CheckFree Payments

Using CheckFree does not mean you can pay your bills at the last moment.

Because many of the merchants you pay are not set up to receive CheckFree payments electronically, CheckFree sends the payment through the U.S. mail from Ohio. Remember, the postal service is sometimes slow.

In addition, because CheckFree payments are accompanied by a payment stub that is different from those the merchant is used to receiving, many merchants process CheckFree payments as "exception items" that must be given special handling.

For these reasons, Intuit advises you to pay bills somewhat earlier than you do now, so that (1) your payments do not arrive at the merchant late, and (2) the merchant's processing does not take so long that your payments are credited late.

CheckFree's Service Guarantee

CheckFree guarantees that your payments will be carried out as you direct. By following the guidelines mentioned below, you can minimize the chance that merchants will credit your payments late. If a merchant does credit your payment late, CheckFree guarantees to verify that the payment was issued on time and to provide you with legal proof of the payment delivery date. If you receive notice of late payments as a result of CheckFree or merchant delays, contact CheckFree by using the message feature of Quicken. (See "Sending Electronic Messages to CheckFree" on page 239.)

Guidelines to Avoid Late Payments

- Be sure you enter the correct merchant telephone number, account number, and address in Quicken.

- Starting from the due date, count back one week (five business days) to determine the payment date.

- Starting from the payment date, count back one week (five more business days) to determine the date to transmit the payment to CheckFree.

Date	Definition	Calculated	Example
Due Date	Date merchant receives payment	—	November 16
Payment Date	Date CheckFree sends payment to merchant	Due Date - 5 business days	November 9
Transmission Date	Date you send instructions to CheckFree to pay bill	Due Date - 10 business days	November 2

For example, suppose you have a bill due on Monday, November 16, 1992. These guidelines advise you to transmit the payment two weeks before the due date in this case.

The transmission date is November 2, five business days before the payment date.

November 1992

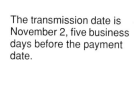

The payment date is November 9, five business days before the due date.

Shaded areas on this calendar are nonbusiness days. If a payment is scheduled or due after a holiday like Thanksgiving, be sure you still allow five business days between the transmission date and the payment date and between the payment date and the due date.

The due date of the bill is November 16.

Run a test to verify payment schedule.

The first time you make a CheckFree payment to a merchant, schedule the payment to occur at least five working days in advance of the due date. Examine the next statement from the merchant to see how promptly they were able to process the payment. Then decide how to schedule your future payments.

$ Before You Start

If You've Never Used CheckFree Before

Check this list before you follow the instructions in this chapter:

☐ You have signed and sent to CheckFree the CheckFree Service Form, along with your voided check. In Quicken, you can use a bank account for electronic payments only if you have authorized CheckFree to use that account by signing this service form and sending the voided check.

☐ CheckFree has processed this form and entered you as a subscriber to the service for a monthly fee. As of the date of this manual, the fee is $9.95, with added charges for more than 20 monthly transactions. Service begins immediately after CheckFree processes your sign-up form. The first month of service is free. See material enclosed in the CheckFree confirmation package for current CheckFree rates and for the terms of your subscription (in the CheckFree Client Agreement).

☐ You have received from CheckFree a confirmation package that contains information you will need when you set up Quicken for electronic payments:
- Your CheckFree Account Number (Personal Security Code)
- The telephone number required for CheckFree transmissions
- The baud rates (modem speeds) that the CheckFree telephone number supports
- Additional information about CheckFree services and rates

☐ You have equipped your computer with a Hayes-compatible modem.

Set it up to use a baud rate specified by CheckFree, and note which port you (or your dealer) attached your modem to. Consult your computer dealer or the modem user manual for help with these tasks. (See "If You Need a Modem" on page 225.)

If You're Currently Using CheckFree Software to Pay Bills

1. **Important**: Use CheckFree software to print the list of merchants you have set up on CheckFree. Then delete every one of the merchants you set up on CheckFree and transmit these deletions to the CheckFree Processing Center.

   If you do not delete these merchants, the CheckFree Processing Center may make errors in processing your payments. Note that any pending payments scheduled for the next few business days are already in process at CheckFree and will *not* be stopped by your deletions. Any payments dated in the future are deleted, so you must reschedule them with Quicken.

2. If necessary, update your Quicken register by importing the historical data in your CheckFree register. You can use Quicken 5 to import transactions (but not merchant names) from CheckFree 3.0. (See "Importing CheckFree Data" on page 506.)

   Important: After you use Quicken 5 even once to make payments, the CheckFree Corporation will no longer permit you to process payments using CheckFree software. The CheckFree software and Quicken 5 are not designed to be used alternately or concurrently. Specifically, you ***cannot*** use Quicken 5 to pay bills and also use the CheckFree software "fixed" merchant payment feature. For recurring bills, use the memorized transactions and transaction groups. (See *Saving Time with Memorized Transactions*, beginning on page 195, and *Entering Transaction Groups*, beginning on page 211.) You'll learn how to record the monthly CheckFree service charge on page 236.

3. The confirmation letter you received from the CheckFree Corporation when you subscribed to the service contains information you used to set up the CheckFree software; you need that information now to set up Quicken for electronic payments:

- Your CheckFree Account Number (Personal Security Code)
- The telephone number required for CheckFree transmissions
- The baud rates that the CheckFree telephone number supports

If you can't find the confirmation letter, copy this information from the CheckFree software setup screens to the appropriate Quicken electronic payment setup screens.

CheckFree categories

If you've used CheckFree categories, you'll notice some differences in the way you handle categories in Quicken:

- The CheckFree merchant list includes category information. With Quicken, the category is associated not with the merchant but with the transaction.

- You handle a recurring payment by memorizing a transaction (with the category information if you choose).

If You've Been Using Quicken 3.0EP or 4.0

You can just continue using Quicken and CheckFree as always. All the information and data you have entered are retained as you begin using Quicken 5.

If You Want to Use Multiple Bank Accounts with CheckFree

If you need to use more than one bank account with CheckFree, contact CheckFree technical support at 614-899-7500 for instructions about how to complete the multiple account sign-up requirements. (You can have as many as five CheckFree bank accounts in a single Quicken file.)

If You Need a Modem

CheckFree sells a modem for $99.00, plus $4.00 shipping. To order a modem, call CheckFree at 800-882-5280. You can also use any Hayes-compatible modem that works at 300, 1200, or 2400 baud (baud is a unit of speed). Most computer dealers carry this type of modem.

 # How Quicken Works with CheckFree

With Quicken, you can send electronic payment instructions directly to CheckFree. When you install Quicken, the electronic payment option is not turned on, but you can turn it on at any time.

After you enable electronic payments in a bank account and set up your modem, you can use Quicken to do any of the following tasks:

- Set up and edit your electronic payee list.
- Write electronic payments.
- Preview your transactions before transmission.
- Transmit your electronic payments.
- Make stop payment requests.
- Inquire about a payment.
- Send electronic mail to CheckFree.

 # Electronic Payment Settings

To turn on the electronic payment capability in Quicken, you need to enter electronic payment settings. This step enables Quicken to set up your modem and access the CheckFree Processing Center. It also causes Quicken to display menu items appropriate for electronic payments.

After you have followed the procedure to turn on electronic payment, you can specify electronic payment for any bank account for which you have a CheckFree account number.

To set or change electronic payment settings:

This procedure assumes you are working with the file you want to use.

1. From the Main Menu:
   a. Choose Set Preferences.
   b. Choose Electronic Payment Settings.
   c. Choose Modem Settings.

Quicken displays the Electronic Payment Settings window.

1200 is the most common modem speed.

```
┌────────────────────────────────────────────────────────┐
│█████████████████████████████████████████████████████████│
│             Electronic Payment Settings                 │
│ ─────────────────────────────────────────────────────── │
│  Serial port used by modem: 1                           │
│         1. COM1              3. COM3                     │
│         2. COM2              4. COM4                     │
│                                                         │
│  Modem speed: 2                                         │
│         1. 300              3. 2400                      │
│         2. 1200             4. 9600                      │
│                                                         │
│  Tone or Pulse Dialing (T/P): T                         │
│                                                         │
│  Telephone number to dial CheckFree Electronic          │
│  Payment Processing Service: 1 000 000 0000             │
│  (Press F1 for additional information)                  │
│                                                         │
│  Turn on Electronic Payment capability (Y/N): Y         │
│ ─────────────────────────────────────────────────────── │
│            F8-Custom Modem Initialization               │
│  Esc-Cancel          F1-Help          ◄─┘ Continue      │
└────────────────────────────────────────────────────────┘
```

Enter the telephone number CheckFree gives you. (This number is an example only.)

2. Enter the number that corresponds to the port to which your modem is attached.

   If you are unsure which port to select, ask your computer dealer which port your modem is attached to, or try COM1 for now. If your modem doesn't respond when you try to transmit, come back to this window and change to other ports until you find the port that works.

3. Enter the number that corresponds to the modem speed (baud rate) required by CheckFree and by your modem.

4. Enter T for a touch-tone (pushbutton) phone or P for a rotary dial phone.

5. Enter the telephone number you received from CheckFree.

   Quicken uses your modem to dial this number exactly as you enter it here. Include any special sequence of digits or characters required (for example, 9 to reach an outside line before you dial the telephone number). Include a comma to indicate a pause, or multiple commas if you need a longer pause between digits.

6. Enter Y in the Turn on Electronic Payment Capability field and press Enter to continue.

7. Stay at the Set Preferences menu and continue with setting up a bank account to use with CheckFree.

Sample telephone number for CheckFree service:

Code to turn off call
waiting (*70)

Digit for a long-distance call (1)

Area code and fictional
telephone number. Your service
number is supplied by
CheckFree for your particular
modem speed and geographic
location.

*70, 1, 800 555 1111

Pauses (commas)

Modem problems?

If you have trouble with a modem that is not completely Hayes-compatible, see
"Customizing Initialization for Your Modem" on page 242.

$ Setting Up a Bank Account for Use with CheckFree

To use a bank account with CheckFree, you can either edit an existing account or set up
a new account. Before you can edit or set up an individual account for electronic
payment, you must have set up Quicken by following the steps in "Electronic Payment
Settings" on page 225.

Note: Only a Quicken bank account can be set up for electronic payment. The bank
account must be the one you specified when you filled out the CheckFree Service Form.

This section provides steps for editing an existing account from the Main Menu. If you
have just completed setting Quicken up for electronic payments, start at step 2. To set up
a new account to use with CheckFree, begin by setting up the account as usual and fill in
information about electronic payments as described starting with step 4 of this procedure.

To set up an existing account for use with electronic payments:

1. From the Main Menu:
   a. Choose Set Preferences.
   b. Choose Electronic Payment Settings.
   c. Choose Account Settings.

   Quicken displays the Set Up Account for Electronic Payment window.

2. Select the bank account and press Enter.

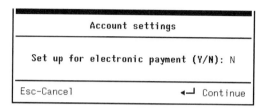

3. Enter Y in the Set Up for Electronic Payment field.

Maximum length 10 characters.

Maximum length 58 characters.

Maximum length 24 characters.

Maximum length 20 characters.

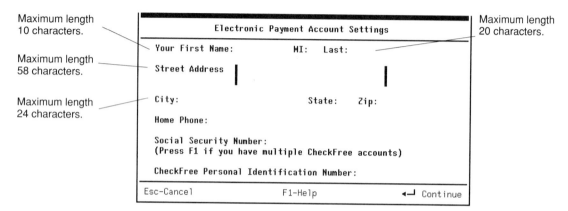

4. Enter your name and address.

Automatic initial capital letter

You don't need to capitalize the first letter; when you press Enter, Quicken automatically capitalizes the first letter in the Name field (and all others) in this window.

If you want the first letter to be lowercase, press Enter to leave the field and then go back and change the first letter to lowercase.

If you don't know the exact state abbreviation, type the first letter of the state to display a list of state abbreviations. Choose the state you want from the list.

Quicken recognizes valid zip codes for your state. If you enter a newly created zip code, you will see the message "Invalid zip for *statename*." Press Ctrl-Z when you see the message, enter the number, press Ctrl-Z again at the message, and Quicken will accept the zip code you entered.

5. (Required) Enter your telephone number, beginning with the area code.

You don't have to type the punctuation characters, such as hyphens or parentheses; Quicken automatically inserts them when you press Enter.

6. Enter your Social Security number (CheckFree System Identification Number) or the alternate identification number sent to you by CheckFree.

   If you have more than one account with CheckFree, the CheckFree Corporation sends you an identifying number based on your Social Security number for each account. Supply the correct identification number here. (See "If You Want to Use Multiple Bank Accounts with CheckFree" on page 224.)

7. In the CheckFree Account Number field, enter the four-digit Personal Security Code given to you by CheckFree.

   In most cases, this number is the one you selected when you sent material to CheckFree as part of the registration process.

   After you type the account number and press Enter, Quicken returns to the Set Up Account for Electronic Payment window. Notice that the account is selected and now has the word "Enabled" in the Electronic Pmts field.

   From now on, when you see a list of accounts, you'll see a small triangle (▲) in the Type field to indicate an account that can be used for electronic payments.

8. Press Esc until you reach the Main Menu.

   You are ready to add payees to the electronic payee list.

$ Adding Payees to Your Electronic Payee List

For Quicken to record an electronic payment, you must first add the payee to the electronic payee list.

You only have to add a payee to the list once; all accounts in the file share the same payees. You can add payees before you begin writing electronic payments or at any time as you write payments. (Quicken transmits changes to the payee list to CheckFree the next time you make payments.)

To add a payee to the electronic payee list:

1. Start at the register or the Write Checks screen.

2. Choose Electronic Payee List from the Shortcuts menu (or press Ctrl-Y).

   Quick Key:
   Press Ctrl-Y at the register to display the electronic payee list.

   (Menu items and control keys for electronic payment work only for accounts set up for electronic payment, so if you don't see Electronic Payee List on the Shortcuts menu, this account has not been set up for electronic payment.)

3. Choose <Set Up a New Payee>.

Quicken displays the Set Up Electronic Payee window.

Maximum length 28 characters.

Enter street number and name on the first line of the address.

Enter apartment or suite number on the second line.

Maximum length 25 characters.

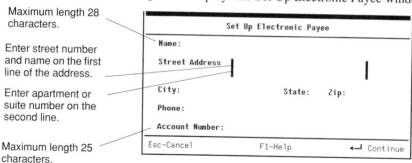

4. Enter the name of the merchant or individual you want to pay.

   If you have multiple customer accounts with the same merchant, you may want to set up that merchant more than once. Quicken allows some extra characters that are not transmitted so you can distinguish the merchants in the merchant list and in reports. See "Duplicate Payees" on page 232.

5. Enter the address of the merchant.

   Important: CheckFree may use this address to mail your payment to the merchant. Take a moment to double-check that you have entered the address completely and accurately.

   If you don't know the exact state abbreviation, enter the first letter of the state. Quicken displays an alphabetized list of state abbreviations. The first state abbreviation that begins with the letter you typed is selected. Press Enter to select that state or use the arrow keys to select the correct name and then press Enter.

   Quicken recognizes valid zip codes for your state. If you enter a newly created zip code, you will see the message "Invalid zip for statename." Press Ctrl-Z when you see the message, enter the number, press Ctrl-Z again at the message, and Quicken will accept the zip code you entered.

6. Enter the merchant's phone number (that is, the phone number you usually call if you have a billing question), beginning with the area code.

   You don't have to enter the punctuation characters (parentheses or hyphens); Quicken automatically inserts them when you press Enter.

   Important: CheckFree uses this number for cross-reference and may need it to contact the merchant for you in case of problems. *An incorrect telephone number may cause payment processing errors*, so take a moment to double-check it.

7. Enter the number this merchant uses to identify you in the Account Number field.

   (Look on the merchant's bill for an account number, a policy number, a loan number, or some similar number.) If the merchant does not use a number, or you don't know it, enter your last name.

   The merchant uses this number to process your payments. Without the number, the merchant may be delayed in crediting your account for the payment. *An incorrect account number may cause payment processing errors*, so take a moment to double-check it. (You can enter up to 25 characters in this field.)

8. Press Enter to record the merchant information. You can add additional merchants or go on to writing electronic payments.

Storing category information

If you have used CheckFree software, you may wonder where to store category, memo, and split transaction information associated with a merchant. With Quicken, you keep this information as part of a memorized transaction.

$ Editing or Deleting a Payee

You can edit or delete a payee as long as you do not have an untransmitted or pending (transmitted but not yet paid) payment for that payee.

If all your payments to this payee have been transmitted and paid:

To edit payee information, select the name in the electronic payee list and press Ctrl-E.

To delete payee information, select the name in the electronic payee list and press Ctrl-D.

If you have outstanding payments to this payee:

If you have either untransmitted or pending payments to this payee, exercise caution before editing or deleting the payee. In both cases, Quicken waits to transmit a payee edit or deletion until CheckFree has processed all untransmitted payments to that payee.

You can edit the payee in the standard way (Ctrl-E) if you have untransmitted payments, but not if you have pending payments (payments that are transmitted but not paid) for that payee. In that case, see "Special technique to edit information for a payee having both untransmitted and pending payments:" on page 232. (Quicken transmits a payee edit the next time you transmit a payment.)

You cannot delete a payee if you have either untransmitted or pending payments for that payee. Use this table to determine whether you can currently edit or delete a payee.

	With payments to a payee:	
	Untransmitted	**Pending (transmitted but not paid)**
Can you edit the payee?	Yes	No
Can you delete the payee?	No	No

Special technique to edit information for a payee having both untransmitted and pending payments:

1. Set up a new payee with correct information.

2. Select an untransmitted payment in the check register and choose the new payee name from the electronic payee list. (Repeat if there are multiple untransmitted payments to this payee.)

   You cannot change the payee for the pending (transmitted but not paid) payments.

3. Quicken transmits the payee changes the next time you transmit a payment. (See "Transmitting Electronic Transactions" on page 237.)

4. After CheckFree pays the pending transaction, you can delete the incorrect payee from the electronic payee list.

Duplicate Payees

If you have two accounts with the same merchant, you may want to set up that merchant more than once. For example, suppose you and your spouse each have your own account at a local department store.

You can set up multiple payees with the same name, but Quicken will ask you to add extra characters to the name to make the name unique. (Quicken does not transmit the extra characters to the CheckFree Processing Center.) These extra characters help you distinguish the two accounts in reports and when you see the merchant list. Here's how the electronic payee list looks with two entries for the same department store.

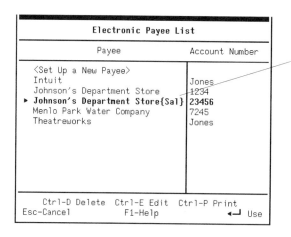

The characters within the braces are not transmitted to CheckFree. They help you distinguish the two accounts.

You can edit an existing payee to add characters in braces at the end. In this example, the Jones family could add {Jim} to the first entry for Johnson's Department Store. If they had thought ahead, they could have added the extra characters in braces when they set up the first entry.

Note: If you change an electronic transaction to a paper check transaction and then print checks, Quicken will not print the characters after the first brace or the brace itself. You might find this feature useful for paper checks as well as for electronic payments.

Writing Electronic Checks

Writing an electronic check is very similar to writing a paper check.

To write an electronic check:

1. Choose Write/Print Checks from the Main Menu.

2. Press F9 to display the screen in electronic payment format.

(Note that the Payment Date and Pay To fields work a little differently than they do when you write a paper check. See steps 3 and 4 for specific information.)

Quicken automatically postdates five working days.

Enter a payee name or choose it from the electronic payee list.

When you have electronic payment set up for an account, and press F9 to make an electronic payment, Quicken clearly labels the window.

F9 toggles back and forth between electronic payment and paper check.

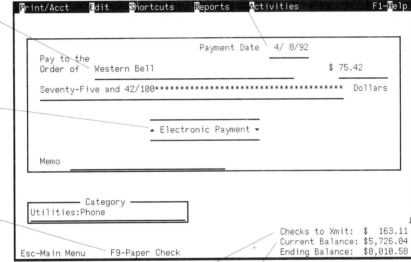

Checks to Xmit tracks the total amount of electronic payments you have written and have yet to transmit.

The Current Balance does not include postdated transactions; the Ending Balance does. (By default, all electronic payments are postdated.)

3. At the Payment Date field, Quicken automatically postdates the check by five days.

4. At the Pay To field, enter the payee name.

If you type the name of a payee who is not in the list, Quicken displays screens so you can select from the electronic payee list or set up the payee.

You can enter just enough letters to uniquely identify a merchant. Quicken fills in the rest of the name when you leave the field.

If the letters you've typed do not identify just one payee in the electronic payee list, Quicken displays screens so you can select from the electronic payee list or set up the payee.

If you have memorized an electronic transaction, you can recall it. Type enough letters of the payee name to identify the payee and press Ctrl-E to recall a payee without displaying a list. You can also use Ctrl-T in the usual way to recall a memorized transaction.

CheckFree will not process a payment that appears to be a duplicate of a previous payment. (It will not process a second payment that has the same information for all of these fields: Merchant, Amount, and Date.)

5. Fill in the $ amount, Memo, and Category fields as usual. (The Memo field is not passed through on CheckFree payments.)

6. Press Ctrl-Enter to record the payment.

    Quicken records the payment and displays an empty check so you can write another if you want. Note that Quicken does not transmit the payment until you tell Quicken to transmit (see "Transmitting Electronic Transactions" on page 237).

Memorizing and Recalling Electronic Payments

You can memorize a recurring electronic payment just as you memorize a paper check. For example, you may want to memorize a payment to a particular merchant with category, memo, and split information.

If you memorize a transaction in the check register, Quicken memorizes it as an electronic payment if the Num field contains the electronic payment symbol >>>>> or the abbreviation E-PMT.

If you have memorized an electronic transaction, choose Recall Transaction (Ctrl-T) from the Shortcuts menu to recall it in the usual way. (See "Saving Time with Memorized Transactions" on page 195.) To recall multiple memorized electronic payments, set up transaction groups. (See "Entering Transaction Groups" on page 211.)

Recalling a payee

If you type Ctrl-E instead of Ctrl-T, Quicken checks to see if the characters you've typed match only one payee in the memorized list. If so, Quicken recalls the payee directly, without displaying the list. If several items match, the list is displayed as usual.

When you recall a memorized electronic payment, Quicken postdates it five business days. Similarly, when you recall a transaction group containing electronic payments, Quicken postdates the electronic payments five business days. It recalls any regular transactions in the group with the current or specified date.

If you recall a memorized electronic payment in the check register or recall it in the Write Checks screen and review it later in the check register, you'll see the electronic payment symbol >>>>> or the abbreviation E-PMT in the Num field.

Postdating transactions for recurring payments

A good way to handle recurring payments is to postdate them. You can postdate and transmit up to 12 transactions per merchant, so you can schedule a full year of payments.

To prevent unauthorized entry to a file set up for electronic payment, use a Quicken file password. See "Setting Up the File Password" on page 439.

 # The Register

The register lists electronic payments just as it lists paper checks. For electronic payments, the Num field distinguishes untransmitted electronic payments with greater-than signs (>>>>>) and transmitted electronic payments with the abbreviation E-PMT (for "electronic payment").

E-PMT marks a transmitted electronic payment.

The double line appears before postdated items.

The >>>>> indicate that the electronic payment has not been transmitted.

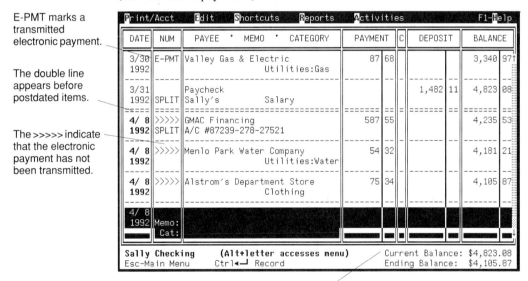

The Current Balance appears only when the register contains postdated items.

Adding Electronic Payments to the Register

To enter payments to be paid electronically in the check register:

1. Start at the last (empty) item in the register.

2. Check the date and change it if necessary to schedule the payment.

3. Enter a single greater-than sign (>) in the Num field to indicate an untransmitted electronic payment and press Enter.

    As soon as you enter one greater-than sign, Quicken fills in the rest of the Num field. When you press Enter, Quicken advances the date, if necessary, so the transaction is dated five working days ahead.

    If the single greater-than sign does not expand to five when you enter it in the Num field, and the greater-than sign in the Num field disappears when you save the transaction, you need to turn on electronic payments for this account. You cannot enter electronic payments if the electronic payment option is not turned on. (See "Setting Up a Bank Account for Use with CheckFree" on page 227.)

    > **Recalling a memorized transaction**
    >
    > You can recall a memorized transaction after step 3, instead of filling in fields. Press Ctrl-T or Ctrl-E. Or, if you memorized the transaction as an electronic payment at the Write Checks screen, you don't even have to enter >. Just start at the last (empty) item and recall the transaction.

4. If you are entering a new payee, type the name of the payee and press Enter.

    If the payee is already in the list, you can press Ctrl-Y to select the payee from the list. For a payee not in the list, the Electronic Payee Not Found window appears. Add the new payee in the usual way.

5. Fill in the rest of the screen as usual.

6. Press Ctrl-Enter to record the payment.

Handling the CheckFree Service Charge

You pay a monthly service charge to use CheckFree, which the CheckFree Corporation automatically charges to your bank account. You will see this charge on your bank statement.

To keep your Quicken register up to date for this charge, add the CheckFree charge to the Service Charge field on the Quicken Reconcile Register window.

Alternately, enter the fee as a transaction at the check register, memorize the transaction, and add it to a monthly transaction group. Execute the transaction group each month. (If you have installed Billminder, it will remind you when a transaction group is due.) Then you can adjust the amount if necessary when you reconcile your check register against your bank statement. (See "Stage 1. Starting Reconciliation" on page 121.)

Transmitting Electronic Transactions

The transactions you transmit to CheckFree can include payments, additions, or changes to the electronic payee list, stop payment orders, and inquiries or messages to the CheckFree Processing Center. You can view a summary of payment and payment-related transactions before you transmit them.

To preview and transmit transactions:

1. Start at the Write Checks screen or the register.

2. Choose Transmit Payments from the Print/Acct menu. (Or press Ctrl-I.)

   Quicken tells you how many payments are ready to be transmitted.

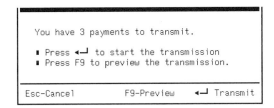

```
You have 3 payments to transmit.

■ Press ◄─┘ to start the transmission
■ Press F9 to preview the transmission.

Esc-Cancel          F9-Preview      ◄─┘ Transmit
```

3. Press F9 to preview the transmission.

All electronic payments are indicated by the abbreviation "Pmt." Quicken places them at the top of the screen in the payment date order.

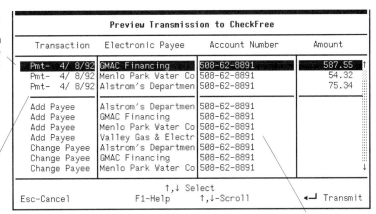

```
Preview Transmission to CheckFree

  Transaction    Electronic Payee    Account Number     Amount

  Pmt-  4/ 8/92 GMAC Financing      508-62-8891          587.55
  Pmt-  4/ 8/92 Menlo Park Water Co 508-62-8891           54.32
  Pmt-  4/ 8/92 Alstrom's Departmen 508-62-8891           75.34

  Add Payee      Alstrom's Departmen 508-62-8891
  Add Payee      GMAC Financing      508-62-8891
  Add Payee      Menlo Park Water Co 508-62-8891
  Add Payee      Valley Gas & Electr 508-62-8891
  Change Payee   Alstrom's Departmen 508-62-8891
  Change Payee   GMAC Financing      508-62-8891
  Change Payee   Menlo Park Water Co 508-62-8891

                     ↑,↓ Select
  Esc-Cancel         F1-Help    ↑,↓-Scroll      ◄─┘ Transmit
```

Quicken separates electronic payments from updates to the electronic payee list with a line.

Quicken transmits payee additions the first time you use them. See page 231 for when deletions are transmitted.

Updates to the electronic payee list appear below the separation line and include the type of transaction, the name of the merchant, and the account number.

4. Make any necessary changes.

   To modify transactions, press Esc twice to return to the register or the Write Checks screen, where you can make any needed changes.

5. Quicken transmits payee additions the first time you use them. Quicken transmits updates to the payee list along with the payments you send; you cannot modify updates in the preview list.

6. When the transactions are correct, press Enter to transmit.

   Quicken initializes the modem and dials the CheckFree Processing Center. As it transmits, Quicken displays messages indicating progress. If you see an error message, try the procedure again and press F1 for Help if the error occurs again.

Note: If you see "Payee not set up" in the Account Number field, you must add the payee to the electronic payee list before transmitting the transaction. Record the transaction again and set up the payee; then transmit again.

How to Get a Confirmation Number

CheckFree sends a confirmation number back to Quicken for each transmission. Quicken stores this confirmation number and automatically uses it if you send an inquiry or a stop payment request regarding the transaction. To see this number, select the transaction in the check register and choose Electronic Payment Inquiry from the Edit menu. You'll see the payment date of the transaction, its transmission status, the merchant account number, and the confirmation number.

Important: Don't void an electronic payment. If you delete or void an electronic payment, Quicken cannot get the confirmation number needed to stop the payment or transmit a status inquiry to CheckFree. Use the Stop Payment Request window instead.

$ Stopping Electronic Payments

After Quicken transmits an electronic payment, you can stop payment on it if you don't wait too long. On the basis of the five days it can take CheckFree to make a scheduled payment, Quicken determines whether you are likely to be able to stop the payment and tells you if it's clearly too late.

CheckFree sends a letter by U.S. mail reporting their action on your stop payment request.

To stop a payment:

1. Select the transaction in the register.

2. Choose Transmit Stop Payment Request from the Edit menu.

   Quicken tells you when the payment is scheduled to be made. If it is possible to stop payment, Quicken asks if you want to do so. If it's too late to stop the payment or the payment has not yet been transmitted, Quicken will let you know.

3. Enter Y if it's still possible to stop the payment.

   Quicken's communication software immediately sends your request to CheckFree. Messages inform you of the progress of the transmission. If the transmission is successful, Quicken marks the payment VOID in the register and records the stop payment confirmation number received from CheckFree. To see the confirmation number, select the transaction in the check register and choose Electronic Payment Inquiry from the Edit menu.

   Important: Timing is critical: Quicken determines whether you can still stop a payment, taking into account the usual five days between the transmission date and the payment date. The CheckFree Corporation does not assess a charge for stop payments performed in this manner. If Quicken tells you that it is too late to stop the payment, you can contact CheckFree by telephone and request a stop payment. CheckFree does assess an additional fee for payments that must be stopped by manual intervention. See the "How to Get the Most from CheckFree" booklet enclosed in the CheckFree confirmation package for details.

Sending Electronic Messages to CheckFree

You can send electronic messages directly to CheckFree by making payment inquiries or by sending electronic mail. If you want to speak with a customer service representative, see the telephone numbers in "Calling CheckFree Customer Service" on page 243.

Making Electronic Payment Inquiries

Remember that CheckFree knows nothing about a payment until you transmit it, so you cannot send a payment inquiry about an untransmitted payment. To get information about an untransmitted payment, you can view it in the check register or preview it as part of the transmission procedure.

To inquire about electronic payments:

1. At the register, select the payment transaction. You can use Find on the Edit menu (Ctrl-F) to locate the transaction.

2. Choose Electronic Payment Inquiry from the Edit menu.

   Quicken displays the Payment Information screen, which shows the account number, the payment date, the date the transaction was transmitted, and the confirmation number. Quicken also determines whether you can still stop this payment, taking into account the usual five days between the transmission date and the payment date.

   Quicken asks if you want to transmit an electronic message to CheckFree regarding this transaction.

3. Check to make sure this transaction is the one you want to inquire about. If it is, enter Y to send an inquiry.

   Quicken displays the Transmit Inquiry to CheckFree window.

4. Fill in the fields. After the date, the reference to the merchant, and the salutation, you can type three lines of text. Quicken supplies the signature line.

5. Press Ctrl-Enter to send the inquiry to CheckFree.

Sending Electronic Mail

You can send CheckFree a message that is not specific to a payment. CheckFree sends a postcard to acknowledge your message.

To send a message:

1. Choose Send Electronic Mail from the Activities menu (or press F6).

   Quicken displays the Transmit Inquiry to CheckFree window, but this time the window contains only the date, the salutation, and the signature line.

2. Type your message in the text area, and then press Ctrl-Enter to transmit the message.

$ CheckFree Troubleshooting

If you have trouble transmitting to CheckFree, try the troubleshooting steps in this section one by one. After each step, try transmitting until you transmit successfully. If you're still unsuccessful, see "Calling CheckFree Customer Service" on page 243.

1. Wait a minute or two and try transmitting again.

   The CheckFree system may simply have been busy when you first tried to transmit.

2. Check that all fields are filled in correctly at the Quicken Electronic Payment Settings window. (To reach that window from the Main Menu, select Set Preferences, then Electronic Payment, then Modem Settings.) Check each field to verify that the information is correct.

3. Check all connections at both ends (modular phone plugs, RS-232-C cable, power cords) to be sure they are securely plugged in and the power is on.

4. Check the modem switch settings, if any. Your modem manual describes the function of each switch. With the modem turned off, set the switches:
   - To originate a call (not to answer)
   - To respond to DTR ("data terminal ready")
   - To recognize commands

5. Dial the phone yourself to be sure that you're getting a dial tone and that when you dial the access number, the CheckFree Processing Center answers with a high-pitched tone.

    a. When you dial yourself, do you have to wait to get an outside line or do you have to add extra digits?

    b. Write down the sequence of digits, characters, and pauses you dialed. An example of a character is an asterisk (*), which many phone systems use as a signal for a special phone feature.

    c. Translate what you've written down into the sequence of numbers, commas, and characters you need to enter in the "Telephone number to dial" field at the Electronic Payment Settings window or the Custom Modem Initialization window. (Use a comma for each pause, or several commas for longer pauses. For example, if you need to dial 9 to get an outside line and then need to wait a second to hear a dial tone, enter 9, in this field.)

6. You may need to include a longer sequence of commands for Quicken to send to the modem before dialing the access number. (See "Customizing Initialization for Your Modem" on page 242.)

7. Try changing the settings at the Electronic Payment Settings window:

    a. Change the serial port from its current setting, typically COM1, to COM2, to see if you've been using the wrong port. Try this step only if you are getting no response at all from your modem.

    b. Change the setting for modem speed and check that the access number is correct for the modem speed. If possible, change to a slower speed.

    c. At the Electronic Payment Settings window, change the setting for tone or pulse dialing. Enter T (touch-tone) if you have a pushbutton phone; enter P (pulse) if you have a rotary phone. (In Alaska, you may need to use P even if you have a pushbutton phone.) If your phone has a switch to select between tone and pulse dialing mode, make sure the switch is set correctly.

8. Ask your computer dealer if your serial port is wired DCE. If it is, you may need a "null modem" cable. Don't be confused by the term "null modem"; all the cable does is switch the connections of two wires.

9. Ask your dealer if your serial card or your modem has nonstandard connectors. If either is nonstandard, get help installing a cable with appropriate connectors.

10. If your computer can be run at a slower speed, try setting it to the slowest speed.

11. Remove any memory-resident programs.

12. Disable the mouse driver.

13. If your modem appears to be operating correctly, but the CheckFree Processing Center does not respond, call CheckFree customer service.

Customizing Initialization for Your Modem

You can customize Quicken to handle special requirements of your modem each time you transmit to CheckFree. You might need this feature to switch your modem to Hayes-compatible mode. Quicken sends these codes to the modem only; do not use the Custom Modem Initialization window to send codes to your phone system.

To handle these special requirements, you need codes that are specific to your modem. To find out what codes you need, *look in the user's manual for your modem*. (Most modem commands must begin with the prefix AT.)

To customize initialization:

1. Starting at the Main Menu:

    a. Choose Set Preferences.

    b. Choose Electronic Payment Settings.

    c. Choose Modem Settings.

    Quicken displays the Electronic Payment Settings window.

2. Press F8 to display the Custom Modem Initialization window.

3. In the Codes field, enter the special letters, digits, and other characters to be sent to the modem.

Enter the correct codes for your modem. (These codes are only an example.)

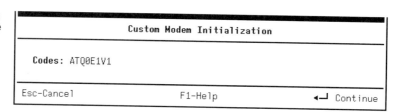

```
┌─────────────────────────────────────────────────────┐
│▐▬▬▬▬▬▬▬▬▬▬▬▬▬▬▬▬▬▬▬▬▬▬▬▬▬▬▬▬▬▬▬▬▬▬▬▬▬▬▬▬▬▬▬▬▐│
│             Custom Modem Initialization               │
├─────────────────────────────────────────────────────┤
│                                                       │
│    Codes: ATQ0E1V1                                    │
│                                                       │
├─────────────────────────────────────────────────────┤
│  Esc-Cancel            F1-Help           ◄┘ Continue  │
└─────────────────────────────────────────────────────┘
```

4. Press Enter.

    When Quicken initializes your modem just before transmission, it will send these characters to your modem exactly as you typed them, adding the keystroke for Enter at the end.

5. Press Ctrl-Enter.

    You will see the Electronic Payment Settings window. You can press Esc repeatedly to return to the Main Menu, or choose Account Settings to set up an existing account for electronic payment.

    If you continue to have trouble, call CheckFree customer service.

$ Calling CheckFree Customer Service

Important: The CheckFree service is a product of the CheckFree Corporation, not of Intuit, so only CheckFree can help you with questions about service, your payments, or any CheckFree charges. CheckFree's technical staff is also trained to help with problems with your modem, phone lines, and other communications puzzles.

If you need help with CheckFree service, payments, or communications:

- Use Quicken's message feature (see "Sending Electronic Messages to CheckFree" on page 239), or access CheckFree customer service through CompuServe EasyPlex (mailbox 72537, 2156) or MCI Mail (checkfree).

Call CheckFree at 614-899-7500 from 8:00 a.m. to 8:00 p.m. Eastern time (as of this printing). Do not call Intuit with these questions; we have no control or knowledge in these areas.

Chapter 14

Working with Multiple Accounts

This chapter tells you how to set up new Quicken accounts, and how to choose an account when you want to work with it.

You can create six different types of Quicken accounts:

- Bank accounts (for checking and savings)
- Cash accounts (to keep track of cash expenditures)
- Credit card accounts
- Asset accounts
- Liability accounts
- Investment accounts

Although you use these different types of accounts to track different parts of your financial picture, you follow the same basic steps to create and use any of these accounts.

$ Setting Up and Using Additional Quicken Accounts

With Quicken, you can set up as many different accounts as you want: up to 255 in the same file.

Whatever type of account you want to set up, the steps are basically the same. You fill in the Set Up New Account window.

Note: Quicken places the new account in the current file. In most cases, you create all your accounts in the same file so that you can produce reports based on transactions from all of them. However, in some cases you might want separate files. If you have more than one file, be sure to choose the one you want before setting up the new account. For more information, see *Managing Files*, beginning on page 449.

Basic steps to set up a new account:

1. Press Ctrl-A, or choose Select Account from the Main Menu (or choose Select/Set Up Account from the Print/Acct pulldown menu).

2. In the Select Account to Use list, select <New Account> and press Enter.

3. Fill in the Set Up New Account window to tell Quicken about the new account.

Enter the number for the type of account you're creating.

Enter the name you want to give the account here.

Enter the balance for the account. Quicken uses this amount as the opening balance in the register.

Enter a description (optional).

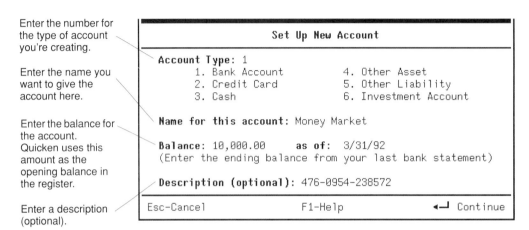

```
                        Set Up New Account

Account Type: 1
      1. Bank Account         4. Other Asset
      2. Credit Card          5. Other Liability
      3. Cash                 6. Investment Account

Name for this account: Money Market

Balance: 10,000.00      as of:  3/31/92
(Enter the ending balance from your last bank statement)

Description (optional): 476-0954-238572

Esc-Cancel              F1-Help              ◄┘ Continue
```

If you set up a credit card account, Quicken displays the Specify Credit Limit window so you can enter your credit limit for the card.

Note: Quicken adds the account name to the Select Account to Use list. In addition, Quicken adds the new account name to the category list. Because the account names are on the category list, you can transfer money from one account to another by typing an account name in the Category field of a transaction. For more information, see "How Transfers Work" on page 252.

Fields in the Set Up New Account Window

Account Type Enter the number that matches the type of account you are setting up:

1. Bank Account — Set up a bank account to keep track of transactions in checking, savings, or money market accounts.

2. Credit Card — Set up a credit card account to keep track of credit card transactions. (See *Tracking Credit Cards*, beginning on page 323.)

3. Cash — Set up a cash account to keep track of cash expenditures or petty cash. (See *Tracking Cash*, beginning on page 333.)

4. Other Asset — Set up an asset account to keep track of things you own, such as your house, capital equipment, or accounts receivable. (See *Tracking Assets and Liabilities*, beginning on page 257.)

5. Other Liability — Set up a liability account to keep track of what you owe, such as mortgages or bank loans. (See *Tracking Assets and Liabilities*, beginning on page 257.)

6. Investment Account — Set up an investment account to track investments such as stocks, bonds, CDs, and mutual funds. (See *Getting Started with Investment Accounts*, beginning on page 265**.**)

Name for This Account — Enter a name for the account. You can use your own name, your bank name, or a descriptive name such as "Checking1," "Visa," or "mortgage."

The name can be up to 15 characters long and can include letters, numbers, spaces, and other characters (except], /, [, : that is, no brackets, slashes, or colons).

Note: Quicken will not accept an account name that is the same as a category name.

Balance — Quicken inserts this amount in the opening balance transaction for this account.

For bank accounts, enter the ending balance and ending date from your last bank statement.

For credit card accounts, use the balance due from your last credit card statement less the payments you made on that statement.

For asset accounts, use the current value of the asset.

For liability accounts, use the current amount owed on the loan; that is, the principal plus all accrued but unpaid interest.

For investment accounts, Quicken does not ask you to enter a balance here. See "Steps for Setting Up an Investment Account" on page 273.

As Of — Quicken inserts today's date. Change it to the ending statement date.

Description *(Optional)* — If you want to record more information about the account than will fit in the Account Name field, enter that information in the Description field.

The description can be up to 21 characters long. For a bank account, you could enter the name of the bank or the account number. For a credit card account, you could enter the credit card number.

Enter Credit Limit *(Optional)* — If you are setting up a credit card account, the Enter Credit Limit field appears in the Specify Credit Limit window. Enter the amount of your credit limit for this credit card. When you enter your credit card limit in this field, you'll see the amount of available credit at the bottom of the credit card account register.

Opening a savings account?

Use Quicken bank accounts for savings, checking, and money market accounts. To set up a savings account, follow the "Basic steps to set up a new account:" on page 246. Enter 1 (for Bank Account) in the Account Type field. For examples of savings account transactions, see "Basic steps to transfer money as you enter a transaction:" on page 254.

Selecting an Account to Use

Quicken maintains a list of all Quicken accounts in the file you're currently using. When you want to use another account, select it from the list (or use its Quick Key).

The triangle indicates a bank account set up for electronic payment.

Use Quick Keys for fast access to another account.

Accounts are arranged by type. For instance, bank accounts are listed first, then credit card accounts.

Press PgDn or PgUp to see more accounts.

```
                            Select Account to Use

                  Current File: DMURPHY in C:\QUICKEN5\
                 Quick                                Num    Ending    Pmts
          Account  Key  Type       Description       Trans  Balance    Due

  ► <New Account>                Set up a new account
    Joint Account   1  Bank▲  Joint FIB                46    8,010.58  *▲
    Sally Checking  2  Bank▲  Sally's FIB              39    4,105.87   ▲
    Steve Checking  3  Bank   Steve's FIB              37    3,405.17  *
    AMX             4  CCard  American Express         15       65.47
    House           5  Oth A  Family House              2  153,775.17
    Sally's 401(k)  6  Oth A  Sally's 401(k)            2    5,678.16
    Mortgage        7  Oth L  Mortgage Due              3  132,766.62
    Criterion Fund     Invst                            3    3,447.00
    Sally's IRA     8  Invst  Yotzvitsky Brokerage      7 ≈ 12,944.81
    Steve's IRA     9  Invst  Assorted mutual funds     6 ≈ 13,941.39  ↓

            Ctrl-D Delete   Ctrl-E Edit   ↑,↓ Select
   Esc-Cancel                      F1-Help                     ←┘ Use
```

An asterisk means you have checks to print; a triangle means you have electronic payments to

Quicken shows the balance at the end of the register, except for investment accounts, for which it shows the market value.

Within each type, accounts are listed alphabetically by account name.

The symbol ≈ appearing before an investment account alerts you that Quicken needs to recalculate the market value.

The Select Account to Use window includes detailed information about your Quicken accounts. The list in the window shows:

- Name of the account
- Quick Key you can use to go to this account by pressing Ctrl-Quick Key
- Type of the account (such as bank, credit card, or investment)
- Description
- Number of transactions in the account
- Ending balance
- Payments due (an asterisk (*) means this account has checks to print; a small triangle (▲) means this account has electronic payments to transmit)

What does the ≈ symbol mean?

For investment accounts, the amount in the balance column is the market value of the account. The amount may have the symbol ≈ next to it. This symbol alerts you that a price change in an investment register or the Update Prices screen could affect the market value of this account, but Quicken has not yet had an opportunity to recalculate the market value. After you choose the account with the alert symbol, Quicken recalculates the market value and removes the symbol.

To use another Quicken account:

1. Press Ctrl-A, or choose Select Account from the Main Menu (or Select/Set Up Account from the Print/Acct pulldown menu).

   Quicken displays the Select Account to Use list.

2. Use the arrow keys to select the account you want to use and press Enter.

   Quicken displays the register for that account on your screen.

Use Quick Keys for fast account access

To change from one account to another quickly, use the Quick Keys listed in the Select Account to Use window.

To use the keys to change accounts, press Ctrl-*<number>*. For example, if you assign Quick Key number 1 to your bank account, you can press Ctrl-1 from any screen to go to your bank account register.

$ Changing Account Characteristics

After you set up an account, you can change the account characteristics:

- The name of an account
- Its description
- Its Quick Key assignment
- The line on the tax schedule related to this account
- The credit limit for credit card accounts

If you rename a Quicken account, Quicken automatically updates any transactions linked to this account through transfers to show the new name. (For more information about account transfers, see *Transferring Money Between Accounts*, beginning on page 251.)

To edit Quicken account characteristics:

1. Choose Select/Set Up Account from the Print/Acct menu (or press Ctrl-A) to display the list of accounts.

2. Use the arrow keys to select the account you want to edit and then press Ctrl-E.

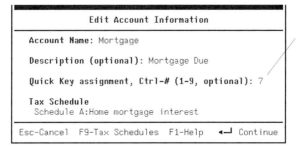

Enter a number from 1 - 9 to assign a Quick Key to this account.

To remove a Quick Key, enter 0.

3. (Optional.) Enter a new name for the account. (Enter the new name over the old name, up to 15 characters.)

4. (Optional.) Enter a description or change the existing one, up to 21 characters.

5. (Optional.) Assign a new Quick Key number by entering a number from 1-9. To remove a Quick Key assignment, enter 0.

6. (Optional.) Press F9 to display the preset tax schedule list and the tax line list. Assign a tax schedule and tax line name to accounts you plan to use for transfers that affect taxes. (See "Assigning Account Transfers to Tax Forms" on page 420.)

7. Press Enter to record the new information.

8. If you chose a credit card account, Quicken displays the Modify Credit Limit window, where you can enter or change the credit limit for this account. To change the credit limit, enter the new amount over the one shown and press Enter.

Deleting Quicken Accounts

Deleting a Quicken account permanently removes all of that account's records from your disk. Once an account is deleted, there is no way to get it back, so be certain you want to delete an account before doing so.

Note: If you have used the account name in the Category field of transactions that transfer money to that account, Quicken replaces the account name with a blank.

To delete a Quicken account:

1. Choose Select/Set Up Account from the Print/Acct menu (or press Ctrl-A).

2. Select the account you want to delete and press Ctrl-D (for delete).

    A message warns that you are about to remove this account from your records permanently.

3. If you are certain you want to delete the account, enter Yes.

    Quicken removes the account from your records.

Deleting an account does not reduce the size of your file. For information about how to create a more compact file, see "Copying a Quicken File" on page 462.

Chapter 15

Transferring Money Between Accounts

A file containing several different accounts allows you to work with each account individually, and also to make transfers between your different accounts.

For example, if you write a check to place money in your savings account, you can have Quicken automatically record it as a deposit in your savings account; you don't need to enter a separate transaction in the savings register.

Savings Account

Credit Card Accounts

Checking or Savings Accounts

Cash Account

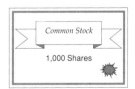

Common Stock

1,000 Shares

Investment Accounts

This chapter explains how to transfer money from one Quicken account to another. When you use more than one Quicken account, you'll find this feature saves you time and helps ensure that transactions affecting multiple accounts are recorded accurately.

You can use account transfers for many types of transactions:

- To record a transfer from checking to savings
- To record a cash advance from your credit card account to your checking account
- To record a loan payment in a liability account tracking your loan balance

In the "from" account (source account), the transaction amount appears in the Payment field; in the "to" account (destination account), the transaction appears in the Deposit field.

For examples of transactions that include transfers, see Chapters 14, 19, and 20, and the chapters in Section E, *Applying Quicken to Your Needs*, beginning on page 341.

> **Why can't I categorize a transfer?**
>
> When you use a transfer, you cannot apply a category or subcategory to the transaction. The transfer account name replaces category information. (Categories track income and expenses, but transfers are neither. Rather, transfers show the movement of funds.)
>
> Transfers appear together on reports, usually near the bottom. If you want all transactions to have Income and Expense categories, do not use the transfer feature. Instead, enter separate transactions in the source and destination accounts.

$ How Transfers Work

It's easy to transfer money from one Quicken account to another. Just enter the name of the account in the Category field when you enter a transaction. When you record the transaction in the source account, Quicken creates a parallel transaction in the destination account. In Quicken, these transactions are linked:

- If you delete one transaction, you delete both; if you change an amount in one transaction, you change that amount in both.

- If the source transaction is a payment or decrease, the destination transaction is a deposit or increase. For example, if you write a check to your savings account and enter the name of the savings account in the Category field, Quicken records a deposit in the savings account for the same amount.

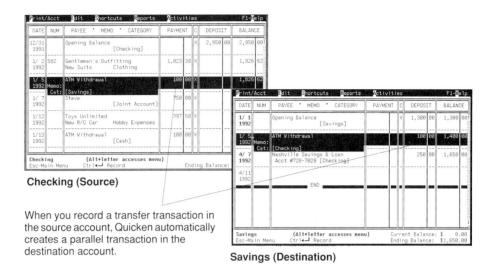

Checking (Source)

When you record a transfer transaction in the source account, Quicken automatically creates a parallel transaction in the destination account.

Savings (Destination)

When you set up a new account, Quicken adds its name to the end of the list of accounts in the Select Account to Use window. In addition, Quicken adds the name to the category and transfer list, so you can select the account for transfers.

When you want to enter a transfer in a transaction, select the account name from the category and transfer list.

Account names are enclosed in brackets.

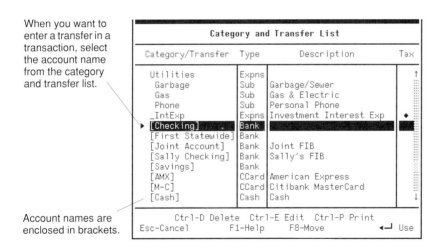

Basic Steps to Transfer Money Between Quicken Accounts

Basic steps to transfer money as you enter a transaction:

1. With the transaction selected in the register (or the check displayed at the Write Checks screen), move the cursor to the Category field.

2. Enter the name of the account to which you want the money to be transferred (or press Ctrl-C to open the category and transfer list and choose the account name from the list).

> **To reach the account name quickly**
>
> In the Category field, enter a left bracket ([ ) and one or more letters of the account name, then press Ctrl-C. The first account that begins with these letters will automatically be highlighted.

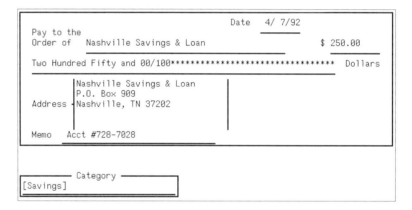

3. When you've finished entering the information about the check, press Ctrl-Enter as usual to record the check.

    Brackets appear around the account name. Quicken always inserts brackets around the account name in transfers. (You don't have to enter them.)

    Note: If Quicken doesn't find the account name in the category and transfer list, the Category Not Found window appears. Because you are typing the name in the Category field, Quicken cannot distinguish it from a category name unless it already exists as an account name. If this happens, enter 2 to select the name from the category and transfer list. The account must already be set up in order to transfer money to it. If you want to set up a new account, select Select/Set Up Account from the Print/Acct menu; then select <New Account> and create the account.

Quicken records the check in your check register *and* creates a parallel transaction in the other account for that amount. Here are two registers showing the transactions that include a transfer:

The account name appears here in the original transaction in the checking account.

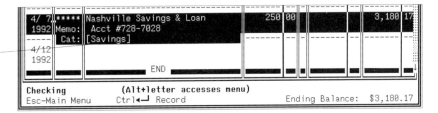

Here's the transaction that was recorded in the savings account as a result of the transfer.

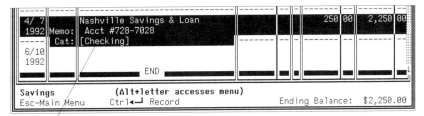

The name of the account from which the transfer was made appears here.

You can enter account names in the Split Transaction window when you want to transfer only part of the total amount of a transaction. You can also include class information with transfer information in the Category field. For example, if you buy an antique table and you want to record the purchase in an asset account called "Personal Assets," you could enter **Personal Assets/Antiques** ("Antiques" is a class set up to record the type of personal asset). However, you cannot enter both an account name and a category name in the same Category field. You'll find more examples of transfers in *Home Uses*, beginning on page 357, and in *Basic Business Uses*, beginning on page 369.

How can I add the check number to a transfer transaction?

Quicken automatically creates parallel transfer transactions that show the date, account name, and dollar amount transferred. (Quicken also copies the payee name, but does not automatically update the payee if the payee changes in the parallel transaction.)

To add additional information to a transfer transaction, edit the transaction in the register.

Changing a Transaction That Includes a Transfer

When you change a transaction that includes a transfer to or from another account, the transaction created by the transfer also changes:

- If you delete a transaction, it is deleted from both accounts.

- If you change the date or amount of a transaction, the information changes in both accounts.

- If you rename an account used in transfers, the account name is changed in the transfer, so your records remain accurate.

However, if the transfer was made in a split transaction, you can change it only from the original transaction: you cannot change it from the account that received the transfer. To locate the original transaction, see "Going to a Transfer Transaction" below.

Splitting a Transfer Transaction

You can also split a transaction created by a transfer. For example, suppose you have a deposit transaction in your Quicken checking account that was created by a transfer. You actually deposited the check at the bank together with another check. To make the correct entry in your register, highlight the deposit created by the transfer and press Ctrl-S. Then in the Split Transaction window, enter the second deposit on line 2. Press F9 to recalculate the total. Then press Ctrl-Enter twice to record the change.

Going to a Transfer Transaction

You can go directly from a transaction that includes a transfer to the parallel transaction in another account. This is useful when you want to see the transaction created by a transfer, and when you want to make a change to a transfer that originated in a split transaction. Such transfers can be changed only in the Split Transaction window of the original transaction.

To go to a transfer transaction:

1. In the register, select the transaction that includes the transfer information. (Or at the Write Checks screen, bring the check containing the transfer information into view.)

2. If the transaction is split, press Ctrl-S to open the Split Transaction window and position the cursor on the line containing the name of the transfer.

3. Select Go to Transfer from the Edit menu (or press Ctrl-X).

   Quicken immediately displays the register for the transfer account and selects the parallel transfer transaction.

Chapter 16

Tracking Assets and Liabilities

If you want to keep detailed track of your total financial picture with Quicken, you can set up and use asset and liability accounts. In these accounts, you can keep track of such things as loan balances, lines of credit, accounts receivable, capital equipment, 401(k) retirement plans, and the tax basis in your home.

Note: Asset and liability accounts are an advanced feature. We suggest that you use Quicken bank accounts for a few months to gain experience that will help you decide how you want to use investment, asset, and liability accounts. Many Quicken users find that Quicken bank and investment accounts are all they need. However, if your finances are complex, or if you want to keep track of them in more detail, asset and liability accounts are available.

Setting up asset and liability accounts

When you set up an asset or liability account using the Set Up New Account window, in the Account Type field, enter 4 for an Other Asset or 5 for an Other Liability account.

Because you also track assets in bank and investment accounts (and liabilities in credit card accounts), Quicken names this type of account an "Other Asset" or "Other Liability" account.

$ About Assets and Liabilities

Assets are what you own; liabilities are what you owe. The difference between your assets and your liabilities is your net worth. The balances in your bank, cash, and investment accounts represent part of your assets. Balances on your credit cards represent part of your liabilities. But they don't give a total picture of your finances. With Quicken, you can enter information about your other assets and liabilities.

For example, you can track your mortgage and car loan balances, line of credit, 401(k) retirement plan, Treasury bills, and real estate held for investment. Or, if you use Quicken in your business, you can track your accounts payable, accounts receivable, and capital equipment.

You can set up separate accounts for these assets and liabilities, and you can include the information from them in reports. Quicken provides a personal Net Worth Report and a general Account Balances Report. Each combines totals from all your accounts to show your net worth.

$ When to Use Asset and Liability Accounts

Set up asset and liability accounts when you want to keep track of the value of your assets and loans not included in other Quicken accounts. Then when you want to look up a loan balance, view an overview of your net worth, or fill out a loan application, you can use Quicken to produce the needed reports. You won't have to dig through file folders to find all the papers you need.

You may not want to create accounts for each of your assets and liabilities. Enter only those that provide the information you need. For example, you might want an asset account in which you record your CDs and Treasury bills, or one in which you keep track of home improvements. You'll find detailed examples in *Home Uses*, beginning on page 357.

If you maintain a single asset or liability account for a group of related assets or liabilities, you can use classes to identify specific items. For example, if you have one liability account in which you keep track of three loans, you could have a class name for each one (for example, "Mortgage," "Car Loan," and "Equity Loan"). When you use classes in this way, you can produce an account balances report that shows subtotals for each class by requesting class detail. For more information, see "Account Balances" on page 173.

Asset account or investment account?

Quicken only calculates performance on investment accounts. If you want to have Quicken calculate a rate of return, choose an investment account rather than an asset account. See "Analyzing Your Investments" on page 300, and "Investment Performance" on page 155.

Some Uses for Asset Accounts

Home Tax Basis

You can use an asset account to keep track of your home improvements over the years. Use your purchase price as the opening balance. Then record each improvement in the register as you make it. When you sell your home, accurate records will allow you to justify a higher tax basis and probably reduce your taxes.

For a detailed example, see "Home Improvements" on page 362.

Accounts Receivable

Businesses can keep up-to-date accounts receivable records in Quicken in an asset account. You'll find a detailed example in "Accounts Receivable" on page 393.

Capital Equipment

If you use Quicken in your business, you can keep a separate asset account in which you list all capital equipment as it is acquired. Then whenever you calculate the current depreciation, enter it in the register. See "Asset and Liability Accounting" on page 380.

Investments

If you have investments that don't fluctuate in value, such as certificates of deposit (CDs) or Treasury bills, you can track them in an asset account. You can record purchases, redemptions, and interest income and keep track of the total value of the investments.

Tracking certain investments that fluctuate in value is more straightforward in an asset account than in a Quicken investment account. For example, use an asset account for your 401(k) or 403(b) retirement plan, especially if you're not told how many shares you have or how the share price changes. You can use asset accounts for real estate, whole life insurance, and personal assets (such as your car, home, antiques).

For more information about what type of Quicken account to use for different types of investments, see "When to Use a Quicken Investment Account" on page 266.

For more suggestions on using asset accounts for personal investments, see "Managing Investments" on page 365.

Some Uses for Liability Accounts

Loan Balances

You can use liability accounts to keep track of loans, such as car loans, home equity loans, mortgages, lines of credit, and owner's equity. When you write a check to make a loan payment, you can transfer the amount of the principal payment to your loan account. Then you can see your up-to-date loan balance at any time. If you think of owner's equity as a loan from the owner to the business, using a liability account is one way to track owner's equity.

See "Asset and Liability Accounting" on page 380 and "Amortization" on page 206.

Accrued Liabilities

Business users can use liability accounts for accrued liabilities, such as sales tax and income taxes payable. When you record an invoice, as part of the split transaction, transfer the sales tax portion of each invoice to a sales tax liability account. This makes it easy for you to keep track of how much sales tax you owe. For more information about transfers, see *Transferring Money Between Accounts*, beginning on page 251. For more information about using Quicken for accounts receivable, see "Accounts Receivable" on page 393.

$ Working with Asset and Liability Accounts

Quicken asset and liability accounts are very similar to Quicken bank accounts. If you've used a Quicken bank account, you already know most of what you'll need to use an asset or liability account.

Basic Steps for Using Asset and Liability Accounts

There are three parts to working with asset and liability accounts—setting up the account, entering transactions, and updating the value of the account.

Setting up separate asset accounts for each liquid investment

Many investors prefer to set up a separate asset account for each liquid investment, rather than grouping investments. If you set up a separate account, you can easily update the balance of the account to reflect a change in market value, using the Update Account Balance window. See "Updating the Value of Your Assets and Liabilities" on page 264.

Setting Up the Account

Follow the instructions in *Working with Multiple Accounts*, beginning on page 245, to set up an asset or liability account.

For the opening balance, follow these guidelines:

- For an asset account for a single asset (such as a CD), the opening balance will be the current value of the asset.

- For a liability account for a loan, the opening balance will be the current loan balance.

- For an asset account for a collection of assets, or a liability account for a collection of loans, enter 0 (zero) as the opening balance. Then, in the register, record a separate transaction for the value of each asset, or the balance of each loan. (The total in the Balance field will display the true opening balance, so you can then delete the opening balance of $0.00.)

In the Category field, enter the name of this account (called a "self-transfer") and a class (for example, [Sally's 401(k)]/Growth). The contents of the Category field are important because they are the source of row headings in your reports. If you enter a self-transfer as the category and each asset or loan as a class, you will prevent these amounts from showing up as uncategorized income or expenses in category-based reports.

For example, suppose you have an account called "Sally's 401(k)," containing three investment funds. Create a separate transaction for each investment fund: a money market fund, a Ginnie Mae portfolio, and a growth fund.

Enter 0 as the opening balance. Once you've entered all the assets, delete this transaction.

Note that the opening balance transaction includes a "self-transfer"; that is a transfer to this account, which is named Sally's 401(k).

Create a separate transaction for each asset.

```
┌─────────────────────────────────────────────────────────────────────────────┐
│ Print/Acct   Edit    Shortcuts   Reports   Activities            F1-Help      │
├──────┬─────┬───────────────────────────┬──────────┬──┬──────────┬───────────┤
│ DATE │ REF │ PAYEE · MEMO · CATEGORY   │ DECREASE │C │ INCREASE │ BALANCE   │
├──────┼─────┼───────────────────────────┼──────────┼──┼──────────┼───────────┤
│ 4/ 1 │     │Opening Balance            │          │  │          │      0 00 │
│ 1992 │     │            [Sally's 401(k→ │          │  │          │           │
│ 4/ 1 │     │Money Market Fund Balance  │          │  │ 1,835 27 │  1,835 27 │
│ 1992 │     │            [Sally's 401(k→ │          │  │          │           │
│ 4/ 1 │     │Ginnie Mae Balance         │          │  │ 1,910 80 │  3,746 07 │
│ 1992 │     │            [Sally's 401(k→ │          │  │          │           │
│ 4/ 1 │     │Growth Fund Balance        │          │  │   985 04 │  4,731 11 │
│ 1992 │     │            [Sally's 401(k→ │          │  │          │           │
│ 4/ 1 │Memo:│                           │          │  │          │           │
│ 1992 │Cat: │                           │          │  │          │           │
├──────┴─────┴───────────────────────────┴──────────┴──┴──────────┴───────────┤
│ Sally's 401(k)    (Alt+letter accesses menu)    Current Balance: $    0.00   │
│ Esc-Main Menu     Ctrl◄┘ Record                 Ending Balance:  $4,731.11   │
└─────────────────────────────────────────────────────────────────────────────┘
```

Entering Transactions

You can enter some transactions directly in the asset and liability registers, or have Quicken record transactions as transfers from another account.

When you write a check in your Quicken bank account to pay a bill that affects an asset or liability, you can have Quicken automatically record the payment in your asset or liability account. For example, when you write a check for a loan payment, you can split the transaction and assign the portion of it that applies to the principal of the loan to the name of your loan account. Quicken will record a parallel transaction for the amount of the principal in your loan account. For more information about transfers, see *Transferring Money Between Accounts*, beginning on page 251.

You may also enter transactions directly in the asset or liability register. For example, enter an increase in the value of an antique or the depreciation of capital equipment as a transaction in an asset register. Enter the sale of a rental property in an asset register, with a transfer to the Quicken bank account that receives the cash. And if you set up an asset account in which to record your accounts receivable, enter the amounts of your invoices directly in the accounts receivable register. (For more information, see "Accounts Receivable" on page 393.)

To see how some asset and liability transactions are entered, see "The Asset Register" below and "The Liability Register" on page 263. The basic steps for entering asset and liability transactions are the same as in Quicken bank accounts. To review the steps for entering transactions, see "Adding Transactions to the Check Register" on page 59.

Updating the Value of Your Account

Periodically you'll want to update your account so its balance is correct. For example, if you have an account representing your 401(k) retirement plan, you may decide to adjust its value periodically to reflect the current value. For more information, see "Updating the Value of Your Assets and Liabilities" on page 264.

$ The Asset Register

To view the register of an asset account:

1. Choose Select Account from the Main Menu, or choose Select/Set Up Account from the Print/Acct pulldown menu (or press Ctrl-A).

2. When the list of accounts appears, select the account you want to use, and press Enter.

The equipment purchase was recorded in this register as a transfer when a check was written from a check register. The amount appears in the Increase field because it increases the value of this account.

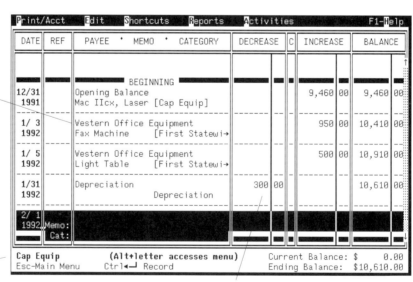

Name of the account.

This decrease transaction was entered in this register to show the depreciation of the assets.

Note: If you haven't set up the account yet, select <New Account> and fill in the Set Up New Account window that appears. For complete information, see "Setting Up and Using Additional Quicken Accounts" on page 245.

 The Liability Register

To view the register for a liability account:

1. Choose Select Account from the Main Menu, or choose Select/Set Up Account from the Print/Acct pulldown menu (or press Ctrl-A).

2. When the list of accounts appears, select the account you want to use, and press Enter.

   Note: If you haven't set up the account yet, select <New Account> and fill in the Set Up New Account window that appears. For complete information see "Setting Up and Using Additional Quicken Accounts" on page 245.

The opening balance shows the initial amount of the loan.

These transactions show decreases in the loan amount. They were each recorded in this register when a check was written from the Joint Account register.

Name of the account.

```
 Print/Acct    Edit    Shortcuts·   Reports   Activities            F1-Help
┌──────┬─────┬─────────────────────────────┬──────────┬─┬─────────┬──────────┐
│ DATE │ REF │ PAYEE  *  MEMO  *  CATEGORY  │ INCREASE │C│ DECREASE│ BALANCE  │
├──────┼─────┼─────────────────────────────┼──────────┼─┼─────────┼──────────┤
│      │     │                             │          │ │         │          │
│      │     │════════════ BEGINNING ══════│          │ │         │          │
│12/31 │     │Opening Balance              │ 18,578 39│ │         │ 18,578 39│
│1991  │     │               [Auto Loans]  │          │ │         │          │
│1/15  │     │GMAC Financing               │          │ │  389 03 │ 18,189 36│
│1992  │     │A/C #87239-278-→[Joint Account]│        │ │         │          │
│2/15  │     │GMAC Financing               │          │ │  394 05 │ 17,795 31│
│1992  │     │A/C #87239-278-→[Joint Account]│        │ │         │          │
│3/15  │     │GMAC Financing               │          │ │  399 08 │ 17,396 23│
│1992  │     │A/C #87239-278-→[Joint Account]│        │ │         │          │
│14/15 │     │Memo:                       o│          │ │         │          │
│1992  │     │Cat:                         │          │ │         │          │
├──────┴─────┴─────────────────────────────┴──────────┴─┴─────────┴──────────┤
│ Auto Loans       (Alt+letter accesses menu)    Current Balance: $    0.00  │
│ Esc-Main Menu    Ctrl◄┘ Record                 Ending Balance:  $17,396.23  │
└────────────────────────────────────────────────────────────────────────────┘
```

The balance in this account shows your current loan balance.

 Using the Cleared Column to Mark Closed Items

In asset and liability accounts, you don't need to reconcile the account in the same way you reconcile a checking account. Instead, use the C (Cleared) column to mark those transactions that are "closed."

Closed items are those that are no longer active as assets or liabilities. For example, if you sell an asset listed in an asset account, such as an antique, or you pay off a loan listed in a liability account, those items are no longer part of your net worth. You won't want to include them in most reports; however, you don't want to delete them from your account, either. (In the event of an audit, you might want to produce a report that includes them.)

The solution is to mark closed items as cleared by entering an asterisk (*) in the C column. Then you can report on all uncleared items by filtering your reports. (For more information, see "Filtering Your Report Data" on page 180.)

Note: When an item is closed, be sure to mark all transactions that relate to it with an asterisk (for example, the transaction for the purchase and sale of an item). Choose Find from the Edit menu to locate the transactions.

Updating the Value of Your Assets and Liabilities

From time to time, you may want to update the value of your assets and liabilities. For example, if you have an asset account for your real estate, you may occasionally want to enter a new transaction to show the increase or decrease in the value of the real estate.

Having Quicken Make an Adjustment

If your asset or liability account includes information about only one asset or liability, you can have Quicken make an adjustment to the balance in the account to update the current value of the account. For example, if you have an asset account for a CD, you can have Quicken enter a transaction to update the current value of the CD.

To have Quicken make an adjustment to the balance:

1. From the register window, select Update Account Balance from the Activities menu. The Update Account Balance window appears.

2. Enter the amount that the balance in the account should be, and press Enter.

   For example, if the statement from your bank indicates that your CD is worth $10,182.64, enter that amount.

   Quicken compares this amount with the current balance in the account and creates an adjustment transaction in the amount of the difference.

   Note: If your asset or liability account includes information about multiple assets or liabilities, you must calculate the current value of *each* asset or liability, combine the individual current values into a total current value, and enter that amount in the Update Account Balance window.

3. Enter a category name if you want one to be assigned to the adjustment transaction Quicken creates.

4. Press Enter to have Quicken create the balance adjustment transaction in your account.

Chapter 17

Getting Started with Investment Accounts

In this chapter you'll learn the basic ways to use Quicken to keep track of your investments in stocks, bonds, mutual funds, and other investments that fluctuate in price. In the following chapter you'll learn some additional ways to handle your investments with Quicken.

With Quicken, you can keep track of purchases, sales, dividends and interest, mutual fund distributions, and stock splits. You can easily update the market value of your investments by entering the current prices straight out of the newspaper. Quicken shows you whether you are making or losing money on each investment and lets you compare the performances of your investments. When tax time comes, you can generate reports of your investment income and capital gains for the year to use when filling out Schedules B and D.

Note: Quicken investment accounts are an advanced feature. If you're new to Quicken, we suggest that you use Quicken bank accounts for a few months to gain experience with Quicken before setting up investment accounts.

When to Use a Quicken Investment Account

Quicken investment accounts help you keep track of investments that fluctuate in price. Stocks, bonds, and mutual funds are examples of such investments.

Quicken can also help you keep track of a collection of investments, such as an account at a brokerage firm. The collection can include investments with a constant price, such as certificates of deposit (CDs), money market funds, and uninvested cash.

Quicken investment accounts are designed for investors who want to track their investment transactions, see the performance of investments, update current market values, and create reports for tax purposes.

Quicken has some limitations. Although it can import data from a file, it can't retrieve prices via modem. While it provides basic tax reports, it doesn't keep track of changes in tax laws. Finally, Quicken doesn't track aspects of sophisticated transactions such as commodities trading or strike prices of options.

The table below suggests what type of Quicken account to use with different types of investments. It's simpler to use an asset account if an investment has a constant share price or no share price and is not in a brokerage account with investments that do fluctuate. (See *Tracking Assets and Liabilities*, beginning on page 257, for information on using asset accounts.) However, you may want to use an investment account to take advantage of Quicken's ability to calculate return on investment.

If you invest in:	Use this type of Quicken account:
Stocks	Investment
Bonds	Investment
Mutual funds	Investment
Collection of investments through brokerage firm	Investment
Real estate investment trusts (REITs) or partnerships	Investment
Unit trusts	Investment
IRA or Keogh accounts	Investment
Variable annuities	Investment
Cash management accounts (CMAs)	Bank for checking part of account Investment for everything else
Money market funds	Bank or asset
CDs or Treasury bills	Investment or asset
Fixed annuities	Investment or asset
Collectibles and precious metals	Investment or asset

If you invest in:	Use this type of Quicken account:
Real estate	Asset
Employer retirement plans (401(k), 403(b), pension)	Investment or asset

Note in the table that the best way to handle a cash management account with a broker is as two Quicken accounts. Use a Quicken bank account for recording checks, so you can keep track of payees and categorize all payments. Use a Quicken investment account for the rest of the investments in the brokerage account. You transfer money between the two Quicken accounts when you buy and sell investments or receive investment income.

$ What You Can Do with a Quicken Investment Account

A Quicken investment account is similar to a Quicken bank account but with additional features. You enter all transactions in the investment register. If you've used a Quicken bank account, you're already familiar with many of the procedures.

You perform three basic functions when you use a Quicken investment account:

- Record transactions in the investment register, to maintain a record of the transactions.

- Update the prices of your investments, so you can see how much they're worth.

- Produce reports, so you can study how your investments are doing and gather information at tax time.

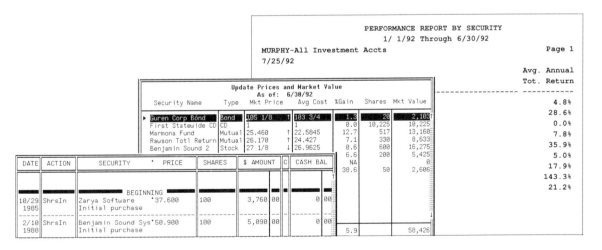

You'll find instructions for the three basic functions later in this chapter and in *Working with Investment Accounts*, beginning on page 305, and "Investment Reports" on page 154.

Before you set up an investment account, read the rest of this section to learn: (1) Quicken's definitions for the terms "security" and "investment account"; (2) suggestions for organizing investments in Quicken; and (3) what types of investment account Quicken has, and the advantages of each. This overview will help you decide how to organize your own investments in Quicken.

Quicken Investment Terminology

Security

Quicken uses the term "security" for a single investment that has a value and (usually) a share price. From Quicken's point of view, a stock, a group of bonds from one corporation, and a mutual fund are all securities because each has a share price, and you own a specified number of shares.

If you want to track the performance of, say, some rare books you own, you may choose to call the books a security in Quicken. On the other hand, there's no point in calling a money market fund on which you draw checks a security. Its price never changes, and you can keep better records if you set it up in Quicken as a bank account.

Investment Account

Quicken uses the term "investment account" for any collection of securities you decide to track as a group. Quicken supplies information about the group as a whole as well as about the individual securities within the group. The account can be a real brokerage account, a single security, or a collection of securities that have a common purpose.

Other Investment Terminology

In the remainder of this chapter, if you're uncertain of the meaning of any terms in "quotes," look for their definitions in "Investor's Glossary" on page 301.

Organizing Your Securities in a Quicken Investment Account

Here are some recommendations about how to group your securities within one or more Quicken investment accounts.

- **Brokerage accounts:** Use a separate Quicken investment account for each actual brokerage account or other managed account you have. If you have a cash management account, set up the checking part as a Quicken bank account.

- **IRAs:** Use separate Quicken investment accounts for your IRA and for your spouse's IRA. (Even if you do not now have securities with fluctuating prices in your IRA, it's a good idea to set up your IRA as a Quicken investment account, as you may want to change the investments later.) This advice applies to other retirement plans that you manage directly, such as a Keogh.

  If you have more than one security in your IRA, put them in the same Quicken investment account, even if the securities are managed by, say, different mutual fund managers. If you transfer an IRA security from one manager to another, Quicken can still track the performance of your IRA as a whole.

- **Securities you hold directly:** If you have a few individual securities you hold directly, you may wish to set each one up as a separate Quicken investment account. Then you can easily reconcile each account with its statement.

  On the other hand, you may prefer to lump the securities in a single Quicken investment account, especially if you have other investment accounts. Then you can subtotal these securities by account on reports and track them as a group.

Two Types of Quicken Investment Account

Quicken has two types of investment account: the regular investment account and the mutual fund investment account. When you set up an investment account, you designate which type it is. You can easily change an account from one type to the other. See "Changing the Type of Account" on page 318.

Regular Investment Account

Most likely, you'll be setting up one or more regular investment accounts. This type of account has the following features:

- It may contain either one or more than one security.

- It may have either a cash balance, as in a brokerage account, or no cash balance.

- Its register displays the cash balance after every transaction and the current market value of the account. It does not display the share balance (total number of shares) of individual securities within the account. (Quicken displays share balances of individual securities in the Update Prices and Market Value screen, which you access directly from the register.)

The advantage of the regular investment account is its flexibility. You can change the securities in it and leave cash in it.

Mutual Fund Investment Account

The mutual fund investment account is designed for a single mutual fund. It has the following features:

- It is restricted to only one security. (You should not have two or more mutual funds in the same mutual fund account.)

- It has no cash in it, only shares of the security.

- Its register displays the share balance (total number of shares) of the single security and the current market value of the security.

- The name of the security and the most recent price, if you enter no new price, appear automatically in the register when you enter a new transaction.

The advantage of the mutual fund investment account is that certain procedures are streamlined. For example, when you write a check from your Quicken checking account to the mutual fund account, the transaction automatically appears in the investment register as a purchase of shares.

Similarities Between the Two Types of Investment Account

Regular investment accounts and mutual fund investment accounts give you the same information about your investments. The main difference is that a cash balance appears in the register for one, and a share balance appears for the other. Quicken allows you to track income, capital gains, and performance of individual securities no matter what type of account they are in.

Setting Up a New Investment Account

Before you set up a Quicken investment account, you'll find it helpful to read "Two Types of Quicken Investment Account" on page 269. Be prepared to tell Quicken which type of account you're setting up.

If you're setting up your first Quicken investment account, you may want to use it for a while and become familiar with it before setting up additional investment accounts.

Three Options for Setup

When you set up a new investment account, you have three options for creating your opening balance. (Remember, if you're uncertain of the meaning of any terms in "quotes," look for their definitions in "Investor's Glossary" on page 301.)

Option 1: Set up fast.

You enter your current investment holdings. For each security in the account, you need to enter the following:

- Name and type (stock, mutual fund, and so on) of security
- Number of shares you now own
- (Optional) "Cost basis" (total cost of all shares)
- Current price per share

From now on, you enter new transactions and new prices.

Advantages:

1. You can get started with the minimum amount of information to gather.

2. You can start using the account right away to see whether you think it's worthwhile to gather and enter more information.

3. Quicken produces accurate reports on performance, income, and changes in unrealized gain for time periods starting now.

Disadvantages:

1. Quicken doesn't have enough data this year for its investment income report to display investment income for the entire calendar year, so you can't use it when preparing this year's Schedule B at tax time.

2. You may have to wait a few months before your investment data is in the range where Quicken can display a valid investment performance report.

3. If you omit the cost basis, Quicken records a zero cost basis for the security. It cannot give you an accurate value for all quantities that depend on cost basis: "average cost per share," "percent gain," total "unrealized gain."

4. If you sell the security, the capital gains report does not display an accurate purchase date. Also, if you omit the cost basis, the "realized gain" is not accurate.

Once you've started using the investment account, you may want to enter historical data later to get accurate reports for earlier periods and in case you sell the security. See "Entering Prior History for Investments" on page 319.

Option 2: Set up for this year.

You enter your investment holdings as of the end of last year. Then you enter all investment transactions for each security since the beginning of this year. For each security in the account, you need to enter the following:

- Name and type (stock, mutual fund, and so on) of security

- Number of shares you owned at the end of last year

- (Optional) "Cost basis" (total cost of all shares)

- Price per share at the end of last year and today

- All transactions (purchases, sales, dividends, reinvestments, and so on) for the current year

As new transactions occur from now on, you enter them.

Advantages:

1. The information you need to gather goes back only to the end of last year and is probably easy for you to find.

2. Quicken displays investment income this year for the entire calendar year, so you can use the investment income report when preparing this year's Schedule B at tax time.

3. Quicken produces accurate reports on performance, income, and changes in unrealized gain for time periods starting with the beginning of this year.

Disadvantages:

1. If you omit the cost basis, Quicken records a zero cost basis for the security. It cannot give you an accurate value for all quantities that depend on cost basis: "average cost per share," "percent gain," total "unrealized gain."

2. If you sell the security, the capital gains report does not display an accurate purchase date. Also, if you omit the cost basis, the "realized gain" is not accurate.

Once you've started using the investment account, you may want to enter historical data later to get accurate reports for earlier periods and in case you sell the security. See "Entering Prior History for Investments" on page 319.

Option 3: Enter all historical data.

For each security in the account, you enter the initial purchase and all subsequent transactions. That is, you need to enter the following:

- Name and type (stock, mutual fund, and so on) of security

- Date, amount invested, and number of shares bought (or price per share) for initial purchase

- All subsequent acquisitions (including reinvestments), sales and gifts, stock splits, and return of capital

- All dividends, interest, and capital gains distributions for the current year

- (Optional) All nonreinvested dividends, interest, and capital gains distributions for prior years. (This data gives you a more complete value for the performance of your security for past years but does not affect Quicken's value for the cost basis.)

- Price per share at the end of last year (and prior years, if available) and today.

As new transactions occur from now on, you enter them.

Advantages:

1. All Quicken reports are complete and accurate.

2. If you sell a security, the capital gains report displays the purchase dates, amounts invested, and the realized gain, so you can use this report when preparing Schedule D at tax time.

3. All your investment records are in one convenient place, making it easier for you to analyze your investments and produce data for tax and other purposes.

Disadvantages:

1. You have to locate data for transactions that occurred in the past.

2. You must spend time entering all prior transactions.

Steps for Setting Up an Investment Account

After you've decided which of the three setup options is best for you and have gathered the appropriate data, follow these steps.

To set up an investment account:

1. At the Main Menu choose Select Account.

Quicken displays the Select Account to Use window.

2. Choose <New Account>.

3. Enter 6 for the account type.

After you enter this account type, Quicken displays the following fields in the Set Up New Account window.

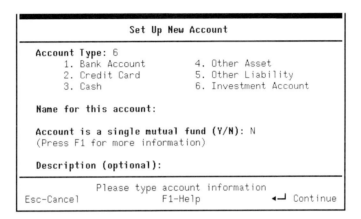

```
                        Set Up New Account

   Account Type: 6
          1. Bank Account          4. Other Asset
          2. Credit Card           5. Other Liability
          3. Cash                  6. Investment Account

   Name for this account:

   Account is a single mutual fund (Y/N): N
   (Press F1 for more information)

   Description (optional):

                  Please type account information
   Esc-Cancel              F1-Help              ◄┘ Continue
```

4. Enter the name for this account.

You may use up to 15 letters, numbers, or spaces. You may not use the characters] / [: within the name.

You may want to use the broker's name or a descriptive name such as "Sally's IRA" or "401(k) rollover." If you're setting up an account with a single mutual fund, you'll probably want to use the name of the mutual fund.

5. Answer **N** if you want to set up a regular investment account.

You may have a variety of securities, including mutual funds, in a regular investment account. You may also have a cash balance.

Answer **Y** only if you're setting up an account with a single mutual fund. You cannot have cash in this type of account.

You can change the type of account later, if you wish. (See "Changing the Type of Account" on page 318.)

6. (Optional) Enter a description of the account.

You may use up to 21 letters, numbers, or spaces.

7. Press the Enter key or F10 to continue.

Note: If you're setting up a mutual fund account, skip to "To finish setting up a mutual fund account:" on page 277.

To finish setting up a regular account:

1. At the Select Account to Use window, choose the new account name.

After reading the message about first-time setup, press the Enter key to continue. You're now ready to enter information for each security in the account.

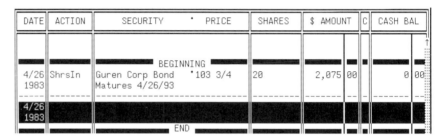

2. For each security, depending on which setup option you've chosen, enter the appropriate date in the first column of the investment register. (See "Three Options for Setup" on page 270.)

- For option 1, enter today's date.
- For option 2, enter 12/31 of last year.
- For option 3, enter the date of your initial purchase or acquisition.

3. Press Ctrl-L to display the action list. Choose Add/Remove shares, and then choose ShrsIn.

Quicken's ShrsIn (abbreviation for "shares in") action has two functions. It allows you to add shares you already own to a Quicken account. It also allows you to enter a purchase of shares for a date in the past, when you were not using Quicken, without deducting the money from a Quicken account.

4. In the Security field, enter the security name.

- If you have not used this name previously for a security in Quicken, press the Enter key to add it to the security list.

  Quicken displays the Set Up Security window.

  You can find instructions for setting up new securities in "Setting Up and Describing Securities" on page 283 as well as on the Help screen for the Set Up Security window.

5. In the Price field (after the raised dot), enter a price as follows.

- For options 1 and 2, enter the cost per share (including commission, fees, or load) if you purchased the security all at one time, or leave the Price field blank.

- For option 3, enter your actual initial cost per share (including commission, fees, or load) or (if you prefer to enter the total cost) leave the Price field blank.

  See "To enter share price:" on page 287 for information about how to enter prices for different types of security.

  Note: If you leave the Price field blank but fill in the $ Amount field, Quicken calculates and fills in the price.

6. In the Shares field, enter the number of shares you owned on the date in the Date field. You may use up to four decimal places.

- **For a stock or mutual fund,** enter the actual number of shares.

- **For bonds,** enter ten times the actual number of bonds (to match the way prices are quoted). Equivalently, enter one hundredth of the total face value of the bonds. For example, if you have two bonds with a total face value of $2000, enter 20 in the Shares field.

- **For a money market fund or a CD,** enter the total value.

- **For a collectible,** enter the number 1.

- **For a precious metal,** enter the number of ounces.

7. In the $ Amount field, enter a dollar amount, including commission, fees, and load, if you did not enter a price.

- For options 1 and 2, you may leave the $ Amount field blank.

- For option 3, the dollar amount should equal the total initial cost.

8. (Optional) In the Memo field, enter a memo.

9. Press F10 to record the transaction.

10. Repeat steps 2 through 9 for each security in the account.

11. For options 2 and 3, enter subsequent transactions for each security. Instructions for the most common transactions are in "Recording Your Investment Transactions" on page 289. Instructions for other transactions are in "More Investment Transactions" on page 306. Temporarily ignore amounts that appear in the Cash Bal field.

12. **If the final amount displayed for the cash balance in this account is correct,** your investment account is now set up. Skip ahead to "Updating Prices" below.

    If the final amount displayed for the cash balance in this account is not correct, continue with steps 13 and 14.

13. Choose Adjust Balance from the Activities menu, and then choose Adjust Cash Balance.

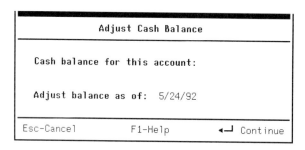

14. Enter your current cash balance for this account.

    Quicken adds a balance adjustment that makes your cash balance correct.

Updating Prices

Your investment account is now set up. Quicken displays the market value of your account in the lower-right corner of the investment register, based on the latest prices you have supplied.

To enter prices for your securities for today, choose Update Prices from the Activities menu for the Update Prices and Market Value screen. For further information, read "Updating the Values of Your Investments" on page 296.

If you set up under options 2 or 3, enter prices for the end of last year as well as for today. Then you can track unrealized (paper) gains or losses and performance for the current year.

To finish setting up a mutual fund account:

When you leave the Set Up New Account window (see page 274), you are at the Set Up Mutual Fund Security window.

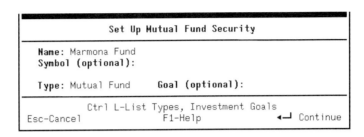

1. At the Set Up Mutual Fund Security window, fill in the information requested.

   Although the name for the security is filled in with the account name, you can change it.

   You can find detailed instructions for setting up a new security in "Setting Up and Describing Securities" on page 283 as well as on the Help screen for this window.

2. Press the Enter key or F10 when you have finished.

   Quicken displays the Select Account to Use window.

3. Use the up and down arrow keys to select the account name, and press the Enter key.

   Quicken displays the Create Opening Share Balance window.

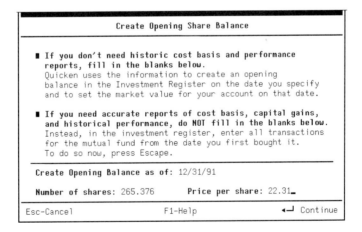

4. If you're entering historical data under option 3 (see "Three Options for Setup" on page 270), press Esc now, and follow the instructions "To finish setting up a regular account:" on page 274, starting with step 2.

   If you're setting up for today or for this year under options 1 or 2, fill in the information requested.

   - For option 1, enter today's date, number of shares you now own, and today's price per share.

   - For option 2, enter the date 12/31 of last year, number of shares you owned then, and price per share then.

   After you enter the price, Quicken displays the investment register with your opening balance filled in. In the Action field, ShrsIn (an abbreviation for "shares in") indicates that you added existing shares to this new Quicken account. Quicken has also recorded the price per share and has used this price to display the market value at the bottom-right of the screen.

In a mutual fund account, this column displays the number of shares you hold.

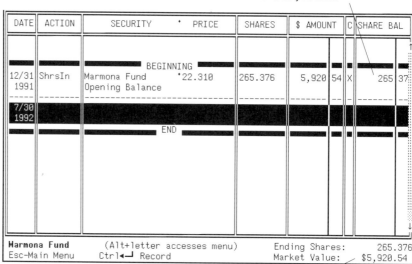

The market value of the account is displayed here.

5. For option 1, your mutual fund account is now set up.

   For option 2, enter transactions for this year. Instructions for the most common transactions are in "Recording Your Investment Transactions" on page 289. Instructions for other transactions are in "More Investment Transactions" on page 306.

6. For option 2, to update the market value of your account to reflect today's share price, choose Update Prices from the Activities menu. For further information, read "Updating the Values of Your Investments" on page 296.

$ The Investment Register

In Quicken you record all investment transactions in the investment register.

DATE	ACTION	SECURITY	* PRICE	SHARES	$ AMOUNT	C	SHARE BAL

DATE	ACTION	SECURITY	* PRICE	SHARES	$ AMOUNT	C	CASH BAL
					.376	5,920 54 X	265 37
		BEGINNING					
10/29 1985	ShrsIn	Zarya Software *37.600 Initial purchase		100	3,760 00		0 00
2/10 1988	ShrsIn	Benjamin Sound Sys*50.900 Initial purchase		100	5,090 00		0 00
12/31 1991	ShrsIn	McKendry MMF *1 End-of-year balance		2,376.826	2,376 83		0 00
1/31 1992	ReinvDiv	McKendry MMF *1 Monthly dividend		9.903	9 90		0 00

Similarities Between the Investment and Check Registers

Quicken's investment register is easy to use because it resembles the check register. If you've been using Quicken for your checking accounts, you already know how to do the following:

- Change the date.
- Move from one field to another.
- Enter information in a field.
- Add a memo for a transaction.
- Record a transaction.
- Add or delete a transaction.
- Scroll through the register.

In this section you'll learn about the fields that are unique to the investment register.

The registers for regular investment accounts and share-balance accounts look similar except for the final column. You'll learn about the other minor differences in this section.

The Action Field

The Action field for an investment transaction describes what is happening to the security or the account. Use it to tell Quicken the following:

- You're buying or selling a security.
- A security is paying interest, dividends, capital gains distributions, or return of capital.
- Money paid by a security is being reinvested in additional shares.
- You're transferring cash or shares into or out of the account.

- Shares are splitting.

- You're paying margin interest.

To enter an action in the Action field:

1. With the cursor in the Action field of the investment register, press Ctrl-L to display the action list.

```
              Action List

▶ Add/Remove shares
  Buy shares
  Capital Gains distr
  Dividend
  Interest
  Other transactions
  Reinvest
  Sell shares
  Transfer cash

  Esc-Cancel        ◄┘ Use
```

Note: The list contains only actions relevant to the type of account you are working with.

(See "List of Investment Actions" on page 281 for an explanation of each action on the list.)

2. Choose the appropriate action.

When you choose most actions, Quicken displays a short list of further choices, each with an abbreviation at the left.

3. Choose the appropriate action from the short list.

Sometimes you are entering a transaction that involves a transfer of cash from one account to another. On the short list, you'll see abbreviations that include an *X* for "transfer." Choose the action type with the *X* if you want to transfer cash to or from another account. Quicken displays a third line for the transaction where you can type the name of the other account.

Shortcuts for choosing an action

- You can bypass the action list by typing the abbreviation for an action in the Action field.

- If you type the first letter or first few letters of the abbreviation, and press the Enter key, Quicken either opens the action list directly to the alphabetically first action with those letters or finishes typing the abbreviation (if what you've typed matches only one action). For example, if you type s, Quicken opens the list to Sell. If you type sh, Quicken opens the list to ShrsIn. If you type i, Quicken enters IntInc.

List of Investment Actions

The following table lists all actions in the order in which they appear for the register of a regular investment account. After each action are the abbreviations and descriptions for the choices.

To learn what action to choose for different investment transactions, see "Recording Your Investment Transactions" on page 289 and "More Investment Transactions" on page 306.

Note: When you're working in the register of a mutual fund account, the action list omits the following actions, which add cash to or remove cash from the account:

Buy	IntInc	RtrnCap
CGLong	MargInt	Sell
CGShort	MiscExp	XIn
Div	MiscInc	XOut

Action Abbrev   **Action Description**

Add/Remove shares

ShrsIn	Add shares to investment account.
ShrsOut	Remove shares from investment account.

Buy shares

Buy	Buy security with cash already in investment account.
BuyX	Buy security with cash transferred into investment account from another account.

Capital gains distr

CGLong	Receive cash from long-term capital gains distribution.
CGLongX	Transfer cash received from long-term capital gains distribution out of investment account.
CGShort	Receive cash from short-term capital gains distribution.
CGShortX	Transfer cash received from short-term capital gains distribution out of investment account.

Dividend

Div	Receive cash from dividend.
DivX	Transfer cash received from interest or dividend out of account.

Interest

IntInc	Receive cash from interest income.
MargInt	Pay for interest on margin loan by using cash from account.

Action Abbrev	Action Description
Other transactions	
MiscExp	Pay for miscellaneous expense by using cash from account.
MiscInc	Receive cash from miscellaneous income.
Reminder	Remind of some pending event associated with investment account (works with Billminder; see "Using Reminder Memos" on page 308).
RtrnCap	Receive cash from return of capital.
StkSplit	Change number of shares as a result of stock split.
Reinvest	
ReinvDiv	Reinvest in additional shares of the security with money from dividend or income distribution.
ReinvInt	Reinvest in additional shares of the security with money from interest distribution.
ReinvLg	Reinvest in additional shares of the security with money from long-term capital gains distribution.
ReinvSh	Reinvest in additional shares of the security with money from short-term capital gains distribution.
Sell shares	
Sell	Sell security and leave cash in investment account.
SellX	Sell security and transfer cash out of investment account.
Transfer cash	
XIn	Transfer cash into investment account
XOut	Transfer cash out of investment account.

The Security Field

In the Security field you enter the name of the security associated with the action. If the action applies to the entire account (an IRA custodial fee, for example), leave the Security field empty.

Note: In mutual fund accounts, Quicken automatically fills in the name of the single security in the account.

To enter a security name:

1. In the Security field, type the name of the security, or choose Security List from the Shortcuts menu to display the security list and choose a name from the list.

   - If the security is not currently on the list, choose <New Security> on the security list to set up a new security. (Or, if you have already typed a name not currently on the list, Quicken offers you a chance to add that name to the list and to describe the security.)

- For detailed instructions, see "Setting Up and Describing Securities" on page 283, or choose Help.

2. Press the Enter key to record the security in the Security field.

Shortcut for entering names already on the security list

In the Security field, type as much of the beginning of the security name as you need to distinguish it from any other name on the list. For example, if only one security begins with *F*, type f. (Lowercase letters work.) If one security begins with *Fid* and another with *Fir*, type the first three letters. Then press the Enter key. Quicken fills in the entire name.

Setting Up and Describing Securities

In regular investment accounts, you may set up securities from the investment register at any time.

In mutual fund investment accounts, you set up the single security in the account when you first set up the account.

To set up a new security:

1. At the investment register, choose Security List from the Shortcuts menu (or press Ctrl-Y).

Quicken displays the Security List window.

The Display column indicates the condition for displaying the security on the Update Prices and Market Value screen. (See "The Update Prices and Market Value Screen" on page 298 for details.)

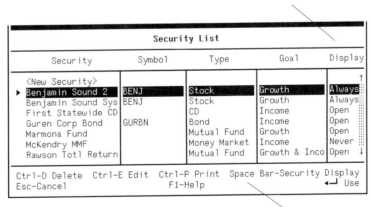

Press the spacebar to change the condition for displaying the security on the Update Prices and Market Value screen.

2. Choose <New Security>.

Quicken displays the Set Up Security window.

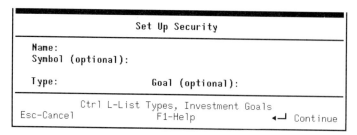

```
                        Set Up Security
   Name:
   Symbol (optional):

   Type:                    Goal (optional):

                Ctrl L-List Types, Investment Goals
   Esc-Cancel                  F1-Help              ↵ Continue
```

3. Enter the name of the security.

   You can use up to 18 letters, numbers, and spaces.

   Quicken uses this name to list your securities in alphabetical order.

4. (Optional) Enter a symbol for the security.

   You can use up to 12 letters, numbers, or spaces.

   Enter a symbol if you plan to export or import price data from a file or to distinguish between different lots of the same security. Otherwise, you don't need one. (For more information, see "Exporting and Importing Prices" on page 312 and "Different Lots for a Security in One Account" on page 314.)

5. At the Type field, press Ctrl-L to view the list of security types. Choose the type appropriate for your security. If none is appropriate, set up and choose a new type.

   See "Security Types" below for more information about types.

6. (Optional) At the Goal field, press Ctrl-L to view the list of investment goals. Choose the goal appropriate for your security. If none is appropriate, set up and choose a new goal.

   See "Investment Goals" on page 285 for more information about goals.

7. Press the Enter key or F10 to record the new security.

Security Types

When you're setting up a security, Quicken asks you to assign a type to the security. When you update prices for all your securities, Quicken displays the securities on the Update Prices and Market Value screen alphabetically within security type, making it convenient for you to enter prices from the newspaper. You can also use types for sorting and subtotaling in investment reports.

The preset list of security types includes the following types:

- Bond
- CD
- Mutual Fund
- Stock.

You can customize this list by adding new types, deleting unused existing types, or modifying existing types. For example, you may wish to add Money Fund, T-Bill, Tax-Free Bond, Option, REIT, Unit Trust, NYSE, NASDAQ, or AMEX.

You can label securities with different types or investment goals (see "Investment Goals" on page 285) to identify the following on your investment reports:

- Taxable vs. nontaxable income
- Securities in your children's or grandchildren's names

You can have up to 16 security types. If you have more than six, press PgDn or PgUp to view the remaining types on the list.

To add a new security type:

1. At the Type field of the Set Up Security window, press Ctrl-L to display the list of security types.

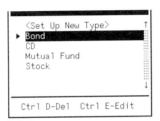

2. Choose <Set Up New Type>.

   Quicken displays the Set Up Security Type window.

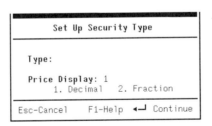

3. Enter a name for the new type. You can use up to 15 letters, numbers, or spaces.

4. (Optional) If you wish prices for this new type to appear as fractions (multiples of 1/16) rather than decimals, enter 2 in the Price Display field.

5. Press the Enter key or F10 to record the new type.

Investment Goals

When you're setting up a security, Quicken lets you assign an investment goal to it. When you create reports, you can sort and subtotal by investment goal. Using goals allows you to group investments within the same account or within different accounts according to the preset choices or any choices that match your own situation.

The preset list of investment goals includes the following goals:

- College Fund
- Growth
- High Risk
- Income
- Low Risk

You can customize this list by adding new goals, deleting unused goals, or modifying existing goals. For example, you may wish to add Retirement, Down Payment, Remodeling, Growth & Income, or Medium Risk. You may use goals to label investments for your children or grandchildren. You may also use goals to distinguish taxable income from tax-free income within the same account, or to designate industry groups (such as technology, energy, consumer products, and so on).

You can have up to 16 goals. If you have more than six, press PgDn or PgUp to view the remaining goals on the list.

To add a new investment goal:

1. At the Goal field of the Set Up Security window, press Ctrl-L to display the list of investment goals.

2. Choose <Set Up New Goal>.

   Quicken displays the Set Up Investment Goal window.

3. Enter a name for the new goal.

   You may use up to 15 letters, numbers, or spaces.

When You Own the Same Security in More Than One Account

Quicken makes it easy for you to track the same security in more than one investment account. You don't have to do anything special. If you've already set up a security for one account, the security appears on the security list for all your investment accounts (within the same file).

Prices, Shares, $ Amounts, and Commissions

Quicken knows that share price, number of shares, and dollar amount are related. If you fill in only two of the three quantities, it will calculate the third quantity from the relationship:

$$\text{Price} \times \text{Shares} = \text{\$ Amount}$$

Prices

To enter share price:

1. With the cursor in the Price field (after the raised dot), enter a share price in fractions or decimals. Quicken keeps track of decimal prices to the nearest 0.0005 and normally displays them to the nearest 0.001.

   - **For a stock or a mutual fund,** enter the actual price per share.
   - **For bonds,** enter one tenth of the actual market value of each bond (to match the way prices are quoted).
   - **For a money market fund or a CD,** enter one dollar.
   - **For a collectible,** enter the total value.
   - **For a precious metal,** enter the price per ounce.

2. To enter a share price as a whole number plus a fraction, leave a space after the whole dollar amount, and use a slash (/) between the numerator and denominator. For example, enter

   36 3/8

Quicken displays prices for stocks and bonds as whole numbers plus fractions (multiples of 1/16) and all other prices in decimals. (You can change this preset format by modifying the security type from the list of security types viewed from the Set Up Security window.) However, if a price for a stock or bond is not an exact multiple of 1/16, Quicken displays it as a decimal.

Number of Shares

To enter number of shares:

In the Shares field, enter the number of shares (to within four decimal places).

- **For a stock or mutual fund,** enter the actual number of shares.
- **For bonds,** enter ten times the actual number of bonds (to match the way prices are quoted). Equivalently, enter one hundredth of the total face value of the bonds. For

example, if you have two bonds with a total face value of $2000, enter 20 in the Shares field.

- **For a money market fund or a CD,** enter the total value.
- **For a collectible,** enter the number 1.
- **For a precious metal,** enter the number of ounces.

If the number of shares is an exact integer, Quicken displays the number without decimals.

Commissions and Fees

When you enter a buying or selling action, Quicken displays the abbreviation Comm/Fee in the second line of the Shares column and allows you to enter a dollar amount for a commission or fee in the second line of the $ Amount column.

After you enter a commission or fee, Quicken adjusts the dollar amount in the first line to include the commission or fee. Quicken even figures out whether to add the commission (in a purchase) or subtract it (in a sale).

Alternatively, Quicken can calculate the commission or fee automatically. Enter values for the price, number of shares, and dollar amount, including commission. If the dollar amount doesn't equal the price times the number of shares, Quicken enters a value for the commission or fee. For example, if you enter a purchase of 100 shares at $15 per share and total cost $1600, Quicken enters a commission of $100 for the transaction.

The Account, Transfer Amount, and Category Fields

When you choose some actions, Quicken includes a third line in the transaction.

The Account and Transfer Amount Fields

Many actions involve a transfer of cash between the investment account and another account. When you choose one of these actions, Quicken displays an Account field and a Transfer Amount (Xfer Amt) field on the third line.

To choose an account for the transfer:

1. At the Account field, choose Categorize/Transfer from the Shortcuts menu.

   Note: Choose Categorize/Transfer, not Select/Set Up Account (on the Print/Acct menu), to choose the account for the transfer. Choose Select/Set Up Account only when you want to display the register of another account.

2. When Quicken displays the account list, choose the account that is the source of the money.

Quicken fills in the Transfer Amount field with the amount in the $ Amount field. However, in a regular investment account, you can change the amount. The difference affects the cash balance of the account.

The Category Field

Two actions (MiscExp and MiscInc, both on the short list under Other Transactions) allow you to associate a category with the transaction. When you choose one of these actions, Quicken displays a Category field on the third line. Choose a category as you do in other registers (choose Categorize/Transfer from the Shortcuts menu).

Cash and Share Balance

For a regular investment account, the farthest right column of the investment register displays the cash balance for the account. When you record a transaction, Quicken automatically calculates the correct cash balance. If you have no cash in the account, the column displays zeros.

If Quicken displays a row of asterisks (*****) in the column, the number is too large for Quicken to display. Quicken displays dollar amounts between -$999,999.99 and $9,999,999.99. Outside of that range, Quicken keeps track of the amount but doesn't display it.

For a mutual fund account, the farthest right column displays share balance. When you record a transaction, Quicken automatically calculates the correct total number of shares of the security you hold in the account.

$ Recording Your Investment Transactions

In this section you'll learn how to record in the investment register the most common investment transactions:

- Buying and selling a security
- Receiving dividends, interest, and capital gains distributions
- Reinvesting income from a security in additional shares of the security.

"More Investment Transactions" on page 306 covers the other investment transactions you can record with Quicken.

Buying and Selling a Security

When you buy a security with money you already have, you pay for it either with cash in the same account or with cash you transfer in from another account, such as your checking account. Quicken distinguishes between these two sources of cash.

- If you're buying with cash in the same account, enter Buy in the Action field of the register. Quicken subtracts the purchase amount from the cash balance in the account.

- If you're buying with cash you transfer in from another account, read "Transferring Money to and from Other Accounts" on page 292. It describes situations in which it may be more convenient to record the transaction from the source account.

  If you're recording the transaction in the investment register, enter BuyX in the Action field. Quicken asks you to name the source account for the cash. Quicken automatically subtracts the purchase amount from the cash balance in the source account.

Similarly, when you're selling a security, Quicken distinguishes between keeping cash from the sale in the same account or transferring it to another account.

- If you're keeping cash from a sale in the same account, enter Sell in the Action field. Quicken adds the sale proceeds to the cash balance in the account.

- If you're transferring cash from a sale to another account, enter SellX in the Action field. Quicken asks you to name the account receiving the cash. Quicken automatically adds the sale proceeds to the cash balance in the receiving account.

If there is an explicit commission added to the purchase or subtracted from the sale proceeds, enter it in the Comm/Fee field. (If you need more information, see "Commissions and Fees" on page 288.)

Loads

A "load" (sometimes called a "front-end load") is a commission built into the purchase price of a mutual fund or other security. A load fund has two share prices: a "Buy" or "Offer" price and a "Sell" or net asset value (NAV) price. Enter the purchase of a load fund at the "Buy" price with no additional commission.

The true market value of your investment is based on the "Sell" or NAV price. If you want to correct the market value, update the price of the fund (see "Updating the Values of Your Investments" on page 296), using the NAV price. The difference between the market value and what you paid is the load.

A "back-end load" is a commission built into the selling price. Funds with these loads have a net asset value (share price) greater than the selling price. Enter the sale of such a fund using the actual selling price.

Accrued Interest

When you buy a bond after its original date of issue, you usually have to pay "accrued interest" to the previous owner. Accrued interest is interest the bond has already earned but not yet paid out.

Enter the bond purchase transaction without including accrued interest.

Enter the payment of accrued interest as a separate transaction. Enter MiscExp in the Action field, the security name in the Security field, the dollar amount, and the expense category _Accrued Int in the Category field. (Quicken adds this category at the end of your expense categories when you set up your first investment account.)

If you paid the accrued interest out of another Quicken account, enter a third transaction to show a cash transfer equal to the accrued interest. Enter XIn in the Action field and the other account name in the Account field.

Dividends and Interest

When you enter the receipt of cash from dividends or interest, tell Quicken whether the cash is staying in the account or being transferred out.

- For cash from dividend income that stays in the account, enter Div in the Action field.

- For cash from interest income that stays in the account, enter IntInc in the Action field.

- For dividend income from a money market fund that is the cash balance of a brokerage account, enter Div in the Action field and use the name of the money market fund as the security name.

- For cash from either dividend or interest income that is being transferred out of the account, enter DivX in the Action field. Quicken asks you to name the account receiving the cash. Quicken automatically adds the income to the cash balance in the receiving account.

  Note: You may wish to memorize a recurring DivX transaction, so you don't have to enter the security name and receiving account each time. See "More Investment Transactions" on page 306.

- For reinvested dividends or interest, including interest that stays in a CD or dividends that stay in a money market fund, see "Reinvestments" on page 292.

An "income distribution" is money a mutual fund pays you as a result of dividends and interest it receives from the securities within the fund. Treat it like dividends in Quicken.

Capital Gains Distributions from Mutual Funds

A "capital gains distribution" is money paid to you by a mutual fund as a result of capital gains the fund earns by selling securities within the fund. The fund usually informs you whether the distribution is for "short-term" or "long-term" capital gains. (You may receive both at the same time. If the fund doesn't tell you whether a capital gains distribution is short-term or long-term, assume it's long-term.) Under U.S. tax law at the time of this printing, short-term capital gains distributions are treated the same as dividends.

- For cash from a short-term capital gains distribution that stays in the account, enter CGShort in the Action field.

- For cash from a short-term capital gains distribution that is being transferred out of the account, enter CGShortX in the Action field.

- For cash from a long-term capital gains distribution that stays in the account, enter CGLong in the Action field.

- For cash from a long-term capital gains distribution that is being transferred out of the account, enter CGLongX in the Action field.

- For capital gains distributions reinvested in new shares, see the next topic, "Reinvestments."

Reinvestments

A "reinvestment" is the purchase of additional shares of a security with money paid to you by that security as dividend or interest income or capital gains distribution. (For a CD or money market fund, you are buying new shares at a share price of one dollar.)

- For a reinvestment of dividend income, enter ReinvDiv in the Action field.

- For a reinvestment of interest income, enter ReinvInt in the Action field.

- For a reinvestment of a short-term capital gains distribution, enter ReinvSh in the Action field.

- For a reinvestment of a long-term capital gains distribution, enter ReinvLg in the Action field.

If you paid a commission or fee for a reinvestment, enter it on the second line of the transaction.

Redemption of Shares for IRA Custodial Fees

In a mutual fund account set up as an IRA or other retirement account, the fund custodian may redeem shares as a custodial fee.

- For redemption of shares as a custodial fee, enter SellX in the Action field. Enter the price and the dollar amount. Also enter the dollar amount of the fee in the Comm/Fee field, to make the net amount of the transaction zero. Enter the name of the investment account itself in the Account field.

Transferring Money to and from Other Accounts

You probably transfer money between your checking or savings account and your investments. For example, you may deposit dividend checks in your checking account, or pay for mutual fund investments with a check.

If you have a cash management account (CMA) with a broker and are writing checks on the cash in the account, we recommend you set up the cash part as a Quicken bank account. You'll be able to print checks, track check numbers, and reconcile easily. You'll then be entering every investment activity affecting your cash balance as a transfer. (However, if you write checks only occasionally and want to keep the cash part in the investment account, enter the checks using MiscExp in the Action field.)

You can enter a transfer between an investment account and a bank account from either register, and it will appear in the other register. The way the transaction appears in each register depends on where you enter the transaction. This section describes what happens in each case.

If you write checks by hand to pay for a security in a regular investment account:

If you write checks by hand, the most direct way to enter this transaction is at the investment register.

To enter the transfer at the investment register:

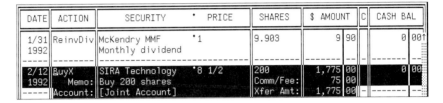

DATE	ACTION	SECURITY	* PRICE	SHARES	$ AMOUNT	C	CASH BAL
1/31 1992	ReinvDiv	McKendry MMF *1 Monthly dividend		9.903	9 90		0 00↑
2/12 1992	BuyX Memo: Account:	SIRA Technology *8 1/2 Buy 200 shares [Joint Account]		200 Comm/Fee: Xfer Amt:	1,775 00 75 00 1,775 00		0 00

1. At the investment register, enter BuyX in the Action field.

2. Enter the security name, price, number of shares, dollar amount, and commission.

3. Fill in the Memo field with the information you want to appear in the bank account register.

4. At the Account field on the third line of the transaction, choose Categorize/Transfer from the Shortcuts menu.

5. When Quicken displays the account list, choose the account that is the source of the money.

6. Press the Enter key or F10 to record the transaction.

7. To view the transaction in the bank account register, select the transaction in the investment register, and press Ctrl-X.

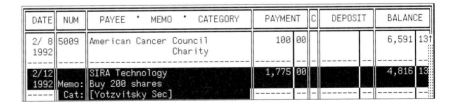

DATE	NUM	PAYEE * MEMO * CATEGORY	PAYMENT	C	DEPOSIT	BALANCE
2/ 8 1992	5009	American Cancer Council Charity	100 00			6,591 13↑
2/12 1992	Memo: Cat:	SIRA Technology Buy 200 shares [Yotzvitsky Sec]	1,775 00			4,816 13

8. In the bank account register, fill in the check number.

If you print checks or prefer to enter checks at the register of your checking account to pay for a security in a regular investment account:

In your bank account, enter the transaction as a cash transfer to another Quicken account. You'll have to go to the investment register to record the security, price, and number of shares.

To enter the transfer at the Write Checks screen or the check register:

1. Fill out the check or register for the checking account.

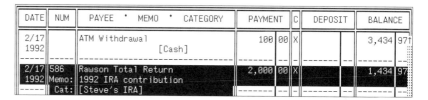

DATE	NUM	PAYEE • MEMO • CATEGORY	PAYMENT	C	DEPOSIT	BALANCE
2/17 1992		ATM Withdrawal [Cash]	100 00	X		3,434 97↑
2/17 1992	586 Memo: Cat:	Rawson Total Return 1992 IRA contribution [Steve's IRA]	2,000 00	X		1,434 97

Whatever you type in the Payee and Memo fields is repeated in the investment register.

2. At the Category field, choose Categorize/Transfer from the Shortcuts menu.

3. Move to the end of the category and transfer list to see your Quicken investment accounts.

4. Choose the investment account containing the security you're buying.

5. To go to the transaction in the investment register, use PgUp or the up arrow key to select the transaction at the Write Checks screen or in the register of the checking account, and press Ctrl-X.

The transaction appears in the investment register as a cash transfer, XIn. The check payee appears in the Security field.

DATE	ACTION	SECURITY • PRICE	SHARES	$ AMOUNT	C	CASH BAL
12/31 1991	ShrsIn	Marmona Fund •22.310 Yearend balance	206.546	4,608 04		0 00↑
2/17 1992	XIn Memo: Account:	Rawson Total Retur• 1992 IRA contribution [Steve Checking]		2,000 00		2,000 00

6. Change the transaction in the investment register, entering BuyX in the Action field and the security name (if needed), price, and number of shares.

If you're buying a security in a mutual fund account:

Quicken knows that you have only one security in a mutual fund account. When you write a check or enter the transaction in your checking account register, Quicken records the transaction in the investment register with the security name, and fills in the number of shares based on the most recent price known to Quicken. Thus, you'll probably choose to record the transaction from your checking account.

To enter the transfer at the Write Checks screen or the check register:

At the Write Checks screen or the register of the checking account, follow steps 1 through 4 on page 294.

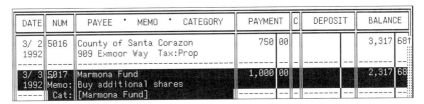

Quicken uses the last known share price to record a BuyX transaction in the investment register. You may need to correct the price and number of shares when you receive your statement.

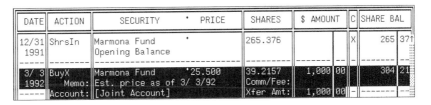

If you're transferring cash out of an investment account:

For investment transactions that include a cash transfer out of an investment account, start at the investment register. You can enter more information about the transaction at this register.

To enter the cash transfer at the investment register:

1. Enter the transaction in the investment register, using the appropriate action.

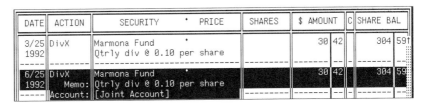

Note: The actions for transferring cash out of an investment account all have *X* in the name. They are CGLongX, CGShortX, DivX, SellX, and XOut. Choose the appropriate action.

2. Fill in the Memo field with the information you want to appear in the register of the bank account.

3. At the Account field on the third line of the transaction, choose Categorize/Transfer from the Shortcuts menu.

4. When Quicken displays the Select Account window, choose the account that is the source of the money.

5. Press the Enter key or F10 to record the transaction.

To view the transaction in the bank account register, select the transaction and press Ctrl-X.

DATE	NUM	PAYEE * MEMO * CATEGORY	PAYMENT	C	DEPOSIT	BALANCE
3/31 1992	5024	Cabinet Supply Warehouse Kitchen Cabinet→[House]	2,002 00			1,034 06↑
6/25 1992	Memo: Cat:	Marmona Fund Qtrly div @ 0.10 per share [Marmona Fund]			30 42	1,064 48

Updating the Values of Your Investments

Quicken makes it easy for you to update the prices of your securities from the newspaper because it lists all your securities in one screen. Quicken uses the prices you enter in that screen to recalculate the market value of each investment account.

To update the prices of your securities:

1. At the investment register, choose Update Prices from the Activities menu, or press Ctrl-U.

Quicken displays the Update Prices and Market Value screen.

For a detailed explanation of this screen, see "The Update Prices and Market Value Screen" on page 298.

To combine lots of the same security, press F8. (Press F8 again to display lots.)

When the lower-left corner reads "All accounts," the screen tells about securities in all investment accounts in the file.

Otherwise, the screen tells about securities in the single account named here. Press F9 to change to the other view mode.

```
                     Update Prices and Market Value
                         As of:   6/30/92
        Security Name      Type   Mkt Price     Avg Cost   %Gain    Shares   Mkt Value

  ▶ Guren Corp Bond      Bond   105 1/8   ↑  103 3/4        1.3        20      2,103↑
    First Statewide CD   CD     1            1              0.0    10,225     10,225
    Marmona Fund         Mutual 25.460   ↑  22.5845        12.7       517     13,160
    Rawson Totl Return   Mutual 26.170   ↑  24.427          7.1       330      8,633
    Benjamin Sound 2     Stock  27 1/8   ↓  26.9625         0.6       600     16,275
    Benjamin Sound Sys   Stock  27 1/8   ↓  25.450          6.6       200      5,425
    SIRA Technology      Stock  11 1/2   ↓                   NA                   0
    Zarya Software       Stock  52 1/8   ↑  37.600         38.6        50      2,606



   Total Market Value                                        5.9             58,426

 All accounts                                          +/-  Adjust Price
 Esc-Register        F8-Combine Lots      F9-One Account   Ctrl◄┘ Record Prices
```

> **Shortcut from the Main Menu**
>
> You can also press Ctrl-U directly from the Main Menu.

2. Check whether the lower-left corner of the screen displays the name of one account or reads "All accounts."

   - To change from "All accounts" to the current account (or the reverse), press F9. (Pressing F9 again brings you back to the first screen.)

   - To go to the screen for a different investment account, press Ctrl-A and choose the desired account.

3. (Optional) If the screen displays separate lots of the same security, press F8 to combine lots for ease in entering prices.

   When you combine lots, the price you enter becomes part of the price history of each lot of the security.

   (If you want to know how to set up separate lots, see "Different Lots for a Security in One Account" on page 314.)

4. Use the up or down arrow keys to select a security. Enter the latest market price.

   For more about entering prices of different kinds of securities, see "Prices, Shares, $ Amounts, and Commissions" on page 287.

> **Shortcuts for entering prices**
>
> - Use the + or – keys to change the price to the next 1/8 (or 0.125).
>
> - Type a quote or ditto (' or ") to enter a price identical to the one above it.
>
> - If a price is unchanged, type an asterisk (*) to indicate that the price is correct for the current date. (The asterisk now displayed disappears.)
>
> - If you make a mistake changing a price and want to return to the estimated price previously displayed, type an asterisk (*).

   The market value changes as you change the price of a security.

5. When you have finished entering all prices, press Ctrl-Enter or F10 to record the prices.

6. If you want to return to the register, press Esc, choose Register from the Activities menu, or press Ctrl-R.

To enter market prices of your securities for other dates:

1. At the Update Prices and Market Value screen, choose Go to Date from the Edit menu, or press Ctrl-G.

2. Change the date to the date for which you wish to enter market prices, and press ⏎.

Shortcuts for going to certain dates

You can go directly to certain dates by using Quick Keys at the Update Prices and Market Value screen.

To go to:	Use this Quick Key:
Previous day	Ctrl-← or Ctrl-B
Next day	Ctrl-→ or Ctrl-N
One month earlier	Ctrl-PgUp
One month later	Ctrl-PgDn

Quicken displays the screen for the chosen date. It shows market prices and market values for the most recent prior date for which you recorded a price in Quicken.

3. Enter correct prices for the chosen date just as you would a current price.

4. To record newly entered prices, press Ctrl-Enter or F10.

The Update Prices and Market Value Screen

The Update Prices and Market Value screen lists securities alphabetically by type.

A security appears on the screen according to how you label it in the Display field of the security list. (Choose Security List from the Shortcuts menu to check.) It appears if:

*   The Display field says "Always."

*   The Display field says "Open," and you own the security (or have a short position in it) as of the date at the top of the screen.

It does not appear if:

*   The Display field says "Never."

*   The Display field says "Open," and you do not own the security (nor have a short position in it) as of the date at the top of the screen.

The Update Prices and Market Value screen summarizes information about each security. The only values you can edit are the market prices.

Market Price: An asterisk (*) next to a market price indicates that Quicken is estimating the share price. As its estimated price, Quicken uses the most recent share price you've entered for a transaction involving this security. An arrow (↑ or ↓) indicates an increase or decrease in share price over the previous known share price.

Average Cost per Share: The average cost per share of a security equals the cost basis (total cost of all shares of this security) divided by the number of shares.

$$\text{avg. cost per share} = \frac{\text{cost basis}}{\text{number of shares}}$$

(If you added shares to an account when you set up the account, and you left the share price and dollar amount blank, Quicken leaves this column blank. See "Entering Prior History for Investments" on page 319 if you want to give Quicken data to calculate the average cost per share.)

%Gain: The percent unrealized (paper) gain (or loss) equals the market price per share minus average cost per share, divided by the average cost per share, expressed in percent.

$$\text{gain} \ = \ \frac{\text{market price per share} - \text{avg. cost per share}}{\text{avg. cost per share}} \times 100\%$$

A negative value is a (paper) loss.

If Quicken doesn't have the data to calculate the average cost per share, it displays "NA" (not available) for the percent gain.

Market Value: The market value for each security equals the market price times the number of shares.

$$(\text{market value} = \text{market price per share}) \times \text{number of shares}$$

Quicken cannot display a market value greater than $9,999,999. Quicken displays a row of asterisks (*******) when the market value is greater than that amount.

To print the Update Prices and Market Value screen on paper or to a file:

1. At the Update Prices and Market Value screen, press Ctrl-P.

2. At the Print Market Value Summary window, choose the printer or type of file.

Viewing Market Values of Your Investments

You can look at the Update Prices and Market Value screen for other dates to get a quick view of how the market values of your investments have changed. (In addition, you can look at a price history of a single security; see "Price History of Securities" on page 311.)

To view market values of your investments for other dates:

1. At the Update Prices and Market Value screen, choose Go to Date from the Edit menu, or press Ctrl-G.

    You may also use the date Quick Keys described on page 298.

2. Change the date to the date for which you wish to view market values, and press the Enter key.

    Quicken displays the screen for the chosen date. It shows market prices and market values for the most recent prior date for which you recorded a price in Quicken.

3. (Optional) If you have set up different lots for the same security, press F8 to view market values for individual lots or for combined lots for each security.

4. (Optional) Press F9 to switch between all accounts and the current account.

5. (Optional) Choose Select/Set Up Account from the Print/Acct menu to view market values for a different account.

6. Repeat steps 1 through 5 to view market values for other dates.

 # Analyzing Your Investments

Quicken takes the information you provide about your investments and produces summaries and reports so you can see what you have and how well you're doing.

Quicken's Output

Quicken gives you information about your investments in seven places:

- The investment register for an account
- The Update Prices and Market Value screen
- The investment reports (five types):
  - Portfolio value report
  - Investment performance report
  - Capital gains report
  - Investment income report
  - Transaction detail report

"Investment Reports" on page 154 describes investment reports in more detail.

The following table summarizes some of the information you can get, and where in Quicken you can get it.

To get:	Look in:
Number of shares of a security	• Investment register (mutual fund accounts only) • Update Prices and Market Value screen • Portfolio value report
Market value of one security	• Investment register (mutual fund accounts only) • Update Prices and Market Value screen • Portfolio value report
Market value of one account	• Investment register • Update Prices and Market Value screen • Portfolio value report
Market value of all accounts	• Update Prices and Market Value screen • Portfolio value report
Current "cost basis" of one security	• Portfolio value report

To get:	Look in:
"Average cost per share" of one security	• Update Prices and Market Value screen
"Unrealized gain or loss" for one or all securities	• Portfolio value report
"Realized gain or loss" for one or all securities	• Capital gains report
"Percent unrealized gain or loss" for one or all securities	• Update Prices and Market Value screen
"Average annual total return" for one or all securities	• Investment performance report
Income and expenses for one or all securities or accounts	• Investment income report

Investor's Glossary

This investor's glossary explains investment terminology Quicken uses in reports and screens.

Cost basis   "Cost basis" equals the total cost to you of a security you purchased; it includes commissions, fees, and mutual fund loads. Your cost basis includes *all* purchases, even reinvestments of dividends and capital gains distributions. However, it excludes the cost of any shares you have sold or given away. Also, cost basis is reduced in a return-of-capital transaction.

- For example:
  - Suppose you buy 100 shares of stock for $2402, including the commission. The cost basis of the stock is $2402.
  - You reinvest a total of $50 of dividends in 2.5 new shares. The total cost basis increases by $50 to $2452, but the cost basis of the original 100 shares is unchanged.
  - The stock goes up in price, and you sell 50 shares for $2000. The selling price doesn't affect the cost basis. The original cost of those 50 shares was $1201 (or half of $2402), so the cost basis of the remaining 52.5 shares is now $2452 less $1201, or $1251.

    Note: Quicken assumes, unless you tell it otherwise, that the shares you sell are the ones you've had the longest. To identify different shares as the ones you're selling, use lot numbers (see "Different Lots for a Security in One Account" on page 314).

After you set up a Quicken investment account, Quicken keeps track of the cost basis of each security. It takes the dollar amount you enter for the first transaction involving a given security and uses this as the cost basis as of the date of the first transaction.

Subsequent purchase costs are added to the cost basis; the cost of shares subsequently sold and any return of capital are subtracted from it.

Average cost per share
The "average cost per share" of a security equals the cost basis divided by the total number of shares.

- For example, if you own 52.5 shares of stock with a cost basis of $1251, the average cost per share is $1251 divided by 52.5 shares, or $23.83 per share.

Quicken displays the average cost per share in the AVG COST column in the Update Prices and Market Value screen.

Unrealized gain or loss
The "unrealized gain or loss" is the difference between the current market value of a security and the cost basis. If the current market value is greater, there is a (paper) gain; if the cost basis is greater, there is a (paper) loss.

- For example, if your 52.5 shares of stock have a cost basis of $1251 but they're now worth $2100, you have an unrealized (paper) gain of $849.

Quicken displays unrealized gain or loss in the Portfolio value report under the heading Gain/Loss. A negative value indicates a (paper) loss.

Quicken also gives you the option of seeing unrealized gain or loss in the investment income report, investment transactions report, and account balances report.

Realized gain or loss
The "realized gain or loss" is the difference between selling price of a security and the cost basis. If you sell it for more than you paid, there is a (real) gain; if you sell it for less, there is a (real) loss.

- For example, when you sell 50 shares for $2000, and the cost basis of those shares is $1201, your realized gain is $799.

Quicken displays realized gain or loss in the capital gains report under the heading Gain/Loss. A negative value indicates a (real) loss.

Percent unrealized gain or loss
The "percent unrealized gain or loss" is the current price per share less the average cost per share divided by the average cost per share and multiplied by 100%. (Equivalently, the percent unrealized gain equals the unrealized gain divided by the cost basis, and multiplied by 100%.)

- For example, if the stock in the previous examples is now worth $40.00 per share, the percent unrealized gain is $40.00 less $23.83, divided by $23.83, or 67.9%.

Quicken displays the percent unrealized gain or loss in the %GAIN column in the Update Prices and Market Value screen. A negative value indicates a (paper) loss.

Average annual total return
The "average annual total return" is a percentage equal to the interest rate on a bank account that would give you the same total return on your investment. It takes into account money earned by the investment (interest, dividends, capital gains distributions) as well as changes in share price. Since it's an annual rate, it acts like a bank interest rate that compounds annually.

- For example, if you invest $10,000 and get an average annual total return of 12.0% over two years, you'd have $12,544 (an increase of $2544, or 25.4%) at the end of the two years.

Average annual total return is not the same as percent unrealized gain or loss. First, average annual total return includes money earned by the investment (for example, dividends received). Second, it depends on the amount of time it takes for the investment to grow to its value at the end of the time period. An investment that earns no income and that doubles in five years has a higher average annual total return than one that doubles in ten years. The percent gain, on the other hand, is 100% in both cases.

Note: Average annual total return is also known as "internal rate of return," or IRR.

Quicken displays the average annual total return in the investment performance report under the heading Avg. Annual Tot. Return. A negative value indicates a loss, which can be either paper or real.

Chapter 18

Working with Investment Accounts

After you know the basic features of Quicken investment accounts described in the previous chapter, you may wish to know about some additional features not covered in that chapter. This chapter tells you about less common transactions. It also explains some timesaving techniques, changing and adding to the information you've stored in Quicken, and reconciling the register.

More Investment Transactions

This section describes how to record transactions that are less common than the ones described in the previous chapter.

Giving and Receiving Securities

When you give or receive shares of a security, without using cash, Quicken treats the transaction differently than it treats a purchase or sale.

- If you're giving shares that are now in a Quicken account, enter ShrsOut in the Action field. Also enter the number of shares (but no price or dollar amount).

  Quicken reduces your number of shares and records a sale with a capital gain of zero, without adding cash to any account.

  Note: If you're transferring the shares to another Quicken account, enter a separate transaction for receipt of the shares in the register of the second account.

- If you're receiving shares, enter ShrsIn in the Action field and the number of shares received. Enter your cost basis for the shares in the $ Amount field.

  Quicken increases your number of shares without subtracting cash from any account.

Entering Stock Splits and Stock Dividends

Stock Splits

When a security declares a "stock split," you are given additional shares. Each share is now worth less than it was before the split, but the total market value of all your shares is unchanged. (In a "reverse split," you receive fewer shares than what you have now.)

If you have more than one transaction for the security on the same day, Quicken places the stock split ahead of the other transactions. For example, if you had 100 shares before a two-for-one split, and you sell 100 shares on the day of the split, Quicken knows you still have 100 shares remaining.

When you record a stock split, Quicken recalculates your average cost per share. Quicken doesn't recalculate the price. For a correct market value, press Ctrl-U and enter the new price. Quicken doesn't change transactions previously recorded in the register.

- For a stock split, enter StkSplit in the Action field. Leave empty the Price, Shares, and $ Amount fields.

- In the Split field, on the third line of the transaction, use numerals to enter the ratio of new shares to old. For example, enter a two-for-one split as 2 for: 1. If you receive one additional share for every three old shares, you now have four (or three plus one) for every three you had before, so enter 4 for: 3.

Stock Dividends

A "stock dividend," which is rare, is a dividend in the form of additional shares *instead of cash*. Most stock dividends are nontaxable. The company issuing the stock dividend will inform you whether it is taxable.

Note: A stock dividend is *not* the same as a cash (normal) dividend issued by a company, nor is it the same as a reinvested cash dividend.

- Enter a nontaxable stock dividend as a stock split. For the ratio of new shares to old shares, add 1 to the number of dividend shares given per existing share. For example, if you receive 0.05 share per existing share, use 1.05 to 1 as the ratio.

- Enter a taxable stock dividend as a reinvested dividend.

Buying on Margin

A "margin loan" is money you borrow from a broker to pay for a security you're buying.

You don't have to tell Quicken you have a margin loan. (If you buy a security and don't have enough cash for it in your account, Quicken displays a negative cash balance.) Alternatively, you may want to set up a liability account for the loan.

- To record interest you pay on the margin loan, enter MargInt in the Action field.

- If you have set up a liability account for the loan, enter XIn in the Action field for the amount you are borrowing at the time, and enter that account name as the transfer account for the money. (Enter an XOut transaction when you pay off the loan.)

Redeeming T-bills or U.S. Savings Bonds

When you buy a T-bill or U.S. Savings Bond, you buy it at a discount from its face value. When you sell it, part of the sales proceeds is interest you've earned while you've held the bill or bond.

- To record interest received when you sell, enter IntInc in the Action field.

- Subtract the interest received from the total you receive. Enter the difference as the dollar amount for the sales transaction.

Return of Capital or Principal

A "return of capital" is money paid to you as total or partial repayment of the money you invested. Return of capital differs from a sale in that you are not the one who initiates the return of capital. For example, a mortgage-backed security (such as a Ginnie Mae) returns capital when the underlying mortgages pay off principal, which is passed on to you. A unit trust returns capital as it sells the bonds within the trust. Note that return of capital, which is not a taxable event, is different from capital gains distribution.

• For a return of capital or principal, enter RtrnCap in the Action field.

Quicken reduces the cost basis of the security by the amount of the return of capital. If you have purchased shares of the security on different dates, Quicken reduces the cost basis of each set of shares in proportion to the number of shares in each set.

Recording Zero-Coupon Bonds

You buy a zero-coupon bond at a discount. While you hold it, its value increases due to the interest it earns. Even though you don't receive this interest (until you sell), it is reported to you every year on a Form 1099-OID as taxable interest.

• To record interest shown on a Form 1099-OID, enter IntInc in the Action field.

• To record the subsequent increase in value of the bond, enter RtrnCap in the Action field of a second transaction. Enter a dollar amount equal to the *negative* of the interest. (The negative RtrnCap increases your cost basis. It thus reduces unrealized gain if you sell the bond or update to the current market price of the bond.)

Selling Short

A "short sale" is the sale of a security you don't own. You deliver to the purchaser shares you borrow from your broker. You hope to buy the security later at a lower price to pay back your broker.

• For a short sale, enter Sell or SellX in the Action field. Before it records the transaction, Quicken warns you that this transaction is a short sale, in case you have entered it in error.

• When you buy the security later, enter Buy or BuyX in the Action field. Quicken calculates your gain or loss on the entire process at that time.

If you're selling short a security you already own in the same account (with the intention of buying additional shares), create different lots for the security. See "Different Lots for a Security in One Account" on page 314.

Using Reminder Memos

Quicken lets you enter a reminder memo in the investment register. For example, you may want to remind yourself that a CD is maturing next month.

If you have installed Quicken's Billminder program, every time you turn on your computer you see a message that you have a reminder, until you turn off the reminder memo.

To enter a reminder memo:

1. Enter Reminder in the Action field.

2. Use one or both lines in the Security field to enter the wording of the reminder memo.

To turn off a reminder memo:

1. In the transaction containing the reminder memo, tab to the Security field.

2. Press the right arrow key to move to the C field.

3. In the C field, enter an asterisk (*) or X.

4. Press Ctrl-Enter or F10 to record.

 # Recurring Investment Transactions

You probably have some regularly recurring investment transactions. Your stocks pay regular dividends, for example. Perhaps you are in an employee stock-purchase plan that invests a certain amount from your salary every pay period. Alternatively, you may be drawing a fixed amount of cash every month from your mutual fund.

Quicken makes it easy to enter recurring transactions in investment (as well as noninvestment) accounts without starting from scratch each time. You can have Quicken memorize a transaction and store it. When you want to use it, you recall it from a list of memorized transactions. You can modify the new transaction (update it, change the share price or amount) before recording it.

Note: If you've already memorized transactions for noninvestment accounts, Quicken keeps them on a separate list from memorized investment transactions.

To memorize an investment transaction:

1. At the register, select the transaction you wish to memorize.

2. Choose Memorize Transaction from the Shortcuts menu, or press Ctrl-M.
    Quicken confirms that you are about to memorize a transaction.

3. Press Enter.

You can memorize transactions with no amounts.

You'll probably find it useful to memorize investment transactions with no amounts. For example, if you reinvest quarterly dividends from a mutual fund, memorize the transaction before you've entered the share price, number of share, and dollar amount. You can fill in the new amounts when you recall the transaction.

Note: Memorized investment transactions for all your investment accounts (within the same file) appear on the same list. If you have the same recurring transaction in two different investment accounts, you don't need to memorize it more than once.

To recall a memorized transaction:

1. At the end of the register, choose Recall Transaction from the Shortcuts menu, or press Ctrl-T.

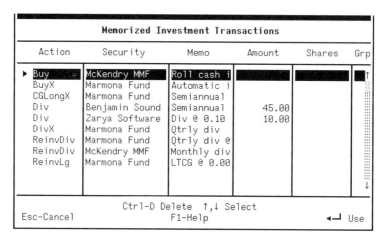

2. Choose the transaction you wish to recall.

   Quicken displays the register, with the copied transaction in place.

3. Make any desired changes to the transaction in the register, and press Ctrl-Enter or F10 to record.

Shortcut for recalling a memorized investment transaction

If you have only one memorized investment transaction for a given action, type the first few letters of the action (as many as make it unique on the list) directly in the Action field of the register. Then press Ctrl-E (instead of Ctrl-T). The entire transaction appears in the register.

To delete a memorized transaction:

1. At the register, choose Recall Transaction from the Shortcuts menu, or press Ctrl-T. The Memorized Transactions List appears.

2. Select the transaction you wish to delete.

3. Press Ctrl-D. After the warning appears, press Enter.

Grouping Transactions That Occur on the Same Date

You may have several transactions in the same investment account that occur regularly on the same date. For example, three bonds may all pay interest on the first day of the quarter. Quicken makes it easy for you to recall such transactions as a group.

Before you can set up a group of investment transactions, you must memorize each transaction in the group (see "To memorize an investment transaction:" on page 309).

You may have used Quicken transaction groups for your other Quicken accounts. If you're not already familiar with transaction groups, you'll find information about them in *Entering Transaction Groups*, beginning on page 211. They work the same way in all Quicken accounts.

More About Your Securities

Price History of Securities

For each security, Quicken keeps track of all prices recorded on different dates. You can view a list of dates and prices, and add or change prices for any date.

To view the price history of a security:

1. At the Main Menu or the investment register, press Ctrl-U to view the Update Prices and Market Value screen.

2. At the Update Prices and Market Value screen, select the security for which you wish to see a price history.

3. Choose Price History from the Shortcuts menu, or press Ctrl-H.

   The Price History window for the security appears. The most recent prices are at the top of the list.

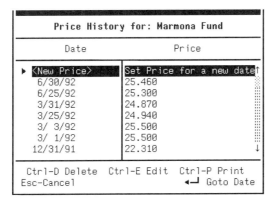

To print the price history of a security on paper or to a file:

1. At the Price History press Ctrl-P.

2. At the Print Price History window, select the printer or type of file. (Note that the earliest prices print at the top of the list.)

To add a price to the price history:

1. At the Price History window choose <New Price>.

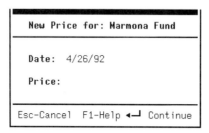

2. Enter the date for the new price.

3. Enter the new price.

   The Price History window reappears. The new date and price are there, in the correct order by date.

To change or delete an existing price in the price history:

1. At the Price History window select the date of the price you wish to change or delete.

2. To change (edit) a price, press Ctrl-E. After making the change, press Enter to record it.

   To delete a price, press Ctrl-D.

Exporting and Importing Prices

Exporting Price Histories of Securities

You can export the price history of one or all securities to an ASCII file. You can then import the price history from the ASCII file into another Quicken file.

Before you export price histories, you must have a symbol for each security whose price history you want to export. You can add symbols by editing your security list. (For instructions, see "Changing Securities, Types, and Goals" on page 315.)

Quicken puts one symbol/price/date on a line in alphabetical order by security name (not symbol) and, for any one security, in ascending order by date. All prices are in decimals. The security symbols and dates are set off by quote marks; the symbols, prices, and dates are separated by commas. For example:

"BENJ",50.875," 2/10/88"
"BENJ",55.625,"12/31/89"

To export price histories to an ASCII file:

1. At the investment register, choose Update Prices from the Activities menu to view the Update Prices and Market Value screen.

2. If you want to export the price history of a single security, select that security.

3. Choose Export Prices from the Print/Acct menu.

4. Choose between exporting the price history of the named security or of all securities.

5. Type the DOS filename to use for the price history. (Quicken creates a file if one with this name does not already exist.)

Importing Security Prices

You can import security price data from an ASCII file. The data must be in standard, comma-delimited, ASCII format with one symbol/price/date per line. ("Comma-delimited" means values are separated by commas, as in the next examples.) Quicken can handle quotes. The following formats are all acceptable:

- ABC, 123.456
- ABC, 123.456, 12/31/91
- "ABC", 123.456, "12/31/91"
- "ABC", "123.456", "12/31/91"

Note: Quicken matches up the prices it imports based on the *symbol*, not the *name*, of the security. If you wish to import prices, you may need to add symbols to the securities on your security list. See "Changing Securities, Types, and Goals" on page 315.

To import price data:

1. At the investment register, choose Update Prices from the Activities menu to view the Update Prices and Market Value screen.

2. Choose Import Prices from the Print/Acct menu.

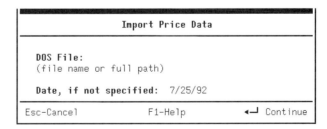

3. Type the name of the ASCII file that contains the price data. If the file is not in the default directory, specify the full path.

4. Change the date in the window, if necessary.

Ordinarily, Quicken uses the date supplied in the file. If there is no date, Quicken uses the date in the Import Price Data window.

Export and import prices to fill in the price history of a new lot.

When you keep track of different lots of a single security (see "Different Lots for a Security in One Account" below), you give each lot the same symbol. When you create a new lot, it has no price history. To give it the same price history as the older lot, export the price history of the older lot to an ASCII file. Then import it from the file. The prices go into the price history of the new lot because it has the same symbol.

Different Lots for a Security in One Account

One reason to use different lots of the same security is when you're selling a portion of your shares and want to identify which shares you're selling. (Unless told otherwise, Quicken assumes you're selling the ones you bought earliest.)

Or, you may sell short a security you already own in the same account, and you want Quicken to know that the short sale is for a different lot of shares.

To create a different lot for an existing security:

1. Set up a security with the same name but add a number after the name.

2. Use the exact same symbol for the security in both lots.

Quicken recognizes lots of the same security by the symbol. If you don't have a symbol for the first security, edit it to give it one. (See "Changing Securities, Types, and Goals" on page 315 if you need instructions.)

3. (Optional) Edit the first security name to add a 1, so you'll recognize that it too is a separate lot.

4. If necessary, revise earlier transactions for the security in the register by substituting the new lot in the Security field.

Combining and Displaying Lots

Lots always appear separately on the securities list, in the investment register, and in investment reports. However, you can combine the lots of one security on the Update Prices and Market Value screen. It is easier to enter new prices if you combine lots.

To combine lots on the Update Prices and Market Value screen, press F8 at that screen. The lots of the same security combine, using the name of the alphabetically first lot name and its most recent price. The number of shares is the total for all lots.

To display your individual holdings for each lot on the Update Prices and Market Value screen, press F8 again. (This key toggles between combining lots and displaying lots.)

$ Making Changes

You can modify your list of securities at any time. You cannot delete a security when you have transactions for it in any of your investment accounts (within the same file); however, you can prevent it from appearing on the Update Prices and Market Value screen.

You can also adjust the cash balance of a regular investment account, adjust the share balance of any security, search for transactions, change transactions, and change the type of account.

Changing Securities, Types, and Goals

To modify an existing security:

1. At the investment register, choose Security List from the Shortcuts menu (or press Ctrl-Y).

   Quicken displays the Security List window.

2. Select the security you wish to modify (edit).

3. Press Ctrl-E.

   Quicken displays the Edit Security window.

4. Make your changes. Then press Enter or F10 to record the changes.

To modify an existing security type:

1. At the Type field of the Set Up Security window or the Edit Security window, press Ctrl-L to display the list of security types.

2. Select the type you wish to modify (edit).

3. Press Ctrl-E. Enter your modification, and press Enter or F10 to record it.

How to drop a security from the Update Prices screen

The Display field in the Security List window determines whether a security appears on the Update prices screen.

- You may wish to drop a security from the Update Prices screen when you no longer own it and don't wish to track it. Select the security in the security list and press the Spacebar until the Display field reads "Open." The security then appears only for dates on which you owned it (or held a short position in it).

- You may wish to drop a constant-price security such as a CD or money market fund from the screen completely. Select the security in the security list and press the Spacebar until the Display field reads "Never."

To modify an existing investment goal:

1. At the Goal field of the Set Up Security window or the Edit Security window, press Ctrl-L to display the list of investment goals.

2. Select the goal you wish to modify (edit).

3. Press Ctrl-E. Enter your modification, and press the Enter key or F10 to record it.

Deleting Securities, Types, and Goals

To delete an unused existing security:

1. At the investment register, choose Security List from the Shortcuts menu (or press Ctrl-Y).

   The Security List window appears.

2. Use the up and down arrow keys to select the security you wish to delete.

3. Press Ctrl-D. After the warning appears, press the Enter key.

To delete an unused security type:

1. At the Type field of the Set Up Security window or the Edit Security window, press Ctrl-L to display the list of security types.

2. Use the up and down arrow keys to select the type you wish to delete. Press Ctrl-D. After the warning appears, press the Enter key.

To delete an unused investment goal:

1. At the Goal field of the Set Up Security window or the Edit Security window, press Ctrl-L to display the list of investment goals.

2. Use the up and down arrow keys to select the goal you wish to delete. Press Ctrl-D. After the warning appears, press the Enter key.

Adjusting the Cash or Share Balance

You can adjust the cash or share balance if you want to make it match what's on your statement, and don't want to use the reconciling process.

Use these adjustments to correct discrepancies caused by rounding off.

To adjust cash or share balance:

1. At the Activities menu of the investment register, choose Adjust Balance.
   - If you're working with a mutual fund account, the Adjust Share Balance window appears.
   - If you're working with a regular account, you're given a choice between adjusting cash balance for the account or share balance for a security within the account. Enter your choice.

2. Enter the date for the adjustment, the correct value for the balance, and the security name (if requested).

   At the Security to Adjust blank, you can press Ctrl-Y to view and choose from the security list.

The adjustment appears in the register with the action MiscExp for cash balance adjustments, and ShrsIn or ShrsOut for share balance adjustments. The memo for the adjustment is "Balance Adjustment."

Finding a Transaction in the Register

You can have Quicken search for a transaction by matching the action, security, price, number of shares, amount, cleared status, or memo.

To search for a transaction:

1. At the investment register, choose Find from the Edit menu, or press Ctrl-F.

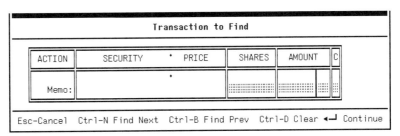

2. In the Transaction to Find window, fill in all the items you want Quicken to match.

   You can use two dots after an action or security (for example Sell.. or Fid..) to have Quicken find any transaction with an action or security beginning with those letters.

3. To find a match in the backward direction, press Ctrl-B. To find a match in the forward direction, press Ctrl-N.

4. To search again, press Ctrl-B to search backward, and press Ctrl-N to search forward to the next match.

5. To clear the window, press Ctrl-D.

Changing a Transaction in the Register

You can go back to a transaction in the register at any time and make changes in it. Quicken automatically calculates related quantities, so it's important to make changes completely and methodically.

To change a transaction:

1. Use PgUp, PgDn, or the up and down arrow keys to select the transaction in the register.

2. If the cursor is not in the Date field, press Home once or twice until it moves there.

3. At each field, make a correction, if desired, and press Enter to move to the next field.

> **Press Ctrl-Backspace to erase an amount.**
>
> It's often easier to erase an amount than to correct it.

4. When the transaction is the way you want it, press Ctrl-Enter or F10 to record it.

If the change affects securities that have subsequent buy or sell transactions in the register, you'll see a message "Recalculating gains & losses…"

Changing the Type of Account

Suppose you set up and use a mutual fund account and then decide you'd like to be able to include another security or a cash balance. You can easily change to a regular investment account. (You can use a parallel procedure to change in the opposite direction *only* if you have a single security and no cash balance in the regular investment account.)

To change to a regular investment account:

1. At the Main Menu, choose Select Account.

2. Select the account you want to change, and press Ctrl-E.

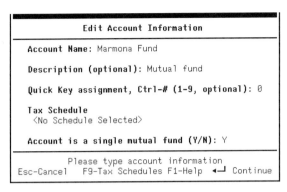

```
┌──────────────────────────────────────────────────┐
│ ████████████████████████████████████████████████ │
│               Edit Account Information             │
├──────────────────────────────────────────────────┤
│  Account Name: Marmona Fund                        │
│                                                    │
│  Description (optional): Mutual fund               │
│                                                    │
│  Quick Key assignment, Ctrl-# (1-9, optional): 0   │
│                                                    │
│  Tax Schedule                                      │
│    <No Schedule Selected>                          │
│                                                    │
│  Account is a single mutual fund (Y/N): Y          │
├──────────────────────────────────────────────────┤
│             Please type account information        │
│  Esc-Cancel   F9-Tax Schedules F1-Help  ◄─┘ Continue│
└──────────────────────────────────────────────────┘
```

3. (Optional) In the Edit Account Information window, change the account name, description, or quick key assignment.

4. Answer **N** for whether the account is a single mutual fund, and press Enter.

$ Entering Prior History for Investments

The more information you give Quicken about your investments, the more complete and accurate your reports and summaries will be.

You may have set up a new investment account by entering a rough estimate of what you paid for the securities. You may have omitted dividends or capital gains distributions that you received since buying the securities.

Here's a guide for what you need to tell Quicken in order to get specific information.

To get:	Tell Quicken:
Accurate market values for a specified date	• Price and number of shares of securities owned on that date
Accurate average annual total return for a specified time period	• Price and number of shares on *day before* beginning of period and on last day of period • All transactions during the period
Accurate capital gains summary (realized short-term and long-term gain or loss) for a specified time period	• Number of shares and cost basis on date at least one year before beginning of period for all securities you have sold • All purchases and sales (including stock splits, reinvestments, and return of capital) from that date to end of period

To get:	**Tell Quicken:**
Accurate income and expense summary for a specified time period	• All transactions during the period • Number of shares owned and price per share at beginning and end of period (if you're including unrealized gains)

To revise the initial shares-in transaction for a security:

1. At the investment register, select the initial transaction for the security.

2. Revise the date, if necessary, to the initial date of acquisition.

3. Using Ctrl-Backspace, erase the price and leave it blank.

4. Revise the number of shares and dollar amount.

   For the dollar amount, enter the amount paid, including commission, fees, and load, or, if you acquired the shares from someone, your cost basis for the shares.

5. Press Ctrl-Enter or F10 to record the revised transaction.

   The revised transaction appears in the register in the correct sequence for the new date.

To enter transactions for dates in the past:

1. Enter additional transactions at the end of the register, correcting the date. (Or, select the first transaction in the register after the correct date. Press Ctrl-Ins to insert a blank transaction above it to fill in.)

   Each transaction appears in the register in the correct sequence for its date.

2. If a transaction involves a transfer of cash out of the account (for example, a dividend paid directly to you), enter the name of the investment account itself in the Account blank. Use this procedure for both types of investment account. In a regular account, it has no effect on the cash balance.

Note: After you've entered the transactions from the past, your cash balance for the whole account or your share balance for any security may be incorrect. Adjust it by choosing Adjust Balance from the Activities menu. See "Adjusting the Cash or Share Balance" on page 317.

Tracking Indexes and Securities You Don't Own

You may want one or more of the popular stock indexes, such as the Dow Jones Industrial Average or Standard & Poor's 500-stock index, to appear on the Security Price and Market Value list.

Perhaps you'd like to follow the price of a security you don't own.

You have two options. Under Option 1 you can track prices. Under Option 2 you can track both prices and performance.

Option 1: Add index or security to your securities list.

Add the index or security to your securities list in the usual way. Then examine it on the list. Be sure that the display field reads "Always." (You may have to select the security and press the spacebar until the display field changes to "Always.")

For an index, you may wish to set up a security type called "Index."

Option 2: Set up an investment account for the index or security.

Follow Option 1, but in addition set up an investment account such as "Index" or "What If."

To enter an index or security you don't own:

1. At the register, enter the date from which you are beginning to track, and enter ShrsIn in the Action field.

2. Enter the name of the index or unowned security in the Security field.

3. Enter the index value or security price in the Price field.

4. Enter 1 in the Shares field.

5. Record the transaction.

Note: If you watch the price of a mutual fund you don't own, be aware that the price may drop because of income or capital gains distributions. When a fund makes a distribution, the share price is reduced by an equal amount (in addition to any changes caused by changes in market value of the underlying securities in the fund).

$ Reconciling the Investment Register

When you get a statement from your broker or other financial adviser, you may wish to reconcile your Quicken investment account with the statement.

Reconciling an investment account is similar to reconciling other Quicken accounts. If you've been reconciling your other Quicken accounts, follow the same procedures.

You reconcile regular and mutual fund accounts the same way, except that you reconcile cash balance in one and share balance in the other. Choose Reconcile from the Activities menu, and follow the directions.

- After you've reconciled the cash balance for a regular investment account, Quicken takes you to the Update Prices and Market Value screen. If you haven't already entered the share prices from the statement, you have a chance to do so now.

- After you've reconciled the share balance for a mutual fund account, Quicken displays the Share Balance Reconciled window. Quicken automatically adds the latest price to the price history for the security.

Chapter 19

Tracking Credit Cards

Credit card expenses are an integral part of most personal and some business finances. This chapter describes several different ways you can handle your credit cards with Quicken, including using a separate Quicken credit card account or entering the information in your Quicken checking account. With each method you can categorize your credit card spending and include the information in reports. The methods vary in the amount of detail that Quicken keeps about your credit card expenditures. The method you choose depends on how you use your credit cards, and how much or how little time you want to spend keeping records of your credit card expenses.

$ When to Use Quicken Credit Card Accounts

Many credit card users will want to use Quicken's credit card accounts. Credit card accounts are particularly useful if you want detailed records of your credit card transactions, or if you pay your credit card charges over time. If you pay off your credit cards in full each month, you may not want to set up credit card accounts. Instead, you can create an expense category for credit card charges, and then enter the payment in your checking account register when you pay the bill.

Use the following information to help you determine the best way to use Quicken to track your credit card transactions and payments. If you're unsure which method to use, start with the simplest method: handle your credit cards through your checking account, as shown in "Handling Credit Cards in Your Checking Account" on page 325. Later, if you decide you want to reconcile your credit card charges, you can open a separate credit card account.

If You Usually Pay Your Credit Card Bills in Full

If you usually pay your credit card bills in full and you want to keep records of only a few individual credit card transactions:

Don't set up credit card accounts. Instead, just record the check that pays the bill in your Quicken bank account. You can split that transaction if you want to assign particular credit card charges or groups of charges to categories. See "Handling Credit Cards in Your Checking Account" on page 325.

This is the fastest way to handle credit cards. However, it won't keep track of your outstanding credit card balance.

If You Pay Your Credit Card Bills Over Time

If you pay your credit card bills over time and you want to keep records of some (but not all) credit card transactions:

Set up credit card accounts. In each credit card account, enter only those transactions you want to keep a record of. (You can use your charge slips, or work from your monthly credit card statement.) You can have Quicken create one transaction covering all the charges you don't want to take the time to enter. See "Working with Quicken Credit Card Accounts" on page 326.

When you're ready to make a payment, have Quicken do it from your credit card account. See "Reconciling Your Credit Card Account" on page 328.

With this method you can keep detailed records of selected transactions without taking the time to enter every credit card transaction.

If You Want to Know Your Outstanding Credit Card Balance at All Times

If you want to know your outstanding credit card balance at all times:

Set up credit card accounts. Enter each credit card transaction in the account from your charge slips as you make purchases throughout the month.

Let Quicken write a check to pay your credit card bill. See "Reconciling Your Credit Card Account" on page 328.

The credit card register shows your card balance and the available credit remaining on the card.

If You Want Records of Every Credit Card Transaction

If you want records of every credit card transaction:

Set up credit card accounts. Enter each credit card transaction in the account. You can use your charge slips, or enter the information from your credit card statement once a month.

Let Quicken write a check to pay your credit card bill when you process your credit card statement. See "Reconciling Your Credit Card Account" on page 328.

This method is best if you want to keep a complete record of your credit card use.

Handling Credit Cards in Your Checking Account

If you usually pay your credit cards in full, you don't need to set up credit card accounts. The example below shows how to keep track of your credit card expenses from your Quicken checking account. With this method, you can keep track of some or all of your credit card purchases by using a split transaction and assigning categories when you write a check to pay your bill. This is the fastest way to handle credit cards with Quicken.

If you want to enter each transaction, or to be able to view your credit card balances in Quicken, set up and use Quicken credit card accounts. Skip this section and go to "Working with Quicken Credit Card Accounts" on page 326.

To track credit card expenses in a checking account:

Suppose your department store credit card statement shows ten new transactions: five are clothing, one is a gift, and four are for miscellaneous items that you don't want to keep a record of. (You don't have to categorize all your credit card transactions.)

1. Write the check for $345.00 to pay the bill. (Don't enter any categories yet.)

2. Press Ctrl-S to open the Split Transaction window.

3. In the first Category field, type Gifts and press Enter twice.

    Quicken displays the total amount of the check in the Amount field.

4. Enter the amount of the gift (88.45) to replace the total now shown (345.00).

5. Press Enter to move to the next Category field.

    Quicken calculates the remainder and inserts it (261.55) in the Amount field.

6. Type Clothing and press Enter twice.

7. Enter the total of all the clothing expenditures (238.34) in the next Amount field and press Enter.

    Press Ctrl-O to use the Calculator to total the charges.

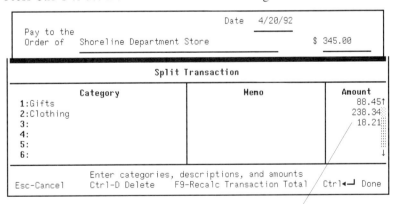

Quicken inserts the remaining amount here. This is the amount for the four miscellaneous items. Leave it blank and Quicken lists it as "Other" on reports.

8. Press Ctrl-Enter twice to close the Split Transaction window and record the check.

From now on, Quicken includes the categorized Gifts and Clothing expenses when you create summary and budget reports.

 # Working with Quicken Credit Card Accounts

A Quicken credit card account is very similar to a Quicken bank account, except that you enter all transactions in the credit card register. If you've used a Quicken bank account, you already know most of what you'll need to use a credit card account.

Basic Steps for Using a Quicken Credit Card Account

Set Up the Account

You should set up a separate credit card account for each credit card you use. The easiest way to set up a new account is to select <New Account> from the Select Account to Use screen (enter 2 for a credit card account). For complete information about setting up accounts, see "Setting Up and Using Additional Quicken Accounts" on page 245. As the opening balance, enter the amount you currently owe on the card. Before actually setting up the account, Quicken also asks you to enter your credit card limit.

Enter Transactions

There are two ways to enter credit card transactions. You can:

•   Save your transaction slips when you charge an item and enter the transactions as they occur throughout the month.

This method provides you with your current credit card balance at all times. It also lets you double-check your charges against those listed on your credit card statement.

OR

•   Wait until you receive your monthly statement and enter the transactions from the statement.

If you don't need to know your balance throughout the month, this method is easy to use. You can also enter some or all of the transactions.

To see how credit card transactions are filled in, see "The Credit Card Register" on page 327. If you want to review how to enter transactions in a register, see "Adding Transactions to the Check Register" on page 59. The basic steps for entering transactions are the same in all types of Quicken accounts.

Reconcile the Statement and Pay the Bill

When you receive the credit card statement each month, use Quicken to reconcile it. Reconciling a credit card statement is similar to reconciling a bank statement: you check off transactions to make sure they're accurate. However, at the end of this process, Quicken automatically creates a transaction to cover any expenses you didn't want to itemize as separate transactions in the account, and writes a check to the credit card company for the amount you specify.

See "Reconciling Your Credit Card Account" on page 328 for step-by-step instructions.

$ The Credit Card Register

To view the register for a credit card account, press Ctrl-A, or choose Select Account from the Main Menu, or choose Select/Set Up Account from the Print/Acct menu. At the Select Account to Use window, select the credit card account you want and press Enter. (Quicken lists credit card accounts with "CCard" in the Type column.)

Note: If you haven't set up a Quicken credit card account yet, choose <New Account> and fill in the Set Up New Account window. For complete information about setting up accounts, see "Working with Multiple Accounts" on page 245.

In the Payee field, enter the name of the store where the charge was made or any other word or phrase you want.

Use the Charge field for amounts you have charged, finance charges, and other fees.

The C (Cleared) field displays an X for transactions you cleared when reconciling your monthly credit card statement.

Use the Payment field to record a credit; for example, for merchandise returned.

Enter category information about credit card charges. Then you can include credit card expenses in reports on your income and expenses.

This payment was made automatically when the credit card statement was processed. The account name tells you what account the check was recorded in.

Account name.

DATE	REF	PAYEE * MEMO * CATEGORY	CHARGE	C	PAYMENT	BALANCE
2/21 1992		Duke of Edinburgh Pub Dining	125 00			3,106 06
2/21 1992		Designs by Rick Flowers Gifts	32 95			3,139 01
2/25 1992		The Topographic Ocean Returned Aquarium			110 98	3,028 03
2/28 1992	Memo: Cat:	Citibank A/C #4128-3748-2984 [Joint Account]			2,731 07	296 96
3/ 2 1992		Carlson Appliances New Microwave Household	325 98			622 94
3/ 7 1992		Pescado Hills Wine Making Hobby Expenses	152 35			775 29

```
Print/Acct   Edit   Shortcuts   Reports   Activities            F1-Help
```
```
M-C                      (Alt+letter accesses menu)    Credit Remaining:$3,203.75
Esc-Main Menu          Ctrl↵  Record                   Ending Balance:  $1,796.25
```

If you record transactions from your monthly statement, enter an asterisk (*) in this field. This step saves you time when you process your statement.

Available credit for this card.

The amount you owe on this account.

Making a Transfer to Another Account

You can have Quicken automatically transfer money from your credit card account to another account, or from another account into your credit card account.

You'll find complete information about how to enter account transfer information in transactions in "Basic Steps to Transfer Money Between Quicken Accounts" on page 254.

For example, if you use your credit card account to provide overdraft protection for your checking account, you can have Quicken transfer the money to your checking account register when you record the charge made to your credit card.

Enter the name of your bank account here to have Quicken record a transfer of funds.

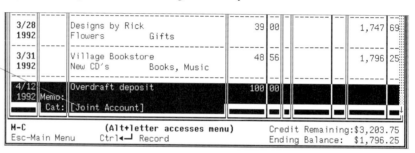

```
------  -------- --------------------------  ------ --       -- ------ --
3/28    Designs by Rick                      39 00           1,747 69
1992    Flowers           Gifts
------  -------- --------------------------  -- --           -- ------ --
3/31    Village Bookstore                    48 56           1,796 25
1992    New CD's          Books, Music
------  -------- --------------------------  -- --           -- ------ --
4/12    Overdraft deposit                   100 00
1992 Memo:
     Cat: [Joint Account]
------  -------- --------------------------  ------ --       -- ------ --

M-C                 (Alt+letter accesses menu)    Credit Remaining:$3,203.75
Esc-Main Menu       Ctrl◄┘ Record                 Ending Balance:  $1,796.25
```

Here is the resulting transaction as it appears in the register for your checking account.

Quicken recorded this transaction in your check register when you entered the transfer in your Master Charge register.

```
------  -------- --------------------------  ------ --       -- ------ --
3/31 5023   National Wildlife Committee     100 00           8,799 39
1992                         Charity
------  -------- --------------------------  -- --           -- ------ --
4/12    Deposit                                     400 00   9,199 39
1992 SPLIT                   Bonus
------  -------- --------------------------  -- --           -- ------ --
4/12    Overdraft deposit                                  100 00  9,299 39
1992 Memo:
     Cat: [M-C]
------  -------- --------------------------  ------ --       -- ------ --

Joint Account       (Alt+letter accesses menu)    Current Balance: $    0.00
Esc-Main Menu       Ctrl◄┘ Record                 Ending Balance: $10,829.39
```

Reconciling Your Credit Card Account

To make sure your credit card account contains accurate information, you should reconcile it each month with your monthly credit card statement. This process also allows you to take advantage of the following Quicken features:

- You don't have to enter every credit card charge. Instead, Quicken automatically creates a single transaction that covers all the charges you did not record individually.

- Quicken automatically enters a transaction that records any finance charges to your credit card account.

- Quicken automatically writes a check to pay your credit card bill.

You reconcile a Quicken credit card statement much as you reconcile a Quicken bank account against a bank statement. You mark transactions as cleared and enter any missing transactions for which you want to keep a record. You must reconcile one monthly statement at a time, in chronological order. (Reconcile your oldest statement first.)

Note: If you enter credit card transactions only from your statement rather than from credit card slips, you can mark them cleared as you enter them. Do this by entering an asterisk (*) in the C (Cleared) column of the register.

To reconcile your credit card statement and pay your bill:

1. At the credit card register, choose Reconcile/Pay Credit Card from the Activities menu.

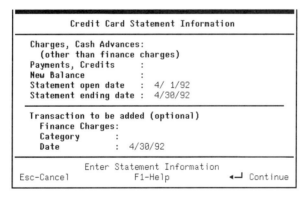

```
              Credit Card Statement Information

   Charges, Cash Advances:
      (other than finance charges)
   Payments, Credits     :
   New Balance           :
   Statement open date   :   4/ 1/92
   Statement ending date :   4/30/92

   Transaction to be added (optional)
      Finance Charges:
      Category           :
      Date               :   4/30/92

                 Enter Statement Information
   Esc-Cancel            F1-Help           ◄┘ Continue
```

2. Fill in the window with the information from your credit card statement:

   a. Enter the total dollar amount of new charges shown on your statement.

   b. Enter the total dollar amount of new payments shown on your statement.

   c. Enter the current balance shown on your statement.

   d. Enter the statement dates.

   e. Enter the total finance charges for the month, any category to which this amount should be assigned, and the date. (Quicken records a transaction for this amount.)

When you've completed the information in the window, Quicken displays a list of uncleared items in the register.

3. Mark each transaction that is listed on your credit card statement as cleared in the register. You can do this in one of three ways:

   • In the list of uncleared items, select each transaction that is listed on your credit card statement and press the spacebar or Enter to mark it as cleared. (An asterisk appears next to each transaction that you mark.)

   OR

   • Press F9 to display the register. Then select each transaction you want to mark cleared and enter an asterisk (*) in the C (Cleared) column.

   OR

   • Press F8 to display a window where you can enter a range of dates and have Quicken mark all transactions with those dates.

4. When you find transactions listed on your statement that are not shown in the register, you can enter them. (Or, if you prefer, Quicken can lump these new charges into one transaction for the remaining amount when you finish processing your statement.)

   Display the register and enter the missing transactions. (Enter an asterisk (*) in the C (Cleared) column when you enter the transaction.)

5. When you finish marking cleared transactions, compare the totals at the bottom of the screen with those on your credit card statement.

   The amount in the Difference field is the difference between the items you've marked cleared and the balance on your statement.

   If the difference is zero (0.00), your account balances. Press Ctrl-F10. Then turn to "Paying Your Bill" on page 332.

   If the difference is not zero and you want Quicken to create adjustment transactions for the difference, press Ctrl-F10. See "Having Quicken Add Adjustments to Your Account" below.

   Or, if the difference is not zero and you want to track down the difference and enter or correct transactions, you can do so now. See "Finding the Difference" on page 331.

Having Quicken Add Adjustments to Your Account

Quicken can make three types of adjustments to your credit card account during reconciliation:

- Opening balance
- Missing charges
- Missing payments

When you press Ctrl-F10 to finish reconciling your statement and there is a difference between the items you've marked cleared and the statement balance, Quicken displays the Adjusting Register window.

This window summarizes the adjustments needed to reconcile the account, which may include opening balance adjustments, missing charges, or missing payments.

The window lists entries appropriate for the differences Quicken has found. When needed, an entry for missing payments appears.

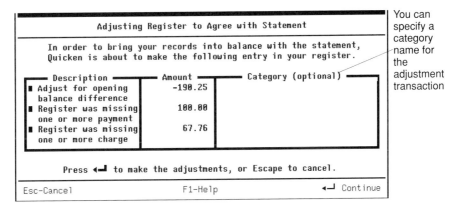

You can specify a category name for the adjustment transaction

Press Enter to tell Quicken to record the adjustment transactions. Then go on to "Paying Your Bill" on page 332.

Finding the Difference

If you want detailed records of all your credit card transactions, you may not want to have Quicken create an adjustment transaction for you. Instead, use the summary information at the bottom of the screen to help you locate the problem.

When you want your credit card account to balance exactly, the method you use is very similar to the one you follow to reconcile a Quicken bank account. See "Finding and Correcting a Current Statement Difference" on page 129 for tips on how to pinpoint the cause of the difference between your account and your statement.

Paying Your Bill

After you reconcile your credit card statement, you can pay the bill by having Quicken write a check or record a handwritten check in the register.

Quicken displays the Make Credit Card Payment window as the last step in reconciling your statement. Fill it in as indicated. Then press Enter to complete reconciliation and have Quicken begin writing the check.

Enter the name of the checking account from which you plan to write the check.

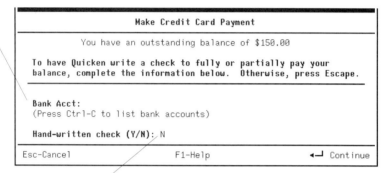

```
                      Make Credit Card Payment

              You have an outstanding balance of $150.00

     To have Quicken write a check to fully or partially pay your
     balance, complete the information below.  Otherwise, press Escape.


     Bank Acct:
     (Press Ctrl-C to list bank accounts)

     Hand-written check (Y/N): N

     Esc-Cancel                 F1-Help              ←┘ Continue
```

Enter Y if you want to record a handwritten check instead of a check printed with Quicken. If you have electronic payment turned on, this field lets you choose between a check printed with Quicken, a handwritten check, and an electronic payment.

When you press Enter to leave this window, Quicken takes you automatically to the Write Checks screen or the register of your bank account, where you can finish writing the check.

If you complete the check with a payee, memo, and address, Quicken automatically uses that information the next time you make a credit card payment on this account.

Making a partial payment

Quicken automatically enters the amount needed to pay the total due on the credit card bill. If you prefer to make a partial payment, change the amount of the check and press Ctrl-Enter to record the payment.

Chapter 20

Tracking Cash

This chapter describes two different ways to record your cash transactions in Quicken:

- You can set up a separate Quicken account in which to record your cash transactions.
- You can categorize your cash spending right in your Quicken bank account.

Both methods let you categorize your cash expenses so that you can include them in reports. The method you choose depends on how much detailed information you want to keep about your cash spending.

 ## When to Use a Quicken Cash Account

Cash accounts are useful if you want to keep detailed records of most cash transactions you make. If you prefer to use cash instead of checks or credit cards, you'll find that by setting up a separate cash account you can easily track what you spend. Just save your cash receipts and enter them in the register for your cash account. You'll also find cash accounts useful if you are often paid in cash. Businesses can use cash accounts to track petty cash.

On the other hand, many people want to track only a few cash transactions. The rest can be simply treated as "miscellaneous" expenses. If that's true for you, don't set up a separate cash account. Instead, enter the information in the register for your bank account, as explained in the next section.

Handling Cash Through Your Checking Account

If you want to track only a few cash expenditures, you don't need to set up a separate cash account. Instead, record checks for cash and withdrawals in your Quicken bank account as usual. Assign these transactions to a category such as "Misc. cash." Then when you have important cash purchases that you want to record, split one of those cash transactions.

Recording a Deposit Less Cash Transaction

Let's say you have a $500 bonus check and you want to get $100 in cash (for as yet unknown uses) and deposit the remaining $400 in your checking account.

Here's how to enter the deposit less cash transaction:

1. Enter the deposit into the register for your checking account. In the Deposit field, enter $400.

2. Press Ctrl-S to display the Split Transaction window.

3. In the first Category field, enter the category you use for bonus income (for example, "Bonus") and press Enter twice.

4. In the Amount field, enter $500 to replace the amount shown and press Enter. This gives you a record of the total amount of your bonus. Quicken inserts the difference between the category amount and the transaction amount on the next line.

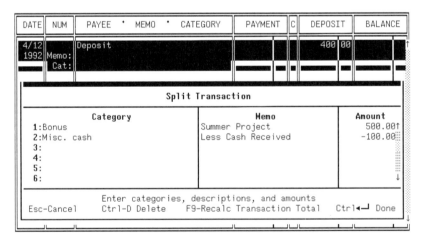

5. In the second Category field, enter the category you use for miscellaneous cash spending. Or, leave it blank and Quicken includes it in a category called "Other" when you produce summary reports.

6. Press Ctrl-Enter twice to close the Split Transaction window and record the transaction.

Recording Important Cash Expenses

Suppose you give $50 cash to a charity, and spend $95 entertaining a client at a business lunch. You want to categorize the first to "Charity" and the second to "T&E:Meals."

Enter the information in the register for your checking account:

1. Select a withdrawal in the register for your checking account that gave you some cash. Pick any one dated on or around the date of your purchases. It is not important which cash-generating transaction you pick. (You can use Find or Go to Date from the Edit menu to help locate the transaction. See "Using Find" on page 63 and "Using Go to Date" on page 65.)

2. Press Ctrl-S to open the Split Transaction window.

3. Move the cursor to the Category field next to the uncategorized cash amount (or next to your category for miscellaneous cash expenses, if you have one).

4. Enter Charity and press Enter twice.

5. Enter $50 to replace the amount shown in the Amount field and press Enter.

6. Quicken inserts the uncategorized remainder in the next Amount field.

7. Enter T&E:Meals as the next category, and $95 in the Amount field.

   Quicken calculates the remainder and inserts it in the next Amount field.

8. Leave the category for this last amount blank, or enter the category you use for miscellaneous cash expenses.

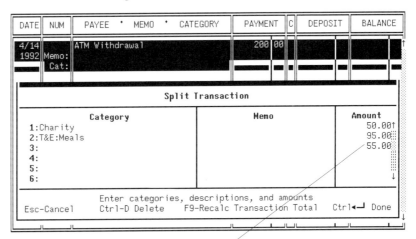

Quicken inserts the remaining amount of the transaction here. If you don't assign a category name, Quicken includes it on reports on a line labeled "Other."

9. Press Ctrl-Enter twice to close the Split Transaction window and record the transaction with the split information.

   From now on, Quicken includes your categorized cash expenses for charity and business entertainment when you produce summary and budget reports.

Working with Quicken Cash Accounts

Use a cash account if you want to keep records of most of the cash transactions you make, or if you get paid in cash. If you need to keep records of only a few cash expenditures, it's easier to do that directly in your checking account register, rather than in a separate cash account. See "Handling Cash Through Your Checking Account" on page 334.

Basic Steps for Using a Quicken Cash Account

Setting Up the Account

See "Setting Up and Using Additional Quicken Accounts" on page 245 to set up a cash account. As the opening balance, enter the amount of cash you now have on hand.

Entering Transactions

You can record transactions in your cash account in two ways:

Enter transactions directly. Enter transactions in the register for your cash account when you want to record how you've spent some cash.

You don't have to enter transactions for all the cash you've spent (see "Updating Your Cash Balance" on page 339). However, you should have transactions that show all the cash you've received, either directly or by making withdrawals or cash advances from your other accounts. Save the cash receipts and other records of your cash transactions. Then enter each one as a separate transaction. If one receipt covers several items that you want to keep track of individually, you can split the transaction. Also enter transactions for cash received directly in the cash transaction register when you're paid in cash or given cash, or when you cash a check without depositing it in another account.

Have Quicken transfer money in. When your money is in one account (for example, a bank account) and you withdraw cash or make a "deposit less cash," you can have Quicken transfer the money to the cash transaction register when you record the original transaction. See "Transferring Cash from Other Accounts" on page 338.

To see how some cash transactions are filled in, see "The Cash Transaction Register" on page 337. The basic steps for entering transactions are the same in all types of Quicken accounts, so to review entering transactions, see "Adding Transactions to the Check Register" on page 59.

Updating the Cash Balance

Regularly (say, once a month), you should update your cash balance. This practice allows you to keep accurate records of your total cash spending and your cash on hand in one simple step, without forcing you to enter every cash transaction you make. To update the cash balance, use the Update Account Balance window in the cash transaction register. See "Updating Your Cash Balance" on page 339.

The Cash Transaction Register

To view the register for a cash account, press Ctrl-A, or choose Select Account from the Main Menu, or choose Select/Set Up Account from the Print/Acct menu.

At the Select Account to Use window, select your cash account and press Enter. (Quicken lists cash accounts with the word "Cash" in the Type column.)

Enter a reference number for the transaction. (Optional.) This is especially useful for petty cash accounts.

Amounts entered in the Spend field show purchases made with cash.

The C field is not used for the cash transaction register.

Dollar amounts in the Receive field indicate increases in your cash on hand.

Categorize your cash expenses so that you can include them in reports about your income and expenses.

This cash account received cash as a transfer when an ATM withdrawal was entered in another register. The account name tells you which account the withdrawal was made from.

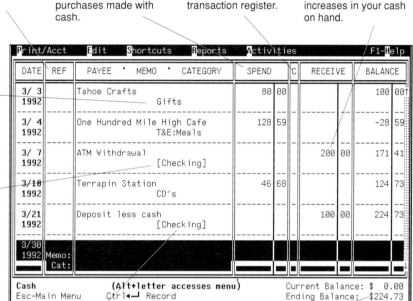

This transaction was recorded when a "deposit less cash" was recorded in the register of a checking account. Again, the account name tells you which account was the source of the cash.

Ending Balance shows the amount of cash you have on hand.

Note: If you haven't set up a Quicken cash account yet, select <New Account> and fill in the Set Up New Account window that appears. For complete information on setting up accounts, see "Setting Up and Using Additional Quicken Accounts" on page 245.

$ Transferring Cash from Other Accounts

For most people, an increase in cash on hand results from a withdrawal from another account (usually the checking account). When you record a cash withdrawal in your Quicken bank account, you can have Quicken "transfer" the amount to your cash account, where it will appear as a transaction showing cash received. You don't have to enter a separate transaction in your cash transaction register. Just enter the name of the cash account in the Category field of the transaction in your check register.

ATM withdrawals, checks written for cash, deposits less cash, and credit card advances are all examples of transactions that you can transfer to your cash account.

You'll find complete information about entering transfer information in transactions in *Transferring Money Between Accounts*, beginning on page 251.

Below is a sample cash transaction register showing deposits made by transferring money from other accounts. The source transactions are shown in the checking and credit card registers.

Cash receipt from a deposit less cash.

Cash receipt from a cash advance on a credit card.

This is the register from the Cash account.

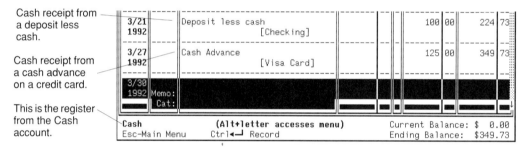

Here's how a deposit less cash was originally entered in the checking account.

This account name tells Quicken to record a deposit for this amount in the Cash account. See the "Deposit less cash" transaction in the cash account.

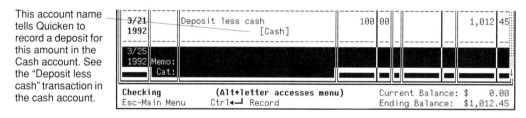

Here's how a cash advance was recorded in a register named "Visa Card."

This account name transfers the amount of the Cash advance to the cash account. See the "Cash Advance" transaction in the Cash account.

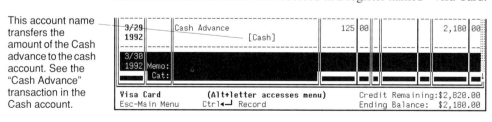

Updating Your Cash Balance

You don't need to reconcile your cash account the way you reconcile your bank account. In cash accounts, you can use the Update Account Balance window to avoid entering every cash transaction. You enter only those cash transactions you want to track in the register. When you update your cash balance, Quicken handles all the other expenditures for you by entering one transaction for the remaining amount of miscellaneous cash expenses.

To update your cash account:

1. At the cash transaction register, choose Update Account Balance from the Activities menu.

2. Enter the amount of cash you currently have on hand in the Update This Account's Balance field.

3. Enter a category name if you want one to be assigned to the adjustment transaction Quicken will create. For example, you can enter the name of the cash account to create a "self-transfer" transaction.

4. Press Enter to have Quicken create a balance adjustment transaction in your account. The transaction will be for the amount of the difference between the previous balance in your account and the amount you entered in the Update Account Balance window.

To quickly update the cash account

If you're in a hurry and want to quickly update your cash account, you can use the Update Account Balance window without specifying a category. Then later, when you have time, go back and split that transaction, allocating the total amount to various items, such as gas, restaurant meals, and groceries.

Chapter 21

Budgeting Your Income and Expenses

You can use Quicken to budget all of your income and expenses or just a few of them. To budget means to compare your actual income and expenses against your planned income and expenses.

Basic steps to budget home or business income and expenses

1. Set up home or business income and expense categories (below).
2. Categorize transactions (page 107).
3. Set up budget amounts (page 342).
4. Create budget reports (page 347).

 # Setting Up Income and Expense Categories

If you categorized your income and expense transactions as you entered them, you've done most of the work required. If you haven't, you can set up categories now. See Chapter 7, *Using Categories*, beginning on page 101, to learn how to set up categories and how to assign them to your transactions. If you want to categorize parts of a transaction with different categories, see "Splitting a Transaction" on page 67.

See page 103 for standard home and business budget categories.

Setting Up Budget Amounts

When you set up a budget in Quicken, you set monthly budget amounts for some or all of the categories and subcategories you use in a special Set Up Budgets screen. (You can also budget amounts for transfers.) Budget amounts for each category can be the same for each month. Or, if you know your income and expenses for a given category will change, you may want to budget differing amounts for different months in the year. For example, if you pay property taxes twice a year, you may want to budget the amount only in the two months in which you make payments.

Budget amounts that vary by month are useful because you can plan for income or expenses that occur quarterly, yearly, or on an irregular basis. You can enter and change monthly budget values at any time.

To set or change budget amounts:

1. In any register, choose Set Up Budgets from the Activities menu.

   Quicken displays the Set Up Budgets screen, where you can enter or change your monthly budget amounts for each category.

The Set Up Budgets screen has a special set of pulldown menus.

File Edit Layout Activities					F1-Help
Category Description	Jan.	Feb.	Mar.	Apr.	May
INFLOWS					
Bonus Income	**1,159**	1,159	1,159	1,159	1,159
Dividend	16	16	16	16	16
Dividend Income	0	0	0	0	0
Interest Income	89	89	89	89	89
Investment Income	0	0	0	0	0
Investment Interest Inc	25	25	25	25	25
Long Term Cap Gain Dist	0	0	0	0	0
Realized Gain/Loss	438	438	438	438	438
Salary Income	7,457	7,457	7,457	7,457	7,457
Short Term Cap Gain Dist	0	0	0	0	0
Unrealized Gain/Loss	0	0	0	0	0
_Other Income	0	0	0	0	0
Total Budget Inflows	9,183	9,183	9,183	9,183	9,183
Total Budget Outflows	5,506	6,170	6,170	6,170	6,170
Difference	3,677	3,013	3,013	3,013	3,013

Quicken calculates all totals automatically, so you cannot edit them directly.

Total Budget Inflows is your total budgeted income for that month.

Total Budget Outflows is your total budgeted expenses for that month.

2. (Optional) Decide whether to enter detail for subcategories.

   For example, do you want to budget separately for federal income tax, state income tax, and property tax? Or do you just want to budget a total amount for "taxes" without estimating the different kinds of tax? If you want to use subcategories for data entry, choose Budget Subcats from the Edit menu.

Note: Quicken remembers any amounts you enter for subcategories even if you hide subcategories and change the category totals. If you redisplay the subcategories, Quicken will restore the sum of the subcategory amounts.

3. To change the amount budgeted for a category in any month, use the arrow keys or a mouse to select the amount in the column for that month and enter the desired amount. For information about shortcuts for setting up budgets, see "Editing Amounts in the Set Up Budgets Screen" on page 344.

    (Optional) You can do any of the following without leaving the Set Up Budgets screen:

    • To print the Set Up Budgets screen with all budget amounts, choose Print Budgets from the File menu (or press Ctrl-P).

    • To export the current category names and budget amounts to a QIF file, choose Export Budget from the File menu. The Export Budget command works like the Export command. See "Copying Budget Amounts from One File to Another" on page 347.

    • You can use the Import Budget command on the File menu to import the category names and budget amounts from a QIF export file. The Import Budget command works like the Import command. See "Copying Budget Amounts from One File to Another" on page 347.

4. When you have finished entering budget amounts, press Ctrl-R to go to the register or Ctrl-W to go to the Write Checks screen.

After you've estimated your income and expenses, you're ready to create budget reports and see you what you've actually earned and spent. "Creating Budget Reports" on page 347 explains how.

Keys and Mouse Actions to Help You Enter Budget Amounts

Use any of the following keys to help you edit budget amounts.

Key	Action
Tab	Move from month to month in the same category.
Shift-Tab	Move back a month.
Up or down arrow	Move up or down one row in the same month.
PgUp and PgDn	Move up or down by page within the budget data.
Quote key (' or ")	Copy the amount from the previous month in the row to the current month.

A mouse works here as it does elsewhere in Quicken. The horizontal and vertical scroll bars may be particularly useful.

• Click the arrows on the horizontal scroll bar to scroll to earlier or later months.

• Click the arrows on the vertical scroll bar to scroll to the next or previous row (or click above or below the scroll box to page up or down).

$ Editing Amounts in the Set Up Budgets Screen

You can use the commands on the Edit menu (Alt-E) in the Set Up Budgets screen to enter or change the amounts that you see in the budget.

Using Your Own Income and Expense Data to Set Up a Budget

You might want to set up a budget quickly by filling in the Set Up Budgets screen with the actual income, expense, and transfer amounts from your account registers. You can extract these amounts from any time period in the current Quicken file, and then copy the amounts to the budget in two different ways:

- You can copy the actual income, expense, and transfer amounts from any number of months up to 12 to any equal number of months in the budget. For example, you can copy actual amounts from October, November, and December of the previous year to the three budget columns for January, February, and March.

- You can have Quicken compute income, expense, and transfer averages for any number of months up to 12 and enter the average amounts in any single month you specify.

To set up a budget with actual data from your accounts:

1. Choose AutoCreate from the Edit menu.

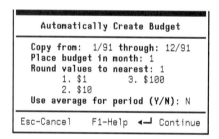

```
  ▀▀▀▀▀▀▀▀▀▀▀▀▀▀▀▀▀▀▀▀▀▀▀▀▀▀▀▀▀▀▀
      Automatically Create Budget

   Copy from:  1/91 through: 12/91
   Place budget in month: 1
   Round values to nearest: 1
        1. $1        3. $100
        2. $10
   Use average for period (Y/N): N

   Esc-Cancel    F1-Help  ◄─┘ Continue
```

2. (Optional) Change the Copy date range.

   The default dates include all transactions from the previous calendar year.

3. In the Place Budget in Month field, enter the number of the first month to which you want Quicken to copy the amounts.

   For example, if you wanted to copy amounts from April, May, and June of the previous year to the budget columns for October, November, and December, you would enter 10, because October is the tenth month of the year and the tenth column in the budget.

4. (Optional) Quicken can round off amounts to the nearest $10 or $100, if you prefer.

5. (Optional) If you want Quicken to compute income, expense, and transfer averages for the date range you specified in step 2 and enter the average amounts in the month you specified in step 3, enter Y in the Use Average for Period field.

6. Press F10 to copy data from your accounts into the Set Up Budgets screen.

Setting Up a Budget Category that Recurs Every Two Weeks

You may have a special category or transfer item that you enter into Quicken every two weeks. For example, you might get paid every other week and record the deposit of your paycheck in a Quicken bank account using the income category Salary. If you want Quicken to budget your estimated salary income as accurately as possible, you should set up the Salary income category as a two-week budget item. That way, Quicken will distribute your estimated and actual salary income at the correct two-week intervals.

To set up a budget item that occurs at two-week intervals:

1. At the Set Up Budgets screen, use the arrow keys to select the category.

2. Choose Two Week from the Edit menu.

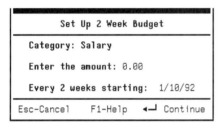

```
            Set Up 2 Week Budget

  Category: Salary

  Enter the amount: 0.00

  Every 2 weeks starting:  1/10/92

  Esc-Cancel    F1-Help   ◄─┘ Continue
```

3. Enter the amount you want to budget in two-week intervals for the selected category.

4. Enter the starting date for the first two-week interval.

   For example, if you are setting up Salary as a two-week budget category for the rest of the year, enter the date of your next payday. If you want to budget at two-week intervals for the entire year, enter the first payday in January.

5. Press F10 to fill in budget amounts calculated at two-week intervals from the current month to all months in the same row.

Copying Budget Amounts To Other Months

Quicken can copy budget amounts across the Set Up Budgets screen in either of two ways:

- **Fill Right**. Copy the amount from the current cell to all cells to the right in the same row. To do this, select the amount you want to copy and choose Fill Right from the Edit menu.

- **Fill Columns**. Copy each of the amounts in the current column to all the columns to the right. For example, you can copy all amounts for January to the rest of the months of the year with one command. Just select any cell in the column you want to copy and choose Fill Columns from the Edit menu. If your cursor is in the March column when you choose this command, the amounts in January and February will not be affected.

Setting Up Budget Amounts for Transfers

The Set Up Budgets screen can include the names of all your accounts under both INFLOWS and OUTFLOWS, in case you want to budget transfer amounts as well as income and expense categories. To turn on the display of transfers, choose Budget Transfers from the Edit menu. (You can turn off the display of transfers by choosing Budget Transfers again.)

The OUTFLOWS section lists all the accounts in your file. You might use the list in this example to budget items such as mortgage payments and transfers to 401K and IRA accounts.

Category Description	Jan.	Feb.	Mar.	Apr.	May
TO Mortgage	0	0	0	0	0
TO Sally Checking	1,100	1,100	1,100	1,100	1,100
TO Sally's 401(k)	200	200	200	200	200
TO Sally's IRA	250	250	250	250	250
TO Steve Checking	1,000	1,000	1,000	1,000	1,000
TO Steve's IRA	250	250	250	250	250
TO Yotzvitsky Sec	300	300	300	300	300
TOTAL OUTFLOWS	11,407	11,407	11,407	11,407	11,407
OVERALL TOTAL	0	0	0	0	0
Total Budget Inflows	11,407	11,407	11,407	11,407	11,407
Total Budget Outflows	11,407	11,407	11,407	11,407	11,407
Difference	0	0	0	0	0

You enter transfer amounts in the Set Up Budgets screen just as you would budget income and expense amounts. Enter all amounts that you intend to transfer to other accounts under OUTFLOWS as TO items. Enter all amounts that you are planning to receive as transfers from other accounts under INFLOWS as FROM items.

You don't have to budget transfer amounts, but budgeting transfers might give you a more complete picture of your cash flow. For example, if you want to budget a monthly transfer of $200.00 from checking to savings, you should enter 200 for INFLOWS from Checking and the same amount for OUTFLOWS to Savings.

$ Changing the Layout of the Set Up Budgets Screen

You might want to display or enter budget amounts by quarter instead of by month. (Choose Quarter from the Layout menu.) You can also specify budgets on a yearly basis. (Choose Year from the Layout menu.)

If you enter budget amounts by quarter or by year, and then choose Month from the Layout menu to switch back to monthly budget amounts, Quicken distributes the budget amounts evenly across the 12 columns in the screen. For example, a $300 amount budgeted for the first quarter of the year will be split evenly among the first three months of the year when you switch back to monthly format. So you can change the budget layout at any time without worrying about how the change will affect your budget amounts.

Copying Budget Amounts from One File to Another

You can copy your budget from one Quicken file to another by using the Export Budget and Import Budget commands. For example, you might want to transfer budget amounts from the Quicken file for one small business to another.

Note: Quicken cannot import category names with the Import Budget command. The file to which you are copying must share the same categories as the file you are copying budget amounts from. If necessary, first copy the categories following the steps in "Copying the Category List from One File to Another" on page 116.

To export budget amounts set up for categories:

1. Select the Quicken file that contains the budget amounts you want to copy.

2. At the register of any account in the file (or at the Write Checks screen) choose Set Up Budgets from the Activities menu.

3. Choose Export Budget from the File menu.

4. In the DOS File field, enter a name for the export file and press Enter.

   Quicken exports the category amounts from the current file to a DOS file.

To import the budget amounts into the second Quicken file:

1. Select the Quicken file to which you want to copy the budget amounts.
   a. Choose Set Preferences from the Main Menu.
   b. Choose File Activities.
   c. Choose Select/Set Up File.
   d. Choose the Quicken file to receive the budget amounts.
   e. Choose any account in the second file.

2. Choose Set Up Budgets from the Activities menu.

3. Choose Import Budget from the File menu.

4. In the DOS File field, specify the name of the export file that you just created and press Enter.

   Quicken imports the DOS file. It replaces budget amounts for the categories in the current file.

Creating Budget Reports

To use budget reports, you must first do two things:

1. Categorize your transactions (see page 107).
2. Set budget amounts for those categories that you wish to budget (see page 342).

Budget reports, as the name suggests, compare actual spending and income with budgeted spending and income. They calculate the difference between the two so you can see exactly where you met your budget, where you exceeded it, and by how much.

Quicken has two types of budget reports:

- Budget reports compare the money you spend and receive in a specific date range with your budget amounts for each category and transfer account. They calculate the difference between the actual and budgeted amounts for each category and transfer account so you can see exactly where you met your budget, where you exceeded it, and by how much. Quicken includes all accounts in the report. This report is not subtotaled by month.

- Monthly budget reports are a variation of the basic budget report. A monthly budget report differs from a basic budget report in the following ways:
  - It calculates the difference between the actual and budgeted amounts by month.
  - It subtotals by month.
  - It includes only bank, cash, and credit card accounts.
  - It is organized by income and expense rather than by cash flow.

To create a budget report:

1. Choose Budget from the Reports menu (or choose Monthly Budget from the Personal Report menu.)

2. (Optional) Change the report dates to cover the time period you want. Quicken sets the first day of this year as the starting date and today's date as the ending date.

3. Press F10.

   Quicken compares the income and expense amounts in your accounts with the budget amounts you set up and displays the report on the screen. See page 349 for a sample monthly budget report.

4. (Optional) Budget reports are a variation of the basic summary report. To report on your income and expenses for a different time period (such as a quarter or a year), choose Column Headings from the Layout menu, just as you would for a summary report. See "Column Headings" on page 178.

5. (Optional) If you want to restrict the data included in the report in any way, use the commands on the Edit menu, just as you would for a summary report. See "Filtering Your Report Data" on page 180.

6. (Optional) To print the report, choose Print Report from the File/Print menu. (For more information about printing reports, see page 164.)

7. (Optional) To memorize a custom report setup for repeated use, see page 193.

A Sample Monthly Budget Report

By default, a personal monthly budget report is organized like a cash flow report. It lists transfers from your asset, investment, and liability accounts under INFLOWS and transfers to your asset, investment, and liability accounts under OUTFLOWS.

This report covers only one month. If your report has a date range that includes more than one month, Quicken creates subtotals for each month.

The Diff column is the difference between what you budgeted and what you actually spent or received.

```
                          MONTHLY BUDGET REPORT
                         1/ 1/92 Through 1/31/92
          MURPHY-Bank,Cash,CC Accounts
          2/ 1/92
                                        1/ 1/92    -     1/31/92
                  Category Description   Actual    Budget    Diff
                  ------------------   --------------------------
          INFLOWS
            Interest Income              105.71     50.00    55.71
            Salary Income            12,083.34  12,000.00    83.34
                                     ----------- ----------- -----------
          TOTAL INFLOWS              12,189.05  12,050.00   139.05
          OUTFLOWS
            Auto Interest              198.52     175.00    23.52
            Auto License               370.00     370.00     0.00
            Automobile Expense          35.00      20.00    15.00
            Books, Music, etc.          60.00      40.00    20.00
            Charitable Donations       100.00     100.00     0.00
            Clothing                 1,065.76     200.00   865.76
            Computer Software          397.52     300.00    97.52
            Dining Out                 375.54     250.00   125.54
            Entertainment              207.42     200.00     7.42
            Federal Tax Withholding  2,870.84   2,350.00   520.84
            Gift Expenses                0.00     150.00  -150.00
            Groceries                  327.87     150.00   177.87
            Hair/Makeup, etc.          175.00     100.00    75.00
            Home Repair & Maint.        35.99     100.00   -64.01
            Household Misc. Exp         40.00     100.00   -60.00
            Insurance                  151.52     200.00   -48.48
            Mortgage Interest Exp    1,093.33   1,000.00    93.33
            Personal Travel            249.99     100.00   149.99
            Property Tax                 0.00     750.00  -750.00
            Recreation Expense         319.51     200.00   119.51
            Social Security Tax        604.16     500.00   104.16
            State Tax Withholding      966.66     800.00   166.66
            Steve's Hobbies            457.58     400.00    57.58
            TO Auto Loans              389.03     200.00   389.03
            TO Mortgage                 65.06      65.06     0.06
                                     ----------- ----------- -----------
          TOTAL OUTFLOWS            10,556.30   8,820.00  1,736.30
                                     ----------- ----------- -----------
          OVERALL TOTAL             1,632.75   3,230.00 -1,597.25
                                     =========== =========== ===========
```

Income categories are shown at the top under INFLOWS and expense categories are shown below them under OUTFLOWS.

These two items represent transfers to two liability accounts from bank, cash, or credit card accounts.

The OVERALL TOTAL at the bottom of the report is your net savings for the month. If the number is positive, you earned more than you spent. If the number is negative, you spent more than you earned.

A Sample Budget Report

By default, a basic budget report is organized by income and expense.

It lists INCOME first and then EXPENSES.

```
                                BUDGET REPORT
                          1/ 1/92 Through 3/31/92
        MURPHY-All Accounts                                    Page 1
        8/13/92
                                      1/ 1/92    -    3/31/92
                 Category Description  Actual    Budget    Diff
                 -------------------- --------------------------
                 INCOME/EXPENSE
                   INCOME
                     Dividend Income        0        60      -60
                     Interest Income      312       150      162
                     Salary Income     36,250    31,500    4,750
                                     --------- --------- ---------
                   TOTAL INCOME        36,562    31,710    4,852

                   EXPENSES
                     Auto:
                       Auto Interest      580       525       56
                       Automobile Expense 166        59      107
                       License            370     1,110     -740
                                     --------- --------- ---------
                       Total Auto       1,116     1,694     -577
                     Books, Music, etc.   274       120      154
                     Charitable Donations 300       299        1
                     Clothing           1,553       600      953
                     Computer Software  1,093       150      943
                     Dining Out         1,155       299      856
                     Entertainment        902       600      303
                     Groceries            614       447      166
                     Hair/Makeup, etc.    365       299       66
                     Home Repair & Maint.  36       299     -263
                     Household Misc. Exp  499       299      200
                     Insurance            455       600     -145
                     Miscellaneous          0       162     -162
                     Personal Travel      463       299      164
                     Recreation Expense   690       599       91
                     Steve's Hobbies    2,430     1,799      631
                     Tax:
                       Federal Tax      8,613     7,050    1,563
                       Property Tax       750     2,250   -1,500
                       Social Security Tax 1,812  1,500      313
                       State Tax        2,900     2,400      500
                                     --------- --------- ---------
                       Total Tax       14,075    13,199      876
                                     --------- --------- ---------
                     TOTAL EXPENSES    26,020    21,764    4,255

                                     --------- --------- ---------
                 TOTAL INCOME/EXPENSE  10,543     9,946      597
                                     ========= ========= =========
```

The basic budget report is not subtotaled by any time period.

Listing all the transactions in a budget category

You can select any category amount in the Actual column of a budget report and choose QuickZoom from the File/Print menu to list all the transactions that make up that budget category. See "Investigating Items in Reports" on page 189. For example, you can select an "Other" item and press Ctrl-Z to list all the uncategorized transactions that make up that item.

Chapter 22

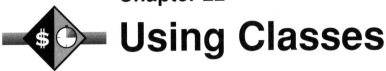

Using Classes

This chapter tells you how to set up and use classes to specify who, where, or for what time period your transactions apply. For example, if you use your personal checking account for both business and personal checks, you can set up and assign transactions to classes named business and personal. If you manage properties, you can classify transactions by property. If you work with multiple clients, you can classify your income and expenses by client. A business can classify transactions by the accounting period to which they belong.

Classes do not replace categories. Rather, they add a second dimension that is unrelated to the category. Use categories to specify what kind of income or expense your transactions are for, and classes to specify who, where, or for what time period.

In some special situations, such as accounts receivable, you may want to use class names for other purposes. The rest of the chapters in this section explain how to use classes for home and business applications.

$ About Classes

Your use of classes can be as simple or as intricate as your finances require. You might use as few as two classes, for example, to distinguish business and personal expenses. Or you might use a number of classes. For example, if you manage properties, you could set up a class name for each property. That way six different utility bills could be marked clearly as expenses applying to six different properties. Or if you work with a number of clients, you could set up a class for each client. Then you could report separately on the income and expenses related to that client.

Use classes when you want to know:	For example:
Who a transaction is for	You, your spouse, your children. Your personal use, or your business. Specific customers, clients, or type of employee for payroll (job grade, for example).
Where the transaction applies	The Eastern region of your company or the Western region. The property on Oak St. or the property on North Ave.
When the transaction occurs	Accounting period one, two, three. Quarter 1, Quarter 2, Quarter 3. Month 1, Month 2, Month 3.
Other information about the transaction that is not income or expense related	

Classes and Categories Work Together

You can apply transactions to classes, to categories, or to both. These two features can provide two different ways of looking at your data. You can use these two features together to clearly identify your income and expenses. For example, if you use your checking account for both personal and business expenses, you can set up one class called personal and another called business. Then you can assign expenses such as supplies or travel to both the category (supplies or travel) AND the class (personal or business). And as you'll discover when you begin to use Quicken's reports, sometimes you may want to use information based on categories and other times you may want information based on classes, or the report you want may use both. You decide which to include in a report when you produce the report.

Before you start classifying transactions, skim through *Customizing Reports*, beginning on page 167. See also the diagram that illustrates Quicken data organization in "How Your Quicken Data Is Organized" on page 450.

Basic Steps for Using Classes

To use classes, you set up class names and assign transactions to classes.

Note: Quicken does not provide a preset list of classes.

Setting Up Class Names

You can set up class names before you enter transactions or as you enter them. When you enter a new class name in a transaction, you can set up the class right then.

Quicken keeps class names in the class list. You can view the class list and change or delete class names whenever you want. You can also print the list, including descriptions.

To set up class names in advance:

1. Choose Select/Set Up Class from the Shortcuts menu (or press Ctrl-L) to display the class list.

2. At the class list, choose <New Class>.

3. Fill in the class name and description and press Enter to set up the new class.

   Use the same conventions for typing class names and descriptions that you do for categories. For more information about names, press F1 for Help.

Subclasses: Note that you do not explicitly specify subclasses when you set up classes. You can use any class as a subclass when you assign transactions.

To print the class list:

1. Choose Select/Set Up Class from the Shortcuts menu (or press Ctrl-L) to display the class list and press Ctrl-P.

2. Enter the number of the printer you are using and press Enter.

Assigning Transactions to Classes

You assign transactions to classes and subclasses by typing the class name in the Category field, or choosing it from the class list (Ctrl-L).

Note: Before you enter a class name in the Category field, enter a forward slash (/). And if you're assigning the transaction to a category as well as a class, enter the category name on the left, before the slash. For example, to apply a transaction to the category Supplies and the class Business, you would enter Supplies/Business. Quicken recognizes all names entered after a slash as class names. (See "Using Subclasses" on page 354 for an example.)

You can assign transactions to classes at the Write Checks screen or in any register.

When you enter a class name in a transaction, Quicken checks to see if the name is in the class list. If not, you can choose from the list or add the new class you entered to the list. If you enter a new category name and a new class name, Quicken will let you add both names, one at a time, to the appropriate list.

For added reporting detail, you can assign transactions to subclasses. For example, if your company has a number of geographic divisions in the Eastern region, you could assign a transaction to both the Eastern region and the New England division, or the Eastern region and the Mid-Atlantic division. When you use subclasses, you enter multiple class names in the same Category field, separated by colons (:), like this: /Eastern:New England. For more information, see the next section.

You can also apply different amounts of the same transaction to different classes. For example, if you deposit several rent checks from different properties at once, you could classify the exact amount of each check to the appropriate class name for that property. This is called splitting a transaction. For complete information about using split transactions, see "Splitting a Transaction" on page 67.

$ Using Subclasses

Subclasses are useful if you want your reports to group and subtotal similar classes together. For example, if you manage properties and one of them is an apartment building with four units, you could have class names for the apartment building and for each of the units. Then when you have an expense for a specific unit, you can assign it to both the apartment building and the specific unit. Create a subclass the same way you create a class. It will look just like a class in the class list. Unlike categories, subclasses are not hierarchical. You can use any class as a subclass.

When you enter a subclass for a transaction, separate the main class from the subclass with a colon (:). Thus, a check for repairs to Main Street, Apartment 1, would have /Main St:Unit 1 in the Category field. And your check for a new refrigerator in Apartment 2 would have /Main St:Unit 2 in the Category field. Quicken could then produce reports giving you subtotals for each subclass (Unit 1 and Unit 2) plus a sum total for the larger class (Main Street).

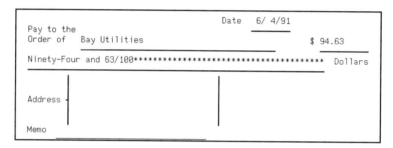

Category name.

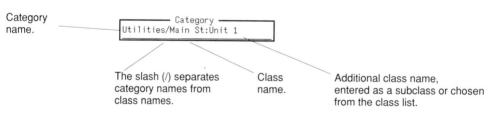

The slash (/) separates category names from class names.

Class name.

Additional class name, entered as a subclass or chosen from the class list.

Important Note: The order in which multiple classes appear in the Category field is critical. Always enter the more general class first, followed by more specific classes. This order ensures that Quicken uses the first class name as the primary class in class reports, and subsequent class names as subclasses. For more information, see "Summary" on page 171.

The suggestions for using subcategories also apply to using subclasses. See "Adding Subcategories" on page 109.

Changing and Deleting Classes

You can change class information or delete a class from the class list. When you rename a class, Quicken automatically changes it in each transaction that was assigned to the old name. When you delete a class, Quicken removes it from the class list and unclassifies any transactions in which that class or class name appears by inserting a blank in place of the class name in the Category field.

Important: The Category field in the register can take a maximum of 31 characters. If you change a class name on the class list to a longer name, the information in the Category field of some transactions could exceed the 31-character limit. If this happens, Quicken deletes all characters after the thirty-first.

To change or delete a class:

1. Choose Select/Set Up Class from the Shortcuts menu (or press Ctrl-L) to display the class list.

2. Choose the class you want to delete or rename.

3. Press Ctrl-E (for Edit) to change the class name or description.

4. Make any changes to the information in the Edit Class window and press Enter.

   OR

   Press Ctrl-D (for Delete) to delete the class.

   A message asks you to confirm that you want to delete the class. Press Enter.

Printing the Class List

You can print the class list, including descriptions.

To print the Class List:

1. Choose Select/Set Up Class from the Shortcuts menu (or press Ctrl-L) to display the class list.

2. Press Ctrl-P.

   The Print Class List window appears.

3. Type the number of the printer you are using and press Enter.

4. Press Enter to print the class list.

Chapter 23

Home Uses

This chapter describes some of the ways you can combine Quicken's features to meet your personal financial needs, from budgeting, to tax preparation, to managing investments.

To make the best use of this chapter, you should be familiar with Quicken's basic features, described in Chapters 4 through 10. However, you don't have to be an expert. In fact, this chapter gives suggestions about how to set up such things as categories and classes to manage specific tasks. Browse through the topics that apply to your situation. In each section you'll find references to information in the other chapters of this book that you'll need to complete each task.

$ Cash Management

Quicken gives you a way to manage cash so you earn more interest without spending less. It does this by helping you pay bills just before they are due. That way, you earn more interest from an interest-bearing checking account.

Here's how to use Quicken to manage cash and maximize interest earned from an interest-bearing checking account:

1. Enter bills into Quicken as you receive them, or at least every week or so.

2. As you enter the bill, postdate the check for when you want to pay it. Remember to allow enough time for the check to be delivered in the mail. See "Writing Postdated Checks" on page 83.

3. Then you have three options for printing and sending the checks:

   - **Option 1**: Let Quicken remind you when it's time to print and mail checks. If you're a hard disk user, Quicken's Billminder feature will remind you even if you are not using Quicken; all you need to do is turn on your computer (see "Automatic Reminders" on page 441).

   - **Option 2:** Print all the checks at once, including postdated ones. The checks print in chronological order. Keep the stack handy and check it every few days to mail the checks as they become due.

   - **Option 3:** Choose the individual checks that you want to print. You can do this at whatever intervals you prefer.

$ Entering Paychecks

Quicken lets you enter your deposited paychecks two ways:

- Enter your net compensation as you would any other deposit.

- Split your paycheck deposit into categories for federal income tax, state income tax, Social Security tax, and so on. If you chose standard Quicken home categories when you set up your account group, you can use the preset income category Salary, and the preset expense categories/subcategories: Tax:Fed, Tax:State and Tax:FICA.

To enter your paycheck as a split transaction:

1. Go to the register of the account where you are depositing the paycheck.

2. Enter "Paycheck" in the Payee field and press Ctrl-S to open the Split Transaction window.

3. Enter the category Salary in the Category field and enter the gross amount of the paycheck in the Amount field. The gross amount is the amount of your pay before any deductions are taken.

4. Enter the deductions from your paycheck for taxes as negative amounts and assign them to expense categories/subcategories: Tax:Fed, Tax:State and Tax:FICA. You may also have deductions for items such as 401(k) contributions, local withholding, medical insurance contributions, and state disability insurance. You can create expense categories for these as needed and use them to identify additional lines in the split. (See the example screen on the facing page.)

5. When you've entered all the deductions, the amount in the Deposit field should equal the net amount of the check. The net amount is the amount you actually receive.

6. After you press F10 to close the split, record the transaction and press Ctrl-M to memorize the paycheck deposit for later use.

   If your paycheck varies from pay period to pay period, reopen the splits and remove the dollar amounts; then memorize the check with no amounts in the splits. Be sure to cancel your changes before leaving the transaction, so you don't record a deposit with no amounts.

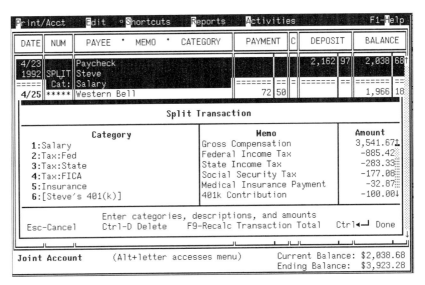

See *Saving Time with Memorized Transactions*, beginning on page 195, for more about memorizing and recalling recurring transactions.

$ Rental Properties

Many people use Quicken to track income and expenses related to rental properties.

If you're tracking several properties, you'll want to pay particular attention to Quicken's category and class features. They can help you record and report on income and expenses from your rental properties. This section highlights some of the ways you can use categories and classes to help manage your properties. You should also review the material in *Using Categories*, beginning on page 101, and *Using Classes*, beginning on page 351.

Using Quicken to track your rental income and expenses consists of four steps:

1. Set up a list of categories for each type of income and expense you track.

2. Set up a class for each rental property.

3. Assign transactions to categories and classes.

4. Produce reports.

Establish Categories

Establish categories based on the specific expenses you have for your properties. You can set up all your category names before you begin entering transactions, or you can create them as you enter transactions. You'll find complete information about categories in

Using Categories, beginning on page 101. Here are some sample category names and descriptions you may find useful.

Income Categories		Expense Categories (continued)	
Category:	**Description:**	**Category:**	**Description:**
Rental	Income Rent Received	Other-Exp	Other Expenses
Late-Fees	Late Payment Fees Received	Other Interest	Other Interest Paid
		Repairs	Repairs
Expense Categories		Supplies	Supplies
		Taxes	Taxes
Ads	Advertising	Travel	Travel Expenses
Commission	Commissions	Utilities	Utilities
Insurance	Insurance		
L&P-Fees	Legal & Prof. Fees		
Mortgage Int	Mortgage Interest		

Establish Classes for Properties

Set up a separate class name for each of your rental properties. For example, if you have a house on Sone Avenue and an apartment building on Toni Boulevard, you'll want separate class names for each. When you record transactions that pertain to one of the properties, you'll assign the property name (Sone Avenue) as a class to the transaction.

Like categories, all your classes can be set up before you begin, or you can create them as you enter transactions. You'll find complete information about setting up and using classes in "Basic Steps for Using Classes" on page 352.

If you have already assigned a set of numbers to your properties, you can use them as the class names. You can enter a description of each class in the Set Up Class window. If you have both name and description, the description will print in reports.

If you have multiple units per location, you can set up a subclass for each unit. For example, you might have Unit 1, Unit 2, and Unit 3 as subclasses for the Toni Boulevard apartment building.

Here are some sample class names and descriptions for properties:

Class or subclass:	Description:
Sone Avenue	Sone Avenue House
Toni Boulevard	Toni Blvd Apt Building
Unit 1	Ground floor, 2 bedroom

Rental properties and tax schedules

You can link rental property categories with specific lines on tax forms by assigning a tax schedule name such as Schedule E:1. For more information, see "Assigning Categories to Tax Forms" on page 416.

Assign Property Transactions to Categories and Classes

Each time you write a check or enter another transaction that covers property income or expenses, assign the amount to a category and class. Here are some examples.

Paying a Bill for a Specific Property

When you write a check to pay for utilities on the Sone Avenue property, enter the following in the Category field: Utilities/Sone Avenue. This assigns the amount of the transaction to the category "Utilities" and to the class "Sone Avenue."

Paying a Bill for a Specific Unit

When you write a check to pay for utilities for a unit in the Toni Boulevard apartment building, enter the following in the Category field: Utilities/Toni Boulevard:Unit 1. This assigns the amount of the transaction to the category "Utilities," to the class "Toni Boulevard," and to the subclass "Unit 1."

Paying a Bill that Covers More than One Property

Now suppose you hire a painting contractor to do some painting on two different properties. You write one check to pay the bill, but you want to keep track of separate expenses by property.

When you write the check, open the Split Transaction window to enter the category (Repairs) and class (property name) to which the amount should be applied.

Enter the category name for the expense (Repairs).

Remember that you can enter a quote mark (") on the second line of the split to have Quicken copy "Repairs" to that line.

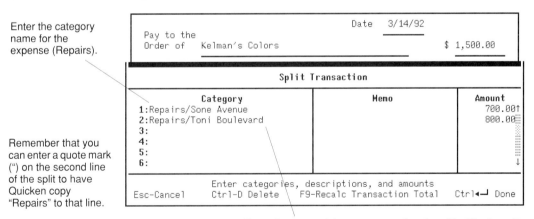

Enter the name of the property as the class (Toni Boulevard).

Recording Rental Income

When you receive rental income, assign the transaction to a category for rental income and include the property name as a class name. This makes your total rental income appear as a separate item when you produce job/project reports and summary reports, and makes it easy to produce reports that tell you when tenants are behind on their rent.

Producing Reports on Your Property Income and Expenses

You'll find job/project and summary reports can be useful in reporting on your properties.

Reporting Income and Expenses by Property

You can produce a report showing your income and expenses for multiple properties. To do this, create a job/project report. (You'll find this report on the Business Reports menu.) In the Job/Project Report window, set the date range to cover the time period you want. Enter a title such as "Income and Expenses by Property." The job/project report automatically creates a row for each income and expense category and subtotals by class (property name). See "Job/Project" on page 151 for an example of a job/project report.

Reporting Income and Expenses for a Single Property

You can produce a report showing your income and expenses for an individual property. Begin by choosing summary report from the Reports menu. In the Create Summary Report window, set the date range to cover the time period you want. Enter a title such as "Income and Expenses for Toni Boulevard." Press Ctrl-Enter to start the report.

To restrict the report to transactions that have been applied to the Toni Boulevard property, choose Filter Transactions from the Edit menu. Then, in the Filter Transactions window, enter Toni Boulevard in the Class Contains field. You can choose to create column headings for any time interval you require.

If you need more information, see "Column Headings" on page 178.

$ Home Improvements

If you own a home, it's important to keep track of all the improvements you make to it. Such a record can save you thousands of dollars in taxes when you sell your home, because home improvements become part of the basis in your home: they reduce the amount of profit you are taxed on.

For example, suppose you purchased a home for $375,000 in 1990. In the interim, you made two improvements to your home. You remodeled your kitchen ($5,500) and installed a smoke detector ($15.97). In 1992, you sell your home for $400,000. At first glance it might seem that your taxable gain is $25,000, the difference between your purchase ($375,000) and selling ($400,000) prices. Not so. Your home basis is $380,515.97. This includes your original purchase price ($375,000) and the two home improvements ($5515.97). So the actual gain you pay taxes on would be only $19,484.03, instead of $25,000.

Note: To simplify this example, we've ignored the expenses of buying and selling the house. However, you can also include these in your home basis.

The IRS differentiates between home improvements, which become part of your home basis, and repairs and maintenance, which don't. Home improvements are generally anything that adds to the value of your home or appreciably prolongs its life.

Here's a brief list of some common home improvements that can increase your home basis (you'll find many more). Notice that these range from small to large items. You may want to consult a tax advisor or accountant to determine exactly what qualifies as a home improvement.

Additional rooms	Drapes	Skylights
Alarm system	Fireplaces	Smoke detectors
Appliances (washer, dryer)	Fixtures	Termite proofing
Bookcases	Heating system	Towel racks
Built-in furniture	Lawn sprinkling system	Venetian blinds
Cabinets	Locks	Wall coverings
Carpeting	Patio	
Doorbells or door chimes	Siding	

Quicken solves the problem of keeping track of home improvements over the decades. Track home improvements by setting up an asset account called, say, "Home Improve." Enter the purchase price as the opening balance. Enter each improvement as a transaction in the register. Or have Quicken enter the transaction by transferring the amount when you write a check or record a credit card transaction.

For example, suppose you're remodeling your kitchen and you buy some cabinets. When you record the check for the purchase, enter the name of the asset account in the Category field. You can enter what home improvement the expense is for ("kitchen") in the Memo field, or you can enter it as a class name after the account name, like this: Home Improve/Kitchen. (To transfer the expense, enter the account name, Home Improve, where you would otherwise enter a category name—in front of the slash.) For more information, see *Transferring Money Between Accounts*, beginning on page 251. Then you can produce a summary report on classes to see the amount you've spent on each major home improvement project.

This transaction was entered as a transfer when a check was written in a Joint Account.

This cash transaction was recorded in this asset account register with the category Home Upgrade.

This asset register tracks home improvements.

```
 Print/Acct    Edit    Shortcuts    Reports    Activities           F1-Help

  DATE   REF    PAYEE   *  MEMO  *  CATEGORY   DECREASE  C  INCREASE   BALANCE

                         ═══ BEGINNING ═══
 12/31         Opening Balance                            152,879 50 152,879 50
 1991          Purch Price + C→[Home Improve]

 1/23          Kevin Harris and Sons                          895 67 153,775 17
 1992          Improvement - B→[M-C]

 3/31          Cabinet Supply Warehouse                     2,002 00 155,777 17
 1992          Kitchen Cabinet→[Joint Account]

 8/14          Viray Hardware                                   15 97 155,793 14
 1992          Smoke detector   Home Upgrade

 8/14   Memo:
 1991   Cat:

 Home Improve        (Alt+letter accesses menu)    Current Balance: $      0.00
 Esc-Main Menu       Ctrl◄┘ Record                 Ending Balance:  $155,793.14
```

Loans and Mortgages

If you want to track the remaining loan balance for your loans, you can set up a liability account called "Loans" or "Mortgage."

When you set up the liability account, use the current loan balance from your monthly loan statement as the starting balance. Then each month when you record each payment in Quicken, categorize the amount of the check that is applied to interest and transfer the amount that is applied to the principal of your loan to the Loans account. (You'll find these amounts listed on most monthly loan statements.) Use the Split Transaction window to categorize the interest and principal. If you use categories for lines on tax forms, such a transaction might look like this:

The Mort Int category was set up as a tax-related category using Schedule A:Home Mortgage Interest as the tax schedule.

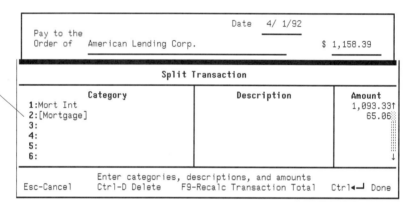

This entry transfers the amount of principal paid to your Mortgage account and enters it as a transaction that reduces the amount of your mortgage.

Amortization

If you have a fixed-rate mortgage, you can set up the loan for amortization in Quicken. First, set up a liability account for the mortgage. Then, create and memorize the payment transaction and set it up for amortization. Once the loan is set up for amortization, each time you record a payment made on the loan, Quicken updates the dollar amount of payments made and calculates the amount credited to principle and interest. For detailed instructions, see "Amortization" on page 206.

$ Managing Investments

You can use Quicken to organize and track your investments. You do this by entering the information in investment or asset accounts. The type and number of accounts you use and how you set them up depends on your individual finances.

You can organize your investments in many ways. The way described below groups your investments into three types:

- Investments that have a fluctuating unit price (such as stocks) or that are in a brokerage account with investments that have a fluctuating unit price

- Investments that don't have a fluctuating unit price (such as CDs)

- Personal assets (such as your car)

You set up and use investment accounts for the first type of investment, and asset accounts for the other two types.

This approach organizes investments in Quicken accounts on the basis of the way you are likely to use the investment. For example, while your car is an asset, its primary value is as transportation. You are unlikely to sell it in order to make another investment such as purchasing a CD. So you record the car in an asset account for personal assets, and you record CDs in an asset account for investments.

When you set up and use investment or asset accounts for your investments, they are automatically included in net worth and account balances reports.

Note: The remainder of this section is about using asset accounts for personal investments. Money market accounts on which you write checks are not included in the discussion that follows. This type of account is best treated as a separate bank account. Then you'll be able to reconcile the account easily. Similarly, stocks, bonds, and mutual funds are not included in the discussion, as they are discussed in *Getting Started with Investment Accounts*, beginning on page 265. If you're not sure what type of investment is suitable for a Quicken investment account, read "When to Use a Quicken Investment Account" on page 266.

Investments Suitable for Asset Accounts

Some types of investments you might keep in asset accounts:

- CDs (certificates of deposit)
- Treasury bills
- Money market funds (used as savings)
- Fixed annuities
- 401(k) retirement plans
- 403(b) retirement plans
- Real estate limited partnerships
- Rental real estate
- Collectibles (art, stamps, and so on)

- Precious metals
- Whole life insurance policies[*]

You can choose to put all these investments in a single asset account or have a separate account for each type of investment. If you have few investments, the simplest way is to set up one asset account for each investment item. For example, you might set up just two asset accounts, "401k" and "CD," which you will use to track the value of a 401(k) retirement plan and a CD (certificate of deposit). This method is simple and straightforward. Another advantage is that you can easily update the value of the investment by using the Update Account Balances window. See "Updating the Value of Your Assets and Liabilities" on page 264.

However, if you want to create one account to hold several investments, you can use Quicken classes to classify different investments in a single account.

Personal Assets

Personal assets are items you own that have resale value, but that you are unlikely to resell because of their usefulness in your daily life. Personal assets include your home, car, jewelry, and other items that have significant value.

You can put all your personal assets in a single asset account for personal assets. You can use this account as a way to organize a list of your valuables for insurance purposes. (You may want to have a separate account for your home to keep track of improvements to your home. See "Home Improvements" on page 362.)

Tracking Investments and Personal Assets

When you set up an asset account, record a transaction in the register for each investment or personal asset. In the transaction, enter the date you purchased the item, what you paid for it, and whom you bought it from.

For investments that pay interest, use the Int Inc (Interest Income) category to record the interest. The interest is then included on reports that show income.

When you buy something new that you want to include in the account, have Quicken transfer the information to your asset account when you record the purchase transaction in your Quicken checking account or Quicken credit card account. To do this, enter the name of the asset account in the Category field of the check or credit card transaction.

Using Classes to Classify Assets

If you have several similar investments in one asset account, you may want to classify them separately. Use a different Quicken class for each investment.

---

[*] Whole life insurance policies are included as an investment, valued at the policy's current cash surrender value. Term life insurance policies are not an investment, because they have no cash surrender value.

It may not be worth classifying your personal assets. However, if you have a number of pieces of jewelry, you may want a "jewelry" class. Or, if you have several antiques, you may want an "antique" class.

Note: Use classes instead of categories. You can assign a class to a transaction at the same time that you record a transfer. For example, if you purchase an antique with a check and want Quicken to "transfer" it to your personal assets account, you can enter {Pers Assets}/Antique. You can enter a class name and an account name in the same Category field; however, you cannot enter both a category name and an account name.

When you produce an account balances report to show net worth, you can choose "Selected accounts" and request to show class detail, which will show subtotals by class. (For more information, see "Account Balances" on page 173.)

Here's how you might enter your paycheck in your checking account to show that $100 is being deducted for the growth fund of your 401(k) retirement plan:

Choose the name of the account for your 401(k) from the category and transfer list.

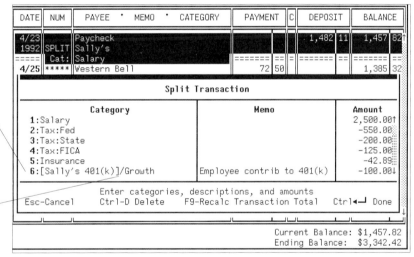

Choose the class name for the fund within your 401(k) from the class list.

$ Net Worth

You can use Quicken to keep track of your approximate net worth. Set up Quicken accounts for all your assets and liabilities. Then you can produce a report that combines the totals in all these accounts and calculates your net worth on the basis of these totals. (See the appropriate chapters in the section *Completing Your Financial Picture*, beginning on page 245, for how to set up and use different kinds of Quicken accounts.)

If you want your net worth as of today, use the net worth report from the Personal Reports menu. (For more information, see "Net Worth" on page 144.)

Here are some typical assets and liabilities you can keep track of in Quicken accounts:

Assets	Liabilities
Cash	Credit card accounts
Checking accounts	Home mortgage
Savings accounts	Other loans
Investments	
Personal possessions	

If you want a report showing your net worth at different intervals, use the account balances report listed on the main Reports menu. You can also have this report provide subtotals for each security or class by choosing "Selected accounts" and requesting detail. (For more information, see "Account Balances" on page 173.)

Chapter 24

Basic Business Uses

Quicken has many business uses beyond paying bills and maintaining a check register. These include bookkeeping, accounts payable, accounts receivable, and reporting income and expenses by job, property, or client. Quicken is used by businesses ranging in size from home businesses to large corporations (who use it for petty cash accounting). It is also used by many nonprofit organizations such as clubs, churches, and charities.

Much of Quicken's power and flexibility comes from its customizability. With Quicken, as with a good spreadsheet program, you need learn only a few functions that can be used in many ways. While Quicken provides some specific preset reports, it also includes a flexible custom report system that can create many different kinds of reports for many different uses. This chapter and Chapter 25 each contain some examples to show you Quicken's potential. As you use Quicken, you're sure to find other ways in which this highly flexible program can help you in your business.

A set of categories and subcategories for business use is provided with Quicken. You can tell Quicken to use them when you set up a Quicken file. You can modify this list or use one of your own. You'll find complete information about setting up and using categories in Chapter 7, *Using Categories*, beginning on page 101.

Quicken's categories can be linked to tax forms and schedules to make tax returns easy to fill in. For information about tax preparation, see *Preparing Your Income Taxes*, beginning on page 415.

$ Cash-Basis Bookkeeping

Quicken is well suited to cash-basis accounting, in which you recognize expenses at the time you write the check and recognize income at the time you receive money from customers. Most proprietorships and small retail businesses use cash-basis accounting because of its simplicity. Larger or more complex businesses usually use "accrual accounting," which Quicken also accommodates (see "Accrual Accounting: Timing of Income and Expenses" on page 383).

Quicken can do the routine bookkeeping work for many businesses. Using Quicken eliminates bookkeeping errors. It has enabled many businesses to do more complete and accurate bookkeeping in much less time than they previously spent. And it creates finished reports that allow the accountant for the business to do his or her job much faster.

Quicken does all this without requiring any double-entry accounting. Double-entry accounting software, as those who have tried it know, can be difficult to set up and rigid, and it requires in-depth knowledge of debit and credit accounting rules.

There are three steps to using Quicken for bookkeeping:

*   Set up a chart of accounts in the form of a list of categories
*   Assign each transaction to a category
*   Create reports

Note: Do not confuse cash-basis bookkeeping with Quicken's cash flow reports. Although the names are similar, they are used differently.

Setting Up a Chart of Accounts

To use Quicken for business bookkeeping, you will want to set up a set of income and expense categories, often called a "chart of accounts." You can start with Quicken's standard set of business categories and modify it for your needs or create your own from scratch. And you can add categories "on the fly" as you type in transactions. You'll find complete information about categories in Chapter 7, *Using Categories*, beginning on page 101, including a list of Quicken's standard business categories on page 103.

Using Chart of Account Numbers

If you have an existing set of chart of accounts numbers, use these numbers as the category names. You can enter a description of each category in the Set Up Category window.

For example:

Category	Description
4001	Sales
4002	Returns
5001	Cost of Sales

Normally, Quicken prints the descriptions in summary reports and arranges them in alphabetic order.

Using category names in reports

If you prefer to print the chart of accounts numbers in reports, choose the Checks and Reports Settings item on the Set Preferences menu, and enter N for the field "In reports, print category Description/Name/Both." (This field is described on page 447.) Your category names should all have the same number of digits, so that summary reports print in ascending numerical order.

Assigning Transactions to Categories

To keep accurate books, you should assign every transaction to a category except the opening balance in the register. If you're running a business from your personal checking account, you might want to assign business transactions to a class for business, as well as to categories.

Assigning a transaction to a category is easy. Just type the category name, or display the category and transfer list (press Ctrl-C) and choose the category. For details, see Chapter 7, *Using Categories*, beginning on page 101.

If a transaction applies to more than one category, use the Split Transaction window to enter each category name and the amount that should be applied to it.

To be certain that you categorize every transaction, Quicken has a feature you can set to require that every transaction be assigned to a category. To set this feature, choose Set Preferences from the Main Menu. Choose Transaction Settings and type Y for "Require Category on transactions." Then press Enter, as needed. Once this feature is set, each time you record a transaction Quicken will ask you to enter a category in the Category field if you haven't already done so.

You might also want Quicken to warn you if you use the same check number twice. If you do, choose Set Preferences from the Main Menu, choose Checks and Reports Settings, and tab to the line "Warn if a check number is re-used". Type Y to turn on this setting.

Creating Reports

Following are two types of reports you can create to help with your bookkeeping tasks:

- P & L Statements (Profit and Loss)
- Transactions by Income and Expense Category

P & L Statements

If you have a cash-based business, a P & L Statement will show your profit and losses. For other businesses, the P & L Statement provides much of the information you'll need.

To create a profit and loss statement, go to the Reports menu (either from the Main Menu, or from the register, or from the Write Checks screen) and choose Business Reports. Then choose P & L Statement from the list of business reports. In the window that appears, type a title such as "Profit & Loss Statement, 3rd Quarter," and set the date range to cover the time period you want. When the report is displayed, you can customize it; for example, the Other Options item on the Layout pulldown menu lets you exclude all transfers from the report.

For an example of how your P & L Statement will look, see "P & L Statement" on page 148. This example is for a business that uses only a few categories to categorize its expenses.

If the report shows a line identified by the word "Other," that means that Quicken found some transactions that were not assigned to a category. For a list of these transactions, create a transaction report in which you restrict the report to transactions without category information. (You do this by typing ~.. in the Category contains field of the Filter Transactions window, available through the Edit pulldown menu.)

Transactions by Income and Expense Category

Transactions by Income and Expense Category shows the "breakdown" of each income and expense category into individual transactions. It also permits you to double-check that transactions were correctly categorized.

To create such a report, go to the Reports menu and choose Transaction (see "Transaction" on page 169). In the Create Transaction Report window, type a title such as "Income & Expense by Category," then set the date range you want. Subtotal by category.

A report that shows income and expenses by category is shown on page 373. Note that Quicken separately totals the transactions assigned to each category and provides separate totals for income and expenses.

$ Reporting by Job, Property, Client, Project, or Department

Quicken can help in billing expenses to clients, tracking actual costs vs. estimates, segregating income and expenses by rental property, and tracking expenses by project or department. This makes Quicken valuable in medical, legal, consulting, and other professional service firms, as well as property management, job-shop manufacturing, construction, and similar businesses.

Note: You'll find a detailed discussion of using Quicken specifically to manage properties under "Rental Properties" on page 359.

```
                        Income & Expense by Category Detail
                           1/ 1/92 Through 1/ 8/92
        DESIGN-Selected Accounts                                     Page 1
        2/12/92

        Date   Acct      Num    Description    Memo      Category      Clr Amount
        -----  --------  ------ ---------------- ----------- ---------------- - --------

               INCOME/EXPENSE
               INCOME

               Design
               ------
        1/ 1 AR          1028 S Robinson Shoes              Design/Job 1   X    500.00
        1/ 1 AR          1029 S Reynolds Markets            Design/Job 2   X    964.50
        1/ 1 AR          1030 S Ace Computer Sal            Design/Job 3   X    556.00
        1/ 1 AR          1031 S Osborne Studios  Ad placemen Design/Job 6  X    380.00
        1/ 1 AR          1032 S Tower Concerts              Design/Job 7   X    413.00
        1/ 1 AR          1033 S Blaine Associate            Design/Job 8        600.00
                                                                          ---------
               Total Design                                               3,733.50

               Printing
               --------
        1/ 1 AR          1029 S Reynolds Markets            Print/Job 2    X    280.00
        1/ 1 AR          1031 S Osborne Studios             Print/Job 6    X    185.45
                                                                          ---------
               Total Printing                                                  465.45

               Production
               ----------
        1/ 1 AR          1028 S Robinson Shoes              Prod/Job 1     X     26.16
        1/ 1 AR          1029 S Reynolds Markets            Prod/Job 2     X     25.00
        1/ 1 AR          1033 S Blaine Associate            Prod/Job 8          200.00
                                                                          ---------
               Total Production                                               251.16

            TOTAL INCOME                                                   4,450.11

               EXPENSES
               Paper Supplies
               --------------
        1/ 1 AP           S Amory Paper & Su                Paper/Job 1    X    -26.16
                                                            Paper/Job 3    X    -11.00
                                                            Paper/Job 4    X    -23.95
        1/ 4 AP             Labels Unlimited                Paper/Job 7         -73.55
                                                                          ---------
               Total Paper Supplies                                          -134.66

               Printing Services
               -----------------
        1/ 3 AP             LaserExpress      2438          Printing/Job 4      -74.00
                                                                          ---------
               Total Printing Services                                        -74.00

               Telephone Expense
               -----------------
        1/ 1 AP             Western Bell      A/C#318-258 Telephone        X   -131.90
                                                                          ---------
               Total Telephone Expense                                       -131.90
                                                                          ---------
            TOTAL EXPENSES                                                   -359.56
                                                                          ---------
            TOTAL INCOME/EXPENSE                                           4,090.55
                                                                          ---------
```

The process of using Quicken for job, property, client, project, or department bookkeeping involves four steps:

- Set up a list of categories based on your chart of accounts. (See "Setting Up Categories" on page 105 for assistance.)

- Set up a list of classes for each of your jobs, properties, clients, projects, or departments. (See the next section.)

- Assign each transaction to a category and a class. (See "Categorizing Transactions" on page 107, or "Assigning Transactions to Classes" on page 353.)

- Create reports. (See "Creating Reports" on page 371.)

Setting Up Classes for Jobs, Properties, Clients, Projects, or Departments

You set up classes on the basis of the type of reporting you want to do. For example, if you work on a number of projects at one time, set up a class for each project. If you work with a number of clients, set up a class for each client. If you have an existing set of job or property numbers, use these as the class names. You can enter a description of each class in the Set Up Class window (be sure to prefix it with the property number). The description will print on summary reports. For complete information about classes, see Chapter 24, *Using Classes*, beginning on page 351.

Sample Class Lists for Client, Job, or Project Reporting

Class	Description
Job 101	101 Jones — First Ave.
Job 102	102 Smith — North Park
Job 103	103 Oak Circle Building

Splitting Purchases Among Jobs

When a transaction includes expenses that apply to more than one job, split the transaction and assign the amount for each job to the class for that job. For example, if you write a check to A & S Building Supply for lumber to be used on both the Smith kitchen (Job 102) and the Jones building (Job 101), the split might look like the example on the next page.

```
                                     Date    3/ 5/92
        Pay to the                         ───────
        Order of    A & S Building Supplies              $  137.03
                   ─────────────────────────────       ─────────

   ╔══════════════════════════════════════════════════════════════╗
   █                        Split Transaction                       █
   ╠════════════════════════════════╤═══════════════╤═══════════════╣
            Category                       Memo              Amount
     1:Lumber/Job 101                                         46.97↑
     2:Lumber/Job 102                                         90.06⋮
     3:                                                          ⋮
     4:                                                          ⋮
     5:                                                          ⋮
     6:                                                          ↓
   ╟────────────────────────────────┴───────────────┴───────────────╢
              Enter categories, descriptions, and amounts
     Esc-Cancel     Ctrl-D Delete    F9-Recalc Transaction Total   Ctrl◄┘ Done
   ╚══════════════════════════════════════════════════════════════╝
```

Creating Reports

You'll find that the job/project report, summary reports, and transaction reports can all be useful in reporting on jobs, properties, clients, projects, or departments.

Showing Income and Expenses by Job, Project, Client, Property, or Department

You can create a report showing your income and expense for each class (property, client, job, department, and so forth). To do this, choose Business Reports from the Reports menu, and then choose Job/Project Report. Type a title such as "Income and Expenses by Job," and set the date range to cover the time period you want.

For a sample of this report, see "Job/Project" on page 151.

Reporting on a Single Job with a Summary Report

Quicken can create an income and expense report for a single job, client, or department. To do this, create a summary report (for complete information, see "Summary" on page 171). In the Create Summary Report window, type a title such as "Smith, Job Summary by Month," and set the date range to cover the time period you want. Subtotal by month by choosing Month as the column headings. When the report is displayed, choose Filter Transactions from the Edit menu and, in the Class contains field, type the class name for the property whose report you want to see; for example, Job 102 to see only transactions involving Job 102. This entry tells Quicken to include only those transactions that have been assigned to that class. The report will show all transactions for that class even if they have different subclasses.

An example is shown on the next page.

Restrict the report to transactions that match a class.

The report will show all transactions for that class even if they have different subclasses.

Press Ctrl-L to view a list of your classes. Select the one you want to restrict the report to and press Enter to copy it into the Class contains field.

```
████████████████████████████████████████████████████████
                    Filter Transactions
_____
 Restrict report to transactions matching these criteria
    Payee contains    :
    Memo contains     :
    Category contains :
    Class contains    : Job 102
_____
 Tax-related categories only    (Y/N): N
 Below/Equal/Above (B/E/A):    the amount:
 Payments/Deposits/Unprinted checks/All (P/D/U/A) : A
_____
 Cleared status is
 Blank ' ': Y  Newly cleared '*': Y  Cleared 'X': Y
_____
 Esc-Cancel           Ctrl-D Reset           ◄┘ Continue
```

Here is the resulting report.

This summary report filtered by class shows income and expenses for a single job.

```
                          Smith, Job Summary by Month
                           1/ 1/92 Through 3/31/92
 DESIGN-Selected Accounts                                   Page 1
 4/ 1/92
                                                          OVERALL
         Category Description       1/92      2/92     3/92      TOTAL
 -------------------------------  --------  --------  --------  --------
 INCOME/EXPENSE
   INCOME
     Design                           0.00  1,810.00    300.00  2,110.00
     Mechanical Preparation           0.00     91.50     54.25    145.75
     Printing                         0.00    280.50     25.50    306.00
     Production                       0.00     50.00    936.67    986.67
     Shipping/Postage               613.51     28.00     28.25    669.76
                                  --------  --------  --------  --------
   TOTAL INCOME                    613.51  2,260.00  1,344.67  4,218.18
   EXPENSES
     Speedy Shipping Services        11.00     28.25     70.00    109.25
     Mechanical Preparation         105.50     54.25     75.00    234.75
     Paper Supplies                   0.00    700.00      0.00    700.00
     Photocopying                    19.00      0.00      0.00     19.00
     Printing Services              250.00     25.50    240.00    515.50
                                  --------  --------  --------  --------
   TOTAL EXPENSES                   385.50    808.00    385.00  1,578.50
                                  --------  --------  --------  --------
   TOTAL INCOME/EXPENSE            228.01  1,452.00    959.67  2,639.68
                                  ========  ========  ========  ========
```

Transactions for a Job or Client by Income and Expense

Quicken can also create a detailed report that itemizes the transactions assigned to each class. For example, let's say you want to see each client's payment history: the dates and amounts of each payment they've made.

- To create a payment history for an individual job or client, choose Transaction from the Reports menu. In the Create Transaction Report window, give the report a name such as "Smith, Payment History." If you want to create a payment history by time period, subtotal by the time period. Display the report. Then, in the Filter Transactions window (from the Edit pulldown menu), limit it to the Smith job by typing Job 102 in the Class contains field, and restrict the report to Deposits.

- To create a payment history for multiple jobs or clients, choose Transaction from the Reports menu. Give the report a name such as "Client Payment History." Subtotal by class. Display the report. Then, in the Filter Transactions window (Edit menu), restrict the report to Deposits.

Note: To see who's late in paying and how much they owe, see "Accounts Receivable" on page 393.

Forecasting Cash Flow and Cash Position

A company can receive cash from other sources beside accounts receivable:

- Bank loans
- Investments in the company
- Interest income
- Repayment of loans to others

If you enter both your expected payments and your expected deposits in Quicken, you can forecast your cash flow. Forecasting cash flow predicts cash surpluses, helping you to figure out whether you can handle new expenses or invest the surplus for highest return. Forecasting also predicts impending cash deficits so you can slow your payables, borrow, or take action to generate more cash.

Forecasting works best if, as in many businesses, your receipt of funds is fairly predictable. If your receipts are unpredictable, forecasting does not work as well.

Here's an overview of cash flow forecasting:

- First, enter your expected payments into your regular check register. (Change the date to the date when you expect to make the payment.)

- Then create a new asset account called "Forecast Deposits" in which to record your expected deposits.

- In the Forecast Deposits account register, enter your expected deposits.

- To view your cash flow, create multiaccount reports by selecting all your checking accounts and the Forecast Deposits account. If you have an account for accounts receivable, include it in your reports as well.

- Be sure to review these deposits regularly and revise any that are no longer accurate. Delete any dated today or earlier so that no deposits are counted twice after they have actually been made in your regular check register.

Caution: Do not enter predicted deposits into your regular checking account. Doing so could lead you to overstate your checking account balance and bounce checks. Instead, create a separate asset account for your predicted deposits, as described above.

Forecast Cash Flow Reports

After entering expected payments and deposits as just described, you can create reports that view your future cash flow in two different ways. Note that Quicken can forecast your cash flow as far into the future as you can predict deposits and payments.

As you use these reports, you might notice that "float" can cover temporary cash deficits. Float is the time it takes for a check you mail to reach your bank and get charged to your account. This can be anywhere from one to ten or more business days. However, it is dangerous to take a risk on float; to be safe, make certain there is never a cash deficit in your cash forecast.

Note: Forecast cash flow reports are not the same as Quicken's business cash flow reports.

Cash Receipts and Disbursements

Cash receipts and disbursements by week is a report used by many businesses. If you're doing cash-basis bookkeeping, you can create such a report. Go to the Reports menu and choose Transaction. In the Create Transaction Report window, type a title such as "Cash Flow Forecast by Week," and set the date range to cover from tomorrow forward. Subtotal by week. Then select the accounts to include, specifying only your checking accounts, your forecast deposits account, and your A/R account (if you have one). Don't include accounts used to track noncash expenses, such as asset and liability accounts.

The next page shows the resulting report. The balance is your cumulative cash position through each week. The report does factor in your bank account balance as of the beginning of the report. A negative balance means you are out of cash as of that date.

To memorize a report format for later use, press Ctrl-M while the report is displayed.

Sources and Uses of Cash

Sources and uses of cash is a report that summarizes your business's cash flow. It shows where your cash is coming from and where it is going. It shows which are your largest sources for cash and which are your largest uses. You may want to direct more management attention to these sources and uses. You can get a Sources and Uses report for your historic cash flow or for your forecasted future cash flow.

Create the report in any of these ways depending upon what you want to see:

- For sources and uses totaled by category, create a summary report totaled by category (choose Category as the row headings) or a transaction report subtotaled by category.

- For sources and uses totaled by payee, create a summary or transaction report and subtotal by payee (choose Payee for the column headings in the summary report; subtotal by payee in the transaction report).

- To see the changes in account balances only, create a summary report with Accounts for the row headings.

A cash flow forecast report sets the date range to cover from tomorrow forward.

```
                              Cash Flow Forecast by Week
                               2/16/92 Through 12/31/92
      DESIGN-Selected Accounts                                          Page 1
      2/15/92
          Date   Acct    Num    Description    Memo      Category   Clr Amount
          -----  ------- ------ -------------- --------- ---------- -  --------

                 BALANCE 2/15/92                                        23,000.00

          2/16 First St **** Smith & Hines               Legal          -1,674.00
          2/16 First St **** Boston Labs     Widgex co   R&D           -12,000.00
          2/16 First St **** Western Bell                Phone             -64.12
          2/16 First St **** State Power Co.             Utilities        -142.87
          2/16 Forecast      Deposit                     Revenue        25,000.00
                                                                       ----------
                 TOTAL    2/16/92 - 2/17/92                             11,119.01

                 BALANCE  2/17/92                                       34,119.01

          2/19 First St **** Transco Office              Office Sup       -932.56
          2/22 First St **** Acme Supply     Inv #45627 Raw Matls      -10,542.00
          2/22 First St **** Eisenhower Inc. Inv #4324  Office            -303.90
          2/24 Forecast      Deposit                     Revenue        32,000.00
                                                                       ----------
                 TOTAL    2/18/92 - 2/24/92                             11,119.01

                 BALANCE  2/24/92                                       54,340.55

          3/ 2 First St **** Florabunda      New Plant   Misc Serv         -50.00
          3/ 3 First St **** Acme Supply     Inv# 456    Raw Matls     -14,889.04
                                                                       ----------
                 TOTAL    2/25/92 - 3/ 3/92                            -14,939.04

                 BALANCE  3/ 3/92                                       39,401.51

          3/ 6 First St **** Ace Fasteners               Raw Matls        -421.87
          3/ 9 First St **** Dravog Printing Inv #1043   Office           -679.00
```

The balance is your cumulative cash position through each week.

```
                                                                       ----------
                 TOTAL    12/24/92 - 12/30/92                                   0

                 BALANCE  12/30/92                                      23,056.64
                                                                       ----------
                 TOTAL    12/31/92 - 12/31/92                                   0

                 BALANCE  12/31/92                                      23,056.64
                                                                       ----------
                 OVERALL TOTAL                                             56.64
                                                                       ==========
                 TOTAL INFLOWS                                          57,000.00
                 TOTAL OUTFLOWS                                        -56,943.36

                 NET TOTAL                                                 56.64
                                                                       ==========
```

- For all these reports, set the report organization to "Cash flow basis" (choose Other Options on the pulldown Layout menu). That way you can clearly see transfers (such as those to a capital expenditure account) as part of the cash outflow.

- Select the accounts to include (Accounts item on the Edit pulldown menu), specifying only your checking accounts, forecast deposits account, and A/R account (if you have one). (For historic cash flow, select only your checking account and A/R account.) Don't include accounts with noncash transactions, such as an asset account that tracks depreciation.

To memorize a report format for later use, press Ctrl-M while the report is displayed.

Asset and Liability Accounting

You can use Quicken's asset and liability accounts to track accounts receivable and accounts payable. You can also use Quicken to track other assets and liabilities; for example, capital equipment and loan principal.

Asset and liability accounting involves three steps:

- Set up asset and liability accounts for each asset and liability you want to track.
- Entering transactions in the accounts.
- Creating reports.

Note: Quicken restricts the total number of accounts you can set up in any one file. (For more information, see "How Your Quicken Data Is Organized" on page 450.) So use fairly broad groupings when determining your asset and liability accounts.

One common use of asset and liability accounting with Quicken is to track depreciation by asset. To do this, set up an asset account in which to record assets as you purchase them. Call it something like "Cap Equip" (for capital equipment).

When you purchase an asset, record it in the register of your checking account. Type the name of the asset in the Payee field. In the Category field, specify a transfer by typing the name of the asset account you created to show depreciation to capital equipment. When you record the transaction, Quicken creates a parallel transaction in the asset account to show the transfer of funds from the checking account to the capital equipment account.

When you're ready to record the depreciation of an asset, enter a transaction in the asset account register. Type the name of the asset as the payee, and the amount of depreciation in the Decrease field. As the category, type Depr Exp, or whatever category name you use for depreciation.

See Chapter 16, *Tracking Assets and Liabilities*, beginning on page 257, for more about setting up accounts to track assets and liabilities.

When you want a report showing depreciation, create a summary report. Use the asset account for the report: report on categories, and subtotal by month (specify Category for row headings, and Month for column headings). Depreciation also appears in a P & L statement.

Creating Reports

Quicken provides two reports you'll find useful in asset and liability accounting: the balance sheet, which is one of Quicken's business reports, and the account balances report, a custom report.

Balance Sheets

When you want a balance sheet showing the company's assets and liabilities as of one date, you can create a balance sheet report. Choose Business Reports from the Reports menu and choose Balance Sheet. Type a title if you want, and make sure the dates shown are those that you want to be combined in the total.

The balance sheet combines the balances in all your Quicken accounts.

Unlike the personal report Net Worth, the business balance sheet shows the difference between your total assets and total liabilities as a line called "Equity." This amount represents the net worth of your business.

Asset and Liability Reports

When you want to create a balance sheet showing the balance at intervals, or if you want to restrict the report to certain Quicken accounts, create an account balances report. For an example of an account balances report, see "Account Balances" on page 173.

Chapter 25

Advanced Business Uses

The previous chapter gave examples of some of Quicken's many business uses, concentrating on cash-basis bookkeeping and asset and liability accounting. This chapter gives further examples of Quicken's business uses: accrual accounting, accounts payable, accounts receivable, invoicing, and payroll.

A set of categories for business use is provided with Quicken. You can tell Quicken to use them when you set up a Quicken file. You can modify this list or use one of your own. You'll find complete information about setting up and using categories in *Using Categories*, beginning on page 101.

$ Accrual Accounting: Timing of Income and Expenses

Many small businesses use cash-basis bookkeeping, but larger businesses often use the "accrual" basis for their accounting. One of the elements of accrual accounting is recognizing income when you bill a customer, instead of when you receive payment, and recognizing an expense when you incur the obligation, instead of when you pay the bill.

Note: Ask your accountant which bookkeeping system is best for your business: cash basis or accrual basis. If you decide to use cash basis, see "Cash-Basis Bookkeeping" beginning on page 370 first.

If you want to track (recognize) income and expenses on an accrual basis, use the following general procedures:

1. Set up an asset account for your accounts receivable (name it A/R) and a liability account for your accounts payable (name it A/P).

2. When you send out an invoice, enter it in the A/R account and assign the transaction to an income category. When you receive a bill, enter it in the A/P account and assign it to an expense category. This technique charges your receivables and payables to income and expense categories at the proper time—immediately.

3. When you receive payments from customers or pay your bills, record the transactions in your A/R or A/P account as transfers to or from your bank account.

See "Accrual-Basis Accounts Payable" on page 387 and "Accrual-Basis Accounts Receivable" on page 396 for details.

Accounts Payable

Quicken organizes your payables so that you know how much you owe, to whom you owe it, and when the payments are due. If you enter all your obligations in Quicken, you can use that information to forecast your cash requirements over the coming months. Quicken lets you track your payables using either cash or accrual accounting.

Cash-Basis Accounts Payable: Postdating Checks

With cash-basis bookkeeping, you don't recognize expenses until payment actually changes hands. To track payables in Quicken, simply enter them as postdated checks.

To track accounts payable with Quicken on a cash basis:

1. In the checking account that you use to pay bills, write a check for each bill as soon as you receive it. For complete information about writing a check, see page 77.

2. Postdate each check to the due date of the bill. For example, if you receive a bill on May 7 and the payment terms are Net 30, you might want to print a check on June 6.

3. Memorize transactions that recur regularly and set up transaction groups for bills that you pay on the same day.

Using transaction groups to save time.

Use transaction groups (see Chapter 12, *Entering Transaction Groups*, beginning on page 211) to reduce keystrokes when typing future transactions. For example, you might write 11 payroll checks every two weeks. Memorize each of these transactions with its typical dollar amount. Assign all 11 to one transaction group. Then, you can enter several months of expected payroll expenses with just a few keystrokes. Later, as you learn the precise dollar amounts, you can change the register accordingly.

Quicken treats the total of your unprinted checks as the accounts payable. It removes an item from accounts payable reports when you do either of two things:

- Print a check.

- Write a handwritten check, go into the register, and replace the five asterisks (*****) in the Num field of the unprinted check with the handwritten check number.

Important: To get a complete picture of your accounts payable, you must enter each item you owe as an unprinted check, even if you don't print checks with Quicken or don't receive bills for some items. If you enter payments in the register, be sure to enter an asterisk (*) in the Num field of the transaction. Then Quicken can forecast how much cash you need to cover all future payments, even those you aren't billed for, such as payroll. Note that Quicken can forecast cash coming in, as well as cash going out, which enables you to forecast your exact cash position. To forecast cash coming in, you'll want to set up a separate Cash Deposits account. For details, see "Forecasting Cash Flow and Cash Position" on page 377.

When Quicken prints your checks, you can choose to print those dated on or before today and hold the remaining postdated checks for future payment. (Just leave today's date next to "Print checks dated through" at the bottom of the Print Checks window.) For more information, see "Fields in the Print Checks Window" on page 94.

Cash-Basis Accounts Payable Reports

Quicken has several useful ways to show your accounts payable.

To see cash requirements by day for a single Quicken account:

1. Look in the account register. All transactions below the double line show checks payable after today's date.

2. Print the postdated portion of the register by pressing Ctrl-P and setting the date range to cover from tomorrow forward.

To see your accounts payable by month:

1. Go to the Reports menu and choose Business Reports.

2. Choose A/P by Vendor.

3. Type a title for the report such as "Accounts Payable by Vendor" and press Enter.

   If you have entered all your payables as postdated checks, the A/P by vendor report shows you unprinted checks due to each vendor, subtotaled by month. If you have entered payments in the register, the A/P by vendor report includes only those transactions with an asterisk (*) in the Num field.

To see your accounts payable by week:

1. Go to the Reports menu and choose Transaction.

2. In the Create Transaction Report window, type a title for the report such as "Accounts Payable by Week."

3. Set the date range to cover from tomorrow forward.

4. Subtotal by week.

5. If you have set up a separate asset account for forecast deposits or accounts receivable, include data from those accounts as well as your checking accounts in the report: choose Selected accounts, then use the space bar to select these other accounts. Run the report. For details on forecasting expected deposits, see "Forecasting Cash Flow and Cash Position" on page 377.

6. To save the report format, press Ctrl-M.

Here's an example "Accounts Payable by Week" report. The balance is your cumulative cash balance through each week. The report factors in your bank account balance as of today, shown as the opening balance on the report. The cumulative balance may be negative if you have postdated only expected payments and not expected deposits or accounts receivable.

```
                        Accounts Payable by Week
                        1/ 1/92 Through 1/15/92
     DESIGN-First Statewide                                        Page 1
     12/31/91
          Date    Num      Description        Memo         Category     Clr  Amount
          -----  ------  ----------------  --------------  -----------------  -  ----------
                  BALANCE 12/31/91                                              35,504.00
          1/ 1 ****   MacWorld          1-year subscri Reference               -20.00
          1/ 1 ****   Western Office Equi Fax machine   [Cap Equip]            -950.00
          1/ 1 ****   Valley Real Estate             Rent Paid                 -400.00
          1/ 5 **** S Chris Jacobson    Payroll        --SPLIT--               -961.16
          1/ 5 **** S Richard Long      Payroll        --SPLIT--             -1,058.11
          1/ 6 ****   Standard Business F 2021          Supplies               -200.00
          1/ 6 ****   Chevron USA       A/C#12345      Auto Leasing            -76.17
                                                                             ----------
                  TOTAL  1/ 1/92 -  1/ 6/92                                   -3,665.44
                  BALANCE  1/ 6/92                                            31,838.56
          1/ 8 ****   Valley Toyota     Honda Accord L Auto Leasing           -104.28
          1/ 9 ****   City of Valley Spri             Business Lice           -23.00
          1/10 ****   Valley News                     Advertising             -245.50
          1/12 ****   Richard Long      Expense Report Meals & Enter          -38.07
                                                                             ----------
                  TOTAL  1/ 7/92 -  1/13/92                                   -410.85
                  BALANCE  1/13/92                                            31,427.71
          1/15 ****   Federal Express   A/C#1111-2222- Shipping               -91.24
          1/15 ****   Western Bell      A/C#318-258-99 Telephone              -131.90
          1/15 ****   Stats 801         1209           Photostats             -37.70
          1/15 ****   Insurance Shield  A/C#2822304-99 Insurance              -150.15
          1/15 ****   Richard Long      Expense Report Meals & Enter          -106.71
          1/15 ****   Valley Courier                  Advertising             -28.00
                                                                             ----------
                  TOTAL  1/14/92 -  1/15/92                                   -545.70
                  BALANCE  1/15/92                                            30,882.01
                                                                             ----------

                  OVERALL TOTAL                                               -4621.99
                                                                             ==========

                  TOTAL INFLOWS                                                      0
                  TOTAL OUTFLOWS                                              -4,621.99
                                                                             ----------
                  NET TOTAL                                                   -4,621.99
                                                                             ==========
```

Accrual-Basis Accounts Payable

If you need to recognize the date you incur an expense as separate from the date you make payment, set up a liability account (see *Tracking Assets and Liabilities*, beginning on page 257). Give this account a descriptive name, such as "A/P" or "Payables." Enter a zero for the opening balance.

When your AP account is set up, use the following general procedures:

- When you receive an invoice or bill, enter it in the AP account and assign the transaction to an expense category. Each obligation you add to the AP account increases your liability.

- Set up and memorize two accounts payable reports: Accounts Payable Summary and Accounts Payable Detail. Use these reports to decide which vendors to pay and how much to pay.

- Record your payments in your checking account as handwritten checks or Quicken checks. When you enter a payment, you transfer the amount to the AP account, where it decreases your liability by the same amount. You can make partial payments on one bill, or write a single check that covers more than one bill. Quicken can track your total liability to any vendor by vendor name. Mark each paid invoice and corresponding payment transaction with an asterisk (*) in the C (for Cleared) column.

Note: A liability is any obligation incurred by your business. Quicken includes all your business obligations, including accounts payable, in the balance sheet report.

Recording an Invoice

Suppose you receive a bill from Standard Business Forms on May 7. You need to record the invoice in your accounts payable account.

To record an invoice in an AP account:

1. Go to the register for the liability account you created for accounts payable.

2. Enter the date of the invoice, the invoice number, the vendor name, the amount due, and assign the transaction to an expense category. The expense category shows up by invoice date in reports like P & L statements and summary reports. You can add a class name if you're interested in tracking costs by job, project, or client:

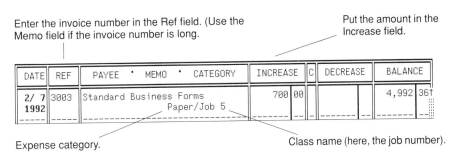

Enter the invoice number in the Ref field. (Use the Memo field if the invoice number is long.

Put the amount in the Increase field.

DATE	REF	PAYEE * MEMO * CATEGORY	INCREASE	C	DECREASE	BALANCE
2/ 7 1992	3003	Standard Business Forms Paper/Job 5	700 00			4,992 36↑

Expense category.

Class name (here, the job number).

3. Press Ctrl-Enter to record the transaction.

When you record the transaction, Quicken automatically increases the total liability in your AP account by the amount ($700.00 in the example).

Recording Credits or Discounts Taken on Payables

Some vendors grant cash discounts to customers for early payment of invoices. A two percent discount for payment within ten days is common. You might also receive a credit from a vendor for returned goods, or to compensate for a billing error. Consider a credit or discount a reduction in the amount assigned to an expense category. You can choose either of two methods to record a credit or discount:

- Select the original invoice and record the credit or discount as a split. The advantage of this method is that you can find all the information about the invoice in one place, the Split Transaction window.

- Enter the credit or discount as a separate transaction. The advantage of this method is that you don't have to search for the original transaction to record your decreased liability to that vendor.

To enter a discount or credit in the Split Transaction window:

1. Use the Find feature (Ctrl-F) to find the original transaction in your AP account.

2. Press Ctrl-S to open the Split Transaction window.

3. Assign the sales discount or credit to the same category as the invoice amount.

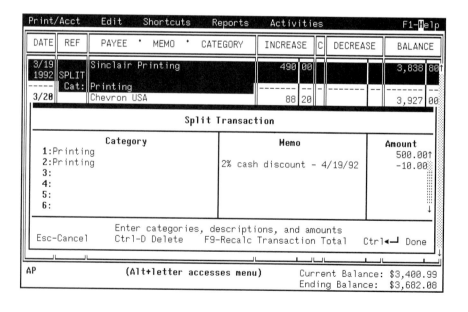

To enter a discount or credit as a separate transaction:

1. Enter a new transaction for the credit in your AP account. (If the original invoice transaction was memorized, press Ctrl-T to recall it to avoid retyping the name of the vendor.)

2. Assign the sales discount or credit to the same category as the invoice amount:

	DATE	REF	PAYEE * MEMO * CATEGORY	INCREASE	C	DECREASE	BALANCE
Payment	3/19 1992	2045	Sinclair Printing Printing	500 00			1,648 80↑

	DATE	REF	PAYEE * MEMO * CATEGORY	INCREASE	C	DECREASE	BALANCE
Credit	3/30 1992		Sinclair Printing Inv.2045/2% Printing			10 00	1,596 58↑

A credit decreases your liability just like a payment.

Accrual-Basis Accounts Payable Reports

If you have entered all your payables as transactions in an accounts payable liability account, Quicken can track your liability by vendor for any time period. Create two Quicken reports before each check run to help you decide which bills to pay.

To see your accounts payable summary:

1. Choose the accounts payable account as your current account. Go to the Reports menu and choose Summary.

2. Type a title for the report such as "Accounts Payable Summary."

3. Set the dates to include all your unpaid AP transactions. For example, set the report date range to include all transactions from six months ago through one week from today.

4. Choose Payee (the vendors) for the row headings.

5. Make sure that Column Headings is set to Don't Subtotal.

6. Make sure the current account is the only account included in the report.

7. Start the report. Filter the report for only those transactions with blank cleared status: choose Filter Transactions on the Edit pulldown menu, and enter Y for Cleared Status is Blank, and N for Newly Cleared and Cleared.

8. When the report is ready, print it, then press Ctrl-M to memorize the report format. From now on, you can select the memorized report by name.

The totals in the accounts payable summary report tell you how much you owe each vendor.

Because you marked each paid invoice and payment with an asterisk (*) in the Cleared field, the report shows only unpaid invoices.

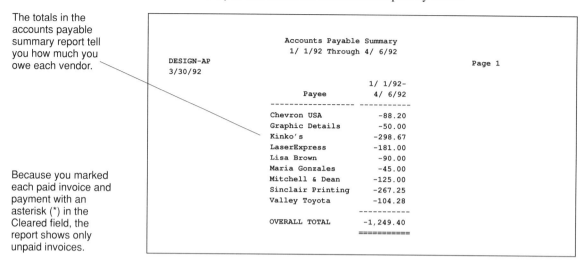

```
                                Accounts Payable Summary
                                  1/ 1/92 Through 4/ 6/92
       DESIGN-AP                                                        Page 1
       3/30/92
                                                    1/ 1/92-
                                        Payee        4/ 6/92
                                  ------------------ ----------
                                  Chevron USA           -88.20
                                  Graphic Details       -50.00
                                  Kinko's              -298.67
                                  LaserExpress         -181.00
                                  Lisa Brown            -90.00
                                  Maria Gonzales        -45.00
                                  Mitchell & Dean      -125.00
                                  Sinclair Printing    -267.25
                                  Valley Toyota        -104.28
                                                     ----------
                                  OVERALL TOTAL      -1,249.40
                                                     ==========
```

To see your payment detail by vendor:

1. Choose the accounts payable account as your current account. Go to the Reports menu and choose Transaction.

2. Type a title for the report such as "Transaction Detail by Vendor."

3. Use the same date range as for the accounts payable summary report.

4. Subtotal by payee (the vendors).

5. Make sure the current account is the only account included in the report.

6. Start the report.

7. With the transaction report displayed, report on blank cleared status only: choose Filter Transactions on the Edit menu, then enter Y for Cleared status is Blank, and N for Newly cleared and Cleared.

8. When the report is ready, print it and then press Ctrl-M to memorize the report format. From now on, you can select the memorized report by name.

Use the transactions by vendor report to get details about the transactions summarized in the accounts payable summary report.

```
                    TRANSACTION DETAIL BY VENDOR
                     1/ 1/92 Through 4/ 6/92
    DESIGN-AP                                              Page 1
    3/30/92
     Date   Num      Description      Memo          Category      Clr  Amount
    -----  -----  ------------------  --------------  ------------------ - ---------
     3/20          Chevron USA                        Auto:Gas            -88.20
                                                                       ---------
            Total Chevron USA                                           -88.20
     3/12          Graphic Details                    Contractor/Job 8   -50.00
                                                                       ---------
            Total Graphic Details                                       -50.00
     3/22          Kinko's                            Photocopying/Job 1 -298.67
                                                                       ---------
            Total Kinko's                                              -298.67
     3/22          LaserExpress                       Photocopying/Job 9 -15.00
     3/25          LaserExpress                       Mechanical Prep/Jo -75.00
     3/26          LaserExpress                       Photocopying/Job 7 -26.00
     3/31          LaserExpress                       Photostats/Job 8   -65.00
                                                                       ---------
            Total LaserExpress                                         -181.00
     3/28          Lisa Brown                         Contractor/Job 8   -90.00
                                                                       ---------
            Total Lisa Brown                                            -90.00
     3/31          Maria Gonzales    graphic design  Contractor/Job 9   -45.00
                                                                       ---------
            Total Maria Gonzales                                        -45.00
     3/28          Mitchell & Dean                    Legal Expenses    -125.00
                                                                       ---------
            Total Mitchell & Dean                                      -125.00
     3/19          Sinclair Printing                  Printing/Job 3     -63.00
     3/25          Sinclair Printing                  Printing/Job 7    -105.00
     3/27          Sinclair Printing                  Mechanical Prep/Jo -99.25
                                                                       ---------
            Total Sinclair Printing                                    -267.25
     3/20          Valley Toyota     Honda Accord L  Auto:Leasing      -104.28
                                                                       ---------
            Total Valley Toyota                                        -104.28
                                                                       ---------
            OVERALL TOTAL                                            -1,249.40
                                                                       =========
```

Entering Payments

After you've printed your accounts payable reports and decided whom to pay, open the checking account where you want to pay the bill and press Ctrl-W to Write Checks. You can make payment in full or in part, or pay several bills with one check.

To make a payment in your bank account:

1. Write a check for the date that you want to pay the bill (March 14 in the example). Create a transfer to AP by entering the AP account name in the Category field.

Invoice reference number or numbers.

AP account name creates the transfer.

Here's how the same transaction appears in the AP account.

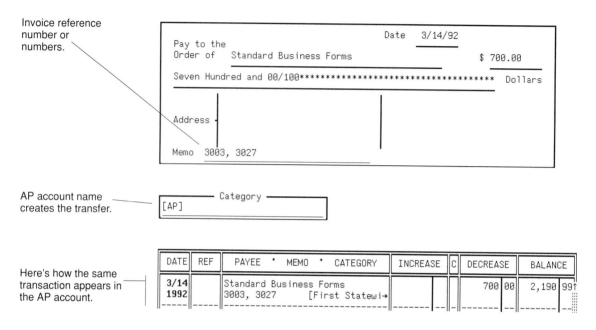

When you record the check, Quicken automatically decreases the total liability in your AP account by $700.00 on the check date. The unprinted check shows up in the A/P by vendor report until you print the check. After you print the check, the payment shows up in your cash flow report.

2. To get meaningful reports, go to the accounts payable register and place an asterisk (*) in the C (for Cleared) field for both the paid invoice and the payment transaction.

Entering recurring transactions

Use memorized transactions (see "Memorizing a Transaction" on page 196) to reduce keystrokes and prevent errors when entering recurring transactions. You can also set up transaction groups to enter bills, invoices, or other payables due at the same time.

When Quicken prints your checks, you can choose to print those dated on or before today and hold the remaining postdated checks for future payment. (Just leave today's date next to "Print checks dated through" at the bottom of the Print Checks window.) For more information, see "Fields in the Print Checks Window" on page 94.

Accounts Receivable

Quicken lets you track your receivables using either cash- or accrual-based accounting. To use Quicken for accounts receivable, you need to set up an asset account (see *Tracking Assets and Liabilities*, beginning on page 257). Give this account a descriptive name, such as "A/R" or "Receivables." Enter a zero for the opening balance.

Note: If your objective in tracking receivables is only to forecast cash flow, see "Forecasting Cash Flow and Cash Position" on page 377.

Cash-Basis Accounts Receivable

In a cash-basis bookkeeping system, you recognize income when you collect from the customer. To track receivables in Quicken on a cash basis, create a separate asset account for receivables and record each invoice or statement that you submit for payment in the asset account register. To time the income correctly, enter the date you expect to be paid in the Date field for each invoice.

Quicken uses the receivables account to monitor the payment status (aging) of your invoices. You can generate reports that show who owes you and how much you're owed.

When you receive payment, you record the amount you collected in the Split Transaction window of the original invoice transaction. The payment is set up as a transfer between accounts receivable and your bank account. To make sure that you recognize the income at the time of collection, check the transaction date and change it from estimated to actual date of payment.

Entering New Invoices

Assemble all your outstanding invoices (or statements, if that's how you bill customers) and type a summary of each into the register of the accounts receivable account you just set up. If you expect to be paid in several installments, enter the invoice in multiple transactions. For example, you could number installments like this:

1074A	First installment
1074B	Second installment

Use these basic steps to enter invoices:

1. Set up an income category; pick something like "Sales" or "Revenue." You can set up subcategories if you want to manage sales by product or salesperson, or track separate items on the invoice such as shipping and sales tax.

2. For each invoice item you enter in the register, enter the expected date of payment in the Date field.

3. Enter the invoice number in the Ref field (or the Memo field if the invoice number is long).

4. Enter the customer's name in the Payee field.

5. Enter the amount of the invoice in the Increase field. (Use the Decrease field for credit memos, where you owe the customer money.)

6. Enter the date you issued the invoice in the Memo field.

7. Assign the transaction to the income category you set up in step 1; for example, Sales. You can add a class name if you're interested in tracking income by job, project, or client.

Note: If you want to keep track of different items in the invoice, enter the invoice amount as a split transaction and assign subcategories. For example, if your invoice covers a product and shipping, you might have separate line items for Sales:Product and Sales:Shipping.

8. Press Ctrl-Enter to record the transaction.

Here's a typical accounts receivable register.

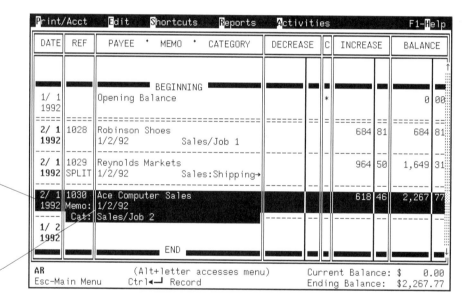

The date in the Date field is the expected date of payment.

The date in the Memo field is the date you issued the invoice.

Entering Payments

When you receive payment from a customer, find the invoice transaction in the accounts receivables register and enter the amount you received in the Split Transaction window.

When you receive payment, two things happen:

- The value of your receivables assets decreases by the amount of the payment.

- The value of your bank account increases by the amount of the payment.

To record a payment in a split transaction:

1. Find the invoice transaction in the account receivables register. (Press Ctrl-F and search by NUM, the invoice number, which you entered in the Ref field.)

2. Change the date of the transaction to the date of payment.

3. Press Ctrl-S to open the Split Transaction window.

   The income category you assigned the transaction to appears on the first line of the split. Or, if you split the transaction when you recorded the invoice, you see the existing split.

4. In the first empty Category field in the split, enter the name of the bank account to receive the payment; for example, [Checking].

5. On the same line of the split, type the dollar amount of the payment as a negative amount, but do ***not*** press Enter.

   (If you accidentally press Enter, Quicken adds a balancing amount in the next line of the split, which you must delete before doing step 6.)

6. Press F9 to recalculate the transaction amount.

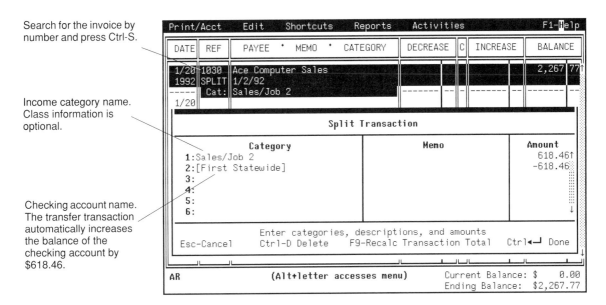

Search for the invoice by number and press Ctrl-S.

Income category name. Class information is optional.

Checking account name. The transfer transaction automatically increases the balance of the checking account by $618.46.

7. Press Ctrl-Enter to close the Split Transaction window.

   If the amount of the transaction is now an Increase, the customer still owes you money on the invoice. If the resulting amount is a Decrease, the customer has overpaid the invoice and has a credit.

8. If the invoice has been paid in full, enter an asterisk (*) in the C (for Cleared) field and press Ctrl-Enter to record the transaction.

Entering Discounts or Credits Granted

To enter a sales discount granted to an account or a credit for goods returned, open the Split Transaction window for the invoice transaction and enter the amount of the discount or credit the same way you record a payment.

Passing Expenses Through to Clients

Sometimes a business purchases supplies or incurs expenses on behalf of clients or customers. For example, a design studio may pass production costs on to the client. You can track these expenses by adapting the method described here for cash-basis accounts receivable.

Record an expense in your checking account. In the Category field, enter a transfer to your asset account. (This could be your accounts receivable account. However, if you often pass through expenses, you might want to open a separate asset account to record them.) The transfer increases the balance in your asset account. When you receive reimbursement from the client, record a deposit in your checking account, again categorized as a transfer to your asset account. The reimbursement reduces or cancels the original increase in amount receivable.

In your asset account, you can link the payment and reimbursement by entering a number in each Ref field, or by entering the original payee's name in the Memo field of each transaction. Now you can track reimbursement with a transaction report.

Accrual-Basis Accounts Receivable

Set up a separate asset account for accounts receivable and then type a quick summary of each invoice or statement you generate into the account. When you receive payment, type a separate transaction into the same account. Then you can get reports showing who owes you and how much you're owed.

Entering New Invoices

Assemble all your outstanding invoices (or statements, if that's how you bill customers) and type a summary of each into the register of the accounts receivable account you just set up. Set up a liability account to track the sales tax you owe the government. If you expect an invoice to be paid in installments, enter a separate transaction for each expected payment.

To enter invoices:

1. Set up an income category; pick something like "Sales" or "Revenue." You can set up subcategories if you want to manage sales by product or salesperson, or track separate items on the invoice such as shipping.

2. For each invoice item you enter in the register, enter the date of the invoice in the Date field.

3. Enter the invoice number in the Ref field (or the Memo field if the invoice number is long).

4. Enter the customer's name in the Payee field.

5. Type the amount of the invoice in the Increase field. (Use the Decrease field for credit memos, where you owe the customer money.)

6. Assign the transaction to the income category you set up in step 1. For example, use the income category Sales.

   Note: If you want to keep track of different items in the invoice, enter the invoice amount as a split transaction and use subcategories. For example, if your invoice covers a product and shipping, you might have separate line items for Sales:Product and Sales:Shipping. For sales tax, enter the name of the sales tax liability account in the Category field of a separate split line item.

7. If you use the balance forward method (see "Entering Payments" on page 398), also enter a class to identify the customer, usually the customer name. For example, use Sales/Jones or Sales:Product/Jones to specify both the income category and the customer name.

8. Press Ctrl-Enter to record the transaction.

   Here's a typical accounts receivable register:

Payment for invoice numbers 1051, 1063.

Invoice assigned to the category Design and classified by job number.

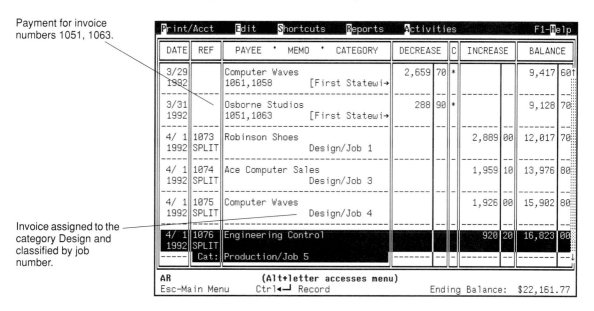

Entering Payments

You can enter payments using either of two methods for tracking accounts receivable:

- The "balance forward" method, in which you track the balance a customer owes you, rather than individual invoices. This method is appropriate if most of the payments you receive apply to multiple invoices. Set up a class for each customer name.

- The "open item receivables" method, in which you track customer payments for each invoice. This method is appropriate if most of the payments you receive are for specific invoices.

Choose one of these methods and use it consistently. (You may want to consult a professional accountant to decide which method is best for you.) Using either method, record the payment in your accounts receivable register and type the name of the checking account in the Category field. Quicken automatically records the amount of the payment received as a deposit in your checking account register.

The balance forward method of recording payment

Enter a separate transaction for each payment you receive in the accounts receivable register. This technique ensures the accuracy of the running balance in your bank account. When entering invoices, use class names to identify each of your customers. You also use class names (usually the customer names) when entering their payments.

To record a payment (balance forward method):

1. For each payment received, type the date you receive the payment in the Date field.

2. Type the customer's name in the Payee field.

3. Type the amount of the payment in the Decrease field.

4. Type the invoice numbers that the payment covers in the Memo field.

5. In the Category field, type the name of the checking account to receive the payment and include the customer's name as the class (for example, Checking/Jones).

The open item method of recording payments

Use the open item method to track the paid status of specific invoices. Enter each payment in the accounts receivable register as a new transaction. This technique ensures the accuracy of the running balance in your bank account. When an item is paid, type an asterisk (*) in the C (for Cleared) field both of the payment transaction and of the invoice transaction to which it applies. (Marking items with an asterisk prevents them from appearing in accounts receivable reports.)

To record a payment (open item method):

1. For each payment, type the date you receive the payment in the Date field.

2. Type the customer's name in the Payee field.

3. Type the amount of the payment in the Decrease field.

4. Type an asterisk (*) in the C (for Cleared) field for the payment transaction.

5. Type the invoice numbers that the payment covers in the Memo field.

6. In the Category field, type the name of the checking account to receive the deposit (for example, Checking).

7. Record the payment transaction by pressing Ctrl-Enter.

8. Find and select the invoice transaction in the accounts receivable register.

9. Type an asterisk in the C (for Cleared) field of the invoice transaction.

10. If you want to track how promptly customers pay, type the date of the payment in the Memo field of the invoice transaction.

11. Press Ctrl-Enter to record your changes to the invoice transaction.

Entering discounts or credits granted

To record a discount or credit granted in accounts receivable, enter it as a separate transaction and be sure to type the amount in the Decrease field, just as you would for a payment.

Accounts Receivable Reports

Receivables by Week

To see your receivables by week, create a transaction report (see "Transaction" on page 169). Set the date range to cover all invoices from first to last. Subtotal by week.

If you wish to memorize this report for later use, press Ctrl-M while the report is displayed.

Receivables by Customer for Open Items

To see your receivables by customer, create an A/R by customer report. (This report is on the Business Reports menu.)

If you clear all paid invoices and payment transactions by typing an asterisk (*) in the C (for Cleared) field, this report lists only your outstanding invoices. The following is an example of the resulting report.

To limit your report to a certain date range, display the report then choose Set Title & Date Range on the Edit pulldown menu.

```
                                A/R by Customer
                             3/ 1/92 Through 4/30/92
        DESIGN-AR                                                    Page 1
        4/30/92
                                                          OVERALL
                  Payee              3/92        4/92      TOTAL
        --------------------     ----------  ----------  ----------
        Ace Computer Sales          404.99      376.97      781.96
        Balloon Adventures            0.00      705.66      705.66
        Blaine Associates           589.03      571.95    1,160.98
        Computer Waves              679.45      595.41    1,274.86
        Engineering Control           0.00      446.19      446.19
        Osborne Studios             682.12    2,059.75    2,741.87
        Reynolds Markets            818.55        0.00      818.55
        Robinson Shoes              463.84      350.00      813.84
                                 ----------  ----------  ----------
        OVERALL TOTAL             3,637.98    5,105.93    8,743.91
                                 ==========  ==========  ==========
```

Quicken can produce a similar report showing only overdue accounts. To adapt your A/R by customer report, choose Set Title & Date Range on the Edit pulldown menu and set the ending date to today's date minus the number of days terms you allow.

To memorize a report format for later use, press Ctrl-M while the report is displayed.

Receivables by Customer on Balance Forward Method

To see your receivables by customer, create a summary report. Set the date range to cover the due dates for all invoices you've issued. Choose Class as the row headings and Month as the column heading.

Press Ctrl-M to memorize the report format.

Customer Payment History

Quicken can also keep a record of how promptly each customer has paid each invoice. This record is called a Customer Payment History.

To track customer payment history, type the date of each payment in the Memo field of the original invoice transaction.

Then, to see each customer's invoice and payment history, create a transaction report and subtotal by payee. Set the dates to include all the invoices.

Income and Expense Reporting of Accounts Receivable

If you run your business on an accrual basis, use the standard business P & L statement for income and expense reporting.

If you run your business on a cash accounting basis, you want your accounts receivable to show up as income when they are paid, not when the invoice is issued. Use the business cash flow report (not the P & L statement) for income and expense reporting.

Also, if you are on a cash basis and have other asset and liability accounts apart from accounts receivable, choose Accounts from the Edit pulldown menu and report on selected accounts. Include all asset and liability accounts except accounts receivable to keep transfers to and from these accounts from appearing in the report. Excluding the accounts receivable account causes transfers from accounts receivable (that is, payments received) to be treated properly as cash inflows.

To memorize this report for later use, press Ctrl-M while the report is displayed.

$ Payroll

Note: This section is for employers only. If you simply want to enter your paycheck into your Quicken account, turn to "Entering Paychecks" on page 358.

If you have employees to pay as part of your business, you need to do payroll. Payroll tasks include making calculations, writing checks with numerous deductions, tracking data for payroll taxes, and filling out payroll tax forms. By far the easiest way to do your payroll is to use the program QuickPay together with Quicken. QuickPay is an add-on utility specifically designed to run inside Quicken.

QuickPay does your payroll for you...

Because doing payroll by hand can be a long and tedious task, Intuit now publishes a dedicated payroll program called QuickPay. Working inside Quicken, QuickPay does the work for you. It calculates each employee's gross pay plus all taxes and other deductions. It then writes the paycheck, records the transaction in your Quicken account, and keeps track of your tax liabilities.

To do the calculations, QuickPay uses built-in tax tables. Subscribe to the Tax Table Update Service, and Intuit will send you immediate updates to these tables whenever your tax rates change.

QuickPay is *the* solution to your payroll needs. We recommend that you try it and see how simple payroll can be. Turn to page 474 for more details, or call Intuit toll-free at **1-800-624-8742** for information and to order the QuickPay package.

If you decide not to use QuickPay, you can still use Quicken by itself to do your payroll, although you will find there is more work involved. Also, you must keep yourself informed of any tax changes so that your tax calculations remain accurate. If you do not intend to use QuickPay but still need to do payroll, read this section.

This section shows you how to set up and use Quicken without QuickPay to do your payroll by hand. After payroll setup, you can use Quicken to do the following tasks:

- Write and print payroll checks
- Calculate employee earnings, deductions from employee earnings, and employer payroll taxes using the Calculator (Ctrl-O)
- Track employee payroll taxes and other deductions from employee paychecks
- Track accrued employer payroll tax liabilities
- Write and print checks to pay for items deducted from the payroll
- Create reports with the information you need to fill out payroll tax forms (see "Filling In Your Tax Forms" on page 410 for details)
- Create balance sheets that show how payroll expenses and related payroll taxes affect net income

Quicken does not do any of the following tasks automatically:

- Compute employee earnings, bonuses, profit-sharing, or any other employer expenses
- Calculate withholding based on number of deductions claimed
- Estimate any deductions from employee earnings
- Figure the various rates and limits for employer payroll taxes

Payroll Setup

Before you start writing payroll checks, you need to do two things: set up payroll expense categories and set up payroll liability accounts.

Quicken offers an assistant that does most of this setup for you. The assistant creates all the basic categories and liability accounts you need to do payroll. You may then need to add other categories and accounts depending on your particular payroll needs, as described in the following pages.

To run the payroll assistant:

1. Make sure the current file is the file in which you will do your payroll (that is, the file containing the checking account from which you will write paychecks).

2. Go to Quicken's Main Menu and choose Tutorials/Assistants.

3. Choose the assistant Create Payroll Support, and start the assistant.

    The assistant asks you to enter your two-letter state abbreviation; for example, CA if you live in California, NJ if you live in New Jersey, and so on.

    When the assistant has finished, Quicken displays the Main Menu.

4. To see the new accounts created by the assistant, go to the register and press Ctrl-A. To see the new categories and subcategories, choose any account and press Ctrl-C.

Setting Up Payroll Categories

The payroll assistant creates the following category and subcategories and adds them to the category list for the current file:

```
┌──────────────────────────────────────────────────────────────┐
│▓▓▓▓▓▓▓▓▓▓▓▓▓▓▓▓▓▓▓▓▓▓▓▓▓▓▓▓▓▓▓▓▓▓▓▓▓▓▓▓▓▓▓▓▓▓▓▓▓▓▓▓▓▓▓▓▓▓▓▓▓▓│
│              Category and Transfer List                      │
│                                                              │
│  Category/Transfer   Type        Description          Tax    │
│  ──────────────────────────────────────────────────────────  │
│     Payroll         Expns  Payroll transaction      ◆ ↑     │
│       Comp FICA     Sub    Company FICA contribution ◆ ░    │
│       Comp FUTA     Sub    Company FUTA contribution ◆ ░    │
│       Comp MCARE    Sub    Company Medicare contrib  ◆ ░    │
│       Comp SUI      Sub    Company SUI contribution  ◆ ░    │
│       Gross         Sub    Compensation to employee  ◆ ░    │
└──────────────────────────────────────────────────────────────┘
```

You use the category Payroll for any company expenses that arise from the payroll. You use the subcategories to break this down into the various contributions your company makes for each employee: Gross, which is the employee's gross pay, FICA (Federal Insurance Contributions Act, or Social Security), FUTA (Federal Unemployment Compensation Tax), MCARE (Medicare), and SUI (State Unemployment Insurance).

For example, when you contribute a FICA payment for an employee, the payment is categorized as Payroll:Comp FICA (for Company FICA). Note that the Comp FICA payment is separate from the FICA withheld from the employee's gross pay, which is handled differently (described on page 404).

In addition to the payroll subcategories that the assistant created, you must add to the category list any others you will need. Some examples of subcategories you may need to add are:

Subcategory name	Type	Description
Comp Dental	Sub	Company private dental insurance contribution
Comp SDI	Sub	Company State Disability Insurance contribution

Make sure you define each subcategory as tax-related. See "Setting Up Categories" on page 105 if you haven't set up subcategories before.

Note: Do not change the category name Payroll. The name must begin with "Payroll" so Quicken can collect information for its payroll report.

Some businesses prefer to set up charge numbers as category names; for example, "5101" for payroll expenses. One solution is to add the charge number to the word "Payroll"; for example, Payroll-5101. (If you do not do this, Quicken will not find the information required for the payroll report. However, you can still create your own payroll report by customizing a summary report: choose Categories from the Edit pulldown menu, then select only those categories and liability accounts you use for tracking payroll. Memorize the report for future use.)

Setting Up Liability Accounts

A business balance sheet should fully disclose the company's liability for payroll-related items owed but not yet paid, such as these:

- Deductions withheld from employee earnings
- Employer payroll taxes
- Retirement pension plans for employees
- Medical insurance for employees

The way to make sure your balance sheet is accurate is to set up liability accounts for payroll-related liabilities and record any increases to those liabilities at the time you prepare payroll checks. The liability accounts track both employee withholdings and employer contributions, since these are all amounts that you owe and must eventually pay.

You need one liability account for each type of liability. Quicken's payroll assistant creates the basic liability accounts you will need. After running the assistant, you will see these accounts in your account list:

```
                          Select Account to Use

                   Current File: BUSINESS in C:\QUICKEN5\
                   Quick                        Num    Ending    Pmts
        Account     Key   Type    Description   Trans  Balance   Due
     <New Account>               Set up a new account                 ↑
   ▶ Payroll-FICA     Oth L   FICA contributions    1      0.00
     Payroll-FUTA     Oth L   Fed unemployment tax  1      0.00
     Payroll-FWH      Oth L   Federal income tax    1      0.00
     Payroll-MCARE    Oth L   Medicare contrib.     1      0.00
     Payroll-SUI      Oth L   State unemploy. tax   1      0.00
     Payroll-SWHCA    Oth L   State income tax      1      0.00
```

Quicken appends your state abbreviation to this account name.

If you have any other payroll liabilities not shown in the list above, you must create an additional liability account for each liability:

- One liability account for each additional type of deduction from employee earnings
- One liability account for each additional payroll-related employer expense not treated as compensation; for example, company-paid medical insurance, or company pension contributions

Some examples of liability accounts you may need to add are:

Payroll-Dental	Dental insurance contribution
Payroll-SDI	State disability tax withheld
Payroll-LWH	Local income tax withheld
Payroll-IRA	SEP-IRA contribution
Payroll-Pension	Pension plan contribution
Payroll-SWHOR	Oregon state tax withheld (for example)

Note: Each payroll liability account name must start with "Payroll" so Quicken can automatically gather payroll report information.

If you need to track both employer and employee contributions for items like SEP-IRAs, pensions, or medical insurance, use the same liability account for both. (Similarly, both employee and employer FICA payments are tracked by the one liability account Payroll-FICA).

If you must handle two different state taxes (for example, if one employee lives in California and another lives in Oregon), add a second account with a name such as Payroll-SWHOR (for Oregon state withholding). In this way, you can keep the two different state withholdings separate.

For each pay period, you will record every deduction, amount withheld from a paycheck, or payroll-related expense in Quicken as a negative transfer from your business checking account to a liability account. Later, you will pay the taxes withheld on behalf of your employees, pay your accrued employer payroll taxes, and pay for other company expenses like medical insurance and pension plan contributions. Your liability for these items will decrease by the amount that you pay.

See *Tracking Assets and Liabilities*, beginning on page 257, if you haven't created a liability account before.

Note: You should have a liability account for each company payroll expense subcategory that you create. Each account must have a unique name, different from the names of any of your categories or subcategories. Be especially careful to distinguish the names of payroll expense categories and subcategories from the names of accounts where you track your liability for employee deductions withheld, employer payroll taxes, and other payroll expenses. For example, the subcategory for company FICA contributions, Comp FICA, is clearly named to distinguish it from the liability account Payroll-FICA.

Writing a Payroll Check

If you have set up all the required categories, subcategories, and liability accounts as described above, you are ready to write payroll checks for your employees.

To write payroll checks, use splits to list the deductions needed for each payroll check. Also use pairs of split entries to track your accrued liability for payroll taxes. As you record each transaction, Quicken keeps track of all deductions and tax liabilities for your payroll tax reporting.

To fill out a payroll check:

1. At the Write Checks screen of your checking account, start a new check by filling in the date and the employee name.

2. Press Ctrl-S to open the Split Transaction window. Assign line 1 of the split to the category Payroll:Gross and enter the gross compensation as a positive amount.

3. On the next lines of the split, enter the names of the withholding liability accounts and enter deductions for each as negative amounts.

    These account names are transfers that increase your liability; they automatically create transactions in the accounts that you name. See "Transfers and Payroll Tax Liability" on page 409 for more information.

    If you type a square bracket ([ ) in the Category field of a split and press Ctrl-C, the category and transfer list opens with the first account name selected.

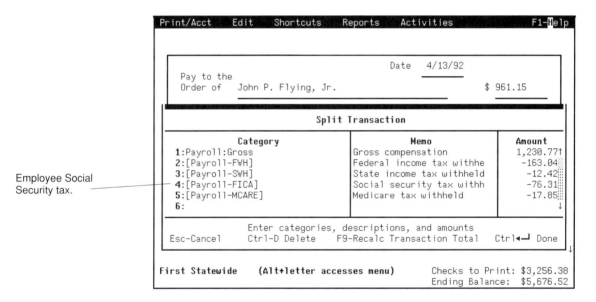

Employee Social Security tax.

4. After entering your liabilities, move down to line 17.

    Leave the remaining lines up to line 16 blank. If you print on voucher checks, Quicken prints only the information in split lines 1 to 16.

5. Assign line 17 of the split to the category Payroll:Comp FICA and enter a positive amount. This amount is your company's FICA (Social Security) contribution. On line 18 of the split, enter the name of the Payroll-FICA liability account and enter a negative amount. This item increases the total tax liability in your Payroll-FICA account. Repeat for your company's Medicare, FUTA and SUI contributions, and any

other employer contributions you are making. These paired line items offset each other, and the net effect on the employee paycheck is zero.

These offsetting entries let you record your payroll tax liability at the time it is incurred. The net effect on the employee paycheck is zero, and these lines do not print on a voucher check.

```
┌────────────────────────────────────────────────────────────────────────────┐
│█████████████████████████████████████████████████████████████████████████████│
│                          Split Transaction                                   │
├──────────────────────────────┬──────────────────────────────┬───────────────┤
│          Category            │           Memo               │    Amount     │
│ 17:Payroll:Comp FICA         │ Company FICA Contribution     │      76.31↑   │
│ 18:[Payroll-FICA]            │ Company FICA Contribution     │     -76.31▒   │
│ 19:Payroll:Comp FUTA         │ Company FUTA Contribution     │      20.00▒   │
│ 20:[Payroll-FUTA]            │ Company FUTA Contribution     │     -20.00▒   │
│ 21:Payroll:Comp SUI          │ Company SUI Contribution      │      10.00▒   │
│ 22:[Payroll-SUI]             │ Company SUI Contribution      │     -10.00↓   │
├──────────────────────────────┴──────────────────────────────┴───────────────┤
│              Enter categories, descriptions, and amounts                      │
│  Esc-Cancel      Ctrl-D Delete    F9-Recalc Transaction Total   Ctrl◄┘ Done   │
└────────────────────────────────────────────────────────────────────────────┘
```

6. Press F9 to calculate the total check amount and press Ctrl-Enter twice to close the split and record the check.

7. Select the transaction and press Ctrl-M to memorize it.

Note: If you prefer, you can record your tax contributions as expenses when paid (instead of doing step 5). But if you accrue payroll tax liability at the time you write payroll checks, you accomplish two tasks at once. You can also create a report that shows exactly how much you owe at any time.

Entering Paychecks in the Register

If you write your payroll checks by hand, you can record them in the register. The procedure is almost the same as filling out a paycheck in the Write Checks screen. The main differences are the following:

- You must enter the net amount of the paycheck in the Payment field before you press Ctrl-S to open the Split Transaction window. The net amount is the amount the employee actually receives.

- When you open the Split Transaction window, the net amount of the check will already be on the first line of the split. You need to enter the category name Payroll:Gross in the Category field and enter the gross amount of the paycheck in the Amount field. Type right over the net amount of the check; the gross compensation you enter will be larger than the net amount.

- On the second line of the split, Quicken makes a compensating negative entry. Enter the deductions and offsetting tax entries as shown in steps 3 to 5 on page 406.

- If you end up with a leftover amount on the last line of the split, your original calculations might not be correct or you might have entered the amounts incorrectly. Check the net amount of the check and all the deduction amounts.

Printing Payroll Checks

If you print on voucher checks, the perforated voucher shows all the wage and deduction information typed on the first 16 lines of the split. If you want, you can omit the category information from the printed voucher checks: choose Checks and Reports Settings from the Set Preferences menu, and enter N in the field "Print categories on voucher checks."

Typing information that shouldn't appear on a voucher check

If you want to include information that won't print on the voucher (such as the company's FICA, FUTA, or SUI contribution), enter the information after line 16 in the Split Transaction window.

See page 85 for complete information about printing Quicken checks.

Speeding Up Payroll

The first time you enter payroll checks, it might be faster to memorize a single check first with no name or dollar amounts, just category and transfer information in each Category field of the splits. (Press Ctrl-M to memorize a selected transaction with splits closed.) Then press Ctrl-T to choose this "skeleton" paycheck from the memorized transactions list and fill in the date, name, and dollar amounts for one employee at a time.

If the compensation for an employee is the same for every pay period, memorize the completed check, including dollar amounts, and recall it each time you need to pay that employee.

See *Saving Time with Memorized Transactions*, beginning on page 195, for information about memorizing and recalling recurring transactions.

Entering Groups of Payroll Checks Automatically

To save time, you can set up a payroll transaction group. As you enter your first batch of payroll checks at the Write Checks screen or in the register, memorize each check as you go. If the compensation for an employee is the same for every pay period, memorize the check with dollar amounts filled in. Otherwise, memorize the check without dollar amounts.

After memorizing a payroll check for each employee, set up a payroll transaction group that includes all the checks. Press Ctrl-J and select an unused group number, then press Ctrl-E to specify the name, frequency, payroll checking account, and next scheduled payday. Once the group is set up, assign each memorized payroll check to the group.

Once you've set up your payroll transaction group, you can press Ctrl-J to choose it from the list of transaction groups at the end of each pay period. When you choose a transaction group, Quicken automatically enters all the transactions in the group in Write Checks (or in the register, if you memorize transactions from the register).

See *Entering Transaction Groups*, beginning on page 211 for more about setting up and executing transaction groups.

Transfers and Payroll Tax Liability

When you write a payroll check, Quicken transfers the deductions that you make from the check for items such as FICA, federal and state withholding, and medical insurance to the appropriate liability account, where the transfers increase your liability. In the previous example, Quicken transfers the federal income tax withheld from the paycheck to the liability account named Payroll-FWH.

Line 2 from the split check on page 406:

| 2:[Payroll-FWH] | Federal income tax withhe | -163.04 |

Register of liability account named Payroll-FWH:

The destination account name is in the Category field of the split; press Ctrl-X to see the other side of the transfer.

Quicken entered an automatic increase of $163.04 in the Payroll-FWH account. Notice the name of the checking account transfer in the Category field.

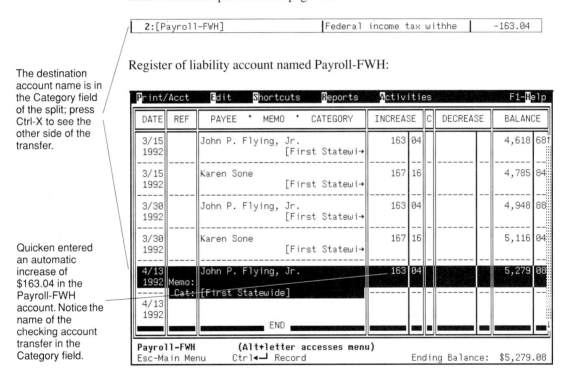

When you review the register for each liability account, the Ending Balance at the bottom tells you the amount currently accrued or withheld and not yet paid. For example, the Payroll-FWH account in the previous example shows a balance of $5,279.08.

The total in your payroll liability accounts may include company contributions as well as deductions from payroll. For example, contributions to FICA or medical insurance can come from either employee or employer.

Paying Taxes Withheld from Payroll Checks

When you write a check to pay for items deducted from the payroll, write it from your checking account, and enter the name of the liability account in the Category field. When you record the check, Quicken enters an automatic decrease in the liability account.

Example

Here's a check written to send a FICA payment to the bank.

This transfer automatically decreases the balance in the liability account named Payroll-FICA.

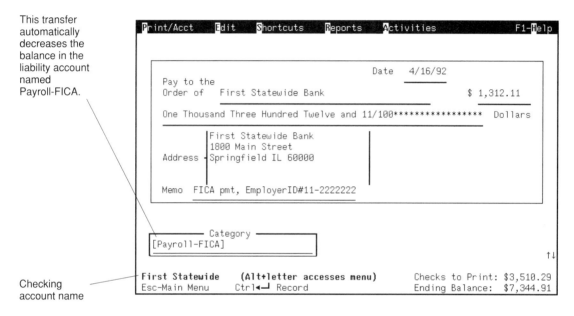

Checking account name

Filling In Your Tax Forms

Once you have written your payroll checks, you can run the Quicken payroll report to get most of the numbers you need to fill in your payroll tax forms. Then you can create customized reports to extract the remaining numbers as described here.

Note that the Quicken payroll report works only if you have set up your accounts and categories as described in this chapter. The report filters your transactions to include only those categories and transfers beginning with the word "Payroll."

The payroll report is available through the Business Reports menu. See Chapter 9, *Personal, Business, and Investment Reports* for details of how to produce the report. You can see a sample payroll report on page 152.

Consult your payroll report for the report items that appear in the following tables. Check the line numbers on each tax form to make sure they haven't changed since this manual was printed.

Note: The payroll report gives the true gross wages figure. If your payroll includes tax-exempt deductions such as 401k, be sure to deduct the total amount of these deductions from the Payroll:Gross figure in the report to calculate the taxable wages. This may apply to Federal, state, or local taxes.

Form W-2 (Wage and Tax Statement)

Form W-2 line item	Payroll report item
9 Federal income tax withheld	TRANSFERS FROM Payroll-FWH
10 Wages, tips, other compensation	EXPENSES Payroll:Gross less 401k and other Federal exempt amounts
11 Social security tax withheld	EXPENSES Payroll:Comp FICA*
12 Social security wages	EXPENSES Payroll:Gross ** less any state exempt FICA deductions
14 Medicare wages and tips	EXPENSES Payroll:Gross ** less any state exempt FICA deductions
15 Medicare tax withheld	EXPENSES Payroll:Comp MCARE*
25 State wages, tips, etc.	EXPENSES Payroll:Gross less state exempt deductions
28 Local wages, tips, etc.	EXPENSES Payroll:Gross less local tax exempt deductions
24 State income tax	TRANSFERS FROM Payroll-SWH
27 Local income tax	TRANSFERS FROM Payroll-LWH

* The IRS now requires separate withholding for the two parts of the FICA tax (Social Security and Medicare). The amounts in Payroll:Comp FICA and Payroll:Comp MCARE are the amounts of the company contributions, but they are the same amounts that the employee pays, so you can use these figures for the "Social security tax withheld" and "Medicare tax withheld" respectively.

** You need to check each employee's gross compensation manually against the wage bases for the two parts of the FICA tax (Social Security and Medicare). If the gross wages exceed the wage bases, enter the wage bases. (Or, if you use a spreadsheet program, you could export the payroll report to a .WK1 file and check the wage bases in a spreadsheet.)

Form W-3 (Transmittal of Income and Tax Statements)

Form W-3 line item	Payroll report item
9 Federal income tax withheld	TRANSFERS FROM Payroll-FWH (Overall Total)
10 Wages, tips, other compensation	EXPENSES Payroll:Gross (Overall Total less Federal exempt amount)

11 Social security tax withheld

EXPENSES Payroll:Comp FICA*
(Overall Totals)

12 Social security wages

To prepare W-2 forms, you had to check the Payroll:Gross amount for each employee against the wage bases for the Social Security tax. Total the line 12 amounts from the individual W-2 forms and enter that total in line 12 for the W-3.

14 Medicare wages and tips

To prepare W-2 forms, you had to check the Payroll:Gross amount for each employee against the wage bases for the Medicare tax. Total the line 14 amounts from the individual W-2 forms and enter that total in line 14 for the W-3.

15 Medicare tax withheld

EXPENSES Payroll:Comp MCARE*
(Overall Totals)

* The IRS now requires separate withholding for the two parts of the FICA tax (Social Security and Medicare). The amounts in Payroll:Comp FICA and Payroll:Comp MCARE are the amounts of the company contributions, but they are the same amounts that the employee pays, so you can use these figures for the "Social security tax withheld" and "Medicare tax withheld" respectively.

Form 940 (Employer's Annual FUTA Tax Return)

Form 940 line item	**Payroll report item**
Part I, Computation of Taxable Wages	
1 Total payments...for services of employees	EXPENSES Payroll:Gross
3 Payments for services of more than...	To compute line 3 for Form 940, check each employee's gross compensation manually and enter only the excess over the minimum paid to individual employees. The payroll report lists the Payroll:Gross amount for each employee. Total the individual Payroll:Gross amounts in excess of the minimum.
Part II, Tax Due or Refund	
2 Total FUTA tax deposited for the year...	TRANSFERS FROM Payroll-FUTA

To complete Part IV, "Record of Federal Tax Liability for Unemployment Tax," create a transaction report restricted to the Payroll-FUTA account. Subtotal by quarter to see your FUTA liability by quarter, plus an overall total. Filter the report to select Payments (in the Filter Transactions window). Memorize this report with the title "940-FUTA Liability by Quarter" for later use.

Form 941 (Employer's Quarterly Tax Return)

Form 941 line item	Payroll report item
2 Total wages and tips subject to withholding...	EXPENSES Payroll:Gross less Federal exempt amount
3 Total income tax withheld from wages, tips...	TRANSFERS FROM Payroll-FWH
6a Taxable social security wages paid	Enter here the same amount you computed for line 12 of Form W-3 (see page 411).
7 Taxable Medicare wages and tips	Enter here the same amount you computed for line 14 of Form W-3 (see page 411).
17 Total deposits for quarter...	TRANSFERS TO Payroll-FWH, Payroll-FICA, Payroll-MCARE.

To complete the section of Form 941 called "Record of Federal Tax Liability," create a summary report with categories as row headings and the pay period (for example, Two Weeks for biweekly employees) as column headings. Filter the report to include only the transfers to the accounts [Payroll-FWH], [Payroll-FICA], and [Payroll-MCARE]. Memorize this report with the title "941-Federal Tax Liability by Month." Then manually add the TRANSFERS FROM amounts for each pay period for each of the three liability accounts (Payroll-FICA, Payroll-FWH, and Payroll-MCARE).

Example of Form 941 "Record of Federal Tax Liability"

Record of Federal Tax Liability (Complete if line 16 is $500 or more.) See the instructions on page 4 for details before checking these boxes.
Check only if you made eight-monthly deposits using the 95% rule ▶ ☐   Check only if you are a first time 3-banking-day depositor ☐

Date wages paid		First month of quarter		Second month of quarter		Third month of quarter
1st through 3rd	A		I		Q	
4th through 7th	B		J		R	
8th through 11th	C		K		S	
12th through 15th	D	2,467.29	L	2,716.56	T	3,187.45
16th through 19th	E		M		U	
20th through 22nd	F		N		V	
23rd through 25th	G		O		W	
26th through the last	H	3,741.70	P	3,832.25	X	5,164.97
Total liability for month	I	6,208.99	II	6,548.81	III	8,352.42

IV Total for quarter (add lines I, II, and III). **This must equal line 16 above** . . . . . . ▶ 21,110.22

You get these numbers from the "941-Federal Tax Liability by Month" report as described above.

If You Decide To Buy QuickPay Later On

The add-on program QuickPay uses the same setup as that described here. It uses the liability accounts Payroll-FWH, Payroll-FICA, and so on to record withholdings. It uses the Payroll category and subcategories such as Payroll:Comp FICA to record your company contributions. So if you later decide to buy QuickPay and let it do your payroll for you, you have already set up Quicken ready for QuickPay to use.

You will need to set up some additional information within QuickPay, such as your company and employee details, so that QuickPay can calculate the paychecks correctly. This is fully described in the QuickPay manual. Once you have set this up, QuickPay takes over the Quicken tasks described in this section and does everything for you.

See page 474 for more details of how Quicken and QuickPay work together.

Chapter 26

Preparing Your Income Taxes

Quicken can greatly simplify the preparation of your Federal Income Tax Return (Form 1040) and related tax schedules, including business-related forms such as Schedule C. Using Quicken helps whether you:

- Use dedicated tax preparation software
- Prepare your own returns manually
- Gather the information to turn over to a tax preparation service

Just gathering information to prepare your return used to take hours. Now that you use Quicken, you can take advantage of Quicken's categories to produce a tax schedule report in just minutes. The report lists the exact amounts to fill in, line by line, on your tax forms and schedules.

Quicken works with tax preparation software.

Quicken works with tax preparation programs such as TurboTax and TaxCut. You can transfer your Quicken data to these programs to fill out and print the tax forms themselves.

💲 Assigning Categories to Tax Forms

Filling in tax returns takes time because you first need to understand what is required on each line of your forms, and then need to gather the figures. If you do the first part when you set up your categories instead of at the end of the year or tax period, Quicken does the second part for you.

You use categories to organize transactions into types of income or expense. Many are not tax-related. For example, whether an expense is categorized as Clothing or Telephone makes no difference to your taxes. But many categories are tax-related: for example, Dividend Income, Mortgage Interest, Charity, and Medical. Each of these can be directly assigned to a certain line on one of your tax forms. Income from dividends goes on the line "Dividend income" of Schedule B, Charity goes on a line in Schedule A, and so on.

When you write checks or enter transactions in the register, you type a category as usual. In this way, you link each check or transaction that affects your taxes to an entry on one of the tax forms. At the end of the year, you run a tax schedule report to summarize all the figures you need to fill in on the tax forms. If you want, you can export these figures to dedicated tax preparation software.

Quicken's standard lists of home and business categories already have tax form information assigned for them, as shown on the next page. Only tax-related categories are assigned to a tax form and line. If you use these standard lists, check the assignments on page 417 to see whether they fit your situation. These assignments are designed to work with tax preparation software. They are for a tax filer with only one W-2 form (one wage earner with one employer) and only one Schedule C. If you have more than one W-2 form or Schedule C, you must have separate categories for each copy of the form. (To assign new categories to tax forms, or change existing assignments, see the steps on pages 418 and 419.) See also "Assigning Account Transfers to Tax Forms" on page 420.

If you create your own categories or add to the standard lists, you must specify the tax form information for each tax-related category you create (see steps on page 418). Be sure to refer to the most recent tax forms available. In general, if an amount should appear on more than one line or on more than one tax form, specify the most detailed location. If you use tax preparation software, check to see where the software requires the amount.

If a category is not tax-related, don't specify a tax form.

If your tax situation is fairly straightforward, you can decide not to enter tax form information. If you don't, you can still specify simply whether or not each category is tax-related, and this enables you to run a tax summary report. This report groups by category, not by line on the tax forms, but is still useful. See "Tax Summary" on page 144.

If you want to transfer Quicken data to tax preparation software, you must enter tax form information.

Any tax form information you enter applies only to the category list in the current file. If you have several files, you may need to enter tax information separately in the category list of each file.

Standard Home Categories

Income Categories

Name	Tax Form & Line
Bonus	W-2:Salary, Copy 1
Canada Pen	
Div Income	B:Dividend Income
Gift Received	
Int Inc	B:Interest Income
Invest Inc	
Old Age Pension	
Other Inc	
Salary	W-2:Salary, Copy 1

Expense Categories

Name	Tax Form & Line
Auto	
Fuel	
Loan	
Service	
Bank Chrg	
Charity	A:Cash charity contributions
Childcare	
Christmas	
Clothing	
Dining	
Dues	
Education	
Entertain	
Gifts	
Groceries	
Home Rpair	
Household	
Housing	
Insurance	
Int Exp	
Invest Exp	A:Investment man. fees
Medical	A:Medicine and drugs
Misc	
Mort Int	A:Home mortgage interest
Other Exp	
Recreation	
RRSP	
Subscriptions	
Supplies	
Tax	
Fed	W-2:Federal Withholding, Cpy 1
FICA	W-2:Soc Sec Tax Withhdg, Cpy 1
Other	
Prop	A:Real estate tax
State	W-2:State Withholding, Copy 1
Telephone	
UIC	
Utilities	
Gas & Electric	
Water	

Standard Business Categories

Preset for Copy 1 of Schedule C or E.

Income Categories

Name	Tax Form & Line
Gr Sales	C:Gross receipts
Other Inc	
Rent Income	E:Rents received

Expense Categories

Name	Tax Form & Line
Ads	C:Advertising
Car	C:Car and truck expenses
Commission	C:Commissions and fees
Freight	C:Other business expense
Int Paid	C:Interest expense, other
L&P Fees	C:Legal and professional
Late Fees	C:Other business expense
Office	C:Office expense
Rent Paid	C:Rent on other bus prop
Repairs	C:Repairs and maintenance
Returns	C:Returns and allowances
Tax	C:Taxes and licenses
Travel	C:Travel
Wages	C:Wages paid

Standard Investment Categories

The standard investment categories are not assigned to tax forms because the tax schedule report does not subtotal investment income by security.

Note:
W-2 = Form W-2
A = Schedule A
B = Schedule B
C = Schedule C
E = Schedule E

Note: See page 425 for details of how to keep your tax form information up to date.

To enter tax form information for a category:

1. At the register or Write Checks screen, press Ctrl-C to display the category list.

2. Select the category you want to add tax information to and press Ctrl-E.

   To set up a new category with tax information, select <New Category> and press Enter.

3. If you are setting up a new category, fill in the name, type, and description.

   See "Setting Up Categories" on page 105 if you need more information about entering category information.

4. In the Tax-related field, enter Y.

   "Tax-related" means that any transactions in this category are relevant to one or more tax forms. (Any categories with Y in this field are included in the tax summary report.)

5. Press F9 to assign tax information.

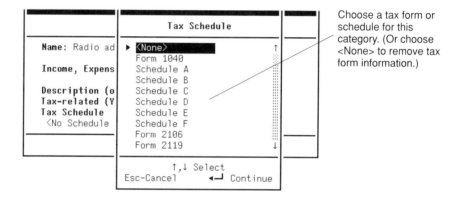

Choose a tax form or schedule for this category. (Or choose <None> to remove tax form information.)

The Tax Schedule window lists all the forms and schedules you may need to file with the IRS. You can scroll through this window using the arrow keys or PgDn and PgUp.

6. Select a tax form or schedule and press Enter.

   (To remove tax form information from a category, select <None>.)

Each category can have only one tax form and line assignment.

If you have a category that may vary in its tax treatment, divide it into separate categories or subcategories for each kind of tax treatment.

For example, if you pay estimated tax *and* have tax withheld, use separate subcategories for the estimated and withheld taxes. Or, if you file a Schedule C and have personal and business categories in the same Quicken file, use separate categories or subcategories for home and for business.

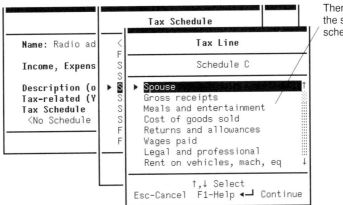

Then choose a line on the selected form or schedule.

The Tax Line window lists all the lines on the selected form or schedule. Again, you can scroll using the arrow keys or PgDn and PgUp.

Note: When you use tax preparation software, the software copies figures from one tax form to another. In these windows, you should choose the form and line where your software requires the amount initially. For example, tax software copies salary information from Form W-2 to Form 1040. So Quicken assigns Salary to Form W-2, and not to Form 1040. (You'll notice the tax line window doesn't include the 1040 line "Wages, salaries, tips, etc.")

7. Select a line and press Enter.

8. If you see the window Schedule Copy Number, type a copy number and press Enter.

You can file (or receive) multiple copies of some schedules and forms (for example, W-2 and Schedule C). If you and your spouse each receive a Form W-2, add subcategories (such as Sally and Steve) to the salary and withholding categories. Assign your salary and withholding subcategories to copy 1 and your spouse's to copy 2. If you file multiple copies of Schedule C, assign all the categories for one business to copy 1, the categories for your second business to copy 2, and so on.

The Tax Schedule field in the Edit Category window displays the tax form and line you selected. (Note: you cannot edit this field directly.) The copy number is displayed too, unless it's copy 1.

9. Press Ctrl-Enter to record the information.

You have now assigned this category to the selected line on the selected tax form or schedule. The tax schedule report will include any transactions having this category (but see below).

To see all your tax form assignments, print the category list. See page 115 for details.

Assigning Subcategories to Tax Forms

You must assign tax form information separately for each subcategory. A subcategory does **not** use the tax form information for the main category it belongs to. If you do not assign the information separately for a subcategory, the corresponding transactions do not appear on the tax schedule report.

The tax form information you assign for a subcategory overrides any tax information for the main category, if this is different.

Assign tax form information for subcategories exactly as described for categories.

Entering Transactions

When you write a check or enter a transaction in a register, you don't need to do anything extra—just enter a category as normal. But remember that the category you enter may affect the figures for your tax forms. For example, if, during a business trip, you write one check to cover both travel expenses and meal expenses, be sure to enter the two amounts separately using a split transaction, because the two expenses are assigned to different lines on Schedule C.

Investments

The tax file Quicken creates for tax software (page 425) summarizes interest and dividend income by Quicken account but not by security name. If you track investments in Quicken mutual fund accounts exclusively *and* all your dividend income is taxable, assign the investment category _DivInc to "Schedule B:Dividend income." Otherwise, do not assign any investment categories (those beginning with "_") to a tax form and line. Instead, gather the tax information for Schedule B as described in "Investment Income" on page 158. To gather information for Schedule D, see "Capital Gains" on page 157.

Some money funds pay tax-free dividends. If you track these in bank accounts, assign the dividends to a category for which no tax information is specified. You may need to add a special category (for example, Div Tax-free) to your list for this purpose.

Assigning Account Transfers to Tax Forms

When you enter a transfer to another account in an account register, you type the name of the destination account in the Category field.

For example, if you contribute to your IRA fund, you might record the transaction as a transfer from your checking account to your IRA account. You enter [IRA] in the Category field in your checking account and Quicken automatically enters [Checking] in the Category field of your IRA account.

Such a transfer between accounts may be tax-related, so you need to assign tax information for certain transfers as well as for simple transactions. You do this by entering tax form details for certain accounts in your account list. In our IRA example, you assign the IRA account to a tax form and line (specifically, "Form 1040:IRA contribution-self"). Any payments into the IRA account will be included in the tax schedule report. Note that you do not need to assign tax form information for the checking account. You assign tax information for only one of the accounts involved in the transfer.

In general, if you use transfers, you should enter tax information only for retirement funds such as IRAs and Keoghs. These are accounts that directly affect your taxes. You should not ordinarily enter tax information for any other types of account. But these are only general guidelines. How you specify tax information depends on how you use your accounts and how you make transfers between them.

If you do not use transfers, you do not need to specify tax information for any of your accounts.

Note that you can specify only one tax form and line number for each account. If you need more for a particular account (for example, if you make a contribution in the same year you receive a distribution), don't assign the account to a tax form and line.

IRA Retirement Account

If you contribute to an IRA account, assign the account to "Form 1040:IRA contribution-self." (This line is for your gross contribution. Manually or using your tax software, you will have to determine how much is deductible.) Note that if you and your spouse each contribute to an IRA, you should track them with two separate IRA accounts in Quicken. Assign your spouse's account to "Form 1040:IRA contribution-spouse." On the other hand, if you draw money from an IRA account, assign the account to "Form W-2P:IRA distributions-gross."

If you make IRA contributions for a given tax year during the following year (for example, in March 1992 you contribute for the year 1991), a tax schedule report for the tax year will not have the correct IRA information. In this situation, it is better not to assign IRA accounts to a tax form and line. Instead, create a transaction report subtotaled by account for the period from January 1 of the tax year to the filing date of the following year. Use all accounts. Filter for selected categories, and select only IRA accounts (which are on the category list after all the expense categories). The report itemizes all transfers to IRA accounts. Subtract the transfers which are for the wrong tax year.

Keogh Retirement Account

Treat Keogh accounts similarly to IRA accounts. If you contribute to a Keogh, assign the account to "Form 1040:Keogh deduction." If you draw money from a Keogh, assign the account to "Form W-2P:Pensions and annuities-gross."

401(k) Retirement Account

The IRS does not require that you report 401(k) deductions from your salary. However, you'll need to specify tax information for your 401(k) account if you use a split transaction to enter your paycheck and show a transfer to your 401(k) account (as in the example in "Entering Paychecks" on page 358).

In the split, be sure to enter your gross salary *before* the 401(k) deduction. Assign your 401(k) account to exactly the same form and line as your salary ("W-2:Salary"). The transfers to your 401(k) account reduce the total for your gross taxable salary.

If you have other pretax deductions from your salary, such as for a healthcare flexible spending account, assign their categories or accounts also to "W-2:Salary."

You do not, in general, need to specify tax information for the following types of account:

Checking, Savings, Cash, Credit Card, Investment Accounts (for Nonretirement Funds)

Transfers between these accounts are simply monetary transactions that do not affect your taxes.

Mortgage Accounts

When you pay the mortgage from your checking account, only the mortgage interest is tax-deductible. You give this part of the payment a category with tax information already assigned ("Schedule A:Home mortgage interest"). The part that reduces your principal is normally not tax-deductible, so you do not need to enter tax information for the transfer.

To assign an account to a tax form:

The procedure is the same as assigning a category to a tax form, except that you start at the Select Account to Use window.

1. Display the Select Account to Use window (Ctrl-A usually takes you there).

2. Select an account and press Ctrl-E to edit the account details.

3. In the Edit Account Information window, press F9.

    Quicken displays the Tax Schedule window.

4. Select a tax form or schedule and press Enter.

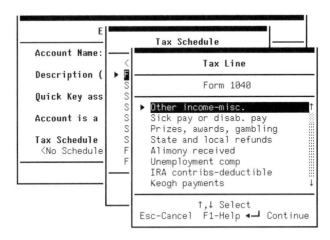

5. In the Tax Line window, select a line and press Enter.

6. If you see the window Schedule Copy Number, type a copy number and press Enter.

   You normally leave this as 1. If you file (or receive) multiple copies of the form or schedule, you can enter a different copy number.

   The Tax Schedule field in the Edit Account Information window now displays the tax form and line you selected.

7. Press Ctrl-Enter to record the information.

   Quicken now assigns the account to the selected line on the selected tax form or schedule. The tax schedule report will include all transfers from this account or to this account.

$ Tax Schedule Reports

The tax schedule report lists the exact figures you need to fill in your Form 1040 and its accompanying forms and schedules, with these qualifications:

- You must check the figures against any limits defined by the IRS (for example, the maximum deduction allowed for IRA contributions). The report simply gives you your personal totals.

- You must have recorded all relevant transactions in Quicken.

- Interest income and dividend income for Schedule B are not subtotaled by payer.

- If you have investment accounts with realized capital gains (following buy and sell transactions), the tax schedule report does not show these realized gains. A message in the report tells you that realized gains are missing. To obtain figures for your realized gains, run a capital gains report (from the Investment Reports menu).

The tax schedule report gathers figures from all accounts in the current file and from all categories that have been assigned to a tax form and line. Several categories or accounts can contribute to the same figure in the report. For example, the line "Salary" on Form W-2 can include both regular salary and bonuses.

Chapter 9, *Personal, Business, and Investment Reports*, beginning on page 139, gives full details of creating reports.

To create a tax schedule report:

1. Choose Personal Reports from the Reports menu.

2. Choose Tax Schedule Report.

3. Enter a report name that states the tax period and a date range that covers the tax period, and press Enter.

   The resulting report lists your transactions, subtotaled for each tax line on each tax form. The example on page 424 shows part of the report for a family's personal taxes.

```
                        Tax Schedule Report - Murphy 92
                            1/ 1/92 Through 8/31/92
        MURPHY-All Accounts                                               Page 1
        8/31/92

          Date   Acct     Num     Description      Memo      Category    Clr Amount
          -----  -------- ------  ---------------- ---------- ---------------- - ---------
                 Schedule A
                 ----------
                 Real estate tax
                 ---------------

          3/ 2 Joint Ac 5016   County of Santa  909 Exmoor  Tax:Prop      X    -750.00
                                                                               ---------
                 Total Real estate tax                                         -750.00

                 Cash charity contributions
                 --------------------------

          1/ 7 Joint Ac 5002    American Heart F            Charity       X    -100.00
          2/ 8 Joint Ac 5009    American Cancer             Charity       X    -100.00
          3/31 Joint Ac 5023    National Wildlif            Charity       X    -100.00
                                                                               ---------
                 Total Cash charity contributions                             -300.00

                 Home mortgage interest
                 ----------------------

          1/15 Joint Ac 5003 S American Lending             Mort Int      X -1,093.33
          2/15 Joint Ac 5010 S American Lending             Mort Int      X -1,092.79
          3/15 Joint Ac 5020 S American Lending             Mort Int      X -1,004.21
                                                                               ---------
                 Total Home mortgage interest                             -3,190.33

                 Schedule B
                 ----------
                 Interest income
                 ---------------

          1/27 Joint Ac          Interest Earned            Int Inc       X      24.56
          2/27 Joint Ac          Interest Earned            Int Inc       X      21.19
                                                                               ---------
                 Total Interest income                                          45.75
```

4. To restrict the report to certain accounts, choose Accounts on the Edit pulldown menu and select which accounts the report should include.

You may need to do this if, for example, your IRA account is a CD you track as a bank account. (You do not have to report the interest it earns.) If you exclude an account for which you assigned tax form information (for example, your IRA account), the report still lists transfers made into or out of the account if the account at the other end of the transfer is included.

$ Tax Summary Reports

A tax summary report is useful if you do not assign tax form information for each category, but simply enter Y in the tax-related field. The report lists transactions and shows your total income and expenses for the tax period for all tax-related categories, subtotaled by category. It includes all accounts in the current file.

(If you want to include only selected accounts, generate the report, then choose Accounts on the Edit pulldown menu, and select the accounts you want to report on.)

The tax summary report looks like the itemized category report on page 143 except that it includes only tax-related categories. Choose the tax summary report from the Personal Reports menu. For details, see Chapter 9, *Personal, Business, and Investment Reports*.

Transferring Data to a Tax Preparation Program

You can transfer data from Quicken's tax schedule report to tax preparation software that calculates your tax and prints completed tax forms. Quicken writes the data to an ASCII file with a standard format compatible with several major tax preparation programs, such as TurboTax and TaxCut.

To transfer tax data to an ASCII file:

1. Create a tax schedule report as described on page 423.

2. At the Report screen, choose Print Report from the File/Print menu.

3. Type 6 to print to a tax file, and press Enter.

4. In the Print To Disk window, enter a file name (eight characters plus extension, DOS format) and press Ctrl-Enter.

   Leave the lines per page as 0 and the width as 80.

   Quicken writes the tax schedule data to the file and then returns you to the Print Report window. See the instructions that accompany your tax preparation program to learn how to use the data file.

Note: The tax schedule report does not include information on realized gains in Quicken investment accounts. Thus, Quicken does not write any information concerning such realized gains to the tax file. Also, if you assign the investment categories _DivInc and _IntInc to Schedule B, the tax file subtotals the amount for each category by investment account but not by security.

$ Updating Your Tax Form Information

If you set up your tax form assignments correctly when you create categories and subcategories, Quicken will take care of gathering the tax information for your tax schedule reports. You can continue to enter transactions without worrying more about it.

However, occasionally the IRS changes the information required on IRS tax forms and schedules. When this happens, Intuit updates its list of tax form assignments, so that each category is reassigned to the correct form and line. This list is contained in a separate file named TAX.SCD. To ensure that your tax information remains accurate, you will need to obtain a new copy of the TAX.SCD file if the IRS makes any changes to the forms you file.

Most changes to IRS tax forms occur in January, and very often affect only specialized forms that most people do not need to file.

If you are a TurboTax user, your Final Edition will include an updated TAX.SCD file in time for you to file your annual returns. All you need to do is copy the file to your Quicken directory as described below.

Even if you are not a TurboTax user, you can request ChipSoft, the makers of TurboTax, to send you a floppy disk containing an updated TAX.SCD file. To order, or for more information about tax form changes, call ChipSoft Customer Sales at **1-800-745-4829 ext. 607** Monday through Friday between 8:30 am and 5 pm Pacific time. Alternately, write to:

ChipSoft, Inc.
TAX SCD Update
6330 Nancy Ridge Road
Suite 103
San Diego, CA 92121-2246

When you contact ChipSoft, specify which floppy disk format you require, 5.25-inch or 3.5-inch. ChipSoft will make a small charge (currently $4.95, payable to *ChipSoft, Inc.*) to cover postage and handling.

When you receive your floppy disk, or your Final Edition, copy the TAX.SCD file to your current Quicken directory as described below.

To update your list of tax form assignments:

1. Exit from Quicken and change to your Quicken working directory or disk drive. For example, if your Quicken program files are kept in the directory C:\QUICKEN5, type cd c:\quicken5 and press Enter.

2. If you received the TAX.SCD file from ChipSoft on a separate floppy disk, insert the disk in a floppy drive.

3. If the disk from ChipSoft is in Drive A, type copy a:tax.scd and press Enter.

   If the disk from ChipSoft is in Drive B, type copy b:tax.scd and press Enter.

   If you have installed your Final Edition on your hard disk, copy the TAX.SCD file from your TurboTax directory instead. Typically, the command to do this would be copy c:\ttax92\tax.scd.

When the copying has finished, you can start Quicken. The new tax form assignments apply to all the transactions already entered, as well as those you enter from now on.

In certain cases, you may also need to make some adjustments by hand to your category list. For example, if a new line is added to a tax schedule, the line will appear in your new Tax Line window. You then need to assign the appropriate category to this new line.

Chapter 27

Setting Preferences

This chapter explains the items on Quicken's Set Preferences menu. Though Quicken comes set up and ready to work, you may want to change some of the settings to suit your own taste or your computer system. For example, you can change the screen colors, whether the program beeps, or how much confirmation Quicken requires when you delete transactions. If you're having trouble getting your printer to work, you may need to change the printer settings. Changing settings is easy, so you can experiment to see what you like best.

Quicken's preset (or default) settings are displayed on the screens and in the illustrations in this chapter. To change them, enter your own information or choose the setting you want.

$ Set Preferences Menu

At the Main Menu, choose Set Preferences to display the Set Preferences menu:

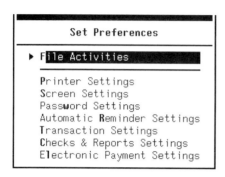

For complete information about the first menu item, File Activities, see Chapter 28, *Managing Files*, beginning on page 449.

$ Printer Settings

Quicken lets you specify three different printer settings, so that you can use up to three different printers. Or, you can use it to set up one printer to work in up to three different ways. For example, you can set up the Report Printer Settings for "draft" mode (when you want to print your reports quickly), and the Alternate Report Settings for "letter quality" (when you want the report to look its best).

Here's how to set or change printer settings:

1. Choose Printer Settings from the Set Preferences menu (or choose Change Printer Styles from the Print/Acct menu).

2. From the list, choose the printer for which you want to make changes:

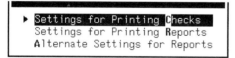

Quicken displays a list of the printing styles available with your printer. The name of your printer is shown selected in the window to the left.

If necessary, use PgUp and PgDn to see all the styles available.

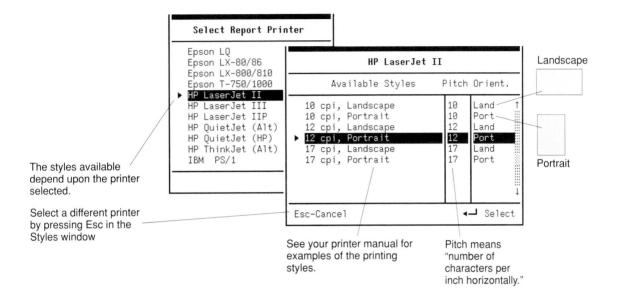

The styles available depend upon the printer selected.

Select a different printer by pressing Esc in the Styles window

See your printer manual for examples of the printing styles.

Pitch means "number of characters per inch horizontally."

3. If you want to select a different printer, press Esc, then select a printer from the Select Printer list and press Enter.

Use PgUp and PgDn to see all the printers listed.

The Select Printer window lists the printers that Quicken supports. If you do not find your printer in the list, choose the name of a printer with which your printer is advertised as compatible. If no name is appropriate, try <Other Dot-Matrix> or <Other Laser> (near the top of the list). If these also give printing problems, see "Calling Intuit for help with unlisted printers" on page 431.

When you select another printer, Quicken displays the styles available with that printer.

4. In the Styles window, select the printing style you want and press Enter.

When you choose a printer and printing style here, Quicken automatically sets the necessary control codes for you. (If you have changed the control codes and simply select the same printer and printing style again, don't worry, Quicken does not reset the control codes.)

Quicken now displays the Printer Settings window.

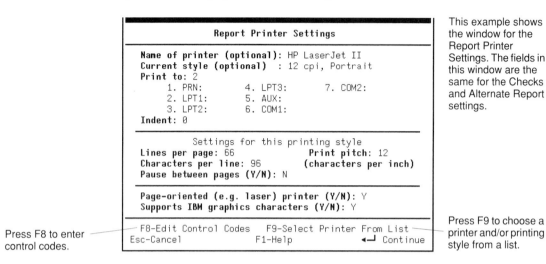

This example shows the window for the Report Printer Settings. The fields in this window are the same for the Checks and Alternate Report settings.

Press F8 to enter control codes.

Press F9 to choose a printer and/or printing style from a list.

5. Make any changes to the settings for the printer in this window.

Most of the time, you won't need to change any of these settings. If you do, see "Fields in the Printer Settings Window" below for an explanation of each field.

6. Press Ctrl-Enter.

Fields in the Printer Settings Window

Name of printer

Quicken inserts the name of the printer you chose from the list of printers. You can type over the name shown if you want to use a different name. Changing the name here does not change the settings assigned to this printer.

Current style

The printing style you chose is displayed here. Change this only if you are defining a different style by entering control codes.

Print to

Enter the number corresponding to the printer port you are using.

PRN:, LPT1:, LPT2:, and LPT3: are parallel ports. AUX:, COM1:, and COM2: are serial ports. Check your computer or printer manuals or consult your dealer if you don't know which port your printer is connected to.

If you choose a serial port, the Serial Port Settings window appears after you complete the Printer Settings window. For more information, see "Serial Port Settings" on page 433.

Calling Intuit for help with unlisted printers

Your printer is not included in the Quicken list of printers, you've tried choosing one of the listed printers that might be compatible with your printer, and you've tried one of the <Other...> printers at the head of the list. But you're still having trouble. Don't worry, Intuit's Technical Support specialists can help you.

Plan to be at your computer when you call Intuit. The specialist will help you follow the procedure in this section and tell you exactly what to type in various fields.

To set up an unlisted printer:

1. On a pad of paper, write down the manufacturer, type, and model of your printer and keep the pad handy for more notes.

2. Have your printer manual available.

   If your printer came with more than one manual, find the one that contains control codes. Look in the index or table of contents for "printer control codes" or "escape control codes."

3. Get to the Select Printer window, if you're not already there:

   a. Choose Printer Settings from the Set Preferences menu.

   b. Choose Checks, Reports, or Alternate.

   c. At the Styles window, press Esc.

4. At the Select Printer window, choose <None>. (Press Home to get there quickly.)

5. Choose the Standard style.

6. At the Printer Settings window, press F8 to display the Printer Control Codes window.

Note:
Your window should not contain any codes to begin with (if you selected <None> as the printer). The examples here are just to show you what control codes look like.

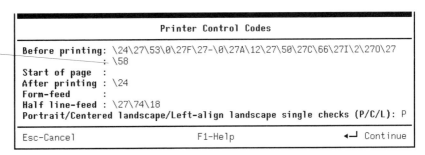

```
                      Printer Control Codes

Before printing: \24\27\53\0\27F\27-\0\27A\12\27\50\27C\66\27I\2\270\27
                 ⊹ \58
Start of page  :
After printing : \24
Form-feed      :
Half line-feed : \27\74\18
Portrait/Centered landscape/Left-align landscape single checks (P/C/L): P

Esc-Cancel                        F1-Help                  ◄┘ Continue
```

7. Telephone the Intuit Technical Support group at (415) 322-2800 Monday through Friday between 5 am and 5 pm Pacific time.

8. The specialist will help you fill in as many fields as necessary in this window.

9. When you have the codes entered correctly, press Ctrl-Enter.

Note: The remaining settings are preset for you when you choose a printer from the list. You probably won't need to change them.

Indent

Specify the number of extra spaces you want Quicken to indent printing on the left. Quicken will move all printing to the right by that number of spaces.

This setting should be 0 unless your printer can print more than 80 characters on a line (96 at 12 pitch, or 136 at 17 pitch). Otherwise, printed text may wrap. A nonzero setting is rarely necessary unless you have a daisy-wheel printer.

Lines per page

(For printing reports or laser checks) Specify how many lines you want Quicken to print on a page. For reports on 11-inch continuous paper, this setting should be 66. For single sheets, the usual setting is 60 for reports and 63 for checks.

Print pitch

(For printing checks) Set this to the "pitch" setting your printer is using when it prints checks. For example, if your printer prints checks at 12 characters per inch, set this to 12. (To measure the pitch, place a ruler on the check and count the characters in one inch.) Note that changing this setting will not change your printer's pitch. You are simply telling Quicken what pitch the printer is already using. (To change printer pitch, select a different printing style (page 429) or see "Entering Printer Control Codes" on page 433.)

Characters per line

(For printing reports) Set the number of characters that your printer can print on one line at the pitch it is using for reports. The setting should be equal to the number of printable columns, minus any indent you have set. For most printers, this number is 80 if the pitch is 10 characters per inch, or 96 if the pitch is 12 characters per inch. If your printer uses compressed type, this number should be 132. You may need to change this setting if you are using a wide printer, if the pitch is other than 10 or 12 characters per inch, or if you have set the indent to a number greater than zero.

Pause between pages

You can have Quicken pause between pages rather than printing continuously. This setting is useful if you are using cut sheet paper rather than continuous computer paper. The pages referred to are pages of paper, not Quicken checks.

Page-oriented (for example, laser) printer

Enter Y here if your printer is a laser printer (or is sheet-fed). This setting affects check printing only.

Supports IBM Graphics Characters

If your printer supports IBM graphics characters, Quicken will use them to generate headings on your reports. If your printer does not support these characters, hyphens and equals signs (− and =) will be used to separate headings from the data in your reports. If you're not sure whether or not your printer supports these characters, you can find out. Enter Y in response to this question. Then print a report. If the report prints correctly, your printer supports graphics characters. If unusual symbols (Ds and Ms) appear across the report, your printer does not support IBM graphics characters, and you should change the setting to N for No.

Serial Port Settings

If you have chosen a serial setting (AUX:, COM1:, or COM2:) to print to, the Serial Port Settings window will appear. This window contains the special settings for serial printers. It comes set for the most popular settings. Consult your printer manual for the specific settings for your printer.

F8 Edit control codes

See the next section.

Entering Printer Control Codes

Quicken, like other software programs, sends two kinds of data to printers: (1) information to print on a check or sheet of paper and (2) instructions about how to print the information (for example, to use letter quality or draft printing or to change the pitch of the printer). The instructions about how to print are called "control codes." Each brand of printer defines its own codes to control its functions.

Most People Don't Need to Fuss with Printer Control Codes

Most people can select a printer from the list provided with Quicken (press F9 at the Printer Settings window) and never need to think about printer control codes. Quicken automatically fills in the necessary control codes for you at a special window. Notice that after choosing a printer you then select a printing style, such as Roman, 10 pitch, portrait, or Draft style.

Be sure to check whether the style list contains an explicit item for what you want to do with your printer before you worry about control codes. If you want to see the codes Quicken fills in for you, go to the Printer Control Codes window (described on page 434).

If your printer is not included in the Quicken printer list, look in the printer's user manual to see if the manufacturer says it is compatible with another brand of printer that is included in the list. You need to read the rest of this section only if you cannot select any printer from the list or if you want to print in a way different from the instructions Quicken sends to your printer.

Note: You must refer to your printer manual to learn the control codes for your printer. The next section explains how to determine what code to enter based on the information in a typical printer manual.

If You Need to Enter Control Codes

You need to enter control codes only if you cannot find your printer in Quicken's printer list or if you want some special printing effect.

The user manual that came with your printer lists the control codes to type in fields at the Quicken Printer Control Code window. Control codes are often combinations of two kinds of characters: printable (and typeable) characters such as "G" or "5" and nonprintable characters such as Esc or Enter. For example, some printers use the code Esc-G for double-strike mode. To enter such a code in a Quicken field, you can't simply press the Esc key, since that would cause Quicken to perform an action (it would remove the Printer Control Code window). The solution is to type the "decimal equivalent" of the Esc character.

When you look in your printer manual, you will find that it gives you two or three formats for each character included in a control code.

ASCII	The key you would press or the letter you would type if you were sending the character to your printer directly rather than setting Quicken up to send it for you.
"Decimal equivalent"	A series of one to three digits that your printer interprets as equivalent to the ASCII syntax for a character.
"hexadecimal" format	Notation of numbers in the base 16. You can ignore this format.

Here's how a typical printer manual presents these three formats for characters in the code to change to double-strike mode:

ASCII code	ESC	G	It's easiest to use the decimal equivalent for all characters.
Decimal equivalent	27	71	
Hexadecimal	1B	47	Ignore the hexadecimal format.

Here's the easiest way to enter the code Esc-G in a Quicken field:

To enter Esc-G, type a backslash and then 27, the decimal equivalent of Esc. Type another backslash and then 71, the decimal equivalent of G.

To go to the next field, press Enter.

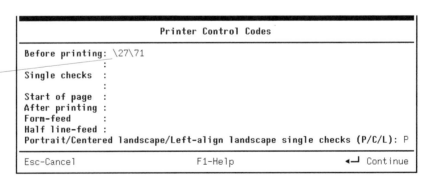

```
                    Printer Control Codes

 Before printing: \27\71
                 :
 Single checks   :
                 :
 Start of page   :
 After printing  :
 Form-feed       :
 Half line-feed  :
 Portrait/Centered landscape/Left-align landscape single checks (P/C/L): P

 Esc-Cancel                    F1-Help                 ◄┘ Continue
```

To enter or change control codes:

1. Consult your printer manual to determine the control codes you need to achieve the printing effect you want.

2. Press F8 at the Printer Settings window.

    Quicken displays the Printer Control Codes window. The window has fields for codes to send to the printer before and after anything is printed, and at the start of each new page. If you selected a printer from the Quicken list, you will see codes that Quicken has filled in automatically. You can add codes for special effects.

3. Type control codes at appropriate fields in the window using the decimal equivalents for all characters. Precede each decimal equivalent by a backslash (\ ).

    We recommend that you use the decimal equivalent even for printable characters such as "G" and "5." If you mix decimal equivalents and printable characters, you must pay attention to the guidelines in the next section to handle cases where printable digits might be mistaken for decimal equivalents.

4. Press Ctrl-Enter when you have finished entering as many fields as necessary.

    Note: The control codes you enter remain in effect until you change printer settings again and explicitly change or remove them.

Guidelines If You Mix Decimal Equivalents and Printable Characters

*   Enter nonprintable characters (for example, Esc, Tab, Enter) by typing the decimal equivalent of the character, preceded by a backslash (\ ). Some nonprintable characters require combination keystrokes, such as Ctrl-C, and they do not display anything on your screen when you press them. For example, to enter Ctrl-C in a field, you might type \03 or \003 in the field.

*   Type any printable character directly by typing the usual key on the keyboard. A printable character is a character such as G or 5 that can be displayed on the computer screen.

*   If you mix decimal equivalents and ASCII codes, you may need a way to keep Quicken from confusing a decimal equivalent with a printable digit. For example, suppose the printer manual shows a code like this:

ASCII code	Ctrl-O	5
Decimal equivalent	15	53

    where 15 is Ctrl-O and the digit 5 is a printable character. In these cases, you must use three digits for the decimal equivalent. You would type \0155 where \015 is the decimal equivalent and 5 is a printable digit. As you can see, it is clearer to type the decimal equivalent for both characters: \15\53.

Fields in the Printer Control Code Window

Before printing Enter the control codes you want sent to the printer before printing any information, following the guidelines in "If You Need to Enter Control Codes" on page 433.

Single checks (This applies only to laser printers.) If you want to insert checks sideways, enter the
(Check Printer only) control codes for sideways printing here.

Note: A single backslash (\) in this field means that the laser printer can handle partial pages of checks in portrait mode (that is, not sideways) and that the printer needs no special codes for partial pages of checks.

Start of page   Enter the control codes to be sent to the printer at the start of each new page. For example, if you have a sheet feeder, you might want to enter the code for a form feed here.

After printing   Enter the control codes to reset the printer to normal after printing.

Form-feed   If you have a sheet feeder and want a form feed at the end of each page, enter the control codes for a form feed here.

Half line-feed   Enter the codes for a half line-feed. This advances the printer by a 1/2 line and is used to align checks.

P/C/L   (Laser printers only.) Enter the code that tells Quicken the correct partial page orientation.

"Portrait" tells Quicken to feed the partial page of checks into the printer in the same orientation as a regular full sheet of checks or standard paper.

"Centered landscape" tells Quicken to rotate the partial page 90 degrees and then to feed the page down the center of the paper path, regardless of its width. Apple's LaserWriter IIs have this type of manual feed.

"Left-align landscape single checks" tells Quicken to rotate the partial page 90 degrees and then to feed the top of the page along the left edge of the paper path.

$ Screen Settings

At the Set Preferences menu, choose Screen Settings to display the Screen Settings menu:

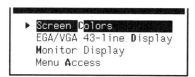

Screen Colors

You can choose the colors or shades for Quicken's monitor display. When you choose Screen Colors from the Screen Settings menu, Quicken displays the Change Color Scheme menu. Choose the colors you want by typing the number of the menu item.

Color Scheme	Comments
1. Monochrome	For one-color monitors that cannot display shades of gray (for example, the IBM PC monochrome display)
2. Reverse Monochrome	As for monochrome, but with black and white reversed
3. Navy/Azure	The setting Quicken normally uses for color monitors

4. White/Navy   -

5. Red/Gray   Helpful for color monitor users who are color blind

6. Shades of Gray   For one-color monitors that can display shades of gray (for example, Compaq one-color monitors, or monochrome VGA monitors)

7. Purple/White   -

8. Green/Yellow   -

Adjust the contrast and brightness controls too

If you have problems seeing the highlighted letters of menu items (for Alt key menus only), try adjusting the contrast and brightness controls on your monitor.

EGA/VGA 43-line Display

Some high-quality monitors (EGA and VGA monitors) can display 43 lines on the screen instead of the normal 25 lines. If you have such a monitor, you can choose 43-line display. Quicken will display many more lines in the check register and in reports.

1. At the Screen Settings menu, choose EGA/VGA 43-line Display.

2. Choose 25 lines or 43 lines.

If your monitor is not EGA or VGA, Quicken tells you the option is not available.

Monitor Display

Quicken can work at two different monitor display speeds: fast and slow. The monitor speed that's best for you depends on how fast your monitor can handle rapid screen changes without "snow" appearing on the screen. (The slow setting is never required for EGA and VGA monitors.) If snow appears on your screen, you probably need to use the slow setting. Here's how to change it:

1. Choose Monitor Display from the Set Preferences menu.

2. Choose Slow in the Screen Update Speed window.

The snow should disappear.

Menu Access

You can access Quicken menu items using either of two different methods: the Alt key method and the Function key method. If you use other DOS software, you may recognize the Alt key method as a new industry standard called "Systems Applications Architecture," or SAA. The Function key method is used by previous Quicken versions and by some other popular DOS software. You work with these two access methods in slightly different ways, so you will want to choose the one you like best.

Using Alt key menus, you choose a menu item by typing the letter that is highlighted in the menu line. Using Function key menus, you choose a menu item by typing the number next to the item.

Alt key menu

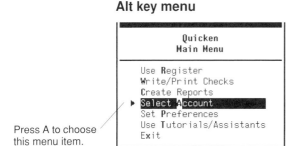

Press A to choose this menu item.

Function key menu

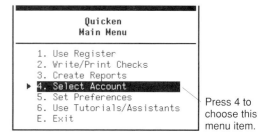

Press 4 to choose this menu item.

Note: With either style menu, you can use the up and down arrow keys to select an item, then press Enter.

Pulldown menus also work differently with the Alt key or the Function key method. In the Alt key method, you use the Alt key to choose a pulldown menu. In the Function key method, you press a function key. For example, in the check register:

Alt key menu

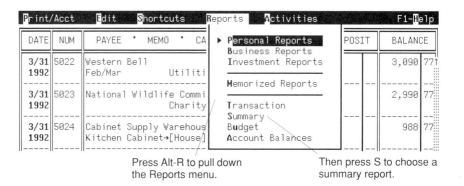

Press Alt-R to pull down the Reports menu.

Then press S to choose a summary report.

Function key menu

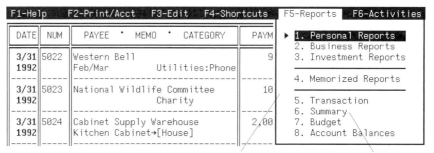

Press F5 to pull down the Reports menu.

Then press 6 to choose a summary report.

With both Alt key and Function key menus, you can use Ctrl-key combinations (Quick Keys) to choose an item directly. For example, if you press Ctrl-S while in the register, Quicken opens a split transaction; you don't need to pull down the Edit menu.

Appendix C, *Quicken Menus*, beginning on page 485, shows all Quicken's menus using the Alt key method of access.

To set the method of menu access:

1. Choose Screen Settings from the Set Preferences menu.

2. Choose Menu Access.

3. In the Menu Access window, enter 1 to change to Function key menus, or enter 2 to change to Alt key menus.

   The menu access method does not change until you exit from Quicken and then start Quicken again.

$ Password Settings

This menu item displays the Password menu, where you can set and change passwords for the current Quicken file.

You can prevent unauthorized access to your Quicken data by requiring a password to be entered before anyone opens your file (called a "file password"). You can also require a separate password (called a "transaction password") to be entered to make changes to transactions before a certain date. Using a transaction password is a means of closing an accounting period.

Note: Quicken's password feature provides a basic level of protection for your data. If you need stronger protection, keep your data on floppy disks and lock up the disks. If your computer has a key lock, use it.

Setting Up the File Password

Caution: If you set up a file password, you will not be able to access the data in your Quicken file without entering the password. Be sure that you write down the password and keep it in a safe place in case you forget it.

When you set up a password, Quicken assigns it to the current file. Make sure that the file that is active now is the one for which you want to assign a password.

To set up a file password:

1. Choose Password Settings from the Set Preferences menu.

2. Choose File Password from the Password Settings menu.

3. Type the password that will be required to use this file, and press Enter.

   You can type up to 16 characters, including spaces. Upper- and lower-case characters are treated the same.

4. Type the password again to confirm it and press Enter.

   Quicken prompts you for the password before allowing you to access this Quicken file again. (Note that the file is currently open, so it can be accessed. To make the password active for this file, select another file first, or exit from Quicken and start Quicken again.)

   When you enter the password to access the file, what you enter is not displayed on the screen.

Changing or Removing a File Password

You can change or remove a password from a file if you want to allow access to it by other individuals. You remove a password by replacing the existing one with a blank.

To change or delete a file password:

1. Choose Password Settings from the Set Preferences menu.

2. Choose File Password from the Password Settings menu.

3. Next to Old Password, type the current password and press Enter.

4. Next to New Password, type the password that you want this file to have and press Enter.

   Or, to remove the password, leave New Password blank and press Enter.

Setting a Transaction Password

In addition to (or instead of) the file-wide password, you can require a password to make changes to transactions prior to a given date (called a "transaction password"). For example, you might want to "close" an accounting period as a reminder that no changes should be made to transactions in the period.

When you set a transaction password, you specify the password you want to set and a date. The date you enter is the date of the last transactions in the register for which this password will be required. Quicken will require that the password be entered before a change can be recorded to any transaction dated on or before this date.

You can make your whole file read-only.

By setting a transaction password dated 12/31/99, you can effectively make a file "read-only." This means you can look at the data, print, and report on it, but you cannot change it without entering the password.

To set a transaction password:

1. Choose Password Settings from the Set Preferences menu.

2. Choose Transaction Password.

   The Password to Modify Existing Transactions window appears.

3. Type the password to be assigned to the prior transactions and press Enter.

4. Type the date through which the password will be required and press Enter.

5. Type the password again to confirm and press Enter.

   The transaction password is active immediately.

You can also change or remove a transaction password. This process is similar to changing the file password, but you choose Transaction Password from the Password Settings menu.

Removing a Forgotten Password

If you forget your password (either a file password or a transaction password) and cannot remove it using the normal procedure described on page 440, call Intuit's Technical Support at (415) 322-2800 for assistance.

$ Automatic Reminders

Quicken reminds you when you have checks which you haven't yet printed, or when your transaction groups are overdue. Quicken offers two reminder methods.

When you start Quicken, a reminder is displayed on the Main Menu for any unprinted checks and transaction groups you have set up. See Chapter 12, *Entering Transaction Groups*, beginning on page 211, for details of how to set up transaction groups.

Another, more comprehensive, reminder system is Billminder. Billminder messages appear earlier, when you start your computer, before you even start Quicken.

Quicken can also remind you to print postdated checks and execute transaction groups several days *before* their scheduled dates. This reminder will help ensure that you pay bills on time if, for example, you don't use Quicken every day.

For both reminder methods, you can define how many days in advance you are reminded that there are bills to pay. Quicken comes set to begin reminding you three days before a scheduled date. For example, if the scheduled date is Thursday, Quicken will first remind you on Monday, which is three days in advance.

This section describes how to set up Billminder, and how to change this advance notice period for both reminder methods.

Billminder

If you have a hard disk, Quicken's Billminder program can help you remember when you have:

- Checks to print
- Electronic payments to transmit to the CheckFree Processing Center
- Transaction groups due
- Action to take about your investments

These can be either overdue or coming up soon (postdated).

When you install Quicken 5 and ask that Billminder be installed, the installation program automatically installs Billminder on your hard disk. It also adds a line to the AUTOEXEC.BAT file to run the Billminder program. Each time you start your computer, Billminder checks your Quicken data directory. If it finds checks to print or other payments that are almost due, it informs you of them.

Here's a sample Billminder message:

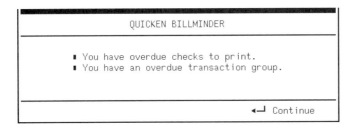

You don't have to use Billminder once it is installed. If you want to stop Billminder from displaying information when you start your computer, you can turn it off as described on page 444.

Billminder and AUTOEXEC.BAT

You may want to change one of the Billminder lines in the AUTOEXEC.BAT file in two cases:

- You have moved the Quicken program to a directory other than the one in which you installed it. You need to change the directory address so that Billminder can find your Quicken files.

- You want to change whether your computer pauses after the Billminder message when you start the computer. A pause is helpful if your AUTOEXEC.BAT executes other programs after it displays the Billminder message.

To make these changes, edit the Billminder line in your AUTOEXEC.BAT file. The exact wording of the Billminder line depends on your version of DOS, and the directory where you installed Quicken. For example:

C:\QUICKEN5\BILLMIND C:\QUICKEN5   (For DOS 3.0 or higher)

BILLMIND C:\QUICKEN5   (For DOS versions lower than 3.0)

To tell Billminder what directory to look in for Quicken files:

• Edit the line to describe the correct directory. For example, if you keep the Quicken program (Q.EXE) in a directory named C:\Q5 and if your version of DOS is 3.0 or higher, you would edit the line so it reads:

C:\Q5\BILLMIND C:\Q5

To have Billminder pause after displaying its message:

• Add /P to the end of the line. Include a space before /P. For example:

C:\QUICKEN5\BILLMIND C:\QUICKEN5 /P

Use this command if you want Billminder to display its message and then pause before returning the DOS prompt to the screen. A message in the Billminder window tells you to press Enter to continue. Delete /P if you do not want Billminder to pause.

Note: Billminder recognizes as the Quicken program directory only the one containing the file Q.CFG. (The file Q.CFG specifies the path to the Quicken data files.) If you specify a directory that does not contain Q.CFG, Billminder displays an error message. Check your directory to be sure it contains your Quicken program files and Q.CFG and then enter the Billminder command again.

To remove Billminder, see "Installation on a Hard Disk" beginning on page 491.

Automatic Reminder Settings

Choose Automatic Reminder Settings from the Set Preferences menu.

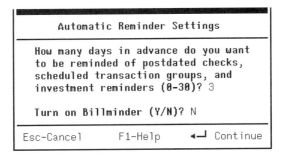

How many days in advance

Enter a number from 0 to 30. This is the number of days in advance that Quicken or Billminder will remind you that there are bills to pay. That is, this number applies to both reminder methods (Quicken's reminder messages and Billminder messages that are displayed when you turn on your computer). When choosing a number, don't worry about weekends, because checks or groups falling on a weekend are treated as falling on the preceding Friday.

Set the days in advance based on your frequency of use. Following are some sample settings for the "days in advance" feature:

Hard disk users using Quicken Billminder:

If you use your computer this often:	Set days in advance to:
Daily (except weekends)	0 days
At least every other day	1 day
At least once every three days	2 days
At least weekly	6 days

Other users:

If you use Quicken this often:	Set days in advance to:
Daily (except weekends)	0 days
At least once every three days	2 days
At least weekly	6 days
At least once every two weeks	13 days
At least once a month	30 days

Turn on Billminder

To use Billminder if you have installed it, enter Y in the field "Turn on Billminder?" To turn Billminder off, enter N.

 # Transaction Settings

Quicken has a number of settings that you can change regarding data entry and the display of transactions in the register.

Choose Transaction Settings from the Set Preferences menu.

```
┌─────────────────────────────────────────────────────────┐
│            Transaction Settings                          │
├─────────────────────────────────────────────────────────┤
│  1. Beep when recording and memorizing    (Y/N): Y       │
│  2. Request confirmation when modifying                  │
│     a transaction                         (Y/N): Y       │
│  3. Request confirmation when deleting                   │
│     or voiding a transaction              (Y/N): Y       │
│  4. Enter dates as MM/DD/YY or DD/MM/YY   (M/D): M        │
│  5. Require a category on transactions    (Y/N): N       │
│  6. Show Memo/Category/Both in register (M/C/B): B       │
│  7. Exact matches on finds and filters    (Y/N): N       │
├─────────────────────────────────────────────────────────┤
│  Esc-Cancel          F1-Help          ◄┘ Continue        │
└─────────────────────────────────────────────────────────┘
```

Fields in the Transaction Settings Window

1. Beep when recording and memorizing

You can turn Quicken's beeping sound on or off. If you turn the beep off, you will not hear beeps when Quicken records, memorizes, or deletes transactions.

2. Request confirmation when modifying a transaction

If this is set to Y, you will be asked "OK to Record Transaction?" when you press Enter after writing a check or adding or changing a transaction in the register. Enter N to turn off this confirmation question. If you enter N, Quicken also disables scrolling in Write Checks, which will allow you to page through unprinted checks more rapidly.

The advantage of having the confirmation questions turned off is that you won't need to use as many keystrokes, especially when changing transactions in the register. The disadvantage is that you won't be stopped and given a chance to consider whether what you have entered is correct before Quicken records it.

3. Request confirmation when deleting or voiding a transaction

If this field is set to Y, you will be asked "OK to Delete Transaction?" when you try to delete a check or a transaction in the register. You will be asked "OK to Void Transaction?" when you try to void a transaction. Enter N to turn off these confirmation questions.

If you enter N, you won't be given a chance to prevent the deletion or voiding once you select it. We recommend that you leave this field as Y.

4. Enter dates as MM/DD/YY or DD/MM/YY

This setting determines the date format Quicken uses when entering dates in the register, when writing checks, and in reports. When this setting is M, dates appear in month/day/year format (MM/DD/YY). If you change the setting to D, dates appear in day/month/year format (DD/MM/YY). This date format is also used on printed checks (unless you choose the three-letter abbreviation for the month — see page 447 for that field).

5. Require a category on transactions

Enter Y and Quicken will check for a category (or a transfer) in every transaction you record. If you don't enter a category, Quicken displays the message "Category Required" (though you can then proceed without entering a category if you want). This reminder is useful if you want to keep complete categorized records of your income and expenditures to use in Quicken reports.

6. Show Memo/Category/Both in register

This setting determines what information is displayed in the register for transactions that aren't selected (on the second line of the Payee • Memo • Category column).

- Enter M (for Memo) to display only memo information on the second line.

- Enter C (for Category) to display only category information on the second line.

- Enter B (for Both) to display any memo text on the left and any category information on the right portion of the line. This is the normal setting. Category information may be abbreviated if it doesn't fit on the line.

7. Exact matches on finds and filters

This setting determines the way the Find feature works when you search for particular transactions in the register. It also affects the filter window when you create a report.

When this setting is set to N, Quicken finds any transactions that contain those characters; the transaction does not need to contain an exact match. For example, if you enter "motor" as the payee, the search will find "Goodfellows Motoring." (This is the standard Quicken 5 method, as described on pages 64 and 183.)

If you set this field to Y, Quicken uses your entry to do an exact match. It will find only those transactions that exactly match the word you entered. However, you can still enter two periods (..) to specify any transaction containing the word. For example, enter "..motor.." to find "Goodfellows Motoring." (This is the method Quicken 4 used.)

See "Using Find" on page 63 for an explanation of the Find feature. See "Using Match Characters to Limit Searches" on page 186 for more information about matches.

$ Checks and Reports Settings

This menu item lets you change the way checks and reports appear.

Choose Checks & Reports Settings from the Set Preferences menu.

```
┌────────────────────────────────────────────────────────┐
│                    Checks and Reports Settings          │
│                                                          │
│   1. Extra message line on check (printed                │
│      on check but not recorded)          (Y/N): N        │
│   2. Change date of checks to date                       │
│      when printed                        (Y/N): N        │
│   3. Print months as Jan, Feb...on checks (Y/N): N       │
│   4. Print categories on voucher checks  (Y/N): Y        │
│   5. Warn if a check number is re-used   (Y/N): N        │
│   6. In reports, print category                          │
│      Description/Name/Both               (D/N/B): D      │
│   7. In reports, print account                           │
│      Description/Name/Both               (D/N/B): N      │
│                                                          │
│  Esc-Cancel          F1-Help            ◄┘ Continue      │
└────────────────────────────────────────────────────────┘
```

1. Extra message line on check (printed on check but not recorded)

You can have Quicken add an extra message line to your checks. This extra message line is printed on your checks, but is not recorded in the check register. The extra message line is useful for such things as typing a charge account number on your check or adding an additional message to the payee. The extra message can be included as part of a memorized transaction, but it is not recorded in the check register. If you choose to have an extra message line, it appears to the right of the address.

To enter a message in the extra message line on the check, press Enter as needed to move the cursor to the extra message line. Type your message and press Enter. The cursor will move to the second line of the address field.

2. Change date of checks to date when printed

When this setting is Y, all checks you print will use the current date, and that date will appear in the register. Postdated checks and checks dated prior to the day you print will all change their dates to the current date. When this setting is N, checks will keep the date with which you originally entered them.

3. Print months as Jan, Feb... on checks

When this setting is Y, the month will be printed on checks as a three-letter abbreviation. For example, 25 Jan '92 or 1 Aug '93. The three-letter abbreviations are always in English, and the day is always printed before the month (regardless of the setting for the field "4.Enter dates as..." in the Transaction Settings window).

This does not affect the display of dates in Quicken.

4. Print categories on voucher checks

When this setting is Y, the category you assign to a transaction prints on the voucher. When this setting is N, the category doesn't print. No matter what this setting is, any descriptions you enter in the Description column of the Split Transaction window print on the voucher.

5. Warn if a check number is re-used

When this setting is Y, Quicken warns if you enter a check number in the register that duplicates an existing check number; that is, if there is another check with the same number in the same account.

6. In reports, print category Description/Name/Both

This setting determines how Quicken displays categories and classes in reports. If you leave the setting as D (for Description), Quicken prints the description when there is one, or uses the category or class name if there is no description. If you change it to N (for Name), Quicken always prints the name and not the description.

7. In reports, print account Description/Name/Both

This setting determines how Quicken displays accounts in reports. If you change the setting to D (for Description), Quicken prints the account description when there is one, or uses the account name if there is no description.

Electronic Payment Settings

This menu item takes you to the Electronic Payment Settings window, where you tell Quicken how to access your modem, your phone line, and the CheckFree Processing Center. Once you have provided this information, you can set up bank accounts for electronic payment. See Chapter 13, *Using CheckFree to Pay Bills Electronically*, beginning on page 219.

Chapter 28

Managing Files

This chapter tells you how to set up and use additional Quicken files. You'll also learn how to back up and restore your Quicken data; delete, rename, and copy files; and change the DOS directory where Quicken stores the data.

Pay particular attention to the instructions for backing up your Quicken files on page 458. You should maintain backup copies of all your Quicken files to guard against accidental loss of data.

How Your Quicken Data Is Organized

Your Quicken data is organized in two main ways: by account and by file. You keep your data in an account, and the account belongs to a file.

You must have at least one file containing at least one account before you can begin to use Quicken. If you ran the First Time Setup when you started using Quicken, the assistant helped you set up your first file containing one account.

Normally, a file contains many different accounts. When you set up a new file, Quicken allows you up to 64 accounts, but you can increase this number up to 255.*

When you have several accounts in one file, you can:

- Use the same categories, subcategories, classes, memorized transactions, transaction groups, and electronic payees in any account in the file. You can use the same securities and memorized investment transactions in any investment accounts in the same file.

- Get reports that consolidate data from all or selected accounts in a file. Quicken organizes transaction data by category. If you like, you can add subcategory and class information to your transactions to get more detail in your reports.

- Transfer amounts from one account to another within the same file.

The figure on page 451 illustrates the structure of Quicken data in a file.

---

* For more information on file size, see "Copying a Quicken File" on page 462.

Quicken File

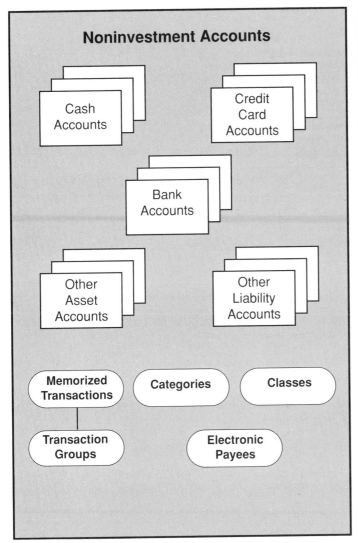

Noninvestment Accounts

Cash Accounts

Credit Card Accounts

Bank Accounts

Other Asset Accounts

Other Liability Accounts

Memorized Transactions

Categories

Classes

Transaction Groups

Electronic Payees

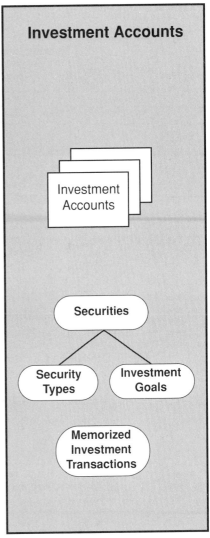

Investment Accounts

Investment Accounts

Securities

Security Types

Investment Goals

Memorized Investment Transactions

Within one Quicken file, all noninvestment accounts share the same categories, classes, memorized transactions, transaction groups, and electronic payees.

Within one Quicken file, all investment accounts share the same securities and memorized investment transactions.

The File Activities Menu

The tasks having to do with files are grouped together on the File Activities menu.

1. At the Main Menu, choose Set Preferences.

2. Choose File Activities.

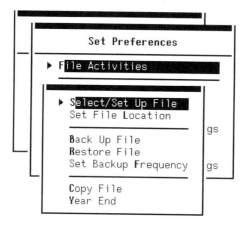

Following is a brief summary of the items on the File Activities menu.

Select/Set Up File. With this item you can select the file you want to use, create new files, delete files, and change the name of a file.

Set File Location. Use this item when you want to use or create a file in a different drive or directory.

Back Up File. With this item you can make a backup copy of any file to floppy disks or to another directory on your hard disk.

Restore File. Use this item to restore a file from your backup copy of it, if the file has become damaged.

Set Backup Frequency. This item allows you to set a timetable for Quicken to remind you to make backups.

Copy File. With this item you can copy a file to another disk, or another directory on your hard disk. You can also shrink a file by copying only part of it (you select the transactions to include in the new copy by entering a range of dates).

Year End. At the end of each year you can "close out accounts" using this item. There are two archiving options, depending on how you want to organize your records. Note, though, that because Quicken can store data indefinitely, there is really no need to close out accounts. This item is optional.

Setting Up Additional Files

If you decide that one file is not enough to organize your data efficiently, you can set up additional files. You can add a new file at any time.

Do You Need More Than One File?

Quicken makes it easy for you to set up additional files. But this doesn't mean that it is a good idea for you to do this. It depends on how you need to arrange your finances. For many Quicken users, one file is all that's ever needed.

Remember that, if you separate your data into several files, you lose several advantages of having just one file:

- Quicken works with one file at a time. Your account list, for example, shows you only the accounts in your current file.

- Reports consolidate data from all accounts in the current file, but not from different files.

- You can transfer amounts only between accounts in the same file.

- All accounts in one file share the same category list. You must set up a separate category list for each file.

For these reasons, you should keep all related data in the same file. Create additional files only if the data in each file is completely unrelated.

You may need more than one file because:

- You run a business that is completely separate from your personal finances. Or you have two completely unrelated businesses. Keeping these in separate files helps to ensure your finances stay separate.

  If there is any regular interaction between your business data and your personal data (or between your businesses), you should keep all the data in the same file. Use classes to distinguish among the different types of transaction. See Chapter 22, *Using Classes*, beginning on page 351, and also "Setting Up Classes for Jobs, Properties, Clients, Projects, or Departments" on page 374.

- You do not have a hard disk, and your data files would otherwise get too big to fit on one floppy disk. See "Copying a Quicken File" and "Year-End Procedures" later in this chapter for details of how to archive old data and keep your current files small.

- You want to start a new file each year, to close each year's accounts. (If you keep your Quicken data on a hard disk, there is no need to start a new file for this reason.)

You do *not* need a separate file for each client or for each project. Use classes to distinguish among these (again, see page 374).

If possible, work with just one file for a while, to appreciate the advantages of having all your data available in one place. Then decide if you need additional files to best organize your data.

Setting Up a New File

To set up a new file:

1. Starting at the Main Menu:

Quick Key:
Press Ctrl-G at the Main Menu to display the Select/Set Up File window.

    a. Choose Set Preferences.

    b. Choose File Activities.

    c. Choose Select/Set Up File.

If you keep your data on floppy disk, Quicken now lets you change disks if you want.

Quicken displays the Select/Set Up File window.

2. Choose <Set Up File> in the window.

Quicken displays the Set Up File window.

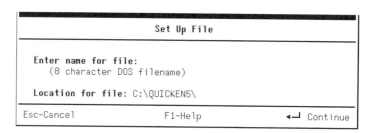

```
                          Set Up File


        Enter name for file:
            (8 character DOS filename)

        Location for file: C:\QUICKEN5\

     Esc-Cancel                    F1-Help              ◄┘ Continue
```

3. In the field "Enter name for file," enter a name for the new file.

You can name the file anything you want, such as "BUSACCTS" or "HOME." Because Quicken will use this name for a series of DOS files, the name must follow the rules for a DOS filename, without an extension. That is, it can be up to eight characters long and can include letters, numbers, and some other characters (such as a hyphen or a number sign). Press F1 at the Set Up File window for the complete rules on DOS filenames.

4. In the field "Location for data files," Quicken fills in the current location for your files. Press Enter to have Quicken create the file in the drive and directory shown.

You can type over the drive and directory if you want Quicken to create the new file in a different location. You can store Quicken files in several different locations if you want. It's simpler, however, to keep them all in the same location because Quicken can list the files in only one location at a time. (Note that each Quicken file is actually composed of four DOS files. See "Program and Help Files" on page 493 for technical details.)

Quicken displays the Default Categories window.

```
┌──────────────────────────────────────────────────────────────┐
│                      Default Categories                        │
├──────────────────────────────────────────────────────────────┤
│  All accounts in a file use the same list of categories.       │
│  Categories help track your income and expenses.  Many people  │
│  who transfer money between home and office like to use both    │
│  Home and Business categories.                                 │
│                                                                │
│    ┌─────────────────────────┬──────────────────────────────┐ │
│    │ Sample Home Categories  │ Sample Business Categories   │ │
│    │       Clothing          │       Advertising            │ │
│    │       Groceries         │       Freight                │ │
│    │       Mortgage          │       Payroll                │ │
│    │       Salary            │       Rent                   │ │
│    │       Utilities         │       Utilities              │ │
│    └─────────────────────────┴──────────────────────────────┘ │
│                                                                │
│    Select a category list: 1                                   │
│        1. Home categories     3. Both Home and Business        │
│        2. Business categories 4. Neither                       │
├──────────────────────────────────────────────────────────────┤
│  Esc-Cancel              F1-Help          ◄┘ Continue          │
└──────────────────────────────────────────────────────────────┘
```

Categories are what make Quicken so useful: they help you understand and organize your finances in the most efficient way. It's important to set up the right list of categories for your new file. We recommend that you use one of Quicken's preset lists of standard categories, which have been carefully designed to work for most homes or businesses. Also, these standard lists already have tax form information defined for them (as described in Chapter 26, *Preparing Your Income Taxes*, beginning on page 415).

You can create the new file with standard category names for home or for business use, or for both, or without category names. If you start with Quicken's standard category names, you can always add, change, and delete category names later. (You can also add the complete list of standard categories for home use or for business use, if you choose the wrong list now; see page 117.) For the complete lists of standard categories, see page 103.

If you choose not to use Quicken's standard categories, you will need to set up all your own categories to organize your data properly.

5. Choose the types of categories you will use with this file:
   - Enter 1 to use Quicken's standard home categories.
   - Enter 2 to use Quicken's standard business categories.
   - Enter 3 to use both the home and the business categories.
   - Enter 4 to create the file without preset categories.

Quicken creates the new file in the specified directory, and displays its name in the Select/Set Up File window. You can create up to 64 accounts in this file. (This number can be increased up to 255 by copying the file; see page 463.)

Choosing a File to Use

When you have more than one Quicken file, you need to be careful to choose the right file to work with. Each time you start Quicken, it assumes you want to work with the file that was active when you last used Quicken. If you want to work with accounts in a different file, you choose the file you want and then choose an account in that file.

Quicken maintains a list of all Quicken files. When you want to use another file, just choose it from the list. At this list you can also get reminder information about any file, such as when the next check is due to be printed.

To use another Quicken file or to get file reminders:

1. Starting at the Main Menu:

   a. Choose Set Preferences.

   b. Choose File Activities.

   c. Choose Select/Set Up File.

   If you keep your data on floppy disks, Quicken now lets you change disks if you want.

   Quicken displays the Select/Set Up File window.

Quick Key:
Press Ctrl-G at the Main Menu to display the Select/Set Up File window.

To see reminders for a specific file, select the file and press F8.

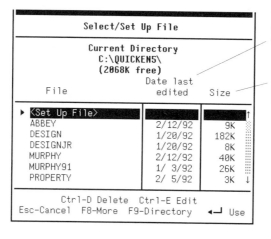

This column shows the date you last made changes to the data file.

Size is the size of the main data file in "K," or thousands of bytes.

2. (Optional) To see some reminder information about one of the listed files:

   a. Use the up and down arrow keys to select the file, and press F8.

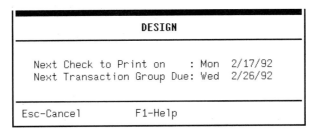

```
┌────────────────────────────────────────────────┐
│████████████████████████████████████████████████│
│                     DESIGN                       │
│                                                  │
├──────────────────────────────────────────────────┤
│                                                  │
│  Next Check to Print on    : Mon  2/17/92        │
│  Next Transaction Group Due: Wed  2/26/92        │
│                                                  │
├──────────────────────────────────────────────────┤
│  Esc-Cancel           F1-Help                    │
└────────────────────────────────────────────────┘
```

   If you have postdated checks, this window shows when the next check is scheduled to be printed. If you have scheduled transaction groups, the window indicates when the next group is due.

   b. Press Esc to return to the Select/Set Up File window.

3. Use the up and down arrow keys to select the file you want to use, and press Enter. (If you don't see the file you want, press F9 to change the directory and look for it in another location on disk.)

4. Type a password if Quicken asks you for one. Then press Enter.

   If the file has only one account, you will see the register immediately. If the file has more than one account, Quicken first asks you to select an account.

Note: You can set and change passwords for files with the Password Settings item on the Set Preferences menu. For more information, see "Password Settings" on page 439.

$ Changing Where Quicken Looks for Data

You can keep your data in any location you like, in a hard disk directory or on a floppy, so long as you tell Quicken where to find it. You use Set File Location to do this.

Quicken can look for data files in only one directory or disk drive at a time. So if it doesn't find a file you know you set up, it's probably looking in the wrong directory or drive. A directory is a portion of a disk that you've asked DOS to set aside and label with a name. (Most people use directories on hard disks; some people also use directories on floppy disks.)

To use a different directory or disk:

1. Starting at the Main Menu:

Alternately, press F9 at the Select/Set Up File window to set the file location.

   a. Choose Set Preferences.

   b. Choose File Activities.

   c. Choose Set File Location.

```
┌─────────────────────────────────────────────────────────┐
│ ▓▓▓▓▓▓▓▓▓▓▓▓▓▓▓▓▓▓▓▓▓▓▓▓▓▓▓▓▓▓▓▓▓▓▓▓▓▓▓▓▓▓▓▓▓▓▓▓▓▓▓▓▓▓▓▓▓ │
│                    Set File Location                      │
├─────────────────────────────────────────────────────────┤
│                                                           │
│  Enter new pathname: C:\QUICKEN5\                         │
│                                                           │
├─────────────────────────────────────────────────────────┤
│                Enter directory and/or drive.              │
│  Esc-Cancel              F1-Help              ◄─┘ Continue│
└─────────────────────────────────────────────────────────┘
```

2. Enter the path name for the directory or drive you want to use.

Typical path name:	If your computer has these disks:
C:\QUICKEN5	Hard disk
B:	Two floppy drives, no hard disk

$ Backing Up a Quicken File

At least once a month (once a week if you use Quicken frequently) you should make a backup copy of each of your Quicken files to guard against accidental loss of data. Quicken does the backup for you in seconds. Back up your data whether you keep data on a hard disk or on floppy disks. This is important insurance because, in the event of a data loss, you can use the copy of the file stored on the backup disk. You might lose data if your hard disk fails or if a floppy disk is damaged.

The first time you back up, we suggest that you make two backup copies of your data and label the disks "Backup Quicken Data 1" and "Backup Quicken Data 2." The second time, back up only to disk 1. The next week, back up to disk 2. Alternate the backup disks from then on. If you follow this plan and a problem develops while you are making your backup copy, you can still use the data on the other backup disk.

The first time you make a backup copy, you will need two blank, formatted floppy disks. Be sure to have them on hand before you begin.

Quicken will warn you if there's not enough room on the backup disk, and will allow you to insert a different disk with more room. Alternately, you can choose to back up the file to multiple disks. If you do this, you must have enough formatted disks ready before starting the backup. Be sure to use Restore File (see page 461) if you ever need to use the backup data from multiple disks; you cannot simply copy it from the backup disks.

You can format disks from within Quicken.

If you have at least 512K RAM, you don't have to exit Quicken to format a floppy disk. Go to the register and select Use DOS from the Activities menu. Then use the DOS FORMAT command. To return to Quicken after using DOS, type EXIT at the DOS prompt.

When you back up a Quicken file, Quicken copies all the accounts in that file to a new file on another disk. You can back up any file from the File Activities menu. Or you can back up the current file at any time from the Print/Acct menu.

To back up the current file:

Quick Keys:
At the Main Menu,
press Ctrl-B (back up)
or Ctrl-E (back up and
exit) to back up the
current file.

1. At the register or the Write Checks screen, choose Back Up File from the Print/Acct pulldown menu.

2. Follow the onscreen prompts to insert your backup disk in a drive. If you have two or more drives, Quicken asks you to type the letter of that drive.

3. Press Enter.

    Quicken makes a backup copy of all the accounts in the current file.

Quick backups to a hard disk or network

If you have a hard disk and type the letter of the hard disk at step 2, Quicken allows you to specify the path to back up to. This feature allows you to make quick backups to a hard disk or to a network.

To back up any file:

1. Starting at the Main Menu:
    a. Choose Set Preferences.
    b. Choose File Activities.
    c. Choose Back Up File.

2. Follow the onscreen prompts to insert your backup disk in a drive. If you have two floppy drives, Quicken will ask you to type the letter of that drive.

    Quicken displays the Select File to Back Up window.

3. Use the up and down arrow keys to select the file you want to back up, and press Enter.

    Quicken backs up the file. Store your backup disk in a safe place.

Setting the Backup Reminder Frequency

Because backing up your Quicken data is an important part of using Quicken, the program can remind you to back up your data at regular intervals.

You can tell Quicken how often you want to be reminded. You do this for each file separately, and can enter a different frequency for each file if you want. You might choose to be reminded weekly, or even daily, for a file you use every day, and only monthly for a file you use infrequently.

To set the frequency of the backup reminder:

1. First, make sure the file you want to back up is the current one. (Choose the file you want to back up at the Select/Set Up File window, if you need to.)

2. Starting at the Main Menu:

   a. Choose Set Preferences.

   b. Choose File Activities.

   c. Choose Set Backup Frequency.

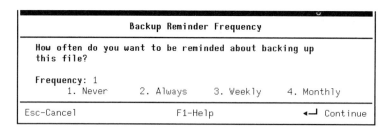

```
                      Backup Reminder Frequency

     How often do you want to be reminded about backing up
     this file?

     Frequency: 1
          1. Never      2. Always     3. Weekly     4. Monthly

     Esc-Cancel                   F1-Help                ◄┘ Continue
```

3. If you do not want to be reminded about making backups, enter 1. Otherwise, choose Always, Weekly, or Monthly.

   "Always" means you will be reminded every time you run Quicken, even if this is several times a day (unless you don't change any data in the file). If you use Quicken only once a week or less often, you can still choose Always as the frequency. Quicken then reminds you to make backups each time you run Quicken. (You do not see a reminder if you do not run Quicken.)

   The reminder frequency you enter applies to the current file only.

Each time you make a backup of this file, Quicken remembers the date you made the backup. If the time period you chose expires, Quicken displays this message when you leave the file or try to exit from Quicken:

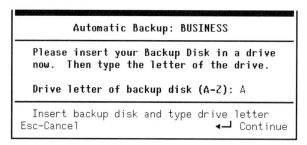

```
           Automatic Backup: BUSINESS

     Please insert your Backup Disk in a drive
     now.  Then type the letter of the drive.

     Drive letter of backup disk (A-Z): A

       Insert backup disk and type drive letter
     Esc-Cancel                      ◄┘ Continue
```

Follow the instructions in the message to make a backup immediately, or press Esc to cancel the message.

Note: Quicken reminds you to make a backup only if you have changed the data in the file. If you haven't made any changes to the file since the last backup, you won't see a reminder.

Restoring a Quicken File

If you are a floppy disk user, you'll never need to restore files. If your data disk is damaged or lost, start using your backup disk.

If you are a hard disk user, you'll need to restore files if your hard disk "crashes." In this event, first reinstall Quicken, following the instructions in "Installing Quicken on a Hard Disk" on page 2. Then restore your files using the following steps.

To restore your file data:

1. Starting at the Main Menu:
   a. Choose Set Preferences.
   b. Choose File Activities.
   c. Choose Restore File.

   The "Select drive to restore from" window appears.

   To restore from a hard disk directory, type C (or the letter of the hard disk drive) and press Enter. Quicken then asks you to specify a directory to restore from.

2. Follow the onscreen prompts to insert your backup disk in a drive and select the file to restore.

   Quicken restores the accounts in the file contained on the backup disk to your hard disk. If your backup is contained on multiple disks, Quicken prompts you to change disks as necessary.

   Note: If Quicken finds a file with the same name on the hard disk, it asks you to confirm that it is OK to overwrite the file on the hard disk. "Overwrite" means that Quicken will erase the file from the hard disk and replace it with a copy from the backup disk.

$ Deleting Quicken Files

Deleting a Quicken file will permanently remove all of the records in that file from your disk. Once records are removed, there is no way to get your account data back except by using your backup disk. Be certain you want to delete a file before doing so.

To delete a Quicken file:

1. Starting at the Main Menu:
   a. Choose Set Preferences.
   b. Choose File Activities.
   c. Choose Select/Set Up File.

2. In the list of files that appears, use the up and down arrow keys to select the file you want to delete, and press Ctrl-D.

   Quicken warns that you are about to permanently remove this file from your records.

3. If you are certain you do want to delete the file, type **Yes** and press Enter.

   Quicken removes the file from your records.

 Renaming Quicken Files

Renaming a file changes the names of the DOS files that contain your account data.

To rename a file:

1. Starting at the Main Menu:
   a. Choose Set Preferences.
   b. Choose File Activities.
   c. Choose Select/Set Up File.

2. In the list of files that appears, use the up and down arrow keys to select the file you want to rename and press Ctrl-E.

   Quicken displays the Rename a File window.

3. Type a new eight-character DOS filename for the account. (You can type right over the old name displayed in the window.)

4. Press Enter.

   Quicken renames the file. The file's order in the list may change.

 Copying a Quicken File

Quicken lets you copy all or part of a Quicken file. You might want to do this if your floppy data disk becomes full, or if your accountant needs a copy.

When you copy a file, Quicken copies the transactions you specify, the memorized transactions list, the transaction groups list, and the category and transfer list. It also removes unused space, so the new file copy may be a little smaller than the original file even if you specify a date range that includes all transactions.

The original file is not changed in any way.

To copy all or part of a file:

1. First, make sure the file you want to copy is the current one. (Choose the file you want to copy from the list of files, if you need to.)

2. Starting at the Main Menu:
   a. Choose Set Preferences.
   b. Choose File Activities.
   c. Choose Copy File.

3. Fill in the fields in the Copy File window.

    To see what to enter in each field, see "Fields in the Copy File window" below.

4. Press Enter to start copying or F9 to specify the number of accounts in the new file.

    Ordinarily, when you set up a new file, Quicken allows you up to 64 accounts. You may increase this number up to the maximum of 255 before starting to copy the file.

5. If you are copying from and to the same floppy disk drive, Quicken asks you whether you want to copy to a different disk or to the same disk. If you specify a different disk, Quicken prompts you when you need to change disks (for a large file, this can be many times).

    Quicken begins copying the file. The old file that you copied from remains in your records. (You can delete it later if you want.)

6. When the copying process is complete, Quicken gives you the option to continue using your original file or start using the new copy. Choose the file you want to work in now.

Fields in the Copy File window

Name of new Quicken file
Enter a DOS filename for the new file (press F1 for rules governing DOS filenames).

Location of new file
Enter the path name showing the drive and directory to receive the copy of the file.

Copy transactions from
Enter the date range of the transactions you want to copy to the new file. For example, to extract only transactions for the year 1991, enter a date range from 1/1/91 to 12/31/91.

Also copy prior uncleared transactions
Tell Quicken whether or not it should also copy prior uncleared transactions by typing Y (for yes) or N (for no).

Prior uncleared transactions are transactions occurring before the date range specified, but which aren't marked with an X.

Note: If you use Quicken to reconcile bank accounts or credit card accounts, or if you keep track of assets with Quicken, it is important to type Y in response to this question. That way Quicken will include uncleared transactions in the new copy of the file, even when they're not included in the date range specified in this window. However, if you do not use Quicken's reconcile feature or keep track of assets in Quicken, you should type N here. Then the copy of the file will include only transactions in the date range, regardless of their cleared status.

Copy all prior investment transactions
Tell Quicken whether or not it should also copy those investment transactions dated earlier than the "Copy transactions from" date (if you have any). To retain historical data, leave this setting at Y for yes.

Note: This question appears only if you have set up investment accounts.

Copying Data from One File to Another

Although you cannot directly transfer information from one file to another, you can easily do so indirectly by using Quicken's Import and Export features.

These features are primarily used to export data in Quicken accounts for use with other software, and to import data into Quicken from other types of DOS files (see "Exporting and Importing Data" on page 500). However, you can also use them to copy data from one Quicken account to another, in the same or a different file. You can also merge data from two accounts into one account using this method.

If you copy data to a different file, you can include more than just the account transactions. You can also include all the associated data:

- Category and transfer list
- Class list
- Memorized transactions list
- Details of other accounts

Quicken adds this information to the new file. It adds the categories, classes, and memorized transactions to the new file's lists, and then it creates each account that existed in the original file. It does not copy all the transactions in these other accounts; however, these accounts will contain any transfers that were made to or from the copied file. For example, if the account you copy contains transfers to a CASH account, a new CASH account is created in the new file. This new CASH account is empty except for the transfers from the copied account.

In this way, you can use Export and Import to copy an account complete with all its associated data. **Note:** This procedure does not copy budget amounts. To copy budget amounts to a different file, see page 347.

To copy data from one Quicken account to another:

1. Make sure that the account you want to copy data from is the current account. If it is not, use Select Account to make it the current account.

2. At the register or Write Checks screen, select Export from the Print/Acct pulldown menu.

```
┌─────────────────────────────────────────────────────┐
│ ▣▣▣▣▣▣▣▣▣▣▣▣▣▣▣▣▣▣▣▣▣▣▣▣▣▣▣▣▣▣▣▣▣▣▣▣▣▣▣▣▣▣ │
│            Export Transactions to QIF file            │
│                                                       │
│                                                       │
│  DOS File:                                            │
│  (file name or full path)                             │
│                                                       │
│  Export transactions from:  1/ 1/92 to:  3/24/92      │
│                                                       │
│  Export Transactions (Y/N): Y                         │
│  Export Categories and Classes (Y/N): Y               │
│  Export Accounts (Y/N): N                             │
│  Export Memorized Transactions (Y/N): N               │
│                                                       │
│  Esc-Cancel          F1-Help         ◄┘ Continue      │
└─────────────────────────────────────────────────────┘
```

3. Enter the name of a DOS file to receive the exported data. You can include the drive and directory if you want.

   You don't have to give the file any particular extension; however, we recommend that you give it the extension .QIF, so you will remember what the file is.

4. Enter the starting and ending dates of the transactions to be exported.

   If you accept the dates Quicken fills in, the export file will contain all the current year's transactions.

5. Choose what should be exported: the transaction data, the category and class lists, the account list, or the memorized transactions list. Enter Y to include each of these.

   If you enter Y in the Export Accounts field, Quicken includes the details of the other accounts in the current file, so that it can recreate the accounts in the new file.

   Quicken begins exporting the data, automatically creating a QIF file. A QIF file has data in the Quicken Interchange Format described in "ASCII File Format (QIF)" on page 501.

6. After the data has been exported, change to the file and account into which you want to copy the data. Set up the account if necessary.

7. Choose Import from the Print/Acct menu.

8. At the Import window, enter the name of the DOS file (including the extension) that contains the data. Include the drive and directory path if necessary.

9. In the Import... fields, specify what you want to import from the QIF file.

10. If you enter Y for Import Transactions, also indicate whether you want special handling for transfers.

    Type Y in the Special handling field only if you have exported from a number of Quicken accounts in the same file and will be using Import to recreate all the transactions. By typing Y, you instruct Quicken to omit transfer transactions that do not increase your net worth. This special handling helps prevent duplicate transfer transactions when you import both the "to" and the "from" accounts involved with transfers.

11. Press Ctrl-Enter.

    Quicken may display an extra message at this point. If you chose to export accounts and you are now in an account with a different name from the account you exported from, Quicken asks you if you want to remain in the currently selected account or create a new account with the same name as the account you are copying from.

12. Select which account is to contain the copied data. If this is the account you are currently in, type 2.

    Caution: If you are in the same file as the original account, you should definitely remain in the current account; otherwise, transactions will be duplicated in the original account.

    Quicken now imports the data into the selected account.

    If you did not choose to copy the category list, Quicken asks you to add each new category to the new account's category list, or select a different category.

If you copied the account list, Quicken also creates the other accounts in the new file if they don't already exist, and makes the transfers to them from the current account. Press Ctrl-A to see these accounts. Some of them may be empty, if no transfers to them were copied over; you can delete unwanted accounts.

A quick way to set up a new file with your existing lists

The preceding procedure gives you a quick way to set up your existing lists of categories, classes, accounts, and memorized transactions for a new file. By using Export and Import to copy everything *except* the transactions from an existing file, you save yourself the trouble of creating these lists. After copying them, you can make changes to the lists at any time.

$ Year-End Procedures

Many people think that you need to "close out your accounts" before continuing to the new year. "Closing out accounts" is required by many accounting packages and means saving all information about completed transactions from the previous year in one file, and continuing the new year with only those transactions that are still open. Quicken does not require you to close out your accounts at the end of a year, or at the close of any fiscal period.

In fact, if you do close out a Quicken file, you forgo easy access to reports covering several years. In many cases, the only reason people close out a year is to protect their data from changes. If you're worried about protecting your data, you can always protect a range of transaction dates with a password (see "Setting a Transaction Password" on page 440). Also, by regularly backing up your data as described on page 458, you needn't worry about losing valuable data.

However, if you want to close a file, Quicken offers two options, depending on how you want to organize your historic files: Archive, and Start New Year. Read about both options, and then decide which one is best for you.

Archiving

The Archive option makes a copy of all transactions in the current file dated earlier than the current year. You give the file copy its own name (for example HOME91) and this copy is for archive only. The current file is untouched and remains your working file—it still contains all your past transactions.

If you select the Archive option once a year, you will eventually have a series of archive files, each containing all transactions up to the end of a certain year. You can give these archive files appropriate names, for example:

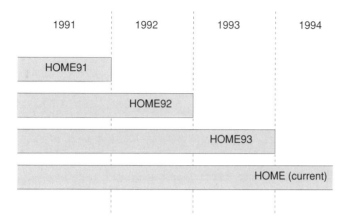

To archive the previous year's transactions:

1. Starting at the Main Menu:

    a. Choose Set Preferences.

    b. Choose File Activities.

    c. Choose Year End.

    Quicken displays the Year End window.

2. In the Year End window, enter 1 for Archive.

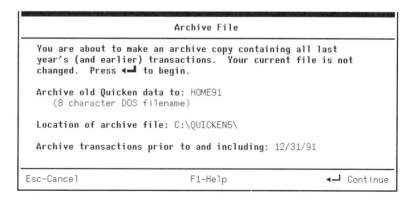

In the Archive File window, Quicken fills in the correct details to archive your file with last year's date appended to the name (for example, HOME91). You can change any of these entries if you want.

3. Change any entries you want in the Archive File window, then press Ctrl-Enter.

Quicken creates the archive file and copies the historic transactions to it. When the copy is finished, Quicken asks you which file you would like to use, the current file or the archive file.

The archive file appears in your list of files.

Making your archives read-only

You should never need to make changes to an archive file. To ensure that nobody does, you can set a transaction password that lets you view (or "read") the file but not make changes without entering the password. Or you can set a file password so that nobody else can view the file or make changes to it. See "Password Settings" on page 439.

Starting a New Year

You can start a new file each year, so that your current file contains only this year's transactions. The Start New Year option copies the entire current file to an archive file, and then deletes any transactions in the current file that are not of the current year. In other words, your current file will go back no further than January 1 of this year. However, investment transactions and uncleared transactions are not deleted, regardless of how old they are.

If you select the Start New Year option at the beginning of each year, you will eventually have a series of archived files, each containing the transactions for just one year. For example:

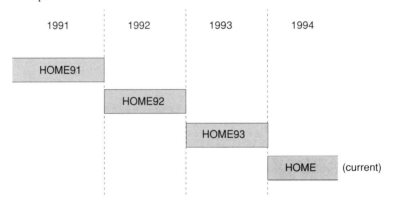

Note: If you want to start using this method part way through a year, run Archive first and then the Start New Year option. Archive creates an archive file without any of the current year's transactions, and then Start New Year creates a current file with **only** this year's transactions. Start New Year also creates an intermediate file containing all transactions—you can delete this file.

To begin a new file for the current year:

1. Starting at the Main Menu:

    a. Choose Set Preferences.

    b. Choose File Activities.

    c. Choose Year End.

    Quicken displays the Year End window.

2. In the Year End window, enter 2 for Start New Year.

3. In the Start New Year window, enter a name for the archive file (for example, you could enter HOME91). Do not include an extension.

4. If you want, change the start date and press Enter.

    Quicken now copies all transactions to the archive file. It then deletes all transactions in the current file earlier than the "older than" date. However, it does not delete any investment transactions nor any uncleared transactions. It then asks if you want to use the current file or the archived copy.

    The archived copy appears in your list of files.

    If you want to protect your archive file from changes, you can set a password for it. See the read-only tip on page 468.

Appendix A

Ordering Checks and Other Intuit Products

This appendix describes Intuit products that work integrally with Quicken to help you complete your financial chores faster and with far greater ease:

- Intuit offers a complete line of checks and envelopes to meet both personal and business needs.

- If you have a payroll, you'll want to consider QuickPay, a software product that works with Quicken to calculate deductions and keep employee records.

- For those who want full customized reports or spreadsheets, the Quicken Transfer Utility will transport your data to Lotus-compatible spreadsheets without additional data management.

The Intuit Supplies Catalog is the best place to learn about Intuit products because it has pictures, more information, and an order form. This appendix answers some common questions about our products. If you have a further question about checks or if you no longer have the catalog, you can call **1-800-624-8742**, Monday through Friday, between 7 am and 5 pm Pacific Time.

To place an order, use the order form in the catalog or select Order Supplies from Quicken's Activities menu in the register to print an order form on your printer.

$ Intuit Checks

The only way to take full advantage of Quicken is to allow the system to print your checks. After all, the system already does most of the work to prepare checks. Why duplicate work by writing checks by hand when printing is so easy? You will save hours of valuable time, avoid clerical errors, and prevent unnecessary financial hassle every month.

Intuit offers checks for continuous-paper printers and sheet-fed printers such as laser and inkjet printers. With Intuit's patented automatic alignment system, you can easily align checks in any continuous printer.

Intuit's Three-Point Guarantee

All Intuit checks are triple guaranteed. We guarantee that:

1. Your checks will be accepted by your bank.

2. Your checks will work with your printer.

3. Your check order will be printed error-free exactly as you submitted it.

If we fail to meet these three conditions, please call right away. We will quickly replace your order or refund your money, whichever you prefer.

Why should I print checks with Quicken?

You should print checks with Quicken for two reasons:

1. Using Intuit checks in conjunction with Quicken will save you the maximum amount of time. Once you've entered your data into the program, you can press a key to print checks in just seconds.

2. Checks printed with Quicken are legible and attractive, which will help you look more organized and professional.

Is it OK to order checks from Intuit rather than from my bank?

ABSOLUTELY. Intuit checks are guaranteed to be accepted EVERYWHERE your checks are accepted now. They're printed to the exacting standards of the American Banking Association and are pre-approved by all banks, savings and loans, credit unions, and brokers across the U.S. and Canada.

How do I write checks away from home?

For checks you might write away from home, such as at the grocery store, just use the paper checks you already have or handwrite a Quicken check. Then the next time you use Quicken, simply enter the transactions into your Quicken check register. When you order your Intuit checks, indicate the starting number to be considerably greater than your personal check numbers. That way, you avoid any confusion or possible duplication of numbers.

For example, if your personal check whose numbers are in the 1000 range, begin your Intuit checks at 3001.

Is having two sets of check numbers a problem?

NO. Quicken can easily manage two sets of check numbers in one account. Moreover, the bank has no concerns about which numbers you use on your checks. Check numbers are for your own records.

Should I have the check number printed on my Intuit checks?

YES. Check numbers are printed with magnetic ink along the bottom of the check where they can be electronically read. When you place a stop payment on a check, the bank's automated equipment reads the magnetic check numbers to find and stop payment on the requested check. Some people have requested that check numbers not be printed on checks to avoid problems in case a check is misprinted in their printer. However, with Quicken's patented automatic alignment system for continuous printers, misprints are minimized.

Where do I get Intuit checks?

Order Intuit checks directly from us. The enclosed Intuit Checks Catalog gives you a complete description of the available check styles and colors. We've enclosed an order form for your convenience. If you need more order forms, Quicken can print them for you. Just select Order Supplies from the Activities menu in Write Checks. Order today and Intuit checks will be in your hands in less than three weeks. For faster service, FAX your order to Intuit at **(415) 322-1597**. If you have questions, call **1-800-624-8742** between 7 am and 5 pm Pacific Time.

Logo Service

Intuit has a selection of hundreds of standard logos that can be printed FREE on your Intuit checks. Just order by number from the catalog. If you want a custom logo, enclose black-and-white, camera-ready artwork with your order. There is a basic one-time $35 set up fee for custom logos. If touchup, typesetting, or rearrangement is required, additional charges may be incurred. Custom logos cannot be ordered by FAX.

More Time-Saving Products

Intuit Double-Window Envelopes

Window envelopes save even more time by eliminating hand addressing of envelopes. Each envelope has two windows. The top one shows the return address printed on the check and the lower shows the mailing address that Quicken prints on the check for you. All you do is sign the check, drop it in the envelope with a stamp, and you're done.

Forms Leaders

Forms Leaders prevent wasted checks. If you have a continuous printer, you need a forms Leader if the tractor feed is above the print head and cannot print on the first check. If you have an inkjet printer, you need an InkJet Forms Leader if you are using standard, 3-to-a-page laser checks and want to print partial sheets.

Deposit Slips

Intuit deposit slips are preprinted with your account number and name and address to save you time. They are available in 2 books of 100 each. When ordering, be sure to enclose one of your current deposit slips.

Endorsement and Return-Address Stamps

To reduce the time it takes to endorse checks and write addresses, use Intuit's endorsement and return-address stamps. These pre-inked stamps are good for over 25,000 impressions. They measure 2 3/8-inches x 3/4-inch, with plenty of space for 5 imprinted lines.

To ensure accuracy when ordering an endorsement stamp, enclose a voided sample check from your checking account.

Payroll with QuickPay and Quicken

QuickPay is the easiest and quickest way to process your payroll. What was once a long and tedious task now requires just a few keystrokes. QuickPay works with Quicken to calculate deductions and keep employee records.

What QuickPay and Quicken Together Can Do for You:

- Calculate gross wages each pay period
- Calculate Federal, state, and local taxes for the United States of America, including the District of Columbia and Puerto Rico. (Sorry, the QuickPay program does not calculate taxes for Guam or the Virgin Islands.)
- Calculate any additional taxes or deductions you specify
- Write payroll checks
- Track your company's liabilities to the government
- Update your Quicken accounts
- Record employee details such as pay and commission rates, social security number, tax exemptions
- Generate payroll reports to help you fill in your tax forms

QuickPay's Special Features:

- Handles all kinds of compensation: salary, hourly, commission, or a combination
- Allows you to specify up to six taxes or deductions in addition to all the standard ones, to apply to all employees or to individuals

- Tracks company loan repayments, 401(k) deductions, tips, union dues, bonuses, car expenses, and many other nonstandard payroll items

- Pays employees daily, weekly, biweekly, semi-monthly, monthly, quarterly, or yearly

- Accommodates an unlimited number of employees

- Keeps year-to-date totals for all employees

Compatibility

Quicken 5 is compatible with all versions and releases of QuickPay. However, you should be aware of one limitation:

- QuickPay version 1.0 does not offer mouse support.

You may also notice one minor inconsistency when running Quicken with QuickPay 1.0, release 3 or earlier. When you run the Quicken Overview tutorial, a message showing the QuickPay version number may obscure part of the screen. To remove the message, exit from Quicken and start Quicken again without QuickPay.

To see what version and release of QuickPay you have, start Quicken with QuickPay, then press V (for Version) or R (for Release) at the QuickPay Main Menu.

Quicken Transfer Utility

The Quicken Transfer Utility offers great flexibility in financial reporting. It works with any spreadsheet that can read and write Lotus 1-2-3 .WKS or .WK1 files. The Quicken Transfer Utility transfers data from Quicken accounts to spreadsheets in Lotus 1-2-3, or Lotus-compatible programs to provide custom reports without typing. It can automatically update spreadsheets with new financial information from your Quicken register.

Custom Reports

The Quicken Transfer Utility actually reads the spreadsheet format, looks through your Quicken accounts, adds up the transactions, and places the correct information in the corresponding cells in your spreadsheet. It does all this for you in seconds, without additional typing. Using the Transfer Utility, you can also consolidate information from more than one Quicken file.

The Quicken Transfer Utility is ideal for custom profit and loss statements, job and client costing, custom budgets, category "spread" reports, and much more.

Compatibility

The Quicken Transfer Utility works with any spreadsheet that can read and write Lotus .WKS or .WK1 files and requires Lotus 1-2-3 release 1A or higher, or a compatible spreadsheet program such as Lotus Works, Microsoft Excel, Microsoft Works, Quattro, PFS Professional Plan, PFS First Choice Version 2, SuperCalc4, SuperCalc5, Symphony release 1.0 or higher, or VP Planner. It runs on any computer that runs these spreadsheets.

Appendix B

If You've Used an Earlier Version of Quicken

First, a note of thanks to you, an experienced Quicken user, for upgrading to our new version. You are our partner in developing products that lift the burden of financial chores from our customers. This version responds to requests from our users for a number of new features, changes, and enhancements.

You know how to use Quicken, so you don't need to read the manual over again. This appendix highlights the new features of version 5, alerts you to some new ways to work, and tells you which sections of the manual describe these new features.

$ Updating Data from Quicken 3 and 4

To update your data means to allow Quicken to make a copy of your data files* in a format that allows you to take advantage of the new features in Quicken 5. Quicken can very quickly and painlessly make a copy of your files in the new format and leave your original files untouched. If you've been using Quicken 3 or 4 and have installed Quicken 5 as described in Chapter 1, *Before You Begin*, beginning on page 1, you're ready to update your data. If you've been using Quicken 1 or 2, please skip to "If You're Upgrading from Quicken 2 or Quicken 1" on page 479.

Note: The files you create or use with Quicken 5 are incompatible with earlier versions of Quicken. Quicken 5 automatically updates your file (account group) the first time you use it. You can't open the file with an earlier version of Quicken after you use the file with

---

* In Quicken 5, we call the files that contain your data "files." We no longer use the term "account group" to describe the way Quicken stores your accounts.

Quicken 5. (You can go back to your original data file, which is untouched when Quicken 5 makes a copy to update.)

To update your file in Quicken:

1. Start Quicken 5 as described in "Starting Quicken" on page 14.

2. If Quicken displays the Welcome to Quicken window, press Esc and Enter to use Quicken's Main Menu. If Quicken goes right to the Main Menu, continue to step 3.

3. Choose Set Preferences from the Main Menu. (In this manual, "choose" means "select the menu or list item and press Enter.")

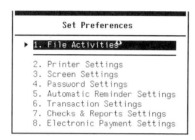

```
                Set Preferences

  ▶ 1. File Activities

    2. Printer Settings
    3. Screen Settings
    4. Password Settings
    5. Automatic Reminder Settings
    6. Transaction Settings
    7. Checks & Reports Settings
    8. Electronic Payment Settings
```

4. Choose File Activities from the Set Preferences menu.

5. Choose Select/Set Up File from the File Activities menu and choose the file you want to update in the Select/Set Up File window. Use the F9 key to change the current directory if necessary.

   Quicken asks whether you want to back up your data before updating.

6. (Optional) We recommend that you choose 1 to back up your data. This backup procedure is the same as that described in "Backing Up a Quicken File" on page 458. If you choose not to back up your data, choose 2 and skip to "Categories in Your Updated File" on page 478.

   Quicken displays the Select Backup Drive window.

7. Insert a backup disk, type the letter of the drive you want to back up to, and then press Enter.

8. Press Enter to continue after Quicken tells you it has backed up the file.

   Quicken makes a copy of your data in the new format and displays the Select Account to Use window when the update process is complete. Choose an account from the list to go to the register for that account. Continue to "Categories in Your Updated File" on page 478.

Categories in Your Updated File

If you used categories in your file (Quicken 3 or Quicken 4 account group), choose Categorize/Transfer from the Shortcuts menu to look at your category list for a moment.

- You might notice asterisks at the beginning of some category descriptions. After you update to Quicken 5, an asterisk in a category description means that the category was not used by any of your transactions. You should delete the categories with asterisks at the beginning of the description, unless you plan to use the categories at a later date. If you want to keep an unused category, delete the asterisk at the beginning of the category description (see "Changing and Deleting Categories" on page 112).

- If you used subcategories in your file, you'll notice that subcategories do not appear as a separate group in the category list after income and expense categories. Subcategories in Quicken 5 always belong to a specific income or expense category, and they are indented in the category list under the category they belong to. When Quicken updated your file, it placed subcategories in the list according to the way you used them in transactions. For example, if you used Insurance as a subcategory for both Auto and Home, you'll find Insurance indented under both Auto and Home in the category list. Quicken treats any unused subcategories as expense categories and indicates that they were never used by placing an asterisk at the beginning of the category description.

$ If You're Upgrading from Quicken 2 or Quicken 1

Quicken 2 Users:

Quicken 5 uses a different file format from Quicken 2. To use your current data files with Quicken 5, you must copy and update them using a program from Intuit.

Note: This process does ***not*** change your data nor any customizing you've done. It simply makes copies of the files in the new format. You still have your original Quicken 2 files.

To receive the data copy and update program and instructions, call the number listed on "Toll-free Product Information and Customer Assistance" on page 530 and ask a customer service representative for the Quicken 2 Copy and Update Utility.

Once you've used Quicken 5 with your data, you cannot go back to Quicken 2 with the updated copy of the data file. You can, of course, return to use the untouched Quicken 2 data files.

Quicken 1 Users:

If you're upgrading from Quicken 1, you need to copy and update your data first for use with Quicken 2 and then for use with Quicken 5. Call the number listed in "Toll-free Product Information and Customer Assistance" on page 530 and identify yourself as a Quicken 1 user who wants to update data to Quicken 5. The representative will be especially glad to help one of our early users.

Summary of New Features

New Features	Page References
Reports	
You can now customize a report to suit your needs *while it is displayed on your screen.*	See the figure on page 163 and "Basic Steps to Customize Reports" on page 168.
In a noninvestment summary or budget report, you can select an amount and use QuickZoom to look at the transactions that make up that amount. From a noninvestment transaction report, you can go to a transaction in the register.	"Investigating Items in Reports" on page 189.
In a noninvestment summary, budget, or account balances report, you can create a more concise report by selecting certain categories to be collapsed into one summary amount rather than shown in detail.	"Collapsing Items in Reports" on page 190.
You can sort a transaction report by account, amount, date, or check number, regardless of how you subtotal it.	"Sort Transactions" on page 177.
Quicken takes advantage of expanded memory (EMS version 4.0) for improved performance and maximum reports.	"Capacity and Memory Usage" on page 492.
You can limit reports to transactions that *contain* the text you type, in addition to the exact match feature of earlier versions.	"Using Match Characters to Limit Searches" on page 186 (see also "7. Exact matches on finds and filters" on page 446).
Categories	
Subcategories in the category list now belong to a specific income or expense category.	Chapter 7, *Using Categories*, beginning on page 101 (see also "Categories in Your Updated File" on page 478).
You can import standard Quicken home or business categories into a file at any time.	"Adding Standard Categories to a File" on page 117.
You can easily merge two categories.	"Merging Two Categories" on page 115.
Taxes	
Quicken 5 can track your financial activity by tax schedule name and line. At tax time, Quicken can print a tax report that groups your transactions by tax schedule and lists which amounts belong on which lines.	Chapter 26, *Preparing Your Income Taxes*, beginning on page 415.

New Features	*Page References*
Quicken can export your tax information to a standard file format compatible with several major tax preparation programs.	"Transferring Data to a Tax Preparation Program" on page 425.
Loans	
Amortization enables you to track loan balances and payments for fixed-rate loans. The automatic payment schedule lets you see each payment split into interest and principal over the life of the loan. A special memorized loan transaction enables you to record payments automatically.	"Amortization" on page 206.
The new Loan calculator lets you do "what if" calculations to see the effect of changing the amount of the loan, the interest rate, or the number of payments.	"Using the Loan Calculator" on page 209.
Mouse Support	
You can use any Microsoft-compatible mouse to work with Quicken 5.	"Using a Mouse with Quicken" on page 26.
Transaction Additions	
The Split Transaction window now accepts percentages and converts them instantly to dollar amounts.	"Entering Percentages in a Split Transaction" on page 70.
You can enter or edit memorized transactions in the Memorized Transactions List window, instead of having to enter or edit a live transaction and memorize it in the register or the Write Checks screen.	"Changing a Memorized Transaction" on page 200.
Press Ctrl-Ins whenever you want to insert a new transaction above the current transaction with the same date as the current transaction. (Ctrl-Ins also works to add a new item to the category list and the class list.)	"To insert a transaction:" on page 66.
Budget Spreadsheet	
The Set Up Budgets screen has special menus you can use to fill in and change your budget. You can also budget amounts for subcategories, if you wish.	Chapter 21, *Budgeting Your Income and Expenses*, beginning on page 341.

New Features	Page References
Tutorials and Assistants	
Quicken 5 has a number of self-running demos and assistants to help you with setting up new files, new accounts, or payroll tracking for a small business. You can also use an assistant to get the sample data file necessary to work through the Quick Tour in Chapter 3.	"Tutorials and Assistants" on page 23.
Expanded Online Help	
Now online Help has bold or colored text that you can use to move quickly to related topics. It also has an expanded index and a new Help Table of Contents.	"Getting Help Information Fast" on page 20.
Investments	
Two new investment actions: MiscInc and ReinvInt.	"List of Investment Actions" on page 281.
More control over the condition for displaying a security in the Update Prices and Market Value screen.	"The Update Prices and Market Value Screen" on page 298.
Support for sixteen security types instead of eight.	"Security Types" on page 284.
Support for accrued interest you pay when you buy a bond.	"Accrued Interest" on page 290.
You can now combine lots for a single security.	"Combining and Displaying Lots" on page 315.
Printing Checks and Reports	
Quicken has many new predefined printer drivers for different printers and print styles.	"Printer Settings" on page 428.
Now you can print checks with the months spelled out in English.	"3. Print months as Jan, Feb... on checks" on page 447.
If you have a laser printer, you can print on three-per-page wallet-size checks.	"Intuit Checks" on page 471.

$ Improved Ways to Work

Improved Ways to Work	Page References
Menus	
The menus you see are the same as those you are used to in earlier versions of Quicken, based on Function keys and numerals. But Quicken 5 has a new menu style in which you press the highlighted letter in a menu item to choose the item. To display a pulldown menu, you press the highlighted letter in combination with the Alt key. If you prefer, you can switch to the new Quicken menu style. Note that the Function keys still work to pull down the new Alt key menus.	"Menu Access" on page 437.
Some Quicken 5 menus and windows have been redesigned for optimum efficiency. Also, the Report screen and Budget Setup screen each have special menus to handle your reporting and budgeting needs.	Appendix C, *Quicken Menus*, beginning on page 485.
When you select a command on a menu or the name of a menu on the pulldown menu bar, Quicken displays a description of the selected item at the bottom of the screen.	"Using Quicken's Menus" on page 16.
Data Entry	
New date shortcut keys.	"Date shortcuts" on page 60.
Quote key (' or ") now copies information from the Memo field in one line of the Split Transaction window to the next line.	"Copying Information from One Line to Another" on page 69.
File and Account Activities	
When you have a file name selected in the Select/Set Up File window, you can press F8 to get information about upcoming payments and scheduled transaction groups in that file.	"Choosing a File to Use" on page 456.
You can assign Quick Keys to any nine accounts in the Select Account to Use window. After you assign a Quick Key to an account, you can press Ctrl plus the Quick Key as a shortcut to use that account without going through the Select Account to Use window.	"Selecting an Account to Use" on page 248.

Improved Ways to Work	*Page References*
Automatic reminders for regular backups, and backup to multiple disks.	"Setting the Backup Reminder Frequency" on page 459 and "Backing Up a Quicken File" on page 458.
More flexible and powerful archive procedures.	"Year-End Procedures" on page 466.
Import and export to QIF now transfer more than just transactions. You can import and export accounts, categories, classes, and memorized transactions.	"Exporting and Importing Data" on page 500.
Install and First Time Setup	
The Install program and first time setup take care of more setup and system configuration than ever before.	Chapter 1, *Before You Begin*, beginning on page 1, and "First Time Setup" on page 15.
Finding and Filtering Transactions	
The filters and search features work the same way they always have. But you can have Quicken 5 automatically search for transactions that contain the text you type, rather than trying to find an exact match. Of course, you can always limit a search by using special match characters (= .. ? ~). If you prefer always to find exact matches, or if your memorized reports depend on finding exact matches, you can switch back to the previous search style.	"Using Match Characters to Limit Searches" on page 186 (see also "7. Exact matches on finds and filters" on page 446).

 # Quicken Technical News

Quicken 5 has system requirements similar to Quicken 4:

- DOS 2.0 or later
- 512K RAM or more
- A hard disk OR two floppy disk drives (one of which must be high-density)

Quicken 5 uses slightly more RAM than Quicken 4 (approximately 20% more). If memory becomes a constraint, consider updating your system to DOS 5.0, which takes up 30K less RAM than earlier versions of DOS.

Important: Although Quicken 5 data files are "upwards compatible" with Quicken 3 and 4 data files, the data format is different. When you first select a Quicken 4 file to use in Quicken 5, Quicken updates the file to 5 format. You can then use the file in Quicken 5. However, once the file is updated to the new format, you will never again be able to use it with Quicken 4. (The data file is not "downwards compatible.") See "Updating Data from Quicken 3 and 4" on page 477. You can, of course, use your original Quicken 4 data files with Quicken 4 because the update process does not change the original files in any way, it simply copies them.

Appendix C

Quicken Menus

This appendix contains menu maps to help you find your way around Quicken's many features. You might find these maps useful for several reasons:

- To get a quick overview of features related to your task

- To learn about Quicken 5's new features, if you are used to a previous version of Quicken

- To see how to access a particular feature

- To see where you are in the program

The menus are shown here in the Alt key style. (If you prefer to use the Function key style, see "Menu Access" on page 437 for how to switch between the two styles.)

Quicken Main Menu

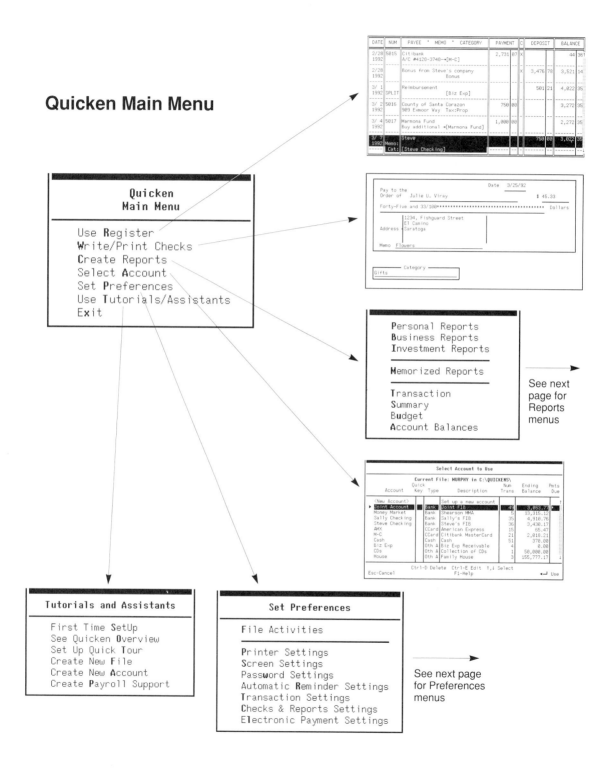

Reports Menus

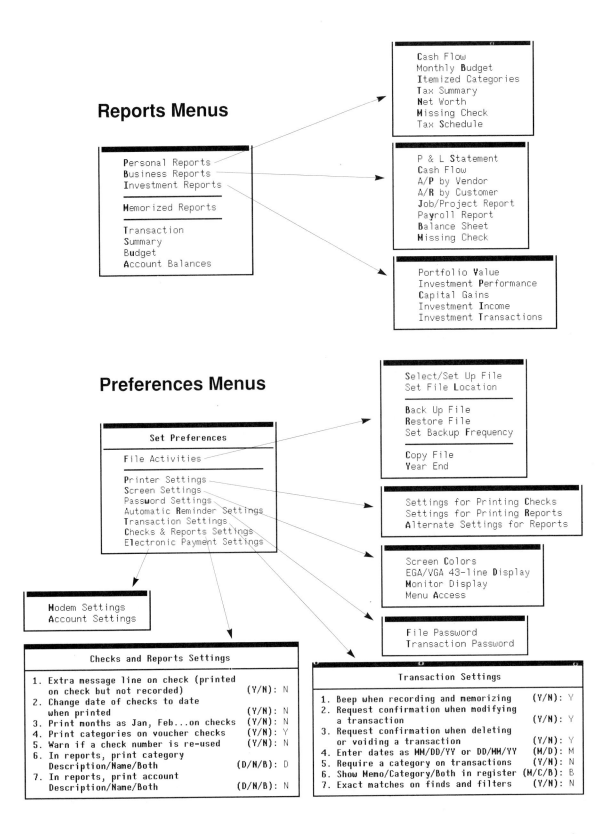

Personal Reports
Business Reports
Investment Reports

Memorized Reports

Transaction
Summary
Budget
Account Balances

Cash Flow
Monthly Budget
Itemized Categories
Tax Summary
Net Worth
Missing Check
Tax Schedule

P & L Statement
Cash Flow
A/P by Vendor
A/R by Customer
Job/Project Report
Payroll Report
Balance Sheet
Missing Check

Portfolio Value
Investment Performance
Capital Gains
Investment Income
Investment Transactions

Preferences Menus

Set Preferences

File Activities

Printer Settings
Screen Settings
Password Settings
Automatic Reminder Settings
Transaction Settings
Checks & Reports Settings
Electronic Payment Settings

Select/Set Up File
Set File Location

Back Up File
Restore File
Set Backup Frequency

Copy File
Year End

Settings for Printing Checks
Settings for Printing Reports
Alternate Settings for Reports

Screen Colors
EGA/VGA 43-line Display
Monitor Display
Menu Access

File Password
Transaction Password

Modem Settings
Account Settings

Checks and Reports Settings

1. Extra message line on check (printed
   on check but not recorded) (Y/N): N
2. Change date of checks to date
   when printed (Y/N): N
3. Print months as Jan, Feb...on checks (Y/N): N
4. Print categories on voucher checks (Y/N): Y
5. Warn if a check number is re-used (Y/N): N
6. In reports, print category
   Description/Name/Both (D/N/B): D
7. In reports, print account
   Description/Name/Both (D/N/B): N

Transaction Settings

1. Beep when recording and memorizing (Y/N): Y
2. Request confirmation when modifying
   a transaction (Y/N): Y
3. Request confirmation when deleting
   or voiding a transaction (Y/N): Y
4. Enter dates as MM/DD/YY or DD/MM/YY (M/D): M
5. Require a category on transactions (Y/N): N
6. Show Memo/Category/Both in register (M/C/B): B
7. Exact matches on finds and filters (Y/N): N

Register and Write Checks Pulldown Menus

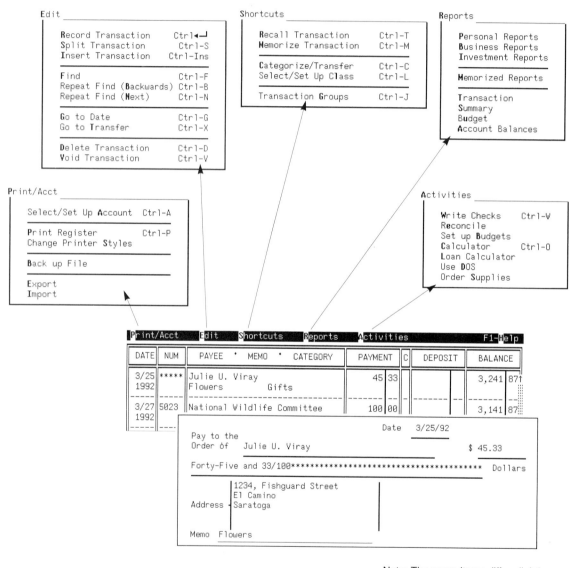

Edit

Record Transaction	Ctrl-⏎
Split Transaction	Ctrl-S
Insert Transaction	Ctrl-Ins
Find	Ctrl-F
Repeat Find (Backwards)	Ctrl-B
Repeat Find (Next)	Ctrl-N
Go to Date	Ctrl-G
Go to Transfer	Ctrl-X
Delete Transaction	Ctrl-D
Void Transaction	Ctrl-V

Shortcuts

Recall Transaction	Ctrl-T
Memorize Transaction	Ctrl-M
Categorize/Transfer	Ctrl-C
Select/Set Up Class	Ctrl-L
Transaction Groups	Ctrl-J

Reports

Personal Reports
Business Reports
Investment Reports

Memorized Reports

Transaction
Summary
Budget
Account Balances

Print/Acct

Select/Set Up Account	Ctrl-A
Print Register	Ctrl-P
Change Printer Styles	
Back up File	
Export	
Import	

Activities

Write Checks	Ctrl-W
Reconcile	
Set up Budgets	
Calculator	Ctrl-O
Loan Calculator	
Use DOS	
Order Supplies	

Print/Acct	Edit	Shortcuts	Reports	Activities	F1-Help

DATE	NUM	PAYEE * MEMO * CATEGORY	PAYMENT	C	DEPOSIT	BALANCE
3/25 1992	*****	Julie U. Viray Flowers Gifts	45 33			3,241 87↑
3/27 1992	5023	National Wildlife Committee	100 00			3,141 87

Date   3/25/92

Pay to the
Order of   Julie U. Viray $ 45.33

Forty-Five and 33/100*************************************** Dollars

Address   1234, Fishguard Street
          El Camino
          Saratoga

Memo Flowers

Note: The menu items differ slightly
for investment accounts.

Quicken adds some items to the
menus if you use the account with
CheckFree.

Report Pulldown Menus

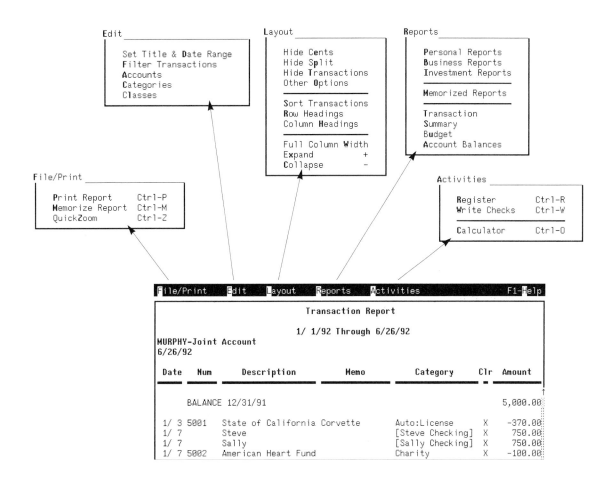

Budget Pulldown Menus

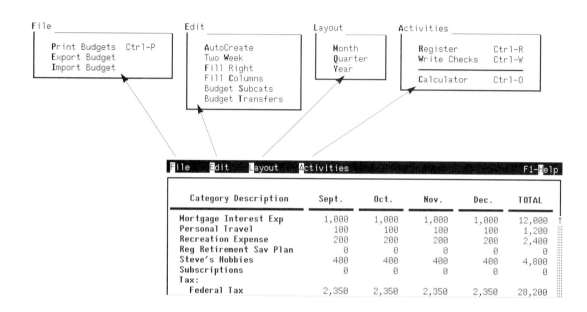

Update Prices Pulldown Menus
(Investment accounts)

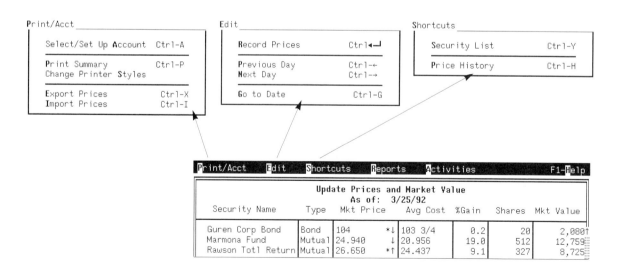

Appendix D

Technical Information

$ Installation on a Hard Disk

To install Quicken on your hard disk, use the automatic installation procedure described in "Installing Quicken on a Hard Disk" on page 2.

Installing Quicken on your hard disk does several things:

- It creates a directory called QUICKEN5 (or the name you specify) on your hard disk.

- It copies the file data from the Quicken Install disk(s) to the directory on the hard disk (other than the Install program itself, which is not copied). This is not a simple copy function. The data is stored on the Quicken Install disk(s) in a compressed format. Installing Quicken restores the files to their executable form before writing the data to your hard disk.

- It creates a batch file called Q.BAT to run Quicken. If there is already a file named Q.BAT, the old one is renamed QOLD.BAT.

- It adds a new line to the end of your AUTOEXEC.BAT file containing the command to run the Billminder program, which will check whether you have any checks to print or transaction groups due. The old AUTOEXEC.BAT file is renamed AUTOEXEC.OLD.

- It modifies or creates a file called CONFIG.SYS to set BUFFERS=16 and FILES=20, if these parameters haven't already been set. It renames the old CONFIG.SYS file, if there is one, to CONFIG.OLD.

  The install program does not lower the buffer and file settings if they are already set higher. If another program set these at lower values, that program will still run with Quicken's higher settings.

- The install program passes the settings for your printer brand and model on to a Quicken configuration file named Q.CFG, which is created the first time you run Quicken. (If you already have a Q.CFG file, your old printer settings do not change.)

Note: If you install Quicken in an already existing directory, your existing data files (that is, your account transactions and so on) are not affected in any way by the installation.

The changes to CONFIG.SYS should improve the performance of your system. The changes to your AUTOEXEC.BAT file activate Billminder, which reminds you of bills that are due whenever you start up your computer. You can turn Billminder off after starting Quicken if you want: see "Automatic Reminder Settings" on page 443. Or, to remove Billminder, copy AUTOEXEC.OLD to AUTOEXEC.BAT. Or use your word processor to remove the Billminder line from your AUTOEXEC.BAT file. (See "Billminder and AUTOEXEC.BAT" on page 442 for details of the Billminder line.)

If your AUTOEXEC.BAT or CONFIG.SYS file is write-protected, the install program does not modify it. Instead you see the message "Your file is write-protected." If this happens, you may need to modify the file yourself as described above.

Don't copy, install.

Quicken is not copy protected, and has no special requirements for the location of its program and data files. It is possible to copy all the files from the install disks directly to your hard disk. However, if you do this, the first time you try to run Quicken you will see a message telling you that you must install first. There is no benefit from copying files, and you will have unnecesary files taking up space on your hard disk.

Capacity and Memory Usage

Quicken's design permits up to 65,535 transactions in a file. This is the total for all the accounts in the file. Because of memory constraints, there's a limit of about 30,000 transactions for any single account. A typical home user will generate from 200 to 1000 transactions per year. Small business users will typically have 300 to 3000 transactions per year.

A regular 5.25-inch floppy disk (360K) has room for about 2500 transactions. A 720K 3.5-inch disk will hold about 5000.

On a hard-disk PC, the number of items you can work with in a single account depends mainly on the amount of memory you have. Quicken requires a minimum of about 300K free plus 16 bytes per transaction. Thus, if you have a 512K machine, and DOS occupies 60K, you will have room for approximately 9,728 transactions per account according to this equation:

$$9,728 = \frac{(512 - 60 - 300) \times 1024}{16} \text{ bytes}$$

The maximum number of memorized transactions, categories, classes, securities, and prices depends on the memory you have. They share the same space, so the fewer of one you have, the more of the other will fit. On a PC with at least 512K of memory, you should have room for at least 325 memorized transactions and at least 1100 categories/classes.

The amount of RAM installed in your PC can also affect the length and complexity of reports you are able to generate. If you request a long and complex report, you may see a message indicating that you do not have enough memory to generate the report. If so, try again with a narrower date range, or restrict the report to fewer transactions. Or subtotal so there are fewer subtotals. If possible, unload any memory-resident programs that may be occupying RAM. Finally, you may wish to add additional RAM to your PC. See also "Not enough memory" on page 528.

If your computer has expanded memory, Quicken uses the expanded memory for overlays and for reports.

$ Program and Help Files

The Quicken install disks contain these files:

INSTALL.EXE	- Installation program
Q.COM	- Program to ensure Quicken is installed correctly
INSTALL.PDM	- Installation program for DeskMate
DESKTOPD.CFG	- Configuration file for installing Quicken in DeskMate

They also contain these files, most of which are in compressed format (see the next page for a list and description of each file in your Quicken directory after installation):

Q51.CMP	~SAMPLE.CDI
Q52.CMP	~SAMPLE.CDT
QHLP.CMP	~SAMPLE.CMT
BILL.CMP	~SAMPLE.CNX
HOME.CMP	Q.ICO
BUSINESS.QIF	Q.PIF
PRINTER2.CMP	QCHECKS.CMP
ASSIST.CMP	TAX.CMP

After installation, your Quicken directory contains these files:

Q.EXE	The Quicken program
Q.HLP	Help file
INSTALL.CFG	First time setup and configuration information
ASSIST.SRC	Text for the tutorials and assistants
TAX.SCD	Tax form information
QCHECKS.DOC	Blank check order form in compressed format
PRINTER2.DAT	Predefined printer setup
BILLMIND.EXE	Program to check for Quicken tasks that are due
HOME.QIF	List of standard home categories
BUSINESS.QIF	List of standard business categories
~SAMPLE.ZDI	
~SAMPLE.ZDT	
~SAMPLE.ZMT	Sample data for the Quick Tour (write-protected format)
~SAMPLE.ZNX	
Q.ICO	Icon file for Quicken running under Windows
Q.PIF	Program file for Quicken running under Windows

These files are not installed on floppy-only systems.

These files occupy approximately 1.2 megabytes of disk space.

When you use Quicken, it creates these files:

In the directory where you keep Q.EXE (usually the \QUICKEN5 directory):

Q.CFG	Configuration/setup information

In the work directory or directories where you keep your data:

Q3.DIR	List of file descriptions/check due dates
filename.QDT	Data file
filename.QNX	Indexes to data file
filename.QMT	Memorized list file
filename.QDI	Dictionary file containing addresses of unprinted checks and memos in split transactions

One of each for each Quicken file

Note: The .QNX index file ("speedup" file) is dispensable. If it is erased or becomes unsynchronized with the data file (for example, if you turn off the computer before exiting Quicken), Quicken automatically regenerates the index file when it is needed. You can also force Quicken to rebuild it by selecting the file at the Select/Set Up File window and pressing Ctrl-Z. Under some circumstances, this procedure can help you to recover a damaged file. (Be sure to make a backup of your files before trying this procedure.)

$ Floppy Disk Information

If you do not have a hard disk, you must have two floppy disk drives, at least one of which must be high-density (5.25-inch 1.2-megabyte or 3.5-inch 1.44-megabyte). You install

Quicken on a high-density disk (your program disk). You keep your data on a data disk in the other drive.

> **Do not remove the program disk from the drive while running Quicken.**
>
> Always keep the Quicken program disk in the drive until you have exited the program. Removing the disk while Quicken is running could cause the program to stop and could lead to loss of data.

If you have a hard disk, we recommend you install Quicken on your hard disk and run it from there. Quicken 5 runs faster and more efficiently on a hard disk. If you wish, you can keep your data on a floppy disk instead of the hard disk. (See "Changing Where Quicken Looks for Data" on page 457.)

Formatting a Floppy Disk

Before you can install Quicken or save data on a floppy disk, you must format the disk.

- The disk for the Quicken program must be a high-density disk that fits your high-density drive.

  - If you plan to install Quicken on a 3.5-inch disk, we recommend you format it as a bootable (system) disk. Then you can use that disk to start your computer and to run Quicken.

  - If you plan to install Quicken on a 5.25-inch disk, format it as a nonbootable disk. There is not enough disk space for the additional files that make a disk bootable.

- The disk for your data should be appropriate for your other drive (either high or regular density). Format it as a nonbootable disk.

To format a floppy disk:

1. Put a blank disk in the drive of the same size and density. (If the drives are identical, put it in Drive B.)

2. Start up your computer with a DOS disk in the other drive.

   If your blank disk is in Drive A, type A instead of B in the following step.

3. To format a nonbootable disk, type format B: and press Enter.

   OR

   To format a bootable disk, type format B:/S and press Enter.

4. When DOS asks if you want to format another disk, type N and press Enter.

If You Run Out of Disk Space

Eventually your data disk will become full. Use Quicken's file operations to reorganize your data. First, use Back Up File to make a backup of your data disk. Then have a blank, formatted disk ready to be used as a data disk.

- If your data disk contains only one file, use Start New Year to create a new, smaller copy containing only transactions you currently need. Change disks as directed to put the new file on the blank, formatted disk. Put away the original disk as an archive.

    OR

    Use Copy File to copy the file to the blank, formatted disk. The copy should be somewhat smaller than the original. Use the copy from now on, and put away the original disk as an archive. Eventually, you will need to use Start New Year to divide the file up.

- If your data disk contains several files, use Copy File to copy all active files to the blank, formatted disk. The copies should be somewhat smaller than the originals. Use the new disk from now on, and put away the original disk as an archive.

    OR

    Use Copy File to copy only some of your active files to the blank, formatted disk. That is, divide your files between two or more data disks. Delete the copied files from the original disk. You then have room for more data on all your data disks.

For details about the Back Up File, Start New Year, and Copy File operations see Chapter 28, *Managing Files*, beginning on page 449.

Caution against using Quicken on a one-floppy system

We do not recommend that you use Quicken 5 on a system with only one floppy disk drive and no hard disk. While it is possible to run Quicken 5, disk space limitations make it impractical over a long period. You cannot use Quicken's Copy File or Back Up File features on a one-floppy system.

$ Starting Quicken with Options

You start Quicken by typing Q at the DOS prompt (called the "command line"), as explained in "Starting Quicken" on page 14.

Quicken also provides several options you can type after Q on the command line to start Quicken in special ways:

- To choose a particular account, file, and/or Main Menu item at the same time you start the program

- To specify which of two methods of menu access you prefer

- To specify which of two definitions of certain keystrokes you prefer

- To tell Quicken not to use expanded memory even if it is present

Starting with a Particular Account or File

When you start Quicken, you can specify the account and/or file that Quicken 5 loads automatically when you first select the register. You can also specify the Main Menu item you want to use to bypass the Main Menu (this works only for Function key menus).

Type the account's name on the command line. Quicken remembers the file you used last time you worked, so you need to specify a file only if you want to switch files. Next are examples of several combinations you might want to try. You should type a space between the different options in the command.

C:> Q checking	Selects the account named "Checking" in the last file used. If the account name has a space in it, see the next example.
C:> Q "home checking"	Selects the account named "Home Checking" in the last file used. If the account name has a space in it, you must put the name in quotes.
C:> Q checking murphy	Selects the account named "Checking" in the MURPHY file.
C:> Q checking C:\accounts\murphy	Chooses the account named "Checking" in the MURPHY file in the directory C:\ACCOUNTS.
C:> Q 1	Starts Quicken and displays the register without first pausing at the Main Menu (Function key menus only).
C:> Q loan 2	Selects the account named "Loan" in the last file used and displays the Write Checks screen without first pausing at the Main Menu (Function key menus only).

Changing the Method of Menu Access

Quicken offers two methods of selecting menu items. You can choose either Alt key menus or Function key menus. The two different methods are compared on page 438. Within Quicken, you can permanently set one method or the other through the Screen Settings menu (see page 439). When starting Quicken, you can switch to the other method just for the one time you run Quicken.

Start Quicken with either of these commands:

Q /A   (Alt key menus)

Q /F   (Function key menus)

The screen examples in this user manual show Alt key menus.

Changing the Key Definitions

You have a choice of two different behaviors for the Home and End keys. Quicken uses the standard key definitions unless you tell it to use the "classic" definitions. (Quicken 3 and earlier versions used the classic key definitions.)

Key	Standard	Classic
Home	Beginning of current field	Top of register
End	End of current field	End of register
Home Home	Beginning of first field of current transaction	Same as Home
End End	End of last field of current transaction	Same as End
Ctrl-Home	Top of register (or press Home 3 times)	Same as Home
Ctrl-End	Bottom of register (or press End 3 times)	Ends Reconcile

With the standard key definition, use Ctrl-F10 to end Reconcile.

If you prefer the classic key definitions, you can use a command line option to start Quicken with these key definitions. After you have used a command line option once, Quicken remembers your preference until you use a command line option to start again. That is, you have to start Quicken only once with an option to get the key definitions you want in future sessions. You can always change to the other definitions by starting with the appropriate option.

Start Quicken with either of these commands:

Q /S   (Standard definitions)

Q /C   (Classic definitions)

The instructions in this user manual use the standard key definitions.

Ignoring Expanded Memory

If your computer has expanded memory, Quicken uses it for overlays and reports. If you don't want Quicken to use the expanded memory, start Quicken with one of the commands below.

You will probably never need to use these options, unless for some reason you have problems with your expanded memory feature.

Q /E1   Do not use expanded memory

Q /E2   Use expanded memory only for overlays

Q /E3   Use expanded memory only for reports

Amortization Formulas

See "Amortization" on page 206 for a description of Quicken's amortization feature. This feature uses the formulas described here to calculate the payments, the principal, and the interest.

If you enter the payment amount, Quicken calculates the principal (the loan amount) as shown here:

$$Principal \ = \ Payment \times \frac{\left[1 - \dfrac{1}{(1+r)^{ny}} \right]}{r}$$

Note: If your loan company uses some other formula to calculate interest rate per period, Quicken's amortization calculations are not accurate.

where n = number of periods per year
y = total years
r = interest rate per period, given by this formula:

$$r \ = \ \frac{Annual \ interest \ rate}{n}$$

Similarly, if you enter the principal, Quicken calculates the payment amount:

$$Payment \ = \ \frac{Principal \times r}{\left[1 - \dfrac{1}{(1+r)^{ny}} \right]}$$

To calculate each line in your payment schedule, Quicken uses the following formulas to base each amount on the principal remaining (as shown in the Balance field on the previous line of the schedule):

$$Interest \ payment \ = \ r \times Remaining \ principal$$

$$Payment \ against \ principal \ = \ Total \ payment - Interest \ payment$$

Exporting and Importing Data

You can export data from a Quicken file to an ASCII file, and import data from an ASCII file into a Quicken file. Both of these capabilities appear as items on the Print/Acct pulldown menu. (The procedure is described on page 464.) The data can be any, or all, of the following:

- Transactions from one account
- Category list and class list
- Account list
- Memorized transaction list

If you import all the above data, you effectively copy an account register complete with all its associated data, including the account list for making transfers.

Budget amounts can be exported or imported separately through the File pulldown menu on the Set Up Budgets screen.

You can also import data from a CheckFree register, to update your Quicken register before you begin using Quicken to transmit payments to CheckFree. (See "Importing CheckFree Data" on page 506.)

The ASCII file has a special format and is called a QIF file, for "Quicken Interchange Format."

Uses for Exporting and Importing

You'll find a number of uses for importing and exporting data. For example, you can:

- Add transactions from another program to your Quicken account or accounts by importing them.

- Transfer information between Quicken accounts on a PC, on a Macintosh, or running under Windows (only transactions can be exported to or imported from Quicken under Windows).

- Consolidate Quicken accounts from different locations. To do this, you export the transactions from a particular register to a QIF file at one location, and then import the transactions to the appropriate register at another location, thus merging the registers. (See "Copying Data from One File to Another" on page 464.)

- Move data from one account to another. For example, suppose you entered a number of transactions in the wrong register. You could then export them from the register and import them into the correct register. (Be sure to delete them from the first register when you have finished.)

- Merge files or change the account type. (See "Copying Data from One File to Another" on page 464.)

- Reconstruct a file's categories, classes, accounts, and memorized transactions in a new file. By using Export and Import to copy everything except the transactions from an existing file, you save yourself the trouble of creating these lists. After copying them over, you can make changes to the lists at any time.

When you export data from a Quicken register, you specify a range of dates. All the transactions in that date range are exported.

ASCII File Format (QIF)

When you export Quicken data, Quicken writes the data to an ASCII file in a specific format. For Quicken to import data from an ASCII file into the Quicken file, the data must be in the same format.

General rules

The format rules for all types of data are given below.

An "entry" can be one complete transaction, account, category, class, or memorized transaction.

* Each item in the entry must appear on a separate line (for example, an amount, a name, or a description).

* A header line identifies the type of data that follows:

Header	Type of data following
!Type:Bank	Bank account transactions
!Type:Cash	Cash account transactions
!Type:CCard	Credit card account transactions
!Type:Oth A	Asset account transactions
!Type:Oth L	Liability account transactions
!Type:Invst	Investment account transactions
!Account	Account list or which account follows
!Type:Cat	Category list
!Type:Class	Class list
!Type:Memorized	Memorized transaction list

* If a file to be imported contains no header line, Quicken treats the data that follows as transaction data.

* If any other !Type is specified when importing, Quicken ignores the data that follows until a valid !Type is found.

* Each entry must end with a ^ symbol.

* Each item begins with a letter that identifies the type of data, followed by the data. The data to include after each header is given on the following pages. The end-of-entry symbol (^) and all items marked with an asterisk (*) are required. All others are optional.

- We recommend that you put list data before transaction data in the QIF file. That way, categories and classes are defined before the transaction data is imported.

- You can add a line to a file to be imported into a Quicken account to force Quicken to give special handling to transfers, regardless of the user setting when the file is imported. (See "Copying Data from One File to Another" on page 464 for the user setting.) Put the following line right after the header line at the top of the file:

!Option:AllXfr

Items for noninvestment accounts

Each item in a bank, cash, credit card, liability, or asset account must begin with a letter that indicates the field for the item in the Quicken register:

D *	Date
T	Amount
C	Cleared Status
N	Num (Check number)
P	Payee
M	Memo
A	Address (up to 5 lines; a sixth line is an optional extra message)
L	Category or Transfer/Class
S	Category/Class in split
E	Memo in split
$	Dollar amount of split
^	End of entry

The order of these items is not important. For additional items in a split, repeat the lines for S, E, and $. The Date item is required in each transaction. If any other item is omitted from a transaction in the ASCII file, Quicken treats it as a blank item.

Items for investment accounts

D *	Date
N *	Action
Y	Security
I	Price
Q	Quantity (Number of shares or split ratio)
T	Transaction amount
C	Cleared status
P	Text on first line for transfers and reminders
M	Memo
O	Commission
L	Account for transfer, or Category
$	Amount transferred
^	End of entry

Note: Securities data cannot be exported or imported.

Items for account information

The account header !Account is used in two places: at the start of an account list, and at the start of a list of transactions to specify which account they belong to.

N *   Name
T *   Type of account
D   Description
L   Credit limit (only for credit card accounts)
/   Statement balance date
$ Statement balance amount
^   End of entry

When importing, Quicken normally displays a menu asking you if you want to use the new account or remain in your current account. Two lines can be included in the QIF file to skip this menu or display it:

!Option:AutoSwitch   Skip the menu: Quicken automatically selects the new account
!Clear:AutoSwitch   Display the menu

When Quicken creates a QIF file, it includes !Option:AutoSwitch before the account list entries and !Clear:AutoSwitch after the account list entries. This allows Quicken to create all the accounts in the list when importing the QIF file. The menu is still displayed.

Items for a category list

N *   Category name:Subcategory name
D   Description
T   Tax-related if included; not tax-related if omitted
I   Income category
E   Expense category
B   Budget amount (only in a Budget Amounts QIF file)
^   End of entry

The entry should specify either I (for Income) or E (for Expense). If no category type is specified, Quicken assumes the category is an Expense category.

Items for a class list

N *   Class name
D   Description
^   End of entry

Items for a memorized transaction list

KC   Check transaction
KD   Deposit transaction
KP   Payment transaction

KI	Investment transaction
KE	Electronic payee transaction
T	Amount
C	Cleared Status
P	Payee
M	Memo
A	Address (up to 5 lines; a sixth line is an optional extra message)
L	Category or Transfer/Class
S	Category/Class in split
E	Memo in split
$	Dollar amount of split
1	Amortization: First payment date
2	Amortization: Total years for loan
3	Amortization: Number of payments already made
4	Amortization: Number of periods per year
5	Amortization: Interest rate (percentage)
^	End of entry

Each entry must end (immediately before the ^ character) with KC, KD, KP, KI, or KE to specify what sort of transaction follows. Apart from this, memorized transaction entries have the same format as regular transaction entries (non-investment accounts) except that no Date or Num field is included. All items are optional. However, if an amortization record is included, all five amortization lines must be included.

Items in a budget amounts QIF file

A QIF file for budget amounts includes two types of data. A header line identifies the type of data that follows:

Header	Type of data following
!Type:Class	Class list
!Type:Cat	Category list

The category and class list items are as shown previously. Up to 12 Budget amount lines can be included in each category list entry. Note that no date information is included.

Example of a QIF File Exported from a Bank Account

The next page shows an example of a QIF file created by Quicken. The file was exported from a checking account and includes, in addition to three transactions, a (short) class list, category list, account list and memorized transaction list.

For convenience, the file is shown divided into two columns. In the actual file, the data consists of just one column.

If you want to see further examples of QIF file format, create some QIF files using Quicken's import and export functions. Then exit from Quicken and use an editor or the DOS command TYPE to view the file contents.

Example of a QIF file

```
!Type:Class
NJob 1
DBeetle Rentals          Class list
^
NJob 4
^
!Type:Cat
NAuto
DCar expenses
T
E
^
NAuto:Service
DCar servicing
E                        Category list
^
NMeals & Enter
E
^
NOffice
DOffice Expenses
T
E
^
!Option:AutoSwitch
!Account
NAmerican Exp
TCCard
L5,000.00
^
NAP
TOth L                   Account list
DAccounts payable
^
NFirst Statewide
TBank
DChecking account
^
!Clear:AutoSwitch
!Account
NFirst Statewide
DChecking account        Account to follow
TBank
^
!Type:Bank
D6/27/91
T0.00
^
D3/19/92
T-59.95                  Account
CX                       transactions
N3115
PRick's Auto
LAuto:Service
^
```

```
D3/19/92
T-27.00
CX
N3116
PRichard Long
MExpense Report
LMeals & Enter
^                        Account
D3/19/92                 transactions
T-161.50                 (continued)
CX
N3117
PType Design
L[AP]
AType Design
A44 Main Street
AValley Springs, CA 95111
A
A
A
^
!Type:Memorized
T-961.15
PChris Jacobson
LPayroll:Gross
SPayroll:Gross
EGross pay
$-1,230.77
S[Payroll-FWH]
EFederal withholding     Memorized
$163.04                  transaction (split
S[Payroll-SWH]           transaction)
EState withholding
$12.42
S[Payroll-FICA]
EFICA withheld
$76.31
S[Payroll-MCARE]
EMedicare withheld
$18.34
KC
^
```

Importing CheckFree Data

> ### Important: Quicken 5 works only with CheckFree 3.0.
>
> Quicken version 5 does not work with versions of CheckFree earlier than 3.0.

If you have been using CheckFree software to make electronic payments, you may wish to import CheckFree register data into Quicken to update your Quicken register one last time before using Quicken from now on to access the CheckFree system. Please read "If You're Currently Using CheckFree Software to Pay Bills" on page 223 before you follow the steps in this section.

When Quicken imports CheckFree data, it simply reads the file where CheckFree stores its register, skipping transactions that match items already in the Quicken register.

Important: If you have set up fixed transactions in CheckFree, you must run the CheckFree software before you import data into Quicken. This step inserts the payments into the CheckFree register so the data is available to Quicken. You don't have to transmit anything to the CheckFree system for this purpose; just start the CheckFree software and exit.

To import CheckFree data:

1. Display the Quicken check register for the bank account you're using to pay bills with CheckFree.

2. Choose Import from the Print/Acct menu.

3. In the File field, type the full path to the directory where the CheckFree program is installed on your computer.

    For example, if you accepted the default installation directory when you installed CheckFree on your hard disk, type: c:\cf in the File field.

    Leave Special handling for transfers set to N.

4. Press Enter to continue.

    Quicken displays the Import from CheckFree File window, which displays a start date for transactions to be imported.

    If this is the first time you have imported CheckFree data, the default start date is 1/1/80. Otherwise, the default is the date of the last time you imported CheckFree data.

5. At the "Import transactions on or after" field, check the start date for importing items. You can change this date if necessary.

    Caution: If you change the start date so that it is later than the last day you imported data, your Quicken register may not contain all electronic transactions. If you do change to a later date than the default, check the Quicken register against the CheckFree register to be sure the Quicken register is complete.

If you reimport CheckFree data using a start date earlier than the last day you imported and if you have changed data, you may get duplicate entries in the Quicken register. Because of Quicken's built-in matching, duplicate transactions are rare, but you should print the CheckFree register and check it against the Quicken register in these circumstances.

6. Press Enter to continue.

Quicken begins importing the CheckFree register. You see each transaction as it is imported.

Each time Quicken encounters a transaction with a category, it checks the Quicken category list.

If the category is in the list, Quicken imports the data about the transaction. If all of your imported transactions have known categories, skip to step 9 below.

If the category is not in the list, Quicken displays a menu so you can choose to set up the category or select a category from the category list. Continue to step 7.

7. Choose Select from Category List.

The category list appears. The category name that most closely resembles the CheckFree category name is highlighted. Use the up and down arrow keys, if necessary, to highlight the category you want and press Enter.

When you have selected a category, Quicken continues importing transactions. If you do not set up or select a category for a transaction that has a CheckFree category, Quicken cannot import the data. Quicken displays a window so you can decide to stop importing data or you can return to the menu to set up or select a category.

8. If you want to stop importing data, at the Quit importing window, press Esc. Press Enter to return to the menu to set up or select a category. If you stop importing data before Quicken has imported it all, your Quicken check register will contain the transactions up to the one at which you stopped. You will need to decide what to do to keep your check register accurate, and that will depend on why you stopped importing. For example, you might want to import again, starting at the date where you stopped importing, and then delete any duplicate transactions.

9. When Quicken has imported all CheckFree data, it displays a message reporting the number of transactions imported.

Now you are ready to set up Quicken to make electronic payments and no longer use the CheckFree software. See "How Quicken Works with CheckFree" on page 225.

Important: After you have used Quicken 5 even once to make payments, Checkfree Corporation will no longer permit you to process payments using CheckFree software. The CheckFree software and Quicken are not designed to be used alternately or concurrently. See "If You're Currently Using CheckFree Software to Pay Bills" on page 223.

Running Quicken from the Windows 3.0 Desktop

Although Quicken is not a Windows-specific application, you can set it up to run from the Windows 3.0 desktop by following these instructions.

Important: Install Quicken first.

Before you follow these instructions, install Quicken on your hard disk as described in "Installing Quicken on a Hard Disk" on page 2.

To set up Quicken to run from the Windows desktop:

1. From Program Manager in Windows, open the group window for the group you want Quicken to be in.

2. Choose New from the File menu.

   The New Program Object dialog box appears.

3. Select Program Item and choose OK.

   The Program Item Properties dialog box appears.

4. Type quicken in the Description text box.

5. Type the complete pathname for the Quicken Q.PIF file in the Command Line text box.

   For example, if you installed Quicken to the C:\QUICKEN5 directory, type c:\quicken5\q.pif in the Command Line text box.

6. Choose Change Icon.

   The Change Icon dialog box appears.

7. Type the complete pathname for the Quicken Q.ICO file in the Filename text box. (If another filename is in the box, the text you type replaces it.)

   For example, if you installed Quicken to the C:\QUICKEN5 directory, type c:\quicken5\q.ico in the File Name text box.

8. Choose OK.

   The Program Item Properties dialog box returns.

9. Choose OK.

   A dollar-sign icon with the name Quicken appears among the other icons in the open group window. If you have a color monitor, the dollar sign is in white against a red background.

Running Quicken from Windows 3.0

At the Program Manager desktop, open the group window for the group containing Quicken, and double-click the Quicken icon.

When you run Quicken from Windows 3.0, it works just the way this manual describes it. Quicken 5 supports the use of a Microsoft-compatible mouse.

Quicken runs best in a full-screen display

Although you can modify Quicken's Q.PIF file (see your Windows User's Guide) to run Quicken in a window with Windows in 386 enhanced mode, we recommend that you run Quicken full screen. If you run Quicken in a window, you cannot see the full width of a Quicken register, and some Quicken screens do not display properly. Also, you cannot use the mouse for Quicken operation.

Note: If you try running Quicken (or any other nonWindows application) in a window and accidentally click the mouse within the window, the application may appear to lock up. To continue work, press Esc. (You can switch between window display and full screen display by pressing Alt-Enter.)

Exiting Quicken

When you press X (or E) at the Quicken Main Menu to exit Quicken the normal way, your data is saved and you return to the group window from which you started Quicken. If you switch to another application while Quicken is running, don't forget to return to Quicken and exit from it. Otherwise, you may inadvertently start running a second copy of Quicken and create a problem in your data.

Appendix E

Questions and Answers

Screen Display

Why does my screen have speckles or "snow" on it?

You need to change the monitor speed. To do this, choose Set Preferences from the Main Menu. Then choose Screen Settings, then Monitor Display and set it to Slow.

What does the "EGA/VGA 43 Line Display" setting mean?

EGA and VGA monitors are special high-quality monitors that can display more lines on the screen. If you have one, the 43 Line Display setting (50, with VGA) will display more of the check register and reports.

Quicken worked fine on one computer, but when I took it to my second computer and tried to use it, all I got was a blank (or amber) screen.

On the second computer, erase the Q.CFG file in your QUICKEN5 directory and try again. (Note: your printer settings will be lost by doing this. Make a note of your settings first if you want.)

The Register

I entered a transaction and it disappeared. Where is it?

Quicken sorts the register by date. Look back in the register by date.

Can I sort the check register by check number?

When you print the register you can have Quicken sort it by check number. However, you cannot see the register sorted in this way on the screen. When you sort by check number, the account balance is not printed.

What does the double line in the register mean?

The items below the double line (with highlighted dates) are postdated. That is, they have dates after the current date. (The current date is the system date. This should be the same as today's date. If it is not, you can change it by typing date and pressing Enter at the DOS prompt. DOS will show you the current system date and let you type a different one.)

Billminder

I have a hard disk; how do I get Billminder to show up when I start my computer?

From the Main Menu, choose Set Preferences. Then choose Automatic Reminder Settings and make sure that "Turn on Billminder" is set to Y.

How do I turn Billminder off?

From the Main Menu, choose Set Preferences. Then choose Automatic Reminder Settings and enter N next to "Turn on Billminder."

Why isn't Billminder reminding me of anything?

Perhaps you do not currently have any of the items that Billminder tracks for you: checks to print or transmit, a transaction group due, or an investment reminder. Billminder will not remind you of postdated entries in the register unless they are checks to be printed.

If you know that Billminder should be showing something, but it still is not, check your AUTOEXEC.BAT file. Be sure Billminder points to your data directory, as described in "Billminder and AUTOEXEC.BAT" on page 442.

Does your AUTOEXEC.BAT file run any other batch files before activating Billminder? If so, insert the word CALL before the other batch file commands. This instructs DOS to return to your AUTOEXEC.BAT file after running these other batch files. (Otherwise, DOS runs the other batch file and does not return to your AUTOEXEC.BAT file, so does not activate Billminder.) For example, if you see the word NET alone on a line, and NET is the name of a batch file, modify the line so that it reads CALL NET. Caution: You should understand the contents of the AUTOEXEC.BAT file before modifying the file.

Reports

How do I get Quicken to create a report for just one account instead of all of them?

Run the report, then choose Accounts from the Edit pulldown menu. Choose Current to include only the current account or Selected to select exactly which accounts in the current file to include.

Why does "Other" appear on my summary reports?

You might see "Income-Other," "Expenses-Other," "Inflows-Other," or "Outflows-Other." These indicate amounts that have not been categorized. To find which transactions contain uncategorized amounts, select the figure in the report and press Ctrl-Z (for QuickZoom). Quicken lists all the transactions that make up the "Other" figure. To categorize one of the transactions, select it and press F9. Quicken takes you to the transaction in the register, where you can add a category.

Alternately, create a transaction report as described in "Searching for Uncategorized Transactions" on page 188. You might prefer to do this if you have many uncategorized transactions.

Why am I still getting "Other" on reports when I have given all of my transactions a category?

Make sure you have been consistent in using subcategories. For example, if you type Utilities:Phone in some transactions, you should not type just Utilities without a subcategory in other transactions.

When I print a transaction report, the payee, memo, and category are truncated too much.

With the report displayed, choose Full Column Width from the Layout pulldown menu. When printing the report, select a compressed printing style if your printer supports it. Or, choose Other Options from the Layout menu and choose "Show memo" only or "Show category" only.

Can I control how splits are displayed in transaction reports?

With the report displayed, choose Show Split from the Layout pulldown menu to show the split transactions details in the report (or choose Hide Split to hide them).

However, if you specify a report that is subtotaled or filtered by category, class, or memo, Quicken shows split transaction detail regardless of what you type at this option (if the filter affects split descriptions).

Why don't my accounts payable items show up in the balance sheet?

If you have been using postdated checks to track accounts payable, set the date at the field "Report balances as of" to a date later than your unprinted checks. Postdated accounts payable items will appear in the balance sheet report.

Why does my report have a line of Ds and Ms?

Your printer probably does not support the IBM graphics characters, which Quicken uses to draw lines. In the Report Printer Settings window, type N at the "Support IBM graphics characters" field. See "Supports IBM Graphics Characters" on page 432.

Writing Checks

Why won't Quicken copy the payee name into the address?

Be sure the cursor is in the top line of the address field. Also be sure that line is empty before pressing the Quote key (' or ").

Do I have to categorize every transaction?

No. Using categories is optional.

Reconciling

When I am reconciling my bank statement, how do I enter new transactions and how do I tell Quicken that I have finished reconciling?

If the list of uncleared transactions is on your screen, press F9 to display the register. To add transactions, press Ctrl-End to go to the end of the register, and then type and record the transaction. (Be sure to type an asterisk in the C field.) To finish reconciling, press Ctrl-F10 and Quicken will tell you if your account balances or not.

Memorized Transactions

How do I change a memorized item or report?

Memorized items: At the register or at Write Checks, press Ctrl-T to recall the memorized transactions list, select the item, then press Ctrl-E to make the changes. Memorized reports: Choose Memorized Reports from the Reports menu. Recall the report, make your changes, and rememorize it by choosing Memorize Reports on the File/Print pulldown menu. You can memorize it with a different report name to retain both your former definition and the new definition. You can also change the name of a memorized report by editing the name on the memorized reports list.

If I set up a transaction group, do I always have to pay all of those bills?

No. Quicken gives you complete control. After you execute the group, you can delete or change any transactions.

Printing

Can I use Quicken with my laser printer?

Yes. You can tell Quicken that you're using a laser in the Printer Settings windows. For more information, see "Page-oriented (for example, laser) printer" on page 432.

Can I reprint a check after I have already printed it?

Yes. Go to the check register and type an asterisk (*) in the check number (NUM) field. This adds the check to the list of unprinted checks. If the check has an address, go to the Write Checks screen, use PgUp to display the check, and type the address on the check.

Why isn't Quicken printing correctly on my printer?

If you are having problems aligning your checks, see "Common Printing Problems and Solutions" on page 97. If you need help setting up your printer, see "Printer Settings" on page 428.

How do I know if I need the Forms Leaders?

When you put paper in your printer, if you cannot print at the top of the first page, you need Forms Leaders.

How can I restore my old printer control codes after installing Quicken 5?

The install program creates a backup copy of your old configuration file called QOLD.CFG. This file contains your old control codes. To restore your old printer control codes, copy this file to Q.CFG. To do this, exit from Quicken and go to your Quicken directory. Type copy qold.cfg q.cfg and press Enter.

Accounts and File Activities

How can I merge files?

Export the data from each account in the file to a separate ASCII file (a QIF file). Then go to the other Quicken file and import the data from each of the ASCII files. See "Copying Data from One File to Another" on page 464.

How can I separate accounts in one file into two separate files?

Copy the file. Delete unwanted accounts and categories from each of the two files. Then use Copy File on each file to reduce the file size. See "Copying a Quicken File" on page 462.

How can I combine two accounts?

Export the data from one account to an ASCII file, and then import it into the second account. See "Copying Data from One File to Another" on page 464.

How do I use Quicken with a menu program or a "program director"?

The path for Quicken is \QUICKEN5 and the executable file is Q.EXE.

I want to keep separate files for each year's data. How do I start new accounts for this year?

From the Main Menu, choose Set Preferences. Then choose File Activities, then Year End. Then choose Start New Year. Specify the first of the new year as the starting date. The new accounts will have the same category, class, memorized transaction, security, price, and memorized reports lists.

If I created an account but assigned the wrong account type, how do I change it?

To change the account type, export its transactions to a DOS file, delete the account and then set it up again with the correct type, and then import the DOS file. (See the steps below.) **Note**: If you change an asset account to a credit card or liability account, or vice versa, be aware that the Increase and Decrease fields will be reversed, so the Balance amounts will be backwards.

To change the account type:

1. **Important:** Make a backup copy of the file for the account whose type you want to change.

2. Start Quicken and choose the account whose type you want to change.

3. Choose Export from the Print/Acct pulldown menu.

4. Enter the name of a DOS file to receive the exported data. Use any name allowed by DOS, for example CHECKING.QIF.

5. Enter the starting and ending dates of transactions to be exported.

   The default dates are from the start of the current year to the date of the last transaction in the account. To include all transactions in the account, enter a starting date such as 1/1/80.

6. Enter Y to export transactions and N for the next three fields, and press Enter.

   (The lists of categories and classes, accounts, and memorized transactions are the same for all accounts in the file, so these options have no effect within the same file.)

   Quicken exports the data.

7. Choose Select/Set up Account from the Print/Acct menu.

8. Select the account and press Ctrl-D to delete it.

9. At the warning screen, type yes and press Enter to confirm that you want to delete the account.

10. Set up the account again, this time selecting the new account type. Enter a balance of 0. (See "Setting Up and Using Additional Quicken Accounts" on page 245 for detailed steps.)

11. Choose the new account.

12. Choose Import from the Print/Acct menu.

13. Enter the name of the DOS file.

14. Enter Y to import transactions, and enter N for the other fields (including the field "Special handling for transfers.") Press Ctrl-Enter.

    Quicken imports the data into the new account.

How do I transfer my category and transfer list from one file to a new file?

Use Export and Import to copy your category, class, and account lists without copying any transactions. The main steps are as follows:

1. Export the lists from any account in the first file to a DOS file. Enter Y in the fields "Export Categories and Classes" and "Export Accounts." Enter N in the other two fields.

2. Select any account in the second file and import from the DOS file.

   For full details, see "Copying Data from One File to Another" on page 464.

How do I enter capital values, such as my home value, into Quicken so they are included in my net worth reports?

Since capital is an asset, create an asset account with an opening balance that is the value of the asset. To depreciate the value of the asset, create an expense category for depreciation, and enter transactions, recording the change in value into the asset's register. Follow the same steps for appreciation, but make it an income category.

How do I deal with projects whose budgets aren't monthly, such as a fixed term project?

The easiest way is to enter the entire budget amount in the month the project is to end; that is, if the project runs from January to May, enter amounts for the entire budget in May. Then, when you create a budget report, set the date range for the report as the term of the project. Don't subtotal. The report will have totals for current expenditures and project budget amounts.

Data Disks and Files

How can I use Quicken on my hard disk and keep the data files on a floppy?

At the Main Menu, choose Set Preferences. Then choose File Activities. Then choose Set File Location. Enter the pathname as A: (or B:).

How do I move my Quicken data that is backed up on a floppy disk onto my hard disk?

Use the Restore File option. At the Main Menu, choose Set Preferences. Then choose File Activities. Then choose Restore File. Quicken will prompt you to insert the disk.

If you have been keeping data on a floppy disk and now want to keep it on a hard disk, tell Quicken the new location to keep the data *before* choosing the Restore File option. At the Main Menu, choose Set Preferences. Then choose File Activities. Then choose Set File Location. Enter the pathname as c:\quicken5 (or the directory where you want to keep your data). Then restore the file from the floppy disk. Quicken copies it to the new location on your hard disk.

How do I change the location of my accounts?

From the Main Menu, choose Set Preferences. Then choose File Activities. Then choose Set File Location. Note that this procedure does not physically move the data. It just tells Quicken to look for it in a different place. (To physically move the data, use Copy File or the DOS command MOVE. Remember that one Quicken file consists of four DOS files.)

How do I remove old data from my accounts?

From the Main Menu, choose Set Preferences, then choose File Activities, then Year End. Finally choose Start New Year. Specify a new file name and the starting date that you want in your current file (for the data you want to keep). The original file is not altered. See "Starting a New Year" on page 468 for details (you don't have to use the start-of-year date Quicken uses as a default).

Back up the original file to a floppy, check the copy you have just made, and then delete the original file from your hard disk.

Categories

How do I rename categories? Will the name change throughout my register?

To rename a category, press Ctrl-C to display the category and transfer list. Select a category, then press Ctrl-E to display the Edit Category window, where you can make changes to information about the category. To rename a class, start by pressing Ctrl-L. When you rename a category or class, it is automatically changed in all transactions where it is used.

Can I categorize a transfer?

Transfers can't be categorized or subcategorized since they simply represent movement of funds. However, if you need to track this information, you can assign a class, such as [CarLoans]/Corvette. See *Using Classes*, beginning on page 351.

When I try to create subcategories, I get this error message: Invalid category name

This happens at the Set Up Category window when you try to create both a category and a subcategory at the same time; for example, Photography:Film. To create a subcategory, enter only the subcategory name (for example, Film) without the category name in front.

The simplest way to set up a subcategory is this:

1. If the category does not already exist, create it. (For example, enter Photography at the Set Up Category window and specify E for Expense.)

2. Highlight the category in the category list and press Ctrl-Ins. Quicken displays the Set Up Category window with S already entered for Subcategory. Enter the other details and press Ctrl-Enter. Quicken creates the new subcategory under the selected category.

You can also create categories and subcategories "on the fly". For example, type Photography:Film in the category field in the register. Quickens leads you through the steps for creating both the category and the subcategory.

Why are my account names in the category and transfer list? What will happen if I select one of them?

Account names appear in the category and transfer list so that you can make transfers to other accounts. If you select one of the account names from the category list, the amount of the transaction will be transferred to that account.

Will my entire category name appear on a report when only part of it shows in the register?

Yes.

Can I combine two categories into one?

You can not directly edit the category names to make them identical. However, there is a simple way of merging two categories (or subcategories). First move one of the categories so that it becomes a subcategory of the other category. Then delete this subcategory. Quicken automatically reassigns all the subcategory's transactions to the category it belonged to. You can merge subcategories using a similar method, by first moving one of the subcategories below the other subcategory. See "Merging Two Categories" on page 115.

Use Find or get a transaction report to check that appropriate transactions now have the same category.

I started using Quicken in the middle of the year. How can I enter a summary of the amounts I've spent to date for various categories?

Enter a single transaction for which the net amount is zero. Use the Split Transaction window to enter the summary amounts for the categories. To get the net amount to equal zero, include a split line equal to the total of the amounts, but with the opposite sign.

Importing Data

Can I import data into Quicken?

You can import ASCII files in the Quicken Interchange Format (QIF) or CheckFree data. Choose Import from the Print/Acct menu. See "Items for noninvestment accounts" on page 502 for Quicken's ASCII import format. When you export a Quicken file, it has this same format.

Special Terms and Messages

I get the message "Reconstructing Index File" when I go into my account.

Quicken maintains an index file that speeds access to your file. If you turn off your computer without exiting Quicken through the Main Menu, the index files are not saved and must be reconstructed. To manually reconstruct the file, choose Set Preferences from the Main Menu, then File Activities, then Select/Set Up File. Use the arrow keys to select the name of the file (don't press Enter), and press Ctrl-Z.

Note: This operation also rebuilds your dictionary file.

What is a dictionary file?

A file of addresses and split descriptions, stored in compressed form. If you shut off the power without exiting Quicken, Quicken will rebuild this file automatically when you restart Quicken.

Running Quicken in a DesqView Window

Can I run Quicken within a DesqView window?

Quicken provides limited support for the DesqView multi-tasking environment. Specifically, the screen output has been designed so that Quicken can run in a DesqView window. See the DesqView user guide for information about setting up Quicken as a "DesqView Aware" application.

Using Quicken on a Network

Can I use Quicken on a network?

Yes. One user at a time can use the Quicken program on a network. If individuals connected by a network have individual copies of Quicken, each can access a common Quicken file (one person at a time). Quicken will not allow more than one person at a time to work with a specific file. If you want to print over a network, be sure you have set the printer port appropriately. See "Print to" on page 430 for how to change the printer port setting. If you do not know which port to use, ask your network administrator.

Keep in mind the terms of your Quicken license: you have the right to make a backup copy of the program for your own use, not to make unlimited copies. In a network environment, each individual who uses Quicken must own a copy of the program. To purchase additional copies of Quicken, see "Upgrades to New Versions and Additional Copies" on page 530.

Using CheckFree

Can I record an electronic payment so I can project cash flow, but defer transmission of the transaction to CheckFree?

Yes. Temporarily remove the >>>>> symbols from the Num field and type an asterisk (*) there. When you want the transaction to be included next time you transmit, remove the asterisk and type a single > in the Num field. Quicken fills the column with angle brackets automatically to signal that the transaction should be transmitted.

Can I print the addresses and phone numbers of my vendors? Can I print a mailing list?

Yes. You can print the Electronic Payee List. See "Adding Payees to Your Electronic Payee List" on page 229 for instructions for displaying the list. Then press Ctrl-P to print the list.

You can use this feature to create a mailing list of payees even if you do not use CheckFree to pay bills. You should read the chapter on CheckFree so that you understand how activating this feature changes Quicken menus (see *Using CheckFree to Pay Bills Electronically*, beginning on page 219). Follow the instructions to turn on the electronic payment feature and then set up payees on the Electronic Payee List. You can select payees from this list when you write paper checks and you can print the list at any time.

At the Write Checks screen, simply press F9-Paper Check to write a paper check instead of preparing an electronic payment.

Investments

Can I produce a report that lists the market values of all my securities on two or more different dates?

Produce an account balances report. Choose Accounts from the Edit pulldown menu, then choose Selected. In the Select Accounts to Include window, choose Detail for each investment account. See "Account Balances" on page 173.

How should I enter a payment from a mortgage-backed security (such as a Ginnie Mae) that includes both interest and principal?

Use the action IntInc for the interest part of the payment. Use the action RtrnCap for the principal part of the payment.

I update the prices for my securities at the end of each quarter, but when I run an investment performance report the returns are way off. Why?

First, make sure the starting date for the report is the day *after* the date for the beginning prices. (The report starts with the *morning* of the starting date, while market values change at the *end* of the day.) Second, remember that Quicken considers dividends and other payments as well as changes in market value. Third, remember that the average annual total return is equivalent to the bank interest rate that would give you the same return on your investment. For example, if you double your money in four months, at that rate you'd double it twice more in the next eight months. At the end of 12 months you'd have eight times your original investment, for a return of 700% (not simply three times the original 100% return over four months).

The cash in my brokerage account is automatically rolled into a money market fund. How should I track it and the dividends it pays?

If you don't write many checks on the money fund, set it up as a security. Then you have two choices. If your brokerage statement shows no cash balance other than what's in the fund, you can treat the money fund as your cash balance. Use the action Div to enter a dividend from the fund. The cash balance will increase. If your statement shows a cash balance in addition to the fund, you may prefer to treat the fund like an ordinary security (number of shares equals dollar value). Use the action ReinvDiv to enter a dividend as a reinvestment in the fund that does not increase the cash balance.

What exactly do the actions ShrsIn and ShrsOut do to my investment?

The action ShrsIn is like BuyX except that Quicken does not require that cash be transferred. Quicken increases the number of shares and the cost basis. The action ShrsOut is like SellX at a price equal to the cost basis per share except that Quicken does not require that cash be transferred. Quicken decreases the number of shares and the cost basis.

How should I enter options (puts and calls)?

Basically, treat an option like a security but give it a distinctive name (such as "XYZ put Aug 40"). If you sell an option you don't already own, Quicken treats it like a short sale. If an option you bought or sold expires worthless, enter the opposite action (Sell or Buy) for the option at a price of zero to close your position. Quicken then records a realized gain or loss. If you exercise a call, close your position with a ShrsOut transaction for the call. When entering the purchase of the underlying security, include the cost of the call as a fee paid (to correct the cost basis).

Can I enter negative dollar amounts in the investment register?

Yes. Use the action RtrnCap with a negative amount to raise the cost basis of a security. Use the action MiscExp with a negative amount to enter miscellaneous cash income.

How does Quicken round off amounts in the investment register?

- **Price:** Quicken keeps internal track of decimal prices to the nearest 0.0005 and normally displays them to the nearest 0.001. It displays exact integers without decimals. If the fourth decimal place is a 5, Quicken displays it; otherwise it rounds to three decimal places. For example, Quicken displays 8.2175 but rounds the price 8.2177 upward to 8.218.

- **Shares:** Quicken displays the number of shares to four decimal places. It displays exact integers without decimals. It does not display zeros after the decimal point unless they are followed by nonzero digits. If there are more than four decimal places, Quicken truncates the additional places. For example, Quicken truncates the number of shares 8.21678 to 8.2167.

- **$ Amount:** Quicken displays dollar amounts to two decimal places. When it calculates the amount from the price and number of shares, it rounds to the nearest 0.01. For example, if you enter 40.3 shares at 8.26, Quicken rounds the dollar amount upward to $332.88.

At the end of each year, you may wish to adjust for the effects of rounding, to make the register match your statements. You can adjust the cash balance or the share balances of individual securities (for instructions, see "Adjusting the Cash or Share Balance" on page 317).

Appendix F

For Canadian Users

Intuit is delighted to have a growing community of Canadian Quicken users.

Here's how Quicken works for Canadian needs:

- Quicken can use the date format usual in Canada (day/month/year). At the Main Menu, select Set Preferences, then Transaction Settings, and on the line "Enter dates as MM/DD/YY or DD/MM/YY" enter D.

  Also, you can choose a three-letter abbreviation for the month when the date is printed on cheques, for example 25 Jan '92 or 1 Aug '93. At the Main Menu, select Set Preferences, then Checks and Reports Settings, and on the line "Print months as Jan, Feb...on checks" enter Y.

- The standard Quicken home and business categories include Canadian tax categories. You can delete the U. S. tax categories.

- Quicken cheques are accepted at all financial institutions in Canada and the United States. You can call **800-268-5779** toll-free for information about ordering cheques and other supplies. Or call **(416) 752-6470** or FAX **(416) 752-1140**. You cannot order cheques by phone because we must have a void cheque to process your order. See the supplies catalogue in your Quicken package for information about ordering from our Canadian cheque printer.

- The Checkfree Corporation does not serve Canada at this time.

Write us:

This page is the only place we've spelled "cheque" and "catalogue" correctly. Tell us how else we can serve Canadians better. We appreciate your comments and suggestions.

Product Development
Intuit
P. O. Box 3014
Menlo Park, California 94026-3014

Attention: Canadian Team

Appendix G

Contacting Intuit

As an Intuit customer, you have full access to technical support at no charge for help with any Quicken problems you can't solve yourself. This appendix suggests ways to save yourself time and long distance charges by checking for the easy answers yourself. If you try these suggestions, you may not need to call or, if you do need to call, the support technician may be able to help you faster because you may already have ruled out common problems.

This appendix also tells you how to contact other departments at Intuit: the supplies and checks order department, and corporate departments.

$ Saving a Phone Call

If you have a question about the way Quicken works, the best way to get an accurate, immediate answer is to try one or all of these self-help approaches first:

1. Press the Help key (F1) to get instant on-screen information from the software.

2. Check the index of this manual for the topic you need.

3. Try the troubleshooting steps in this appendix.

If you take the steps listed above and still can't find the answer, call Technical Support, using the phone number on the last page of this appendix. We want our customers to get the answers they need as quickly as possible. Tell the support specialist that your question was not answered in Help or the manual. We will add the information to the manual and Help as soon as possible, so future customers will benefit.

$ Error Messages

Usually, when Quicken can't perform an action for some reason, you see a message that explains the problem, such as the following:

```
┌─────────────────────────────────────────┐
│ ███████████████████████████████████     │
│            No Checks to Print            │
├─────────────────────────────────────────┤
│                                          │
│   You must write and record checks       │
│   before you can print checks.           │
│                                          │
├─────────────────────────────────────────┤
│ Esc-Cancel                               │
└─────────────────────────────────────────┘
```

Messages such as the above are normal occurrences with straightforward solutions. The next section explains those problem messages that are most likely to puzzle you.

Rarely, a user encounters a Quicken message that includes an error number and instructions to call Technical Support. You cannot solve such a problem without help from Intuit. If you see an error message, write down the error number and turn to "Contacting Technical Support" on page 531 for the phone number of our Technical Support group.

Problem Messages

Data Error Reading Drive.

This message usually indicates a problem with your hard disk drive. Use Quicken's Copy File feature to move the current file to another location. Choose Set Preferences from the Main Menu, then File Activities, then Copy File. Enter a new name for the file, then accept all the other default settings (the date range includes all transactions). See page 462 for full details of the copy feature. (You can also move files with the DOS COPY command.)

Dictionary/QDT/QDI file is full.

Your file has reached the limit of information that can fit in one of the four DOS files that comprise a data file. You can easily make your file smaller so you can continue to work. Use Quicken to back up the file and then make a copy of the file that excludes older transactions. From the Main Menu, choose Set Preferences. Then choose File Activities and Back Up File. After you have backed up, use Year End to make a copy that excludes older transactions and continue work with the smaller copy.

Disk is full.

If you get this message when you are using a hard disk for your working data, free up more space on your hard disk. If you see this message when you are backing up to the hard disk and if you have multiple hard disks or a network drive, you can back up to that drive.

You are more likely to get this message if you are working with data that you store on a floppy disk. Make sure you are not using a disk with other files on it. If you are not, your Quicken file may be too large to fit on a single floppy disk.

Use Quicken to back up the file and then make a copy of the file that excludes older transactions so that you can continue to work with a smaller file that will fit on one floppy disk. From the Main Menu, choose Set Preferences. Then choose File Activities and Back Up File. After you have backed up, use Year End to make a copy that excludes older transactions and continue work with the smaller copy.

Note: The Quicken Backup feature automatically prompts you to insert another floppy disk if your file is too large to fit on one floppy.

Error Accessing Disk

Use Quicken's copy feature to make an exact copy of the current file, including all accounts. As it makes the copy, Quicken rebuilds your file, which should correct the problem. Choose Set Preferences from the Main Menu, then File Activities, then Copy File. Enter a new name for the file, then accept all the other default settings (the date range includes all transactions). See page 462 for full details of the copy feature.

Error in Q.EXE file

Try installing Quicken again from floppy disk (see Chapter 1). If you still have problems, you may have a damaged sector on your hard disk. (To diagnose the state of your hard drive, ask about hard disk utility programs at your computer store.) Try installing Quicken in a different location on your hard disk, by specifying a different directory during installation. Then use Quicken's copy feature to copy your files to the new location.

Another possibility is that your computer has picked up a virus. You can eliminate most viruses with a virus industry program available at computer stores.

Error 5000 or
Error 5300

This indicates a problem with your index file. It's easy to reconstruct it. First make a backup of your current Quicken file (as a routine safety measure). Then list your files (press Ctrl-G at the Main Menu). Select the file that you were working with when you got the message, but *don't* press Enter. Press Ctrl-Z. Quicken reconstructs the index file.

File damaged: 1 or more splits will not be copied
Some split data lost

When Quicken detects that a file is damaged, it automatically attempts to correct the problem. Quicken has attempted to correct a damaged file, but it could not correct the problem completely. Check your data to find the split information that Quicken could not recover. If you have a backup of the file, use it as your working copy or at least use it to compare transactions to discover the lost information.

A common cause of file damage is turning off the computer before exiting Quicken. Always exit from Quicken before turning off the computer.

Index and data files are inconsistent

Follow the onscreen instructions for rebuilding the index. This problem can be caused by turning off the computer before exiting Quicken or by data errors on your disk drive.

Memorized list file is missing/damaged

Quicken cannot find the .QMT file that is one of the four DOS files that comprise your data file. Or the .QMT file has been damaged. Try using the DOS COPY command to copy the .QMT file from your backup disk. The .QMT file contains your lists of memorized transactions. If you have not added many categories, classes, securities, or memorized items since your last backup, you can now continue to use your file.

If you have made many changes or if you do not have a backup, call Intuit's Technical Support group and ask for a copy of the "QMT file rebuild utility." See page 531.

Not a valid Quicken account/file

You may see this message if you try to open a Quicken file that you have backed up to a disk using the DOS BACKUP command. Use the DOS RESTORE command to copy the file to your hard disk before you open the file with Quicken. Enter the command this way: RESTORE A: C:\QUICKEN5\filename.* and press Enter, where filename is the name of the file (this example restores from drive A to the Quicken directory C:\QUICKEN5). If the problem persists, call Intuit Technical Support.

In the future, use Quicken's Backup feature to back up your file to more than one floppy disk.

Not enough memory

Quicken 5 uses slightly more memory than Quicken 4. If your data file becomes very large or if you request a very long and complex report, you may see a message reporting that Quicken needs more memory. See "Capacity and Memory Usage" on page 492 for estimates of how many transactions you can have.

If you see a message about memory, try one or more of these solutions:

- Exit to DOS and unload any memory-resident utilities (such as a calendar, notepad, keystroke program, or QuickPay). Then start Quicken again in the usual way.

- If you have at least 512K of memory in your computer, buy expanded memory.

- Update your system to DOS 5.0, which frees 30K of memory.

- Back up your file and then use the Year End function to restrict your Quicken data to fewer transactions. See "Year-End Procedures" on page 466.

- If you see the message when you request a long and complex report, restrict the date range or the transactions to shorten the report or create your report with fewer subtotals.

- See "Copying a Quicken File" on page 462. When you copy a file, Quicken removes unused space, so the new file will be a little smaller.

⊞ Troubleshooting

This section explains general steps to narrow down a problem before you call Intuit.

When you call Intuit with a problem, the support technician leads you through steps to identify and solve the problem. You can do some of this exploration yourself to eliminate possibilities that don't require technical expertise. The key to troubleshooting is trying the most basic approach first.

- Try the procedure again, starting at the beginning. Examine screens and any windows where you filled in fields to be sure you are asking the program for what you want. Some examples:

  - If a report does not include the information you want, be sure you have typed the correct starting and ending dates for data to include or used the filter settings you want.

  - If checks do not print, be sure you are recording checks at the Write Checks screen rather than in the register.

- Try a related procedure. For example, if you have a printing problem, check that the printer is working by trying to print something else. If you have trouble printing checks, try printing a report. If you can't print from Quicken, try printing from a word processor. If nothing prints, you know the problem is related to the printer, not the software. Check the printer connections.

- If something used to work, think about what has changed. For example, if Billminder can't find your data, did you move the data on your hard disk without changing the data location in the Billminder line of your AUTOEXEC.BAT file?

Mouse problems

Quicken 5 works with any Microsoft-compatible mouse. If you have problems when using your mouse with Quicken, for example:

- You don't see a mouse cursor at Quicken's Main Menu

- The mouse works inconsistently in different areas of Quicken

then follow these troubleshooting steps, in the order suggested here:

1. Make sure your mouse is installed correctly. Does it work with other programs? Using a mouse, like using most programs, is usually a two-step process: installing and running.

2. Check your cable connections. Make sure each connecting cable is securely fastened to the appropriate "port" on your computer. The ports are usually located at the back of the computer. Refer to your mouse manual to find out which port to use.

3. Load the mouse driver software. The "driver" is a program which controls the mouse while you are running another program. Some programs automatically load the mouse driver, so you may have been using the mouse with these programs without

needing to load the driver first. But Quicken requires you to load the mouse driver separately before starting Quicken.

Usually, a one-line command loads the mouse driver. Check your mouse manual to find this command. Be sure the command refers to the directory where you installed your mouse software. You can add this command to the ***beginning*** of your Q.BAT file, so that the mouse driver is automatically loaded before you start Quicken.

4. Check your PATH statement. The PATH statement is a DOS command and is usually included in your AUTOEXEC.BAT file. Amend your PATH statement, if necessary, to include the directory where you installed your mouse software. For example, PATH C:\MOUSE

5. Test your mouse. Most mice come with testing utilities which ensure the mouse is installed correctly.

6. Reinstall the mouse. Perhaps the first attempt did not correctly install the mouse software.

7. Make sure you have the latest mouse driver from the mouse manufacturer. Quicken may require the latest version of the driver program which controls your mouse. Call the mouse manufacturer (or supplier) to get the latest release of the mouse driver software (which is usually sent free of charge).

Toll-free Product Information and Customer Assistance

Intuit provides toll-free product and order information for new versions of Quicken, Quicken upgrades, and Intuit checks. The toll-free number is **1-800-624-8742**. Call between 7 am and 5 pm Pacific Time. Call this number also for customer service on orders that have been placed.

Note: You cannot reach the Technical Support group through the toll-free number. See "Contacting Technical Support" on page 531 for the phone number for technical questions.

Upgrades to New Versions and Additional Copies

Intuit offers upgrades to existing versions of the software at a special price. To be eligible for the special upgrade price, be sure to send in your registration card. If the registration card is lost, send us a postcard with your name, address, daytime phone, and the version name and number of your Quicken program. We'll register you as a Quicken user.

Note: If you are upgrading from version 1 or 2, call to order a kit with software and instructions to copy your Quicken 1 or 2 data so that it can be used with Quicken 5. (See page 479 for more information.)

You can also order additional copies of Quicken by calling Intuit. Give your friends our telephone number, not an unauthorized copy of the program.

Check Orders

If you want to write and print checks with Quicken, you need to order Intuit checks. The checks are approved by all financial institutions and are universally accepted. To order your personalized Intuit checks, see the catalog and order form enclosed in the Quicken package. If you need a check order form or want additional forms, you can print forms by choosing Order Supplies from the Activities menu.

Note: You cannot order checks over the phone because we must have a copy of one of your checks. See the order form for instructions on ordering via Fax.

Corporate Calls

If you need to reach other departments at Intuit (except for Technical Support), use the corporate phone number: **(415) 322-0573**.

$ Contacting Technical Support

Have you:

- Pressed the Help key (F1) to get on-screen information?
- Used the index of this manual to find the information here?
- Tried the troubleshooting steps in this appendix?

If you still can't find the answer to your question, call our Technical Support group at **(415) 322-2800** Monday through Friday between 5 am and 5 pm Pacific time. This group can help you with questions about how Quicken works. Be sure you have sent in your registration card.

Note: If the question concerns CheckFree services or payment processing, please call CheckFree Technical Support at **(614) 899-7500**. Only Checkfree Corporation can help you with questions about service, your payments, or any CheckFree charges. CheckFree's technical staff is also trained to help with problems with your modem, phone lines, and other communications issues.

Be Prepared When You Call

If you call Intuit's Technical Support, you will get an answer to your problem faster if you are ready:

- Be at your computer with Quicken on the screen, ready to follow instructions.

  The support specialist can troubleshoot best if you're ready to step through the sequence that led to the problem.

- Know exactly what you did before the problem occurred, and the exact wording of any message appearing on the screen. If you have several questions, write them down.

- Know what version of Quicken you are using. Type V at the Main Menu and Quicken will display the version number.

- Know your system. If the following information is relevant to your problem, find it before you call:
  - Hardware type and model number and amount of memory (RAM) installed.
  - Operating system version.
  - Monitor type.
  - Printer manufacturer, type, and model.
  - Network configuration, if any.

- Have a pencil and paper handy to take notes.

You can also write our Technical Support group at this address:

Technical Support Group
Intuit
P. O. Box 3014
Menlo Park, CA 94026-3014

Please include the information listed above and on the previous page. **Important:** Also include your day and night phone numbers, the best time to call, and a FAX number (if available).

$ Phone Numbers

If you want information about:	Contact:	At this number:	During these hours:
Problems with Quicken	Technical Support	415-322-2800	Monday - Friday 5 am - 5 pm Pacific Time
Quicken upgrades and supplies	Customer Assistance	800-624-8742	Monday - Friday 7 am - 5 pm Pacific Time
Your suggestions to improve this manual or the Help text	Reader Comment Line	800-468-8487 (800-INTUIT-7)	Anytime (Record a message)
CheckFree problems and payment processing	CheckFree Technical Support	614-899-7500	Monday - Friday 8 am - 8 pm Eastern Time
Tax form changes, or the file TAX.SCD (see page 425)	ChipSoft Customer Sales	800-745-4829 ext. 607	Monday - Friday 8:30 am - 5 pm Pacific Time

Index

D

G

H

M

N

O

Q

R

S

T

Symbols

As a Quicken owner, you're eligible for special offers from Intuit. You'll be using these two attached coupons as your proof of ownership of Quicken Version 5 / IBM®.

When Intuit announces a special offer, just return the *specified* coupon. Each announcement will specify the exact coupon number (1 or 2) required.

If requested, please fill out your name, address and any other information on the coupon's reverse side. ☞

SPECIAL OFFER COUPON
Quicken Version 5 / IBM®

Use this coupon to qualify for Intuit's special offer to Quicken owners. The offer announcement indicates which specific coupon is requested to qualify. The specified original coupon *must* be returned. A copy or facsimile is *not* acceptable.

1

SPECIAL OFFER COUPON
Quicken Version 5 / IBM®

Use this coupon to qualify for Intuit's special offer to Quicken owners. The offer announcement indicates which specific coupon is requested to qualify. The specified original coupon *must* be returned. A copy or facsimile is *not* acceptable.

2

QUICKEN® CUSTOMER SUGGESTIONS CARD

Name: _____

Address: _____

_____

City, State, Zip: _____

Daytime Phone Number: (_____) _____

I use Quicken for: ☐ Home ☐ Business ☐ Both

☐ Type of Business: _____

Suggestions: _____

_____

_____

_____

*If you are mailing this card from outside the U.S., please send it in an envelope with proper postage to assure delivery.

IBM 5.0

08/91

SPECIAL OFFER COUPON #1

Quicken Version 5 / IBM®

Name: _____

Street: _____

_____

City: _____ State: _____ Zip: _____

Phone Number: _____

Additional Information: _____

☐ Check Enclosed ☐ MasterCard ☐ Visa ☐ American Express

Card # _____ Exp. Date _____

SPECIAL OFFER COUPON #2

Quicken Version 5 / IBM®

Name: _____

Street: _____

_____

City: _____ State: _____ Zip: _____

Phone Number: _____

Additional Information: _____

☐ Check Enclosed ☐ MasterCard ☐ Visa ☐ American Express

Card # _____ Exp. Date _____

BUSINESS REPLY MAIL

FIRST CLASS MAIL   PERMIT NO. 18   MENLO PARK, CA

POSTAGE WILL BE PAID BY ADDRESSEE

INTUIT

ATTENTION: CUSTOMER SUGGESTION
PO BOX 3014
MENLO PARK CA 94026-9959